Tibet and the British Raj
The Frontier Cadre
1904 - 1947

Alex Mckay

Published in commemoration of the 50th anniversary of Tibetan people's uprising and the arrival of the Tibetan Government and people in exile

LIBRARY OF TIBETAN WORKS AND ARCHIVES

Copyright © 2009: Alex McKay

ALL RIGHTS RESERVED

No part of this publication may be reproduced, stored in a retrieval system, or transmitted in any form or by any means, electronic, mechanical, photo-copying, recording or otherwise, without the prior permission of the publisher.

ISBN: 978-81-86470-92-3

Published by the Library of Tibetan Works and Archives, Dharamsala, H.P. 176215, and printed at Indraprastha Press (CBT), Nehru House, New Delhi-110002

Contents

Foreword to the Second Edition	v
Foreword by Dr. Michael Aris	ix
Acknowledgements	xiii
Glossary	xix
Maps	xxii
Prologue: 'We could run the whole show'	xxiii
Introduction: 'To avoid incurring the hostility of the Chinese Government'	1
1. 'He may yet be an Indian Ruling Chief'	19
2. 'An extremely mad scheme?'	33
3. 'A conversion almost as remarkable as Sir F. Younghusband'	49
4. 'I became Tibetanised'	67
5. Growing up 'with a profound belief in the British Empire'	87
6. 'The strange laboured breathing of men and mules'	97
7. 'Tom-foolery on the part of Laden La, Tsarong and others in Lhasa in 1924'	115
8. The Weir Years, and 'The right hand of every Political Officer'	133
9. 'Passed to the Heavenly Fields'	149
10. 'One distinct forward move'	161
11. Gartok: Edge of Empire	177
12. 'Keeping the Tibetans happy'	185
13. 'They've all got something special about them'	205
14. 'We want a united Tibet'	219
15. 'Nothing left to which objection could be taken'	239
Epilogue: 'Today we are no longer masters of the Residency'	247
Appendix One: The Tibet Cadre; biographical details	255

Appendix Two: The Government of India's Officers in Tibet;
    dates of service 259
Notes 271
Bibliography 311
Index 329

Foreword to the Second Edition[1]

In 1997, Curzon Press (sadly now extinct), published the first edition of this work, which was a greatly revised version of my 1995 doctoral thesis from the School of Oriental and African Studies, London University. I am indebted to Curzon's eventual inheritors, Taylor and Francis, for permission to bring out the second edition with the Library of Tibetan Works and Archives in Dharamsala (H.P., India). LWTA are a particularly apt publisher, for not only is this a work of Tibetan history, but it was also at Gangchen Kyishong that my systematic research for the book began in 1989, while I waited out the summer in its congenial surrounds until the SOAS academic year started.

It would not be possible to write quite the same book today. The foreword was written by Professor Michael Aris (1946-1999), who is sadly no longer with us (and his wife, the Burmese Nobel Prize winner Aung San Suu Kyi still remains in the captivity Michael was then defiantly hopeful might end). The last British representative in Lhasa, Hugh Richardson (1905-2000), whose assistance was invaluable, has also passed on. Indeed all but one of the eye-witnesses to the British period in Tibet that I interviewed for this work have left us.[2] The charismatic Sikkimese princess "Coo-coo-la" (Princess Pema Tsedeun Lacham Kusho, 1924-2008), has also passed away more recently.

But there have been a number of significant contributions to our knowledge of some of the people and events outlined here since this work was first published. The issue of Russian involvement in Tibet has been meticulously examined by several scholars,[3] while Michael Carrington has demolished long-standing denials of wide-spread looting on the Younghusband mission,[4] a theme expanded in Charles Allen's recent *Duel in the Snows*.[5] The latter provides the most balanced and well researched account of that mission so far.

Frank Ludlow's English school in Gyantse has been examined in two articles by Michael Rank,[6] and Isrun Egelhardt has now given us properly researched and balanced studies of the German "Schäffer mission" to Tibet in 1938-39.[7] As well as adding considerably to our knowledge of its aims and achievements, her work has highlighted the extent to which the British sources used here to describe the mission are bitterly biased against the Germans.[8] Thus my account, (particularly in regard to Kaiser [K. Bahadur Thapa]), must be considered regrettably one-sided.

We note also that Julie Marshall's bibliography,[9] without which no serious study of the subject could proceed, is now easily available, and that an authoritative list of Western and Japanese visitors to Tibet has been established.[10] A privately published account by Dr W.S. Morgan of his time in Lhasa with the Gould mission has given us perhaps the best and most original account of "old Tibet" available,[11] while the diaries of Heinrich Harrer's companion Peter Aufschnaiter are now available in English.[12] There also is a popular account of the experiences of the American bomber crew who crashed near Samye in 1943.[13]

On the Tibetan side, Tsarong Shape's son has published a biography of his father,[14] a number of reminiscences of life in pre-1950 Tibet by members of the exile community have appeared,[15] as has a collection of accounts by three non-elite local servants of the colonial enterprise.[16] Tharchin, the Tibetan Christian, has found a comprehensive biographer,[17] and there have been further studies of the Christian missionaries' approaches to Tibet.[18] In the wider context, steps have been taken towards the economic analysis of Tibet in the pre-communist period,[19] and the immediate post-colonial period has been subject to two major studies.[20]

In my own work since 1997 I have looked more closely at contemporary events in Sikkim, which relate in many ways to those to the north.[21] I have also tried to understand the British period in Tibet in the wider context,[22] concluding that the Younghusband mission and its establishment of a British position in Tibet were far from unique, but rather replicated a common pattern of British imperial expansion in the 19th century. That model, and the ideologies behind it, may in the wider context be profitably examined in the light of Frederick Jackson Turner's famous conclusions in regard to the European

Foreword to the Second Edition vii

settlement of the American West.[23] Finally, I have also discussed the medical encounter in this region, analysing the expansion of Western medicine ('biomedicine') into the Tibetan cultural world against the background of colonial modernisation, while incidentally shedding more light on the character and activities of the Medical Officers who are mentioned here more briefly.[24]

Research into the British officials who served in Tibet has also been continued, with particular reference to photographic archives and private letters and diaries, particularly by Roger Croston. He has located a considerable number of people who visited Tibet in the British period, notably the 1941-42 Lhasa Radio Officer, Henry Baker, as well as the relatives of many others. A tribute to Croston's achievements was the gathering he organised in Oxford on 30 May 2008, which was attended by His Holiness the Dalai Lama. The Tibetan leader met personally with 230 people from 40 families whose members had travelled in Tibet between 1880 and 1950. Croston has also been active in encouraging the publication of memoirs of the period, and, sadly, in acting as obituarist as the ranks of survivors of the British period fade.[25]

* * *

In the earlier volume, perhaps thankfully, a paragraph on the subjects' sex lives was somehow lost in the editing process. It concluded that technical and military personnel formed occasional liaisons with Tibetans, marriage as in the case of Telegraph sergeant 'Bill' Luff and 1940s Radio Officer Reginald Fox), and less official ties that produced children with Tibetan women, as in the case of another Telegraph sergeant in the early period.[26] But the officer class seem to have remained celibate there, for in the 20th century celibacy for the single officer had come to be considered a duty (and one not then seen as unusual, as one officer pointed out to me).

Some controversy was generated by one aspect of my argument that there was a British plan to remove the 13th Dalai Lama from secular power in the 1920s. In writing of Rai Bahadur Laden La's role in those events, I did not make it explicit enough that (if I am correct in the thesis), this was Major F.M. Bailey's plan and that there is no evidence that Laden La did other than follow his orders. Dekyi and

Nicholas Rhodes have demonstrated that Laden La actually was certified as suffering a nervous breakdown after this period, and strongly argued that as a Tibetan Buddhist he would not have acted against the Dalai Lama.[27] A most pleasing development of this issue has been the subsequent publication of the Rhodes's biography of Laden La, an important member of that greatly neglected class of intermediaries in the colonial process.[28]

But if the opportunity to revisit one's earlier work brings with it the temptation to "improve" it, that is a temptation I have resisted. To draw on a parallel from the film world, the Director's Cut is invariably longer, but very rarely an improvement. The original text, which generally seems free of glaring errors of fact, is thus untouched, and if there are errors of judgment, they remain. Of course there could have been changes. The importance of maintaining the flow of information from Tibet as a factor in the policy-making of both British India and China needs deeper analysis and emphasis. On reflection the role of Captain W.F. O'Connor is also understated here; he had a remarkable range of contacts throughout the empire and beyond, and much of his influence was behind-the-scenes.[29] But O'Connor's eventful life is worthy of a study of its own, one that goes beyond his bland autobiography.

Finally I would note that there was one aspect of the original work that entirely escaped notice. *Tibet and the British Raj* is a study of a group of men at the centre of a power structure, in this case the British colonial enterprise. It demonstrates how the Tibet cadre were to an extent bred, and certainly educated and trained, to think and act in a particular manner which was consistent with the aims of their superiors in the imperial chain of command. I tried to imply – obviously too implicitly – that such a process would produce similar results in different times and places. Thus I emphasise here the suggestion that the production of the ideology and actions of what the Italian Marxist-influenced philosopher Antonio Gramsci called the 'intellectual class' of any power structure, be it colonial, national, theocratic, or otherwise, is generally developed by this model of training.

Alex McKay
Belbora
February 2009.

Foreword

Recent years have seen an intensive scholarly reappraisal of the Western encounter with Tibet. Studies have ranged from considerations of high imperial policies famed by the mandarins of Whitehall and Delhi to the adventurous lives of major players in the 'Great Game'. The common assumptions and expectations that infuse the accounts of travellers who wandered on the Roof of the World have been laboriously analysed. Changes in Western attitudes to Tibetan Buddhism have been mapped and plotted. The well-populated lunatic fringe that claimed initiation into the deepest secrets of the Tibetan spiritual tradition have been given centre stage. Even the unlikely influence of Tibetan architecture on that of the West has been the subject of a thesis. At a more abstract level, Tibetan society and statehood have been explored to see if Western concepts are relevant, and Tibetan philosophy has been looked at from the viewpoint of trends in modern Western philosophy. The movement in the West which has made Tibet one of the most popular political causes is also examined. In short, there hardly remains a corner of Western engagement with Tibet that has not been the subject of one or more conference, thesis, monograph, chapter or article.

This evident trend towards introspection, found in so many other spheres of Western 'post-modernism', is sometimes pursued at such a distance from the main object of study, namely Tibet, and it excludes such a self-indulgent tone and flavour that it can only cause annoyance and frustration to those who seek to understand Tibet from the perspective of that country's own traditions and literary heritage. The whole approach sometimes seems to proceed from the assumption that the Western impingement on Tibet is inherently more significant and interesting than Tibet itself or the Tibetan view of Tibet. In this strange inversion of priorities there is sometimes an arrogance and self-importance that reminds one, oddly, of the superior attitudes of an earlier generation of colonial triumphalists. Tibet disappears, as before, in a fog of ambition and fancy, in a hall of distorting mirrors.

It is the great merit of Alex McKay's remarkable and meticulous study of the 'apostolic succession' of British officers who served in Tibet that it avoids the pitfalls of post-modernism while exemplifying its main virtues. The British encounter with Tibet is shown, at the very personal level of individual experience, to have been integral to Tibet's own internal development and present fate. The author's sensitivity to Tibetan aspirations derives not only from his use of sources and studies that do justice to the Tibetan viewpoint but also from the insights and sympathies of many in the gallery of the frontier cadre who became, to some extent, 'Tibetanised'. Above all this book allows one to identify those fundamental preconceptions of Tibet we have inherited unconciously from earlier British writings. The work enhances our self-awareness while preserving Tibet as the main focus.

The author argues, in my view very convincingly, that the most lasting contribution made by the British who served in Tibet lay in the powerful historical image they constructed of an independent Tibetan state. The writings of Sir Charles Bell and Hugh Richardson, and to a lesser extent of Sir Basil Gould, continue today to exert a powerful influence on both the scholarly and less scholarly communities. I hope I may therefore be forgiven for pointing out something that seems to have escaped the notice of the present author in his search for the attitudes these writers held in common: Bell, Gould and Richardson were all the product of my own university's course in Classical Studies, the Oxford Greats School (or Literae Humaniores). The study of the texts of Greek and Latin history, philosophy and literature seems to have prepared them for approaching and trying to understand a much more distant culture in its totality. Close acquaintance with the values of thought and conduct in classical tradition must have brought unconscious expectation that the history of Tibet could be understood in familiar, universal terms. All three gained proficiency in the Tibetan language, the *sine qua non* for any real understanding of Tibetan life and thought. Certainly they grew up in a period when the 'omnicompetent generalist' ruled the day: there was no aspect of Tibetan life of the past or present that did not interest them. If increasing specialization in Tibetan studies and the profusion of historical sources now available has rendered some of their writings a little dated, the total picture they painted has endured with great effect. Hugh Richardson, the last senior member of the frontier cadre, now in his ninety-first year, continues to bridge the gap between the lost world of the generalist and the modern specialist. The author or co-author of wide-ranging works of survey, he is also the foremost Tibetan epigraphist. I had the privilege of editing his *Ceremonies of the Lhasa Year* (Serindia, 1993), and two substantial papers just completed sit on my desk as I write.

There is a painted image of a British diplomat still surviving in the Norbulingka, the Dalai Lama's summer palace in Lhasa. When I saw it several years ago I assumed it to be a portrait of Hugh Richardson, though I now think the figure may perhaps symbolize the whole line of officers who represented Brititsh India in Tibet. He stands beneath the throne of the young Dalai Lama as one of a group who served and supported the 'god-king' before the collapse of his state – close relatives, tutors, ministers, courtiers, favourites, attendants and guardian divinities. The painting is done in a peculiar mixture of Tibetan tradition and modern kitsch. It fits the convention of depicting foreign emissaries bringing tribute to a Buddhist potentate, but it also serves as a most apt symbol of how, as McKay describes, the British came finally to be accepted in Lhasa as 'honorary Buddhists'. This was principally the result of the bonds of trust and friendship they had formed with Tibetans at many levels of Lhasa society, outside the immediately imperial context of their encounter. The force of the image can only be appreciated when set against the Tibetan view of the British in the years leading up to the terrible bloodshed caused by the Younghusband mission of 1904. Then the British were depicted in some Tibetan writings, and with good reason, as foreign demons bent on destroying the land of religion.

The frontiersmen's image of an independent Tibet was developed, as McKay demonstrates so well, to serve the British political aim of maintaining a buffer between India and China. It stood then and continues to stand now at total variance with the Chinese image of Tibet as an integral part of China. The image ultimately failed in its purpose because of Tibet's rejection of modernity and China's own ambitions to secure the boundaries of its empire. Any future solution to the difficult problem of Tibet's status will have to recognize the fact that in some periods the Tibetans certainly entered into a formally subservient relationship with China – but one that allowed them, practically throughout history, to manage their own affairs. The true picture is complicated further by loose or disputed frontiers on all sides and the survival of so many quasi-independent Tibetan polities on the fringe owing little allegiance to any central Tibetan or Chinese government. Whatever constitutional arrangements may be made on paper to redefine the relationship (and there is little prospect of this happening as things stand today), real hope for the future must depend primarily on an increased awareness of Tibetan identities on the part of the Chinese people and leadership, and a clear perception of Tibetan sufferings of the past and present. There have been fleeting glimpses that such a realization is possible, even perhaps one day inevitable. Stranger things have happened in history.

Michael Aris
St Antony's College, Oxford
March 1997

Acknowledgements

The accounts of travellers who visited Tibet before the Chinese take-over in 1950 stress how remote that land was, and how few Westerners ever ventured there. Yet that image of 'forbidden Tibet' is, like so many of our ideas about that country, a myth. Far more Westerners visited Tibet in the first half of this century than travelled to Himalayan kingdoms such as Bhutan, Zanskar, or even Nepal.

This gap between perception and reality was the inspiration for this work. After visiting Tibet in 1984 and 1986, I began to study the history of Western visitors to that land, and discovered that although there was no comprehensive account of the British presence, more than one hundred officials had lived and worked in Tibet during the 1904-47 period.

The story of the officers of the Raj in Tibet turned out to be a very human one. It involved individual triumphs and failures, danger and excitement, as well as boredom and bureaucratic routine, set against a backdrop of a land which, rightly or wrongly, still holds a unique place in the Western imagination. Many of the events which will be described here took place within living memory, yet in a vanished era when imperial officers looked at world maps liberally coloured in the reassuring pink that designated them as part of the British empire, and when it was not impossible for men to imagine that parts of Tibet might even acquire that pink tinge.

Mr James Cooper of the Tibet Society U.K., and Mr Hugh Richardson CIE OBE, the former Head of British Mission Lhasa, both guided me on the paths necessary to undertake this study. I carried out preliminary work on the topic as an undergraduate at the London University School of Oriental and African Studies (SOAS), under the supervision of the now Professor of South Asian History, Peter Robb.

Professor Robb then agreed to supervise my doctoral thesis on the subject, a decision for which I have remained thankful. I have benefited a great deal from his sage guidance and professional expertise, and I could not have wished for a better mentor. In addition to the great debt I owe Peter Robb, I also benefited from the assistance provided by a number of other lecturers at SOAS, who gave me far more time and support than I had the right to expect. In particular I wish to acknowledge the help of Dr David Morgan, and of Drs Avril Powell, Michael Hutt, Humphrey Fisher, Julia Leslie and Professor Timothy Barrett. I am also grateful for the unfailing courtesy and friendly support offered by SOAS History Department secretaries, Mary-Jane Hillman, and Joy Hemmings-Lewis, and of the South Asian Centre secretary, Janet Marks.

This current work represents a substantially revised development of my doctoral thesis (as noted in the bibliography), which was necessarily more concerned with theoretical matters. Specialist readers seeking a more academic context for this study may, I hope, still refer to that thesis with some profit.

Research for this work was carried out in British and Indian archives and libraries, amidst battered files, some still tinted with the dust of Tibet. Occasionally these turned up a direct personal link to the imperial era, as when I came upon a hand-written note in faded ink predicting, in reference to one officer's file, that 'I can't imagine that anyone will ever read it'.[1]

This archival research was supplemented by a series of interviews with veterans of the British period in Tibet and their relatives, who are listed separately in the bibliography. I owe a great debt to those individuals, whose insight has been invaluable, and whose hospitality and support provided the most rewarding memories of my research. I am particularly grateful to Mr Robert Ford CIE and Mr Allen Robins for their comments on my work. I am also grateful to the following descendants of Tibet cadre officers for their assistance and for allowing me access to private papers; Maybe Jehu, Mrs Dekyi Khedrub, Dr Ian Battye, Anne Battye, and Mrs Desiree Battye, Mr & Mrs B.G.Cartwright, Mrs Olga Worth, L.J.Mainprice, and Mr & Mrs R.Mouland.

My research in India was supervised by Dr P.S.Gupta of Delhi University, who opened a number of doors for me. I was grateful for the support of Professor Kumar, Director of the Nehru Library, and particularly for the hospitality and friendship of Chandrani Ghosh, Prabhu and Bidhu Patel and family, and the Gangully family.

In Dharamsala, Geshe Tenzing Tethong kindly arranged my interview with His Holiness the 14th Dalai Lama of Tibet and permission for my wife to accompany to me, and I am particularly grateful to His Holiness for his kind support and for sharing his childhood memories of the British period. My thanks also to the management and staff of the Tibet Hotel for their assistance at that time, and to writer and intellectual Jamyang Norbu, an informative and entertaining host.

In Kalimpong we were indebted to Tim and Nilam Macdonald both for their kindness and hospitality at the Himalayan Hotel (where I was fortunate enough to find the amiable and informative Dr T.W.Pemba a fellow-guest), and for their assistance in my research into the Macdonald family. Dr Keith Sprigg, formerly of SOAS Linguistics Department, and his wife Mrs R.E.Sprigg (also of the Macdonald family), proved both delightful hosts and a mine of information concerning people and events on the Tibetan frontier. My thanks are also due to Namgyal Tsering and George Tsarong for their assistance.

In Gangtok I was helped by a large number of people, many of whom, as serving government officials, must remain anonymous. However, I may thank Admiral R.H.Tahiliani, His Excellency the Governor of Sikkim, and his ADC, Captain Sakhet Jha, who were kind enough to show us the Governor's residence, *Raj Bhavan,* the former British Residency.

I am pleased to acknowledge the specialised advice and assistance of Dr Alastair Lamb, the acknowledged authority in the field of Anglo-Tibetan diplomacy, for his kindly support and stimulating suggestions. In addition, I have benefited from specialist advice from Dr Clive Dewey of Leicester University in particular, and from Professor Michael Fisher of Oberlin College, Ohio, Professor Nikolai Kuleshov of the USSR Academy of Sciences, Dr A.J.Stockwell of

Royal Holloway College, London University and Dr Michael Aris of St Antony's College, Oxford.

Messers Scott Berry, James Cooper, John Bray, John Billington and Tsering Shakya in England, and Alex Andreyev in St Petersburg have all provided regular advice on their areas of Tibetan expertise, and enthusiastic support for my work. I am particularly grateful to John Bray for his proof-reading, and for his stimulating comments and suggestions on several versions of this work. My thanks also to Malcolm Campbell of Curzon Press for the confidence he has displayed in my work, and for his benign stewardship of this project.

Thanks are also due to Mr Henry Hall, Secretary of the Indian Political Department Association, Mr T.A.Heathcote, the Royal Military Academy Sandhurst librarian, Mr D.R.C. West, Marlborough School Honorary Archivist, Pema Yeshi of the Library of Tibetan Works and Archives, Dharamsala, and Mrs A.M.Lucas, Royal Geographical Society Librarian. Sheleen Folkes (Oriental and India Office Library), and Lionel Carter (Cambridge South Asia Library) have been particularly helpful in assisting my more obscure enquiries. My thanks are also due to Marina de Alarcon of the Pitt-Rivers' Museum, Oxford, Mr Richard Blurton, of the British Museum, and Juliana Crowther of the Cambridge University Museum of Archaelogy and Anthropology, for their assistance in locating suitable illustrations.

Unpublished Crown Copyright documents in the Oriental and India Office Collection appear by permission of Her Majesty's Stationery Office.

My late father, Colin McKay, proved the most meticulous of proof readers; with later assistance from Danny Shaw, Dr Sanjoy Bhattacharya (SOAS), and in particular, John Bray and Stephen Tucker, who have both made a number of valuable suggestions; any remaining errors of language are my own. I owe a special debt to my wife, Jeri, for her support and encouragement in various continents over the years that this project has unfolded. Her contribution has been a major one.

Finally there are those whose good influences have been less direct, but highly valued. My thanks to Mrs Beryl McKay, Fiona and Bob Bullivant, Terry Lehane and Linda Palmer, Jim and Caroline Carver,

Terry and Geneen, and to the many friends and travel companions who have helped in so many ways.

Some sections of this work have previously appeared in specialist journals. I am indebted to Dr David Morgan, editor of the *Journal of the Royal Asiatic Society*, for permission to quote from two articles, and to Professor J.A.Mangan, editor of the *International Journal of the History of Sport*, Dr Michael Hutt, editor of *South Asia Research*, and Mr John Billington, editor of the *Tibet Society of the United Kingdom Newsletter*, for permission to publish excerpts of articles, as listed in the bibliography.

The research for this project was funded by a British Academy Major Scholarship. Fieldwork in India was undertaken with the financial assistance of the British Academy, the Central Research Fund of the University of London, and the School of Oriental and African Studies, London University. The writing was completed during an Associate-Fellowship at the International Institute for Asian Studies, Leiden, The Netherlands, under the auspices of the Leverhulme Trust (U.K.). My thanks are due to the Leverhulme Trust, in particular the Secretary, Mrs Jean Cater, and to the IIAS. I am particularly grateful to the IIAS Director, Professor Wim Stokhof, technical expert Manuel Haneveld, to secretaries Kitty Yang-de Witte and Karin van Belle-Foesenek, publication editor Paul van der Velde and to my colleagues there, in particular Dr Michel Hockx, for their support and assistance.

None of these individuals and organisations are, of course, responsible for the conclusions herein. In acknowledging the great debt I owe to all those mentioned here, I naturally accept full responsibility for all opinions, and any errors.

A.C.McKay, 1997

Glossary of foreign Terms

INDIAN LANGUAGES

The following words are of Sanskrit or Persian origin, but were all used by the Tibet cadre in the form given below.

Babu Clerk; particularly used to describe Bengalis, often a derogatory term.
Bodhisattva Mahayana Buddhist ideal: one who renounces nirvana to help others attain it.
Chowkidar Watchman.
Dak bungalow Government rest-house (lit: post house).
Durbar Court, government of an Indian Princely state, (also) assembly of notables.
Izzat Honour; charismatic authority.
Kazi Properly, a judge trained in Islamic law; used as a title by the Sikkimese ruling family.
Khanates Central Asian states, e.g. Bukhara, Khiva.
Lepcha Indigenous peoples of Sikkim.
Mantra (Tibetan: *sngags*) Esoteric formula in words, frequently repeated for spiritual purposes. The most reknowned Tibetan mantra being *Om Mani Padme Hum*.
Pandit Usually 'Scholar' or learned person, applied to British-trained explorers of Tibet in the 19th century.
Purdah Veil; as worn by Muslim women. The practice of seclusion of women.

Rai Bahadur	British Indian title; higher rank.
Rai Sahib	British Indian title; lower rank.
Sahib	'Lord/Master', generally applied to British officials.
Shikar	Hunting, shooting.
Topee	Type of headwear designed to keep off the sun; much favoured by British colonial officials.
Toshakhana	Government store of gifts received and to be given, treasury, (lit: 'treasure-house').

TIBETAN

The following Tibetan words are generally given in the spelling form commonly used in British official documents. In the absence of an accepted standardised form of Tibetan transcription I have avoided the use of academic forms of Tibetan in the text, but they are given here in brackets.

Amban	(am ban) Diplomatic representative in Lhasa of the Manchu Emperor.
Bön	(bon) Tibetan religious sect.
Chipa	(phyid pa) Non-Buddhist; 'outsider'.
Dapön	(mda' dpon) Senior military rank.
Dzasa	(dza sag) High rank or title; 'duke'.
Gelugpa	(dge lugs pa) Leading Tibetan Buddhist sect (to which the Dalai and Panchen Lamas both belong).
Jongpon	More correctly, dzongpön; (rdzong dpon) District administrator.
Kashag	(bka' shag) Council. The senior government body of four officials to whom all government business was referred.

Glossary of Foreign Terms xxi

Khenchung	(mkhan chung)
	Monastic official, inc. Gyantse Tibetan Trade Agent.
Lönchen	(blon chen)
	Chief government minister.
Mani	(ma ṇi)
	As in 'mani wall'. Long piles of stones etc, inscribed with *mantras*.
Mönlam	(smon lam)
	Festival of the New Year (Tibetan calendar). (*Mönlam Chenmo*, "Great Prayer Festival").
Nangpa	(nang pa)
	Buddhist; 'insider'.
Nyingma	(rnying ma)
	Sect of Tibetan Buddhism.
Shapé	(zhabs pad)
	Title of the members of the Kashag.
Trangka	(trang ka). Unit of Currency.
Ula	('u lag)
	Free transport provided by villages to those travelling on government business; part of village tax requirement.

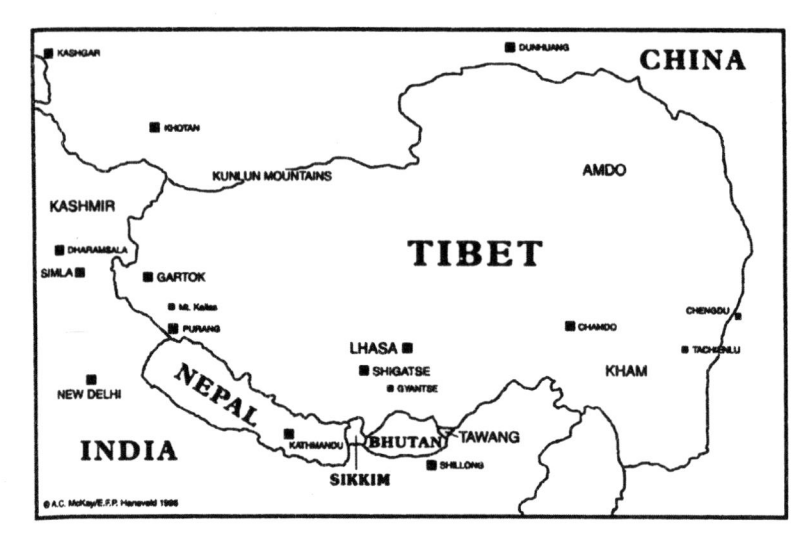

Map 1 Tibet (1914 Boundary)

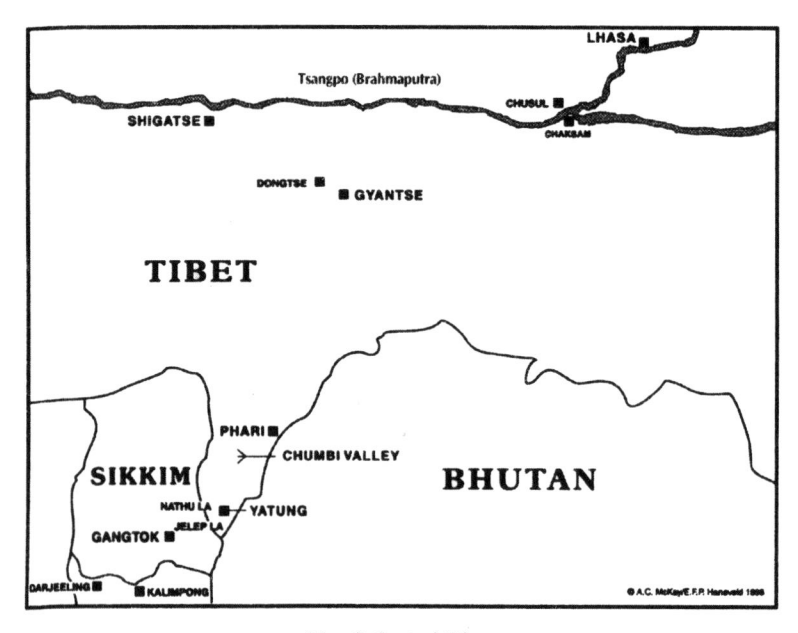

Map 2 Central Tibet

Prologue

'We could run the whole show'

On the morning of 23 September 1904, Lieutenant-Colonel Francis Younghusband rode south out of the Tibetan capital, Lhasa, en route to India. That night he walked from his camp into the surrounding mountains where, as he later wrote,

> I...gave myself up to all the emotions of this eventful time. My task was over and every anxiety was passed...I was insensibly suffused with an almost intoxicating sense of elation and goodwill. This exhilaration of the moment grew and grew until it thrilled me with over-powering intensity...All nature and all humanity were bathed in a rosy glowing radiancy; and life for the future seemed nought but buoyancy and light... that single hour on leaving Lhasa was worth all the rest of a lifetime.[1]

Younghusband had good reason to be euphoric. Despite the Tibetan Government's determination to prevent foreigners from entering Tibet, he had led a diplomatic mission which had fought its way to Lhasa and forced them to sign the 1904 Anglo-Tibetan Convention. This treaty gave the British a firm foothold in Tibet and had great symbolic significance. It ended Lhasa's diplomatic isolation and sent a signal to Russia, Britain's main imperial rival in Central Asia, that Tibet was within the British imperial sphere of influence.

The Anglo-Tibetan Convention allowed the Government of India to open three Trade Agencies ('marts') in Tibet. These were to be sited at Gyantse, 120 miles south-west of Lhasa, at Yatung, in the Chumbi Valley just across the border from Sikkim, and at Gartok, in far-off western Tibet. The most important of these was the Gyantse Agency, which was to be the focus of the British presence until the late 1930s, when they established a mission in Lhasa.

In addition to the official Convention, Younghusband had personally negotiated a separate agreement with the Tibetans, which allowed the Gyantse Trade Agent the right to visit Lhasa 'whenever necessary'. Younghusband and his patron, George Nathaniel Curzon, Viceroy of India from 1899-1905, regarded this as the most important result of the mission.[2]

Curzon and Younghusband had originally planned to station a British representative in Lhasa itself, a post for which Younghusband would have been the obvious choice. They considered that with a British agent at Lhasa, 'we could practically run the whole show'.[3] But in London, the British Government was anxious to avoid upsetting the other great powers with interests in Central Asia. While reluctantly sanctioning Younghusband's mission, they had refused to permit the appointment of a British representative in the Tibetan capital. The separate agreement allowing the Gyantse Agent to visit Lhasa was Younghusband's attempt to circumvent Whitehall's restrictions and salvage something of the mission's original aim.

Younghusband's separate agreement also imposed a large indemnity on the Tibetans, to punish them for fighting against the mission. This was to be paid over a 75 year period. Until the repayments were completed, British forces were to occupy and administer the Chumbi Valley, a strategically-important wedge of Tibetan territory dividing Sikkim and Bhutan. This meant that for all practical purposes the Chumbi would become part of India.

The mission to Lhasa was the peak of Younghusband's career. Within weeks of his departure his political masters in London had rejected the two key elements of his separate agreement with the Tibetans. Whitehall refused to allow British agents to visit Lhasa under any circumstances and ruled that the fine imposed on the Tibetans be greatly reduced, allowing repayment over just three years, whereupon the Chumbi was to be returned to Tibetan administration.

Younghusband had been given a last-minute opportunity to remain in Lhasa. The day before his departure he had received authorisation to remain there and renegotiate the agreement concerning the Chumbi Valley. Younghusband chose to ignore the opportunity. Having announced the mission's departure, he felt he would forfeit the Tibetan's trust if he remained, a trust he had done everything in his power to gain. Had he known then that it would be 16 years before another British officer would be permitted to visit Lhasa, it is unlikely that he would have left as the principal object of the mission, as far as Curzon and Younghusband were concerned, was the establishment of British influence at Lhasa.

Younghusband had been an ideal choice to lead a mission to Lhasa. Like General Gordon of Khartoum or Lawrence of Arabia, he was something of a visionary, and well aware of the symbolic and historical significance of leading a mission to the 'forbidden city' of Lhasa. Although a man of action, he was an open-minded and progressive thinker who got on well with people of all races and inspired great loyalty among the men he led. His quiet nature and endless patience made him ideally suited to negotiating with the Tibetans, whose approach to crisis was much less hurried than the British.

Younghusband had been born in 1863, at Murree, in the Himalayan foothills on the north-west frontier of India. In the tradition of the time, he returned to Britain for his schooling, and, after Clifton College and Sandhurst, he had joined a cavalry regiment in India. Younghusband made his name in the late 19th century, playing the 'Great Game', the clandestine struggle between Russian and British Indian frontiersmen for control of the territory between their empires. He had been at the Relief of Chitral, led a mission to Kashgar in Chinese Central Asia, and, most notably, had undertaken a pioneering journey from Peking to Hunza (in what is now northern Pakistan), by way of the previously unmapped Murtagh Pass. He had even found time to travel to South Africa while on leave from India, to report on the Jameson Raid for the London *Times*.

After leaving Tibet, Younghusband served in the much-sought-after post of Resident in Kashmir, before retiring in 1909. In retirement he increasingly devoted his attention to exploring those mystical aspects of the human spirit into which he had been initiated on that Tibetan mountainside. But he continued to advise his successors on the frontier and his ideas continued to influence Anglo-Tibetan policy. His name remained synonymous with Tibet in the British mind and he became one of the legendary figures in the mythology of the empire.[4]

When Younghusband left Lhasa he was accompanied by the senior civil officers of the mission, including his nominal second-in-command, John Claude White, the Political Officer Sikkim. White had been responsible for dealing with the Tibetans during the previous decade and had expected to be given command of the mission to Lhasa, but he was unpopular both with the Tibetans and with Curzon and his supporters. Although he was the obvious candidate to lead a mission to Lhasa, Curzon preferred a man with no experience on that section of the frontier, a clear indication of his opinion of White. Younghusband was initially sympathetic to White, knowing that he had expected to be given command of the mission, but that sympathy soon vanished. He found White 'arrogant' in his dealings with the Tibetans and 'appallingly unfit' for the diplomatic tasks required.[5]

Denied the possibility of a glorious culmination to his career by the appointment of Younghusband to lead the mission, White served in Gangtok for four more years before he retired. Although theoretically in charge of the British Trade Agencies in Tibet, his authority had been fatally undermined. White became an increasingly embittered figure who directed much of his resentment at the newly appointed Gyantse Trade Agent, Captain W.F. 'Frank' O'Connor.

The Irish-born O'Connor was an extremely able and ambitious officer, who had become Younghusband's 'right-hand man' on the mission to Lhasa. He had been educated at Charterhouse and the Royal Military Academy Woolwich, and when he arrived in India in 1895 he had joined an artillery regiment in Darjeeling, in the Himalayan foothills. There, as O'Connor later wrote, he was 'captivated by the glamour of the unknown...almost entirely unexplored country': Tibet.[6] Surmising that Tibet would be of strategic importance in the future, he began to study the country and its language and became the first and for at least ten years the only, British officer able to converse fluently in Tibetan.

Officially, O'Connor could not travel to Tibet. The Tibetan Government refused to admit foreigners into its territory and theoretically the Government of India did not allow Europeans to cross its northern borders. In practice, however, such journeys were fairly common, particularly by army officers on shooting trips. The Government of

India generally turned a blind eye to these excursions as they provided valuable intelligence on routes into, and conditions within, Tibet.

Within months of his arrival in Darjeeling, O'Connor had been tempted into crossing the border, joining White on a brief excursion through Tibetan territory. The following year he ventured across the frontier for three days before being discovered by local shepherds. After a 'free fight with...fists, sticks and stones', O'Connor retreated as quickly as possible back into Sikkim, a journey so exhausting that two of his coolies collapsed and died en route. As O'Connor noted, however, 'the information then acquired proved useful later on when the [Younghusband] Mission crossed...by the same route'[7]

After a routine admonishment for breaching frontier regulations, O'Connor was promptly summoned to work in the Intelligence Branch of the Quarter-Master General's Department at Simla, a hill-station north of Delhi, which was the seat of British India's government during the hot season. In Simla, O'Connor compiled reports on the Tibetan border areas under the direction of General Hamilton Bower, himself a Tibetan explorer of note.[8] Although O'Connor then obtained a transfer to the war-torn North-West Frontier Province (an almost compulsory step for an ambitious army officer) he retained his interest in Tibet and spent his leave periods travelling in the Tibetan border areas.

O'Connor was a man of strong views whose opinions on Tibetan matters were highly regarded by the Viceroy, Lord Curzon, with whom he had several meetings in Simla. For a young frontier officer, this was a significant mark of esteem and when Curzon began to plan a mission to Tibet O'Connor was an obvious choice. An indication of his growing reputation was that the Indian Army Commander-in-Chief, Lord Kitchener, and the Indian Foreign Secretary, Louis Dane, both supported his application to join the mission.[9]

By January 1903, O'Connor was in Darjeeling preparing for the yet-to-be announced Tibetan Frontier Commission, which became known as the 'Younghusband mission'. He was appointed mission secretary because of his knowledge of Tibetan, but his actual duties were much wider, for, like Younghusband, he was naturally adept at gathering intelligence, and equally brave and resourceful in combat. His post as mission secretary was, in effect, that of intelligence officer.[10]

Younghusband relied a great deal on O'Connor during the mission. When, in a characteristically bold move, Younghusband decided to ride into the camp of the opposing Tibetan forces to personally negotiate a settlement (a risky enterprise which could well have ended in his death), he took just two men with him: one was Frank O'Connor. O'Connor did venture to suggest that the plan was 'a bit risky', but he was no stranger to risks himself. After he had been wounded in the shoulder leading an attack on Tibetan positions during fighting at Gyantse, Younghusband ordered him to avoid combat for the remainder of the mission. O'Connor was just too valuable to lose.[11]

O'Connor was left in Gyantse as Trade Agent after Younghusband's party returned to India, but he did not remain there long. On 10 October 1904, just 10 days after the Trade Agency was opened, he rode the 60 miles to Shigatse, Tibet's second-largest town. Shigatse was the seat of the Panchen Lama, Tibet's second-highest religious figure and as will be seen, O'Connor had great plans for him.

O'Connor travelled to Shigatse with a small party of officers whom Younghusband had deputed to inspect the Gartok Trade Agency site in western Tibet. The expedition continued westwards, racing against the onset of winter, which would close the passes from Gartok to India and force them to endure the extreme cold of a western Tibetan winter.

The Gartok mission was under the command of Captain Cecil Rawling and consisted of four British officers accompanied by 35 'native' assistants, and 144 pack animals. Rawling had, like O'Connor, previously made an illicit visit to western Tibet, but he was to play no further part in Anglo-Tibetan relations and was killed in action early in World War One. Two other members of the party, Captain Ryder (later Surveyor-General of India) and Lieutenant Wood similarly pass out of our story. But the fourth member of the expedition was Lieutenant F.M.'Eric' Bailey, a young officer who had made his name on the Younghusband mission. He was to become one of the most important figures in the Anglo-Tibetan history.

Bailey, like Younghusband, was born in India, the son of a Lieutenant-Colonel in the Indian Army. After schooling at the Edinburgh Academy, Wellington, and Sandhurst, he returned to India in 1900, aged just 18. Bailey was ambitious and quickly realised that 'in these days nothing important happens in India itself. To get on one must learn about the neighbouring countries'.[12]

Serving with the 32nd Sikh Pioneers at Siliguri, south of Darjeeling, he became friends with O'Connor, who encouraged him to learn Tibetan. Bailey was taken on the mission to Lhasa and Younghusband then selected him to accompany Rawling's mission as he considered that Bailey's basic knowledge of Tibetan was 'likely to prove useful'. Younghusband also wanted Bailey to be made Trade Agent at Gartok, but the Government of India decided to economise by posting an Indian employee there.[13]

While Rawling's party carried out valuable survey work, they were obviously anxious to reach India. The expedition stayed in Gartok for just one day, although that was long enough for them to realise that this desolate Tibetan outpost was unlikely to be of any political importance. The party hurried on over the 18,700ft Ayi-la pass, and reached British India on Christmas Eve, 1904. Bailey had no real opportunity to distinguish himself officially on this journey, but it added to his Tibetan experience, and he did appear for breakfast one morning having already shot a wolf; just the sort of distinctive incident that made an officer a name among his contemporaries.[14]

* * *

By the end of 1904, the British had thus established their influence in Tibet. They had opened three Trade Agencies inside its borders and British-Indian troops were in temporary occupation of the Chumbi Valley. Although Younghusband's official role there ended on his return to India, his trusted deputy Frank O'Connor remained in Gyantse to carry on his policies. While forbidden by his own government to visit Lhasa, and nominally under the orders of the Political Officer Sikkim, J.C. White, O'Connor was, in effect, the Raj's first permanent ambassador in Tibet.

Younghusband, O'Connor, White and Bailey were the pioneers of the British presence in Tibet and their influence and reputations lived on throughout the Anglo-Tibetan encounter. Although the popular image of Tibet is of a remote and seldom-visited land, they paved the way for well over 100 British officials who were to serve there during the ensuing 46 years. What follows is the story of those men and their era.

Introduction

'To Avoid Incurring the Hostility of the Chinese Government'

The Anglo-Tibetan encounter in the 1904-47 period had a significant and enduring effect on Tibet and its neighbours. It brought the Tibetans into contact with new technologies and ways of thinking and it shaped the modern European understanding of that land. Many of the problems raised by the encounter remain important issues today. Officers of the British Raj were at the centre of this encounter, yet the role played by these 'men on the spot' has been largely forgotten, although the historical records of the British presence in Tibet provide an almost complete chronicle of every individual who served there and clearly distinguish the key men, who formed a distinct group. They reveal how and why this elite body of imperial frontiersmen thought and acted as they did and prove that these officers exerted a considerable influence on events, ideas, and policies in the region.

The Tibetan frontiersmen formed a small, homogenous cadre with a distinct institutional identity, which was recognised by other government officials. In the absence of an established title, I refer to these officers collectively as the 'Tibet cadre', a term used here specifically to refer to 20 officials, on whom this study will focus. These were the officers who served for more than one year in the senior positions which significantly influenced the encounter between Tibet and the British Raj. Those positions were: the senior post of Political Officer Sikkim, Bhutan and Tibet, the office of Trade Agent Gyantse and, after 1936, the post of Head of British Mission Lhasa.* One name

---

* A list of the Tibet cadre officers, with biographical details, is given in Appendix 'A'.

absent from this group is that of Younghusband, who did not return to Tibet after his 1903-04 mission. But as the cadre's 'founding father', his influence is always apparent.

As a result of their background, character, education, training and imperial service, Tibet cadre officers shared certain values and attitudes which shaped their perception of Tibet, and of their duties there. This collective character was formed and expressed in a particular historical era and to understand the perspective of the 'men on the spot' we must understand the ethos in which they functioned. This study therefore examines the character, role, and actions of the most influential officers in the Anglo-Tibetan encounter within the wider context of the frontier zone in which they were located and the historical era in which they functioned.

This is not a history of Tibet, or of the Tibetans' reactions to the British presence, which are generally referred to only in as much as they affected British aims and actions. Nor does it perpetuate images of Tibet as a land of magic and mystery where spiritual masters preserve esoteric wisdom; the concerns of the Raj were much more prosaic. It is, ultimately, a study of men (no women were in positions of power there) and how their ideas and actions affected events on the periphery of empire, 'betwixt and between' cultures European and Asian.

The theories of social scientists are largely ignored here. While Tibet, Sikkim, China, British India, and indeed the Tibet cadre, may all have been what Benedict Anderson called 'imagined communities'[1], constructed according to the demands of competing power structures, they existed in a specific time and place. While the cultural context in which the cadre existed has now vanished, that context is important because of its effects today on real people, places, and events.

Imperial history today is commonly criticised as defending elite power structures at the expense of the 'voices' of marginalised groups within the indigenous society. Yet the subjects of this study were not all British officers, three were local born. It must also be remembered that British imperial policy was determined through compromise. Discussion often ranged throughout the chain of command from Whitehall to the frontier and along this chain can be found many dissenting views, British and Asian, and many representations of marginalised power structures. There were alternative perspectives on the frontier, and they are represented in both official and private archives. Even where the censor has been at work, there are records of what was censored, and which 'voices' were suppressed. While we cannot ever fully recreate the ethos of a past era, we can use these sources to understand a great deal about how the Tibet cadre thought, why they did so, and what effect their thinking and consequent actions had.

In addition to the main narrative describing the Tibet cadre's role in the events of the 1904-47 period, this work is concerned with two main issues. The character of cadre officers and how this affected their actions and, secondly, the image of Tibet which the cadre constructed. This image shaped our historical understanding of that land, but it was produced by the Tibet cadre for a particular political purpose.

This study is based on, and reflects the perspective of, English-language sources. The issues raised could be considered from Chinese, Tibetan, and Russian viewpoints through the use of their sources. There are always varying perspectives on historical events, and there was much that the British did not know about Tibet. Their power to influence events there was limited, and the Tibetans naturally sought to use their ties with Britain, China and other powers to their own advantage.

References to 'the Tibetans' conceal many varying perspectives within Tibetan society, and generally only represent the prevailing view of the Lhasa ruling elite. The term cannot be taken as indicating a unanimous, collective opinion. Those who seek a deeper understanding of the Tibetan perspective in this period should consult, in particular, the major works of K.Dhondup and Melvyn Goldstein listed in the bibliography, while those concerned with Anglo-Tibetan policy at the highest diplomatic level – and much besides – should turn first to Alastair Lamb's monumental *Tibet, China & India 1914-1950*, a comprehensive and authoritative work on which I have relied a great deal.

Spellings used here are those employed by the British at the time; 'Peking' for example, rather than 'Beijing'. In the case of Chinese these generally follow the Wade-Giles system. In the case of Tibetan they generally follow a system devised by W.F.O'Connor for the

Government of India, except that the term 'Panchen Lama' is used rather than the term 'Tashi Lama' which was often favoured by the early cadre officers. Tibetan transliterations are given in the glossary. Proper names, place names and terms such as 'Dalai Lama', which are commonly known in English, have not been italicised.

The term 'state' is used in the general sense. The term 'Raj' is used to represent not only the Government of India, but its various supporting structures, administrative, social and ideological. 'Tibet' refers to the polity ruled by the Dalai Lamas in the period 1913-50, not that area now designated as the Tibetan Autonomous Region of China. Eastern Tibet refers to the Kham, Amdo and Derge regions bordering China. 'Political officer' is used to denote members of the Indian Political Department in general, whereas the term 'Political Officer' refers specifically to the post of Political Officer Sikkim. On occasion I refer to Political officers collectively as 'Politicals', the term commonly used at the time.[2] Officers' ranks are given at the time of service. Cadre officers' final ranks are given in Appendix 'A'; brief biographies of other important figures are given in the endnotes.

* * *

Before commencing the history of the Tibet cadre it is necessary to understand the basic structure of both Tibetan and British Indian Government, as well as something of the nature of imperial frontier policies, and to outline the events which led to the British presence in Tibet. Specialists will be aware that this introduction simplifies many complex issues in summarising these points.

The Tibet cadre were officers of the British imperial Government of India and while tremendously powerful in their own locality, were actually located at the lower levels of the administrative chain of command.

In the 1904-47 period, India was officially ruled by the British parliament, and administered by the India Office at Whitehall. The India Office was headed by the Secretary of State for India [hereafter, the Secretary of State], who was a member of the British Cabinet. British-Indian relations were thus separate from relations with foreign states such as China and Russia, which were the responsibility of the Foreign Office.

The British Government appointed the Viceroy of India, who held supreme power during his term of office. Although theoretically subject to the orders of the India Office, the Government of India was largely self-financing and maintained a great deal of autonomy, the extent of which depended largely on the ability of the Viceroy to influence or even dominate, the Secretary of State.[3]

India's foreign relations were the responsibility of the Indian Political Department, which was in effect the diplomatic corps of the Government of India. This department came under the personal control of the Viceroy and was responsible for relations both with the 'Princely states' (self-governing territories within the borders of British India) and with neighbouring states whose affairs were of direct consequence to India, such as Nepal, Afghanistan, and Tibet.

Political Department officers were selected either from the Indian Army or the Indian Civil Service (hereafter, the ICS), although occasionally officers from the Indian Police and the Provincial Civil Services were also admitted.[4] An approximate balance of two-thirds Indian Army and one-third ICS officers was maintained by a complicated intake formula. Officers were theoretically 'on deputation' to the Political Department from their original service, but in practice they normally remained members of the Political Department until retirement.

Political officers served in both the Indian Princely states and in external postings. No distinction was drawn between areas of service; 'lean and keen for the frontier, fat and good-natured men for the states' was the popular maxim.[5] Officers could also serve a term in the Secretariat, the administrative headquarters of the Department, which consisted of a small staff controlling the activities and postings within the service. The Secretariat office was situated (after 1911) in Delhi, or at Simla during the summer months.[6]

The decision-making process within the Political Department depended on a hierarchical passage of paper. Reports from the positions in Tibet were forwarded to the Political Officer in Sikkim, who added his own comments before sending them to his headquarters. These reports were considered and commented upon at the Secretariat and might be shown, officially or unofficially, to other relevant departments.

If important, they were passed via the Foreign Secretary to the Viceroy, and thence to the India Office in London, which in turn reported to the British Government.

This process could also work in reverse. A question about a Tibetan matter from a British MP could be passed down the chain to an officer in Tibet, whose report would pass up the chain again. Each officer in the chain could add comments and each department would consider these comments before adding their own suggestions. Of course many of the individuals involved knew each other personally, and would correspond privately as well as officially, often by-passing the established chain of command.

Policy-making thus involved each link in the chain from Tibet to British parliament. As a result, although the opinion of the 'man on the spot' was theoretically highly valued, in practice it was liable to be overruled at any or every higher level.

* * *

The establishment of a British presence in Tibet was a direct result of the Younghusband mission, which was the culmination of a long process of British Indian expansion towards Tibet.

Tibet had emerged as a united tribal federation in the seventh century AD. and had submitted to Mongol authority in the 13th century. In 1642, Mongol forces intervened in Tibetan internal struggles on behalf of the Gelugpa sect of Tibetan Buddhism. They made the hierarch of the Gelugpa sect, the 5th Dalai Lama, the effective ruler of Tibet. To their followers, the Dalai Lamas were successive rebirths of Chenrezi, the *bodhisattva* of compassion. The 5th Dalai Lama later awarded his senior teacher, the Abbot of Shigatse's leading Gelugpa monastery, the title 'Panchen Lama' ('Great Scholar'), thereby instituting a second important power structure within Tibet.

In 1720, the Mongols' overlordship was inherited by China's Manchu Ch'ing dynasty. In 1774, the 8th Dalai Lama was still in his minority, and, although Tibet was ruled by a Regent, the long-serving 3rd Panchen Lama had acquired a considerable degree of power and autonomy. Therefore, when the Governor-General of

Bengal, Warren Hastings, wanted to open ties with Tibet, he sent his envoy, George Bogle of the Bengal Civil Service, to the court of the Panchen Lama.

Bogle's mission went well and after the Panchen Lama died in 1780 (and Bogle a year later), Hastings continued to seek ties with Tibet. He sent Captain Samuel Turner to Shigatse in 1782 after the Panchen Lama's incarnation had been discovered. Although they established good relations with their Shigatse hosts, Bogle and Turner achieved little of lasting value. The Lhasa authorities refused to permit them to visit the Tibetan capital and, after Hasting's departure from India, British contacts with Tibet virtually ceased and did not resume for more than a century.

During the 19th century, most of the territory to the south of Tibet came under the control of the British Raj. Nepal became a British ally and when the Nepalese invaded and defeated Tibet in 1855, the Tibetans assumed they must have had British support. As the Raj increased its power to the south of the Himalayas, the Tibetans became increasingly fearful of British intentions. Encouraged by their Chinese overlords to regard foreigners as a threat to their religion and fearing the expansion of British power, the Tibetan authorities increasingly resisted any attempt by Europeans to enter their territory.

Between 1750 and 1900 only three Westerners visited Lhasa; Thomas Manning, an eccentric English private scholar in 1811, and two Lazarist priets, Huc and Gabet, in 1846. As it became increasingly isolated from changes in the outside world, Tibetan society became more conservative and insular.

Tibet's desire for isolation presented problems to the Government of India. No formal ties existed between India and Tibet, there were no diplomatic representatives and no established mode of inter-governmental communication. When the British sought to raise issues with the Tibetan Government they had no means of communicating with Lhasa, a situation that became intolerable to the Raj.

In the late 19th century, Whitehall and the Government of India came under pressure from powerful trading lobbies wanting to open Tibet to free trade. More significantly, there was an increasing concern over the security of India's northern frontier. Safeguarding the security of India against threats real or imaginary was always a powerful concern, and British Indian strategists raised the fear that Russia's rapid expansion into Central Asia would culminate in their gaining influence in Tibet. While very few officials of the Raj seriously expected a Russian invasion, their involvement in Tibet was seen as liable to pave the way for the infiltration of Russian influence into Nepal and the British Indian Himalayas, with a potentially destabilising effect on India.

There was also a less quantifiable stimulus to opening Tibet to European intrusion: a contemporary spirit of enquiry demanded that the 'unknown' should become 'known'. Tibet's policy of isolation increasingly produced, in the European imagination, a series of enticing images of a hidden spiritual enclave on the 'Roof of the World', which might preserve esoteric knowledge which the rest of the world had lost. Thus, ironically, Tibet's determination to preserve its isolation only succeeded in making it more alluring to many European minds.

As Europeans were prevented from obtaining information in Tibet, the Raj began to send local employees to collect the information which the imperial government needed. They trained a number of 'native' surveyors, known as *pandits*, in such clandestine arts as measuring distances by the number of carefully measured paces they took. The *pandits* made a series of extraordinary journeys through Tibet disguised as pilgrims, secretly compiling maps of the country.[7]

While *pandits* gathered geographical data, valuable political information was collected by the Tibetan-speaking Bengali school teacher, Sarat Chandra Das. Das had been first headmaster of the Bhotia Boarding School in Darjeeling, which was opened in 1874 specifically to develop local youths who could mediate in dealings with the Raj's northern neighbours.[8] After some years Das was given a nominal government post as a school inspector, freeing him to travel to Tibet in 1881-82. Chandra Das travelled in the company of Urgyen Gyatso, a Sikkimese lama from an aristocratic family, who had also been employed as a teacher at the Bhotia School.[9]

Whereas *pandits* travelled among the lower social classes, Das sought a different society. Just as Political officers were directed to 'cultivate the friendship of the local Ruling Chiefs', Das was under instructions to 'cultivate the friendship of influential persons'.[10] He spent more than a year in Tibet, visiting Lhasa in 1882. When the Tibetan Government later discovered this, and correctly assumed that he had been spying for the British, the strength of their reaction underlined the Lhasa Government's determination to preserve Tibet's isolation. They executed Das's principal sponsor, the Panchen Lama's Prime Minister, Kyabying Sengchen Tulku, an incarnate lama from Dongtse Monastery (near Shigatse). In addition, the Dongtse ruling family, the Palhes, close associates of Sengchen Tulku, were severely punished. These events were later to provide the British with ready-made allies in Shigatse.[11]

After their return from Tibet, Das and Urgyen Gyatso were employed as Tibetan specialists, and given such tasks as examining Political Department candidates in Tibetan language. But neither man had any significant political influence on Anglo-Tibetan relations in the 20th century. Their journeys were part of the process by which British India extended its influence over the periphery. Local employees could be used to map new territory, locate its power sources, and establish communication with them. Yet when contacts were established – or refused – British officers took over the process. Thus when Curzon sought to force Lhasa to open relations with India, he turned not to the Tibetan-speaking Bengali, but to Younghusband, a British officer who had never been to Tibet.[12]

One of the biggest problems the British had in opening relations with their northern neighbour was that it was unclear who really controlled it. Towards the end of the 19th century the Manchu emperor's rule over Lhasa had diminished to the point where his authority was little more than ceremonial overlordship, represented by two officials known as Ambans and their military escort.

Tibet's remoteness made it a hardship posting for these Chinese representatives. The officials sent were generally of poor quality and China's own internal weaknesses prevented her from imposing stronger rule. Since the 9th-12th Dalai Lamas all died before, or shortly after, taking office, real political power in Lhasa was contested by the Ambans and a succession of Tibetan Regents.

As China was theoretically the supreme power in Tibet, the British originally assumed they could solve Tibetan issues through discussion with the Chinese. In 1885 China agreed to a mission from the Government of Bengal visiting Lhasa, but this had to be abandoned at the last minute when it became clear that the Tibetans regarded the mission as an invasion force. The troops Lhasa sent to resist the mission, however, entered Sikkimese territory, which the British regarded as being within their sphere of influence.*[13]

After unsuccessful attempts to negotiate a solution with China, the British dispatched an expeditionary force to Sikkim in 1888-89, which expelled the Tibetans. J.C.White, a Public Works Department engineer 'on loan to the Political Department' for the duration of the expedition, was then appointed to the newly-created post of Political Officer Sikkim. In effect, this gave White control over Sikkim and he was later given responsibility for relations with Bhutan and Tibet, although he remained resident in Gangtok (the Sikkimese capital).

The Government of India had yet to realise that Peking could no longer enforce its will in Lhasa and they continued to try to obtain the right to station an officer in Tibet through negotiations with China. The Chinese, fearing that they would lose any vestige of their influence in Lhasa if the British began to negotiate directly with the Tibetans, agreed to discussions. These resulted in the 1890 Anglo-Chinese Convention and its attached 1893 Trade Regulations, which allowed for the opening of a British Trade Agency in Tibet. Although none of their representatives were at the talks, the Tibetan's policy of isolation was recognised by the British. They agreed that their Trade Agency would be situated at Yatung, just across the border from Sikkim, rather than at Phari, the main Indo-Tibetan border trading centre.

The Tibetan Government refused to accept that they were bound by Anglo-Chinese agreements. When White went to Yatung in May 1894 to open the Trade Agency, he found a wall had been built around the site to isolate it. The Government of India were, by the 1893 Regulations, entitled to 'send officers to reside at Yatung to watch the

---

* Sikkim, which stood on the easiest route from Calcutta to Lhasa, had come under British influence following the Treaty of Tumlong in 1861. It became a British protectorate under the Anglo-Chinese Convention of 1890.

conditions of British trade at that mart'. But they realised there was little point and awaited new developments, for there seemed no obvious need for an urgent solution. Thus in 1895, when the 13th Dalai Lama came of age and took power in Tibet, his country remained relatively secure in its isloation.

Unlike his immediate predecessors, the 13th Dalai Lama survived into maturity and established his secular authority at Lhasa. He became a strong and determined national leader, surviving periods in the political wilderness to lead his country to independence, albeit an independence no major power recognised.

* * *

The arrival of Lord Curzon as Viceroy of India in 1899 marked the beginning of a new era on India's north-east frontier. Curzon was an enormously commanding personality, who increasingly concentrated power in his own hands. Totally self-assured and often arrogant, he was admired rather than liked by most of his supporters. Unlike many Viceroys, he had travelled widely in Asia, and was one of the great imperial strategists. Having seen at first-hand the expansion of the Tsarist Russian state into the tribal confederacies and *khanates* of Central Asia, he regarded this as a major concern. As a committed imperialist he respected the Russians' right to imperial expansion. But he believed British interests demanded that India, 'the Jewel in the Crown' of her empire, be secured from Russian influence. He saw it as his duty to ensure that the challenge was met and defeated by action safely beyond the frontiers of India.[14]

Soon after Curzon's arrival, there were indications that Russia was becoming involved in Tibet. British suspicions centered on Agvan Dorzhiev, a monk from the Russian Buriat Mongol region where Buddhism predominated.[15] Dorzhiev had studied at Drepung monastery in Lhasa and risen to be an attendant of the Dalai Lama. Although on one occasion he had travelled through India, the British had very little reliable information about him (his name appears in their records in numerous different spellings). They suspected, however, that he was supplying Tibet with modern weapons and aiming to bring Lhasa into the Russian sphere of influence.[16]

When it became officially know that Dorzhiev had travelled to St.Petersburg to contact the Russian Government at the Dalai Lama's behest, Curzon made two attempts to open communications with the Tibetan leader. He sent letters to him through intermediaries, but they were both returned unopened. Curzon saw this refusal by an Asian potentate to accept a letter from the Viceroy of India as a deliberate blow to British prestige. He began planning a mission to Lhasa to remove Russian influence from Tibet and bring it within the Raj's sphere of influence.

By late 1902, Curzon had selected the dynamic Political officer, Francis Younghusband, to lead the Lhasa mission. Younghusband greatly admired Curzon and shared his views on frontier policy. He developed a great personal loyalty to the Viceroy and admitted that 'if he [Curzon] thought that in the end I had failed him I should have been miserable for the rest of my days'.[17]

This meant that while Younghusband was theoretically answerable to the Government of India and ultimately the British Government, in practice he represented the interests of Lord Curzon. This personal chain of loyalty was to be characteristic of the British presence in Tibet. Just as Younghusband supported Curzon, to whom he owed his appointment, so too did O'Connor have a personal loyalty to Younghusband, who had promoted him. O'Connor in turn acted as patron to his own loyal protégé, F.M.Bailey.

Younghusband's mission was therefore following Curzon's policies, and Younghusband himself was determined to reach Lhasa and end Russian influence there. His mission crossed the frontier in 1903 with a large military escort, which inevitably clashed with the Tibetan army. The British Indian forces were more professional, and were equipped with far superior weapons. They inflicted a series of heavy defeats on the local troops as the mission slowly advanced towards Lhasa. On 30 July 1904, the 13th Dalai Lama fled into exile in Mongolia. Four days later the British forces entered his capital. Younghusband negotiated with the remaining Tibetan authorities, and the Convention between Great Britain and Tibet was signed in the Potala Palace on 7 September 1904. Tibet's isolation was now ended. The British, who had actually found almost no trace of any Russian influence, momentarily held supreme power at Lhasa.

* * *

The acquisition of power brings with it the need for strategies to secure or to expand that power. For the Raj, the security of India's northern frontier was the primary concern in its dealings with Tibet. In the early 19th century, the massive Himalayan mountain chain had provided a 'natural frontier'* between India and China. Consequently little attention was paid to the north-east frontier. Even when it became apparent that China's authority over Lhasa was purely nominal and that the Tibetans were not prepared to establish any diplomatic relations with the Raj, it was still possible to disregard that problem. Tibet did not pose a threat to India. Only when it appeared that Russia had developed links with Lhasa was it agreed that action on Tibet was necessary.

The policy the Government of India adopted at the turn-of-the-century was designed to prevent Russia from gaining influence in Tibet, while making some concession to the trade lobby and those forces arising out of contemporary spirit of enquiry. This policy was largely the creation of Lord Curzon, with the support of senior officials such as the Indian Foreign Secretary Louis Dane, who was in day-to-day charge of the Political Department.

Curzon sent Younghusband to Lhasa to force the Tibetans to end their dealings with Russia and, incidentally, to enforce free trade between Tibet and India. He did not intend to bring Tibet into the British empire; that was never a practical proposition. What mattered was that Tibet accept British guidance in affairs which affected the security of India's northern border. The ideal model later emerged in Bhutan. Their foreign relations and defence were controlled by the Government of India, but, at least theoretically, they retained internal autonomy.

Curzon's policy was recognised in British India as one of two possible frontier policies. Either the frontier could be defended by

---

* 'Natural frontiers' are those imposed by geography; rivers, lakes, coastline and so on. In British India, mountains were considered, as Royal Geographical Society President, and Superintendent of Frontier Surveys, Sir Thomas Holditch, stated, 'the most lasting, the most unmistakable and the most efficient as a barrier'; Holditch 1916, p. 147.

garrisons of troops, or it could be defended by 'buffer states' beyond the frontier. 'Buffer states', those which separated two empires, usually came under the influence of one of those empires, and tended to eventually be taken over completely by the imperial power. This meant that while frontier garrisons were an essentially defensive policy, 'buffer states' implied a 'forward' policy.[18]

'Forward' policies were those which involved an expansion of imperial responsibilities beyond existing boundaries. The classic exposition of the consequences of this policy was by General Sir John Jacob, on the Sind frontier in the 1850s, who stated that, 'to enable this red line to retain its present position...it is absolutely necessary to occupy posts in advance of it.'[19]

The Tibet cadre, in common with imperial frontiersmen in other empires, generally favoured 'forward' policies. When people who were not under their authority created problems, the obvious solution often seemed to be bringing them under imperial authority. They also knew that that could benefit their career; most heroes of the empire were frontiersmen who had brought new territory under control.[20]

Although 'forward' policies were favoured by those at the periphery of empire, they were much less popular with those at the centre. As national security was probably the Government of India's primary concern, its officials could see advantages in expanding their authority in Tibet, but India's frontier policies were governed by financial limitations. Government had to adopt the most economical policies and was thus extremely reluctant to extend its responsibilities. Annexing Tibet, with its primitive economy and no infrastructure, would have been financially impossible for the Raj.

'Forward' policies were even less attractive to the home government, not for economic reasons, but because Whitehall's global perspective gave it an aversion to expanding the frontiers of empire. Both Russia and China strongly opposed any extension of British influence in Tibet and after World War One they were joined by Japan, America and later Nazi Germany, all of whom employed varying degrees of anti-colonialist rhetoric in regard to the British presence in Tibet. Whitehall was particularly concerned to avoid alienating the Chinese, with whom

British trade ties were considered of great economic importance, and thus wanted to solve Tibetan issues by wider regional agreements with China and Russia.

As the British Government at Whitehall ultimately controlled the Government of India there was never any possibility of Tibet being taken into the British empire; Whitehall neither considered it, nor would have allowed it. The Tibet cadre saw advantages in having some measure of control or influence at Lhasa, and also saw benefits in an independent Tibet, but Whitehall's view was very different. They recognised China as having 'suzerain' power over Tibet. The term 'suzerain', however, had no specific or agreed meaning, and has never been properly defined in the Tibetan context. But a lack of specific definition was not uncommon in Anglo-Tibetan affairs, and had advantages to all powers concerned.[21]

The interests of the home and imperial governments often clashed in areas of foreign policy. Measures India considered essential to safeguard its security could be strongly opposed by Whitehall because of their effect on British foreign relations. As Whitehall mistrusted the imperial frontiersmen and opposed their plans for expanding British authority, the home government increasingly exerted its authority and limited India's expansionist tendencies.

Curzon's years as Viceroy were of seminal importance to Anglo-Tibetan relations and were in many ways the most confident era of the Raj, but they marked the high tide of empire on India's north-east frontier. A new anti-imperialist Liberal Government was elected in Britain after the Boer War had swung public opinion against overseas adventures and when Curzon left India at the end of 1905, the age of British imperial expansion was practically over.

In a reversal of the circumstances during the Curzon period, 1905-10 saw a weak Viceroy and a strong Secretary of State, and the Government of India was ordered to follow Whitehall's orders regarding frontier policy. Younghusband received a foretaste of this new era when Secretary of State St.John Broderick personally gave him a copy of his despatch to the Viceroy, dated 2 December 1904.

Questions [wrote Broderick] of Indian Frontier policy could no longer be regarded from an exclusively Indian point of view, and the course to be pursued in such cases must be laid down by His Majesty's Government alone.[22]

Implementation of obviously 'forward' policies towards Tibet was now blocked by Whitehall. The Tibet cadre, though keen supporters of the 'forward school', had to accept Whitehall's opinion that

> The large commercial interests of His Majesty's Government in China make it necessary to subordinate policy in Tibet to the general policy of the British Government in China and to avoid incurring the hostility...of the [Chinese] Government.[23]

Acceptance did not mean agreement. The cadre were frustrated by the restrictions imposed on them by the Government of India, usually, though by no means exclusively, at Whitehall's behest. They often railed at the 'Old maids who weave our destiny in Simla', and at the British Foreign Office whose officials they rightly judged to be totally biased in favour of China. When one cadre officer visited the Foreign Office in 1949 he found 'an icy Chinese expert, Paul Grey, in charge of the Far East...and he simply smiled bleakly when I tried to tell him of Tibet's position.' Another complained that 'I don't think the young pup who was dealing with Tibet...knew where it is on the map.'[24]

Despite British fears, Russian influence in Tibet was always very limited. The cadre found that its real enemy was China, who wanted to bring Tibet into her empire. There was no dispute between the two powers over the ideological model which Lhasa should follow, for China was herself modernising on the Western model. The point of dispute was who would control the process.[25]

The British and the Chinese struggled to establish a controlling influence in Tibet throughout the 1904-47 period. Both sent representatives to influence and control the country. They used similar methods, copied the other's initiatives, and constantly measured their opponent's successes and failures against their own. The slightest indication of Tibetan preference for one country's ideas, actions, and even sports and pastimes, was seized upon as evidence that the Tibetans favoured that country and hence its policies.[26] Both sides claimed their involvement was in the Tibetans' best interests, but the Tibetans' desire for isolation and control of their own affairs was totally ignored.

* * *

Younghusband's forces did not encounter a modern nation-state as Europeans understood it. Tibet had no standard procedure for conducting relations with its neighbours, nor did it have a bureaucratic class. While Tibetan traders travelled widely in Asia, their central economic system was primitive and functioned largely by barter. There was no industrial or mechanical development and even the wheel was only used in a religious context, not as a means of transport.[27]

While Tibet was not a modern nation-state and was largely oblivious to the outside world, Tibetans had a definite identity. This was based on racial, cultural and linguistic distinctness from their neighbours and on the collective understanding of a shared history, mythology and traditions.

Although there were non-Buddhist elements in Tibetan society, the outstanding feature of that culture was its Buddhist religion. Tibetans defined themselves primarily in religious terms and spiritual matters constituted the central feature of their unique social system. Tibet was a Buddhist traditional state, defining itself by its centre and sacred spaces. As will be seen, the Anglo-Tibetan encounter forced the Tibetans to confront the differing perceptions of national and state identity held by traditional and modern societies. Their perspective on the 1904-47 period was naturally very different from the British perspective.

Chapter One

'He may yet be an Indian Ruling Chief'

On 1 October 1904, with no formalities beyond raising the flag, the Gyantse Trade Agency began operations in Chang Lo ['Willow garden'], a country house which the Younghusband mission had used as its Gyantse base. In addition to local employees, O'Connor had a number of European staff. There was a British officer of the Indian Medical Service [hereafter, the IMS] and a military escort consisting of 50 Indian soldiers, which was normally under the command of a British officer. There was also a European Head Clerk to oversee clerical staff recruited from the Darjeeling area, two Indian Army telegraph sergeants responsible for communications and a third in charge of supply and transport.

We do not know what instructions were given to O'Connor by Younghusband or his government. If he was given written instructions, they would have been similar to the orders issued to the Gartok Trade Agent, who was instructed to 'furnish a weekly diary giving particulars of routes traversed, of the trade prospects and of such political information as he may be able to gather'.[1]

Lord Ampthill, who acted as Viceroy while Curzon was on leave, cautioned the Politicals that

> We must be very careful that anything we do does not even wear the appearance of establishing a political centre at Gyantse...and I hope that the Department...will refrain from intrigue.'[2]

Ampthill's view was ignored. O'Connor understood that his real purpose reflected the largely unwritten aims of Curzon and Younghusband. He was supposed to establish his influence over the Tibetan leadership, although with the Dalai Lama having fled Lhasa it was not immediately apparent who those leaders were.

Three days after the signing of the 1904 Anglo-Tibetan Convention, the Chinese authorities in Lhasa had issued a proclamation deposing the exiled Dalai Lama. Younghusband had co-operated with China's Amban while he was in Lhasa and had encouraged, if not initiated, this move.[3] Although the Tibetans threw mud at the proclamation, Younghusband and the Amban were not concerned with their opinion. Deposing the Dalai Lama created a power vacuum which both parties hoped to use to their advantage.

After he fled into exile, the 13th Dalai Lama temporarily faded into insignificance in British eyes. He was just one of many local rulers that they had deposed during the expansion of the empire. The Trade Agents reported rumours of his whereabouts, but no European had yet met him, and he seemed a shadowy figure, doomed to fade into obscurity. The British saw his flight as cowardly. But in the perspective of the Lhasa Government it was a practical decision reflecting his symbolic status as the embodiment of Tibetan indentity: like the colours of a British regiment, the Dalai Lama had to be saved.

When the Tibetan leader fled Lhasa, he escaped towards the Mongolian capital, Urga [now Ulan Bator], where Mongolia's political and religious ruler, the 8th Jebtsundamba Khutukhtu, had his court. He fled there because the Tibetans had strong religious ties with the Mongolians, who were predominantly followers of Tibetan Buddhism. Oddly enough the Khutukhtu, like most of his predecessors a Tibetan by birth, had apparently foreseen the Dalai Lama's arrival. In 1903 he had predicted that Tibet's leader would soon come to Urga; a prediction which had then seemed highly unlikely.[4]

The Dalai Lama reached Urga in November 1904. For the last 28 days of the journey he was carried in a palanquin by the escort which the Khutukhtu sent to welcome him. The welcome, however, was soon outstayed. Religious offerings which had previously gone to support the Khutukhtu were now offered to the Dalai Lama and his court, and playing host to the Tibetan party rapidly drained Mongolian funds. In addition, the Jebtsundamba Khutukhtu conspicuously failed to maintain the moral standards expected of a Buddhist monk. He was an active bi-sexual, suffered from syphilis, and drank heavily.

Despite this embarrassing situation, the Dalai Lama was safe in Urga, not least because there was a Russian consulate there. Agvan Dorzhiev had accompanied the Dalai Lama into exile, and acted as go-between with the Russian Consul. Seeing an opportunity to advance Russian interests, the Consul deployed Cossacks to protect the Tibetan leader.[5] Russia, however, was too pre-occupied by internal problems and with the Russo-Japanese war to get seriously involved in Tibet.

In the absence of the Dalai Lama, Tibet's nominal ruler was the Abbot of Ganden Monastery, who had been appointed Regent. Ganden, along with Sera and Drepung, was one of Lhasa's 'Big Three' monasteries, which all had considerable power, wealth, and political influence. The Ganden Abbot was of particular importance as he, rather than the Dalai Lama, was also the head of the Gelugpa sect. The Abbot was an elderly but much respected religious figure whom Younghusband considered 'more nearly approached Kipling's Lama in "Kim" than any other Tibetan I met'.[6] But the Regent had little knowledge of, or interest in, the secular world, and was unprepared for the machiavellian ways of diplomacy.

Once the Dalai Lama had fled, the question of control at Lhasa became extremely complex. The Ch'ing dynasty was in terminal decline and it was their failure to control Tibet which had created the need for the Younghusband mission. China was simply not strong enough to enforce her control, and hence to exclude Russian influence from Lhasa. Although the British Government were prepared to give the Chinese full authority, the Tibet cadre realised that China's rule would be strongly opposed by the Tibetans, which would mean continued instability on the frontier.

As Whitehall refused to countenance any extension of British power in Tibet – which to the frontiersmen seemed the obvious solution – the search began for a suitable Tibetan who could control his country and with whom the Raj might negotiate a lasting solution. This was not a simple matter. Tibet's traditional power structure was a complicated system of 'checks and balances' which devolved the power of the Dalai Lama among various monastic and aristocratic factions and the British were not familiar with the way in which this complex power structure worked.

With Whitehall refusing to allow the cadre any direct contact with officials in Lhasa, the one obvious candidate for the leadership of Tibet was the Panchen Lama. He had an independent power structure in Shigatse, with his own court and officials, tax-paying territory and even foreign policy. The Dalai Lama was not necessarily his superior in the eyes of many in Shigatse, who regarded the Panchen Lama as their supreme sovereign in both the secular and religious realms. He was the obvious man for the cadre to deal with.[7]

So it was that O'Connor set off for Shigatse in October 1904, hoping to befriend the Panchen Lama. There was a promising start. When O'Connor and his party arrived the Panchen Lama, a somewhat nervous young man in his early twenties, welcomed them. He told O'Connor that he was delighted to renew the friendship which he had established – in his previous incarnations – with Bogle and Turner. O'Connor then remained in Shigatse for more than a month and had several private meetings with the Panchen Lama before he had to return to Gyantse.[8]

O'Connor's efforts to cultivate the friendship of the Panchen Lama were hindered by the fact that the Gyantse Agency was a days' ride from the Panchen Lama's Shigatse monastery. In fact, the cadre soon realised that all three Trade Agencies were in the wrong location, both in terms of trade, and politics. As Curzon had originally planned for a British mission in Lhasa, little thought had been given to the location of the Trade Agencies. Yatung had been chosen instead of Phari as a goodwill gesture, while Gartok had been chosen as it was believed to be the most important trading centre in western Tibet. In fact it was the site of an annual trade fair which lasted for around two weeks, and was otherwise virtually deserted.

Gyantse was selected because it appeared a commercially important meeting-point of trade routes from India, Shigatse and Lhasa. But Shigatse was home to the Panchen Lama and the leading merchants and was far more important both as a trading and political centre.[9] O'Connor and subsequent Trade Agents at all three Agencies frequently recommended relocating the Agencies, but that would have required renegotiating the 1904 Treaty. The Tibetans had only signed that because Younghusband's troops had fought their way to Lhasa. They had no interest in renegotiations; as the 13th Dalai Lama put it

> Why do the British insist on establishing trade marts? Their goods are coming in from India right up to Lhasa. Whether they have their marts or not things come in all the same. The British under the guise of establishing communications, are merely seeking to overreach us.[10]

* * *

O'Connor had made a promising start to his attempts to befriend the Panchen Lama, but he faced fresh problems on his return to Gyantse. If the Tibet cadre were to succeed in promoting the policies they favoured (and consequently advance their own careers), they had to ensure that they were Whitehall's only official source of information on Tibet. Other voices, which might promote policies opposed by the cadre, had to be silenced.

One threat to the cadre's position was already apparent. Following the 1893 Anglo-Chinese Trade treaty, British officers serving in the China Maritime Customs Service were posted to Yatung. These officers had little or no contact with the Government of India prior to 1903, when the Customs officer Captain W.R.M.Parr was attached to the Younghusband Mission.

Parr was a colourful and argumentative character who informally raised a complex issue of international law. He claimed that the presence of China Customs officers meant that the trade marts were technically Chinese Treaty Ports, which would mean that legally they were open to all foreigners. If that was the case, the Government of India would lose its preeminent place in Tibet. 'This', ruled Indian Foreign Secretary Louis Dane, 'we cannot allow'. But in September 1904, the hard-drinking Captain Parr was replaced by a more ambitious officer, Mr Vincent Henderson, who immediately challenged the Government of India.[11]

Henderson made a brief visit to Gyantse in December 1904 and officially refused to recognise the right of the Government of India, in the person of Trade Agent O'Connor, to be advised of his movements and motives within Tibet on the grounds that he was an officer of Tibet's suzerain power, China. Unofficially however, Henderson got on well with O'Connor, and he revealed that China planned to get rid of the Trade Agencies. He also told O'Connor about his own ambitions – a posting in Lhasa as 'advisor' to the Ambans, which he hoped would mean 'practically running the country'. O'Connor promptly warned his government that 'Henderson, nice fellow that he is, is a very dangerous and skilful opponent to us and the sooner he leaves...the better.'[12]

What concerned O'Connor was not just that Henderson represented the Chinese Government and its plans to take control of Tibet, but that he was not under the Government of India's authority. Maintaining the imperial government's authority required that it be seen as the highest, and undivided, authority in the region. If that authority was seen to be successfully challenged, even by other British elements, the Raj's prestige would, it was held, be damaged throughout the 'East'. This was also an issue which reflected the wider struggle between the Government of India and the 'China hands' in the British Foreign Office. In this debate, the cadre naturally represented what they saw as India's interests.

The cadre made prestige the weapon with which they removed the China Customs officers from Tibet. They began to argue that they needed to present a particular type of European to the Tibetans in order to maintain their respect and claimed that these officers were 'not of a particularly refined type and add little to our prestige'. They warned that the Tibetans 'believed that the Chinese must be superior to us [because they are] employing Englishmen in their service.' O'Connor also alleged that they ill-treated the Tibetans, which reflected badly on all British officers, and he warned that the Customs men might influence the Tibetans to act in ways detrimental to the Raj's interests.[13]

The Government of India agreed and asked Whitehall to order the removal of European officials in Chinese employ from Tibet. This took time, and was apparently done informally, to avoid creating an issue in which Sir Robert Hart, the powerful Head of Chinese Customs, would intervene to safeguard the prestige and interests of his own force. But, in April 1907, Henderson was replaced by a Chinese officer. Six years later, the Chinese service, apparently forgetting the previous difficulties, attempted to send another British officer on an inspection visit to the redundant Chinese Customs post at Yatung. They hastily backed down in the face of strong opposition from the Government of India, which instructed frontier officials to prevent the officer from crossing the border. The principle of Delhi's control over all British officials in Tibet was now firmly established.[14]

* * *

O'Connor settled into life at Gyantse. He had a great personal interest in Tibet and its people, and he cultivated friendships at all levels of Tibetan society. He attended monastic ceremonies, collected folksongs from villagers and entertained secular officials at the Agency. But while personally fascinated by the local culture, O'Connor's growing expertise was of wider significance. It enabled him to obtain practical information about personalities and events in Tibet which were of great political importance. Obtaining this type of information was a central part of the cadre's role.

The Raj did not rely solely on the cadre for information on Tibet. Nepal maintained a representative in Lhasa, who regularly forwarded lengthy reports on the situation there to his government in Kathmandu. These reports, much of which were based on rumour, were of mixed value, but they were passed on by the Nepalese Prime Minister to the Raj's representative in Kathmandu.[15]

Another valuable source of intelligence were the Christian missionaries who worked on the Chinese side of the eastern Tibetan frontier. As Lhasa steadfastly refused to allow them to work in Tibet, the missionaries supported increased British or Chinese authority, believing this would result in their being allowed into Tibet. In fact, the cadre consistently opposed allowing missionaries into Tibet in deference to Lhasa's strong opposition to any threat to their Buddhist faith, but they did not tell the missionaries that.

Consequently missionaries such as the Reverend J.R.Muir and Mr J.H.Edgar sent long reports on conditions in eastern Tibet which were forwarded via Peking to India. The missionaries were, in effect, unpaid spies. Much of the information they provided was obviously of military value. One report from Muir, for example, notes that 'I have made out a small map which will show better the disposition of the troops on the frontier'. The missionaries, whose converts were usually Chinese, not Tibetan, clearly enjoyed their clandestine role. Edgar, for example, actively solicited intelligence assignments.[16]

The Trade Agents' presence inside Tibet greatly extended British information-gathering capability there. Among their sources were the British Indian Buddhists who resided in Tibet, such as the half-brother and the son of the Maharaja of Sikkim. They lived on estates outside Gyantse and were regular providers of 'valuable information about Lhasa and Tibetan affairs'.[17] Lhasa's Ladakhi community were another source of information, as were Indian traders. They could travel more freely in Tibet than the Trade Agents, and were expected to deal with the Agents in the normal course of their business.

Agency staff also obtained information. Mission servants passed on gossip from the bazaars and what passed for popular opinion. Even the Medical Officer was involved. He treated private patients from the wealthier sections of Tibetan society, knowledge of whose fitness or otherwise could be of value. Theoretically the Medical Officers were bound by their oath of confidentiality and the cadre officers were not allowed to ask them about private cases, but the Medical Officers generally worked closely with the cadre, and there can have been few secrets between them.[18]

Prior to 1904, the Chinese authorities in Tibet used couriers to communicate with Peking. When the British introduced a telegraph and postal service, the Chinese began to use it because it was much quicker than their own arrangements. But the cadre gained invaluable insight into Chinese plans because the letters and telegrams which they sent were routinely intercepted and read in India before being forwarded to China. The system was not foolproof, however. Mail from the Japanese in Lhasa passed unread, because there was no-one available in India who could read that language.[19]

Foreign travellers were largely excluded from Tibet at this time, but those who did manage to enter were seen as particularly reliable sources. Teramoto Enga, a Japanese who travelled through Tibet disguised as a Mongolian, called on O'Connor on his way to India, and reported that he had seen two Russians accompanying an arms caravan arriving in Lhasa. O'Connor, in an effort to confirm this, promptly sent to Lhasa what he called 'a special secret agent...with instructions to obtain if possible letters or any scraps of writing left behind by the party'.[20]

'Secret agents', usually British employees, were sent out both by the Trade Agents and by the Political Officer Sikkim. Most of them were local employees at the Gangtok Residency or at the Trade Agencies. Nonetheless, O'Connor referred to 'the very unsatisfactory medium of secret agents', apparently due to the limited results they obtained. One problem was that in such a close-knit society, the Tibetans 'doubtless knew well enough what they were doing'.[21]

'Secret agents' may have been of dubious value, but the network of friendly contacts which O'Connor had built up was vital to intelligence-gathering. Trade Agents were provided with a monthly 'Secret Service allowance' to pay informants and the lists of those who received these funds reveal the wide range of informants used. Those listed naturally include nationals whose interests coincided with those of the British – such as Indian traders, Bhutanese officials, and the Nepalese representative in Gyantse (who received a regular monthly payment of 50 rupees). But O'Connor's contacts were wide-ranging. Villagers were rewarded with one or two rupees, servants of Lhasa officials and clerks at the Panchen Lama's monastery received 10-50 rupees. The Gyantse Jongpon's clerk and 'a Gyantse monk' were regular paid informants and a number of other monks from monasteries throughout Lhasa and central Tibet also profited. No possible source was ignored. O'Connor even managed to obtain informants in the Chinese army and there were regular payments to a 'Chinese Agent from Lhasa' – presumably an employee of the Ambans.[22]

Perhaps the most valuable informant O'Connor obtained was the Panchen Lama, who carried on a secret correspondence with the Gyantse Agent using 'slate' letters, a common means of secret correspondence in Tibet. Letters were written on slate, and entrusted to a messenger who could quickly erase the writing if there was any threat of its falling into the wrong hands. One such message O'Connor received confirmed Teramoto's news of Russians in Lhasa. With or without the knowledge of the Panchen Lama, O'Connor also arranged that his Prime Minister provide a copy of the weekly report of the Shigatse representative in Lhasa; for which it was agreed 'to pay the agent well for his trouble'.[23]

This information gathering process was by no means one-sided. Though they denied it, Britain, China, Russia and other powers such as Japan all spied on Tibet and on each others' activities there. The Tibetans certainly watched the British, and in 1908 one of the Gyantse Agency clerks was dismissed on charges of reporting to the Chinese in Lhasa. The Tibetans could be refreshingly honest about it. When one visitor in the 1930s asked the 'guides' she was given by the Tibetan Government if they were reporting her activities to the Dalai Lama, the Tibetans replied, "Of course".[24]

* * *

The secret correspondence with the Panchen Lama was a measure of how far O'Connor had succeeded in gaining his trust. The next step came in September 1905, when O'Connor returned to Shigatse to invite the Panchen Lama to visit India. The Prince and Princess of Wales were to visit India and various frontier nobles who were considered British allies were invited to meet them. White, the Political Officer in Sikkim, suggested inviting the Panchen Lama. O'Connor had doubts as to the wisdom of this proposal because it would be strongly opposed by the Chinese, who were bound to see it as a threat to their authority.

O'Connor advised White that if the Panchen Lama was to be invited, he should be given guarantees of support and protection against China. White, however, did not forward O'Connor's telegram to his government, for which failure he was later censured and O'Connor probably did promise the Panchen Lama some measure of protection.[25]

O'Connor persuaded the Panchen Lama to take up the invitation and remained in Shigatse for two months while arrangements for the visit were made. The preparations were time-consuming. The Government of India assumed that the Lama's party would consist of around 30 accompanying officials and retainers; the Panchen Lama himself felt that a party of more than 1,000 was necessary. O'Connor arranged a compromise figure of 300. Their departure was kept as secret as possible to avoid alerting the Chinese, and the official invitation was only given a few days before the departure was due. O'Connor even managed to cut a day out of that period when he found the calendar the Tibetans used was so complex they were not sure what day it was.[26]

O'Connor was determined that the Panchen Lama be treated with the ceremony appropriate to a religious figure of enormous influence throughout the Himalayas. The Tibetans, like the British, placed a great deal of emphasis on the maintenance of prestige which manifested in great concern for the smallest details of ceremonial etiquette. This led to what now seems a bizarre correspondence, in which O'Connor sought to ascertain how far the Viceroy would advance to meet the Panchen Lama, and vice versa. This was an important consideration in Tibetan etiquette, but it led even Louis Dane, a strong supporter of O'Connor, to comment that, 'Really these Tibetan officers are very unreasonable', and to pronounce that, 'We are not Buddhists and cannot pay this extravagant spiritual homage.' But O'Connor insisted, and eventually a minor official in Calcutta was deputed to count the number of steps at the entrance to the Viceregal residence, although the official concluded ironically that the 'number of paces to be taken in each case [is] unascertainable.'[27]

This correspondence symbolised the problem which the Raj had in choosing the appropriate response to cultural issues. Should they impose Western solutions, or should the local cultural context govern policy formation?[28] Officers such as O'Connor considered that respect for local traditions enhanced the dignity of the British by demonstrating their understanding of what the local people considered 'civilised' behaviour. The opposing view was held by officers such as White, or later by Bailey. They believed that it was 'inconsistent with the maintenance of dignity to pander too much to native ideas'. Thus

White believed that O'Connor should 'simply have told the [Panchen] Lama what he is expected to do'. As will be seen, O'Connor's ideas were to emerge as the more successful tendency in dealing with Tibet.[29]

It was clearly stated that the aim of inviting the Panchen Lama to India was to impress him and the plan succeeded. He was duly dazzled by the might of the Raj, quite literally so in the case of electric lights. The Tibetans had never seen them before and spent considerable time trying to blow them out. A special train was provided to take the Panchen Lama to Rawalpindi, where he was introduced to the Royal couple and to the Indian Army Commander-in Chief, Lord Kitchener. He also attended a review of Indian Army troops. Although suitably impressed by the march past of 53,000 soldiers, the Panchen Lama was worldly enough to send two of his attendants to the rear of the parade-ground to check that it was not just the same troops marching round in circles![30]

The Panchen Lama and his party, with O'Connor in attendance, then visited several sacred Buddhist sites before they were received by the Viceroy in Calcutta. After a second meeting with the Prince of Wales, they returned to Tibet in February 1906. At this point, O'Connor took leave and Lieutenant Bailey, the promising young veteran of the Younghusband mission, was appointed to relieve him in Gyantse. O'Connor remained in Calcutta for several months dealing with Tibetan affairs, in close consultation with Foreign Minister Louis Dane, before returning to England for the first time since his arrival in India, 11 years before.

Dane and O'Connor were allies. They were both Irish and were both keen supporters of the 'forward' views of Curzon and Younghusband. What they discussed in Calcutta was obviously how to use the Panchen Lama to their best advantage. Dane subsequently suggested two possible ways in which he could serve the Raj. If the Chinese installed him as the nominal leader of Tibet, British India would have a friendly neighbouring ruler. It could then accept Chinese authority in Lhasa because the alliance would 'effectively settle the unruly Tibetans and exclude Russian influence'. Dane went as far as to request details of historical precedents concerning the Chinese deposition of the 6th and 7th Dalai Lamas. But Dane also considered an alternative possibility. The Panchen Lama, he noted, 'may yet be an Indian Ruling Chief' – in other words, he still felt that Tibet might well be drawn into some form of association with the Raj.[31]

These plans were almost destroyed by external events however. Late in 1905, Lord Curzon resigned. His replacement, the Earl of Minto, was a much less dominant figure, who lacked Curzon's wide knowledge and experience of Central Asia. Soon afterwards a new Liberal government was elected in Britain which strongly opposed any further expansion of the empire. The new Secretary of State for India, John (later Lord) Morley, was totally opposed to what he called 'Curzonism', and was determined to bring government in India more firmly under the control of Whitehall. When O'Connor visited Morley in London, Morley made it clear to him that Whitehall would not support any extension of British responsibility in Tibet and that it hoped to settle Tibetan issues through negotiations with China and Russia. With a strong Secretary of State and a weak Viceroy, the power structure of the Curzon period was suddenly reversed; initiative and authority had passed from the periphery to the centre.

Chapter Two

'An extremely mad scheme'?

Although the British Government hoped that talks with China and Russia would settle outstanding issues in Tibet, China took advantage of Whitehall's cautious approach and began asserting her power. The Tibetans, with no really effective functioning government of their own, had little option but to accept China's increasing authority. But although Whitehall's refusal to allow the Raj to send its representatives to Lhasa had been a serious blow to the 'forward school' of frontier policy, it had not destroyed the cadre's hopes that British influence in Tibet could be advanced through an alliance with the Panchen Lama. With O'Connor going on leave, the hopes of the 'forward school' rested on his protégé, F.M.Bailey.

Bailey did not lack guidance. He received frequent letters from O'Connor (whose illegible scrawl must have tested his code-breaking skills) and regular advice from Younghusband in Kashmir. This was usually sent via Bailey's father because Bailey's superior, the Political Officer Sikkim, was still J.C.White, who would not approve of Younghusband's interference. As Bailey's father was also a former Indian Army officer, Younghusband found him an ideal go-between for passing on advice.[1]

Younghusband reminded Bailey's father that the Gyantse post was 'ostensibly that of a *trade* agent', and that Bailey had best 'stick to trade – keep clear of politics'. This was, Younghusband admitted, 'all very different to what I should have liked', but he considered that 'Our only chance of getting more in the future is by going slowly now.' While Bailey was told to avoid politics, ensuring the flow of information was still of paramount importance, the Trade Agencies were, in the eyes of the 'forward school', 'listening posts' in Tibet. Younghusband wrote directly to Bailey concerning rumours of the Dalai Lama returning to Tibet and asked 'when can you make yourself useful by getting information?'.[2]

Younghusband regarded Bailey as an 'excellent fellow', who 'ought to go far', an opinion he had formed on the mission to Lhasa, where Bailey had showed 'pluck and common-sense and tact...and...a very happy knack of getting on with Tibetans'.[3] Younghusband therefore offered Bailey the patronage that was almost a pre-requisite for career progress under the Raj. But the young Bailey was an ideal candidate for promotion. In addition to being capable and intelligent, he was modest, personable and charming. Tall and strongly built, he was clearly a most promising frontier officer. But he was now in a most unpromising post.

There was little prospect of Bailey devoting much of his time to trade, as Younghusband had suggested. The term 'Trade Agent' was a convenient fiction, which owed its usage to political circumstances. Although Whitehall had prevented Curzon from stationing British officials in Tibet for political purposes, pressure from British and Indian trading interests mean that they had accepted the need for British officers to oversee trade in Tibet. But by placing them under the Political Department's command, the Government of India ensured that the Agents' role would be political and diplomatic. As Curzon observed, 'The distinction between a trade or political officer is not mutually exclusive after all'.[4]

One role the Trade Agents were not qualified for was that of *Trade* Agents. Had trade been a priority in Tibet, some officers with customs experience would presumably have been sought, but none of the cadre had any background in trade or commerce, indeed the word 'trade' carried pejorative connotations in official British Indian circles and those who made their living from it were at the lower end of the Raj's social scale.

Although they did their best to help Indian traders, the Trade Agents made only token efforts to live up to their name. In April 1906 Bailey wrote that 'I don't send in any reports on trade as I can get no information here.' However, in the following month, government ordered the Agents to submit quarterly trade reports, 'noting especially the measures which have been taken to foster it'. But the reports submitted were notable for their lack of precise information, and were, compared to the long and detailed reports from Agencies such as Kashmir, brief and perfunctory. Bailey's first quarterly report stated that trade figures were 'so unreliable' that he 'thought better to omit them altogether'. Later reports gave figures, but they remained unreliable.[5]

Even the Political Officer regarded trade reports as being of little importance. One quarterly report was not passed on to government for four months, because White 'overlooked' it while preparing for a trip to Bhutan. In September 1908, the order to submit quarterly trade reports was rescinded without explanation, doubtless to relief all round.[6]

The main reason trade figures were unreliable was smuggling. Apart from the main passes, the Nathu la and the Jelep la, there were at least 12 other passes into Sikkim alone, and trade was measured only through the Jelep la. As the Political Officer noted, 'nothing is easier than to pass by night, or to go through the fields' to avoid a trade registration post. The British relied on figures given by trade registration posts manned by the Chinese; no check was kept by the Tibetans, who did not appoint a Trade Agent to Gyantse (which they were required to do under the terms of the 1904 Treaty) until January 1907. In one report the Political Officer allowed 30 per cent 'for the customary under-valuation' of figures given by the Chinese, whose trade registration post was, the cadre reported, 'principally active as an intelligence bureau'.[7]

What efforts the Agents did make to increase trade were largely unsuccessful, and any expansion in trade was generally the result of an increase in established trade rather than new trade. Tibet's external trade was localised, finely balanced and regularised by tradition. There was no mechanism for altering it and its localised character meant that vast annual fluctuations could be caused by factors such as the weather or a shortage of pack-animals. Trade was largely in the hands of intermediaries, such as the Tromowa people of the Chumbi Valley, and these groups had a vested interest in maintaining the status quo. The Tromowas sent large annual bribes to Lhasa to maintain their profitable monopoly. They controlled the limited supplies of pack-animals in their territory and saw no benefit in allowing competing Indian merchants to use their animals.[8]

Tibet and China actively resisted British attempts to foster Indo-Tibetan trade. Their opposition took many forms. A high-caste Hindu trader in western Tibet was discouraged by the slaughter of a yak outside his tent; traders from India were harassed and had their goods impounded on various pretexts. Indian shopkeepers were charged exorbitant rents, and the Tibetans, responsible under the 1904 Treaty for repairing the trade route to India, allowed it to fall into disrepair. But the biggest obstacle to encouraging trade was that Tibetan currency was of no value in India. Indian merchants were usually forced to rely on barter. The Agents were able to overcome the problem to some extent by exchanging Tibetan currency for rupees, but, until a bank was set-up in the 1920s, that was limited to the amount of local currency that the Agency required. As a result, few Indian traders broke into the Tibetan market.[9]

European traders fared no better. Most were discouraged by the lack of infrastructure, and the occasional adventurous merchant found little encouragement to remain. Apart from Annie Taylor, an eccentric missionary who opened a shop at Yatung as a means of entering Tibet, and who was not concerned with material profit, only two European trading companies ventured into Tibet in the early years. An Anglo-Indian representing a New York carpet firm visited Gyantse in August 1906, having read an optimistic account of the Gyantse carpet trade in a book on the Younghusband mission. Unfortunately, the report was 'quite inaccurate' and he returned after a few days.[10]

A Darjeeling hotel owner travelled to Gyantse in August 1907 with the idea of setting up in Tibet as a tea trader but he was unable to find accommodation and was charged heavily for transport. Before returning, he and an Indian trader sent reports from Gyantse to the Government of India suggesting that the Trade Agency be moved to Shigatse. As they stated that O'Connor had done 'his best' to assist them, O'Connor had probably encouraged them to add their weight to his unanswered calls to relocate the Agency in the Panchen Lama's domain.[11]

The Agents did advance a number of well-considered schemes for increasing trade, particularly in regard to tea. Tea shops were opened in several locations in the Chumbi Valley to promote the Indian brew and an Indian company was given a contract to supply the Gyantse Agency.[12] But in addition to the difficulties of finance and transportation, the Tibetans simply preferred their tea in the form of compressed bricks which the Chinese supplied. The Indian tea industry was unable to manufacture these bricks to the necessary standard and, in addition, much to the Indian tea-promoters' frustration, the Tibetans simply never developed a taste for Indian tea.

Events in the late 1906 ensured that trade would be of even less interest to the Gyantse Agent. In the wake of the Younghusband mission, the Chinese were determined to establish complete authority in Tibet. As Henderson of the China Customs had warned O'Connor would happen, the Chinese began to try to get rid of the British Trade Agencies.

* * *

Bailey had continued O'Connor's attempts to form a close relationship with the Panchen Lama. Bailey had escorted him on his return to Shigatse in February 1906, and, like O'Connor, had got on well with him. Diplomacy naturally involves the presentation of ceremonial gifts and exchanges of compliments, but the officers of the Raj went beyond that. They established personal friendships based on mutual trust and affection. Consequently the diplomatic screens could be put aside, as when Bailey played records on his wind-up gramophone to entertain the Panchen Lama. The Tibetan greatly enjoyed the music, particularly the songs of Scottish music-hall entertainer, Harry Lauder, and the meeting went on much longer than scheduled. Hearing the sound of trumpets outside, Bailey suspected he was outstaying his welcome and asked if he should leave. "No, don't stop" replied his host, "they're only worshipping me".[13]

The Panchen Lama invited Bailey to visit Shigatse again late in 1906, but Whitehall, in an example of how the new government was making its influence felt on the frontier, refused to allow Bailey to accept the invitation. The Political Officer Sikkim took no chances when he decided to visit Shigatse in October that year. Whitehall, much to their displeasure, were only informed after the event. The Political Officer, however, returned with interesting news. He reported that the Panchen Lama 'opened his mind to me. He wanted to be independent of Lhasa and to deal with the British Government as an independent State'.[14]

While the Tibet cadre officers were cultivating the friendship of the Panchen Lama, the Chinese had been considering how they could enforce their authority over Tibet. Unlike the cadre, they had access to Lhasa and on 8 September 1906, a new senior Amban, Chang Yin-tang, arrived in the Tibetan capital with a mandate to reorganise China's position. Chang set about establishing his authority in Lhasa and introduced various measures designed to modernise Tibet's institutions and bring both their administration and cultural practices in line with Chinese custom. One example of these reforms was his order that 'sky burials' – where the bodies of the dead were cut up and fed to the vultures – be replaced by burial in the Chinese fashion.[15]

Chang appointed another Chinese official, a Mr Gow, as his representative in Gyantse. Gow was the man the British Trade Agent had to deal with and he was to prove every bit as determined to establish Chinese authority as his superior.

On 21 November 1906, Gow told Bailey, 'in most discourteous language', that all the Agency's future dealings with the Tibetans had to be made through the Chinese authorities. Bailey, somewhat taken aback, referred matters to his government. He was awaiting a reply four days later when regular supplies which the Agency obtained from the local Tibetan authorities were delivered by a uniformed Chinese. Bailey ordered the Chinese to leave and when he refused, 'seized him by the ear and kicked him out of the place in front of all the Tibetans'. On reflection, Bailey realised he had acted unwisely and seized the initiative by sending a written complaint about the man to Gow. On this occasion, Gow sent 'a very humble apology': but it was to be the last time he backed down.[16]

Bailey, however, was transferred to the Yatung Trade Agency in December 1906 and escaped the worst consequences of Gow's campaign against British influence. O'Connor returned to Gyantse after his home leave in spectacular style. He had two cars, a Clement which was intended as a gift for the Panchen Lama and his own Peugeot, carried up over the mountains and he and another driver brought them to Gyantse. These were the first, and for twenty years the only, motorised vehicles to be brought to Tibet. But they were no match for Tibetan 'roads' and the Agents soon went back to riding horses, which could move much more quickly across country.[17]

Upon learning that Mr.Gow had never made an official call on Bailey, which, as the newcomer he was bound by diplomatic etiquette to do, O'Connor resolved not to call on the Chinese: the two communicated only in writing and apparently never met. But O'Connor soon found that Gow had succeeded in totally isolating him from the Tibetans. When the Panchen Lama invited him to the Tibetan New Year celebrations during February 1907, at which O'Connor hoped to present him with the car and two Newfoundland terriers, the Chinese refused to allow the visit to go ahead.[18]

In his memoirs, O'Connor reflected that China's determination to control Tibet was 'very natural', but at the time he found his position depressing in the extreme. Gow's actions effectively undermined all of O'Connor's attempts to advance British interests in Tibet. Gow had even prevented the Tibetans attending a free medical dispensary operated by the Medical Officer at Gyantse. He even protested that the smallpox inoculation campaign carried out under the dispensary's auspices was British interference in Tibetan internal affairs, which was forbidden under the terms of the 1904 Treaty. Gow also made various petty difficulties for O'Connor personally, such as preventing him obtaining willow cuttings for the Agency garden.[19]

It was in the course of this debacle that O'Connor proposed a policy which, if accepted, would have changed the map of Central Asia. In February 1907 he suggested that India should encourage the

Panchen Lama to declare his independence from Lhasa and create a separate state in southern Tibet, ruled from his Shigatse headquarters. The British would then recognise and support the new state. With a British representative and his military escort in Shigatse, and British arms supplies to the new state, neither China nor Lhasa would be in a position to prevent the break-away. British India would then have a friendly 'buffer-state' on its northern border, from which it could ensure that Russian influence was excluded.[20]

Since the Dalai Lama had fled, O'Connor and his fellow cadre officers had worked assiduously to cultivate an alliance with the Panchen Lama, who then seemed the only figure with sufficient authority to rule Tibet, or at least that part of it that bordered British India. He had succeeded in obtaining the trust of the Panchen Lama, who had indicated that he wanted to be independent of Lhasa. Louis Dane, with whom O'Connor had worked closely, had foreseen that the Panchen Lama might become an Indian Princely ruler. The proposal was thus the logical culmination of O'Connor's efforts since the Younghusband mission.

In retrospect, the only surprising thing about this plan was that it had not been advanced earlier. Indeed, had O'Connor persuaded the Panchen Lama to declare independence immediately after the Younghusband mission, while Curzon was still Viceroy, and the plan had been presented to Whitehall as a *fait accompli*, it would surely have succeeded.

O'Connor's plan was consistent with 'forward school' thinking. Tibet itself was too large for the British to protect militarily, but a southern state centered on Shigatse could have been supported; would have provided a forward position for British interests beyond the Himalayas; and had the potential to be drawn into a closer relationship with British India in due course. In the world of imperial *realpolitik*, it was a masterly scheme.

O'Connor's plan was never acted on, although Viceroy Minto saw its advantages. The Secretary of State, Lord Morley, committed to reducing the British presence in Tibet to the minimum and mindful of Russian opinion, was appalled by the idea. Although he agreed to protest to Peking about Gow's actions, Morley totally rejected O'Connor's proposal.

One leading observer has stated that this proposal 'suggests that O'Connor was not fully in touch with the depths of Tibetan history and religious feeling'.[21] But while his understanding of the wider geopolitical implications was limited, O'Connor and other early cadre officers saw Tibet from the perspective of the Panchen Lama. To them he was a known ally and the Dalai Lama was an unknown enemy. The British had been welcome in Shigatse since the time of Bogle and Turner and it was natural that the cadre should sympathise with its ruler's aspirations. O'Connor failed, but his plan had merits then which are easily overlooked today.

* * *

One reason O'Connor's plan to support the Panchen Lama failed was that he lacked any support from his immediate superior, J.C. White. The Political Officer described O'Connor's plan as an 'extremely mad scheme' and he recommended that O'Connor be removed from his post.[22] White's conclusion, however, was not a purely professional judgement. Differences over the Panchen Lama's visit to India had bought to a head the tensions that had arisen between the two men.

White was the worst type of imperial officer; arrogant, intolerant, petty and self-seeking. As a former Public Works Department officer he lacked the social status of his successors and, in consequence, he had an obsessive concern with his income and social standing. He had little or no empathy with the Tibetans and spent as little time there as possible. He preferred Sikkim, where he was 'a little god',[23] who ran the state as his own personal fiefdom.

White had been appointed to Sikkim when the region was of little importance and no ambitious officer wanted to serve there. He had expressed the necessary 'forward' views on frontier policy to gain the initial approval of Lord Curzon, but as the region gained prominence, White's faults became increasingly apparent.

On the Younghusband mission, senior personnel became divided into two camps, one supporting the dynamic Younghusband, the other supporting the military commander, General 'Retiring Mac' MacDonald, whom one commentator assessed as 'one of the most contemptible men who ever wore the king's uniform'.[24] White was firmly in the MacDonald camp, and Younghusband relied on O'Connor as his 'right-hand man'. Accordingly, while White and O'Connor had been at least cordial acquaintances in the past, any friendship that may have existed between them did not survive long into the mission.

Although White is included here as one of the Tibet cadre because of his long occupation of the senior post in Gangtok, his character and attitudes were the reverse of other cadre officers. Yet history recalls White as one of the great pioneers of the frontier, probably because later commentators have accepted at face-value what the Viceroy of the time described as White's 'extremely self-laudatory' memoirs, entitled *Sikhim and Bhutan*.[25] As the title suggests, White was not overly concerned with Tibet. But even in regard to Sikkim he left a legacy of problems. Indeed, one of his proudest boasts was that he turned Sikkim into a revenue-producing state, but he did so by importing Nepalese labour, which created communal problems, the consequences of which are still felt today.

Not only were White's policies short-sighted, his conduct was appalling. He considered himself poorly paid, and between 1898 and 1912 he bombarded government with petitions for an increased pension. He was granted some extra benefits in 1902, but in 1904-06 he overpaid himself 500 rupees a month. His half-hearted explanation left the government doubting his '*bona fides*' and this earned him an official censure, one of five he received between 1904 and 1908. While, in the mores of the empire at that time, one censure might be overlooked and could even be seen as a positive indication that an officer had 'character', five was too many. Despite this, when White applied to stay at his post after retirement age, his superiors were careful to word their refusal to extend his term 'so as not to hurt his feelings', apparently in consideration of his long service in an isolated post. In retirement, White was employed as an agent to the King of Bhutan in a state revenue-producing scheme there, but was dismissed over an expenses claim and died soon after.[26]

O'Connor found working under White's control increasingly difficult to endure and the Secretariat found itself having to mediate in a series of disputes between the two frontiersmen. Late in 1906, when White went on leave and a junior officer relieved him, O'Connor took advantage of the situation by obtaining the right to correspond directly with his government rather than through the junior officer in Gangtok. After White returned in January 1907, O'Connor, as his government realised, 'made use of the order...to ignore his superior officer even more than before'.[27]

White was particularly incensed when O'Connor's report on the Panchen Lama's visit to India was submitted. He asked that O'Connor be made to apologise for various 'extraneous and objectionable matter' in the report, and demanded that he be made to rewrite it to give more prominence to White's part in the visit. Government declined to order O'Connor to apologise, but allowed White to add material on his own involvement.

The continual clashes between White and O'Connor eventually forced the government to order them to 'sink your private differences and work together...without friction, in the interests of government.' In fact, in the Secretariat, sympathies were generally with O'Connor, whose difficult position was recognised, not least by Louis Dane. They realised that 'a saint could quarrel with Mr. White'.

O'Connor also had to deal with the problems arising from the theft of a large amount of money left at Gyantse after the Younghusband Mission. He had taken receipt of the boxes of money from the army and placed them in a storeroom under guard. A hole in the roof of the storeroom went unnoticed until the boxes were checked in May 1905, when it was discovered that the money had been replaced by sand and stones. Finding no evidence as to who had taken it (although it was presumed to have been members of the original escort), O'Connor promptly conducted his own court of enquiry and wrote the money off. Government was less sanguine, and, after a long-running investigation culminating in a formal court of enquiry in July 1907, O'Connor was censured for his failure to guard the treasure properly. White was able to avoid ultimate responsibility as the theft had occurred before he was officially given control of the Agency, and he offered no support to O'Connor.

***

O'Connor's problems continued to mount. As China increased its control over Tibet their agent in Gyantse, Mr Gow, succeeded in his efforts to isolate the Trade Agency. After 5 March 1907, O'Connor was completely cut-off from any contact with the Tibetans.[28]

The Tibetans often expressed political opinion and gossip about political events in song and O'Connor's plight did not go unnoticed. He reported that Tibetan coolies were now singing 'You'd better not go to Changlo (our post) if you don't want your throat cut'. O'Connor took his frustrations out in his official reports, claiming that

> There can I think be no doubt that a part at least of the hostility and bitterness displayed towards us by the Chinese officials in this country is due to jealousy. They recognise that we are their superiors in science and in honesty.[29]

The final straw for O'Connor personally, as a typically sports-loving ex-public schoolboy, came when a sports day was held in Gyantse. He was not invited, and it was Mr Gow who presented the prizes while O'Connor stayed home.[30]

By the time his main supporter, Louis Dane, was made Lieutenant-Governor of the Punjab in May 1907, O'Connor's position had become untenable. Government was concerned that his withdrawal should not seem to be in response to Chinese pressure, and talks in Simla with the Chinese over the trade regulations (to which the Chinese sent Mr Chang from Lhasa), provided a suitable opportunity to withdraw O'Connor.

In his last days in Gyantse, O'Connor had had the satisfaction of reporting that he was again in contact with the local Tibetan administration. Whitehall's protests had finally had some effect in Peking and the isolation of the Trade Agency ended. China even withdrew Gow, who outlasted O'Connor in Tibet by only a few weeks. But Gow had succeeded in greatly damaging the Trade Agency's prestige and forcing the removal of the highly-rated O'Connor. Gow was promoted to a post as Director of Telegraphs in Mukden [now Shenyang], Manchuria; his work in Tibet successfully completed.

O'Connor spent eight 'painful' months of wrangling with the Chinese negotiators in Simla. When his role there ended, he was sent to accompany the heir-apparent to the throne of Sikkim on a world tour. O'Connor never returned to Tibet.[31]

* * *

By the end of 1907, the British had lost or surrendered most of the benefits Younghusband had achieved in Tibet, allowing China to fill the power vacuum the mission left in Lhasa. Although the pace of her advance slowed after Chang left Lhasa for talks in Simla, China was clearly bringing Tibet into her empire. Chang's work in central Tibet was matched by a ruthless campaign in the eastern Tibetan borderlands, carried out by General Chao Er-feng, who succeeded in bringing most of that traditionally restless area under Chinese administration.

The British, however, still controlled the administration of the Chumbi Valley. The Chumbi was of great strategic importance because it was the only route by which an invasion of India from Tibet could realistically be carried out by modern troops. By occupying the Chumbi Valley, the British ensured that, even if Russia took-over Tibet, they could not use it to mount an invasion of India.

In Lhasa, Younghusband had tried to salvage some concrete benefit from the mission by imposing an indemnity on the Tibetans, under Articles Six and Seven of the 1904 Convention, of 7,500,000 rupees towards the expenses of the mission. Whitehall had originally instructed Younghusband that repayment of any indemnity imposed on the Tibetans should be spread over three years, but allowed him to be 'guided by circumstances in the matter'. Younghusband duly used this leeway to the fullest. As he advised Louis Dane, spreading the repayments over 75 years meant that

> I do not see the slightest prospect of our ever being able to give Chumbi up whatever His Majesty's Government may say about not occupying any part of Tibet.[32]

But Younghusband's hopes of annexing the Chumbi were swiftly quashed when Whitehall reduced the indemnity to 2,500,000 rupees, to be repaid over three years. The British actually had no idea of whether the Tibetans could afford to pay this amount, but the question never arose because Tibet came under Chinese control. The Chinese realised they could demonstrate their authority over Tibet by repaying this money themselves. The cadre understood the symbolic significance of this, but were unable to prevent it. Thus, when the Chinese made the final payment, the Government of India had to withdraw its troops from the Chumbi Valley.

The Tibet cadre objected to the hand-over of Chumbi, claiming that 'we have many excuses for keeping it'. They argued that India would be justified in retaining it on two grounds; legally, because of breaches of the 1904 Agreement by the Tibetans, and morally, because (they claimed) the people of the Chumbi preferred British to Chinese or Tibetan rule. But Whitehall did not consider the treaty breaches – such as the Tibetan's failure to maintain the roads on the trade route – were serious enough to justify an action which would have aroused international protest. The cadre's claim that the Chumbi people preferred British rule was dismissed in a scribbled aside: 'Was there ever a pioneer of the forward policy who did not find the trans-border people dying to be annexed?'.[33]

On 3 February 1908, the order was given to withdraw from the Chumbi. After delays due to the usual shortage of pack-animals, British forces there withdrew to India. The Yatung Trade Agency remained in British hands, but the officer there was no longer in administrative charge of the valley. In a last attempt to salvage something from their withdrawal, the Yatung Agent handed over the Chumbi to the Tibetan, rather than the Chinese authorities, who were advised of the hand-over by letter. The Chinese, however, apparently convinced the local Tibetans that the British had withdrawn under Chinese pressure.[34]

Whitehall's policy of reducing British involvement in Tibet meant that they now began to question the need for a military escort at the Gyantse Agency and even the need for a British Agent. In January 1908, after India had defended the need for the Trade Agent's escort on the grounds that Gyantse was 'full of bad characters, brigandage is rife and the monks of the large monastery are hostile', the Secretary of State asked the Viceroy whether it would not be possible to station a 'native agent' at Gyantse.

who presumably would not require special protection. Can it be said that trade requirements are such as to justify employment of a British officer at Gyantse when on political grounds H.M. Government consider it desirable to withdraw him?[35]

On 20 April 1908, Britain signed an Agreement with China and Tibet amending the 1893 Trade Regulations, which had governed the operation of the Trade Agencies. Britain agreed to withdraw the Gyantse escort when China had arranged 'effective police measures at the marts and along the routes to the marts'. This was the third treaty concerning Tibet into which Whitehall had entered since watering-down the Younghusband Agreement, and in each of these Britain had signed away more of its power to influence events in Tibet. In the 1906 Anglo-Chinese Convention they had agreed not to interfere in the administration of Tibet or to annex any Tibetan territory. In 1907, by the Anglo-Russian Convention (which sought to end Anglo-Russian competition in Central Asia through an overall regional agreement), Britain recognised China's 'suzerainty' over Tibet, agreed to deal with Tibet only through China, and agreed not to send British officers to Lhasa. The Tibetans, now firmly under Chinese rule, were excluded from contributing to any of these agreements, although they were present during the negotiations for the 1908 Agreement.[36]

An active British presence in Tibet seemed to be coming to an end. Whitehall was content to allow China to take-over the country and it seemed certain that the Trade Agencies would be reduced to a token presence. The supporters of Curzon and Younghusband had been outmanoeuvred and were clearly out of favour. When White retired in 1908, Morley, in what he called 'a moment of pure, wicked joy',[37] vetoed the appointment of O'Connor to replace him.

O'Connor subsequently wrote to Bailey and advised him 'to get away from Gyantse as soon as possible' and Bailey obtained a transfer to India in June 1909.[38] For the next six months, the Gyantse Medical Officer, Lieutenant Robert Kennedy, acted as Trade Agent; no-one else seemed to want the job. Tibet was no longer a posting sought by ambitious Political officers. In Yatung, in a symbol of the downgrading of that position, it was decided to appoint a local employee as Trade Agent.

The Tibetan frontiersmen who had once been at the forefront of policy formation were now reduced to voices crying in the wilderness. It seemed clear that Curzon's 'forward' policy had been routed by Morley's 'backward' policy. But events in China, and the vision of one cadre officer, were to provide an unexpected reprieve for Younghusband's successors.

Chapter Three

'A conversion almost as remarkable as Sir F.Younghusband'

After Lord Morley's refusal to approve O'Connor's appointment as Political Officer Sikkim in 1908, the position was given to Charles Alfred Bell. The architects of the Younghusband era 'forward' policy in Tibet had all now departed, or were soon to depart, from positions of influence in Tibetan policy, and Morley hoped that the Tibetan frontier would now return to its former obscurity. Bell, unlike the outspoken O'Connor, was an officer who appeared, at first glance, to be the sort of prudent bureaucrat who could be relied upon to keep the frontier quiet.

Charles Bell had been born in India and educated at Winchester and Oxford, before joining the ICS in 1891. He then served for nine years in various districts of Bengal, Bihar and Orissa, before his health declined. In 1900, he was posted to Darjeeling, a healthy environment but then a backwater for an ambitious officer. There Bell found his destiny. He developed an interest in Tibet, learning the language well enough to compile a dictionary and a grammar textbook, and making a brief journey across the border in August 1902. Called upon to survey a possible cart route from Bhutan to the Chumbi Valley, his report was a model of clear and concise thinking, which brought him favourable attention.[1]

As was often the case in the empire, having reported on the area, Bell was henceforth considered the expert and he was given administrative charge of the Chumbi Valley in 1904-05. On three occasions he acted as Political Officer Sikkim while White was on the Younghusband mission or on leave and when White retired, Bell succeeded him.

Bell was very much the scholar-administrator of ICS tradition, devoting his spare time to the study of Tibetan language and culture. Frontiersmen such as Younghusband, O'Connor and Bailey, with their military backgrounds and more dynamic approach, initially underestimated Bell's abilities. They regarded him as 'a *babu*...possibly alright [sic] in an Indian district but...not the man for the frontier'.[2]

When an officer took over such a post, he needed to establish his authority, both with the local people he dealt with and with his own government. Much of White's authority had been undermined by O'Connor, and Bell ensured that there would be no repeat of that situation by selecting officers for the Gyantse and Yatung Agencies with whom he was personally compatible. His most important choice came in 1909, when his government decided to appoint a local employee as Yatung Trade Agent. Bell offered the position to the Anglo-Sikkimese David Macdonald, a quiet and modest man, who, like Bell, was easy to underestimate.

Macdonald's father, a Scottish tea-planter, had left India when Macdonald was six years old. He did, however, leave Macdonald's mother, a Lepcha, well-provided for, with the then-generous sum of 20 rupees a month for David's education. She dressed him as a Tibetan in order to enrol him in the Bhotia Boarding school in Darjeeling.[3]

David (born Dorje), Macdonald became a Christian under the influence of his wife, the Anglo-Nepalese Alice Curtis, and entered local government service. He assisted Bell in his language studies, and was then taken on the Younghusband mission, where he briefly acted as Younghusband's interpreter after O'Connor had been wounded. Macdonald became favourably known to most of the significant figures involved in the mission, both British and Tibetan, and avoided being identified with either of the factions that developed among its officers. After it ended, he was placed in charge of classifying and cataloguing the 400 mule-loads of relics which were taken from Tibet to India, and in the course of this work he became acquainted with Lord Curzon.

Clearly a capable and talented man, Macdonald attracted the favour of a number of senior British officials, of whom Bell was to be the most significant. Being of mixed race, Macdonald was in particular need of this patronage to overcome the Raj's prejudice against 'Anglo-Indians'.

Perhaps because he was Anglo-Sikkimese, and stood just over five foot tall, Macdonald's authority was severely tested by the local people and by his own staff when he became Trade Agent Yatung. Locals began using part of the Agency land as a cremation ground, withheld transport, and demanded various fees which had not previously been imposed. Macdonald overcame each problem through an intuitive understanding of the situation which enabled him to reach conclusions by no means obvious to the outsider. For example, after a peon fired a rifle one evening at what he claimed was an intruder, Macdonald sacked him on the dubious premise that 'no thief would dare to commit theft on the Agency grounds at this time of night'.[4] Whatever the logic the testing process ceased and he was soon given a much more significant opportunity to demonstrate his abilities.

The situation in Tibet was about to change. By 1908 it was clear to the exiled 13th Dalai Lama that he could not expect Russian assistance, and he began to consider whether his country's best interests lay in some kind of accommodation with China. The Chinese were similarly concerned to reach an accommodation with the Tibetan leader, and in September 1908 the Dalai Lama arrived in Peking for talks with the Emperor.

The Dalai Lama's presence in Peking meant that he was now accessible to European visitors. But in accordance with the 1907 Anglo-Russian Convention forbidding either nation to intervene in Tibetan internal affairs, British and Russian officials in Peking agreed to pay purely formal calls on him and avoid discussion of political matters.

O'Connor, however, was then in Peking accompanying the Sikkimese prince on his world tour. The prince's desire to meet the Dalai Lama provided the excuse for O'Connor to become the first Government of India official to meet the Tibetan leader. The forthright O'Connor was much less reticent than the British officials in Peking. He discussed the past and present political situation in Tibet with the

Dalai Lama, whom O'Connor found to be 'a man of striking and strongly-marked personality...Altogether a more vivid, and far more formidable, personage than his brother Lama of Shigatse [the Panchen Lama]'.[5]

Individuals on opposing sides of the 'Great Game' were rivals, rather than enemies. Players in what the Russians called 'The Tournament of Shadows' almost invariably got on well when they met. Relations between British and Russian representatives were marked by mutual respect, rather like those between international sportsmen today. So when O'Connor met Agvan Dorzhiev, who remained part of the Dalai Lama's large entourage, they found they had much in common.

O'Connor described the Buriat, whose presence in Lhasa had so troubled Curzon, as 'a stout, cheery-looking monk...of intellect and character'. O'Connor advised Dorzhiev that the British Government bore the Dalai Lama no ill-will, and were prepared to enter into friendly relations with him if he returned to Lhasa.[6] O'Connor had no official authority to make these statements, but his reassurances, along with the honourable reception given to the Panchen Lama during his visit to India, seem to have convinced the Dalai Lama he had nothing more to fear from the British.

In November 1908, the Dalai Lama met the Emperor and the Empress Dowager of China. He considered himself their equal, in a relationship between 'priest' and 'patron'.[7] But they conferred on him the subtly humiliating title of 'Loyal and Submissive Vice-Regent', and ordered him to return to Lhasa and to obey the commands of the Chinese Ambans after he returned. But within weeks of this meeting, the Emperor died, followed soon after by the death of the Empress Dowager, events which the Tibetans attributed to the lack of respect they had shown to the Dalai Lama.

After the necessary mourning period, the Tibetan leader journeyed slowly back to Lhasa, arriving on Christmas Day, 1909. The British generally felt that he would now have little option but to obey Chinese authority, and that, as one India Office official put it, 'it is pretty clear now...that we should have put our money on the wrong horse if we had supported him'.[8]

Early in 1910, 2,000 troops from General Chao Er-feng's forces in eastern Tibet were dispatched to Lhasa. Although the Chinese claimed these troops were sent to police the trade marts, as allowed for under the 1908 Anglo-Chinese Agreement, both the cadre and the Tibetans regarded the troops as an invading army, sent to enforce Chinese control in Tibet. Whitehall, however, ultimately accepted the Chinese explanation.[9]

There was great tension in Lhasa when the troops arrived. Hailey's comet, which the Tibetans regarded as an omen of war, had recently appeared, and the number of troops was far greater than the Ambans had insinuated would be sent. When Chao Er-feng's troops opened fire on the crowds that greeted their arrival, the Tibetans (and the British) naturally interpreted this as a hostile act. There may have been a more prosaic explanation. The British Consul in Chengdu was later told by one of the foot-soldiers that the shooting was 'a bluff to conceal weakness. "We were scared and hoped to scare them".' Whatever the truth, these events led the Tibetans to fear for the safety of the Dalai Lama. On the night of 12 February 1910, the Tibetan leader again fled into exile, but this time he fled south to India.[10]

Chinese troops set off in hot pursuit of the Dalai Lama and his party, but were delayed by Tibetan troops at Chaksam Ferry, the point 40 miles south of Lhasa at which the Tsang po (Brahmaputra) river must be crossed. The Tibetans, armed with just 34 rifles, were under the command of the 24 year-old Chensal Namgang (later to be better known by the title Tsarong Shapé), who became the outstanding secular figure in modern Tibetan history. The Tibetans dug in on the rocky southern shore of the Tsang po and the Chinese force of around 200 soldiers had to cross open, sandy ground to reach the river. The Tibetans, reportedly killing 70 Chinese soldiers for the loss of two of their own, were able to hold them off for long enough to give the Dalai Lama a good headstart.[11] By-passing Gyantse where there was a large Chinese garrison, the Dalai Lama was able to reach Phari, where the Chinese garrison was too small to pose any threat. There he was greeted by Mr W.P.Rosemeyer, a calm, unassuming Anglo-Indian who was responsible for maintaining the British telegraph lines in Tibet and Sikkim.

On his own initiative, Rosemeyer allowed the Dalai Lama to shelter in the Phari *dak* bungalow, one of a series of 11 bungalows which the British had built along the Gangtok-Gyantse route to house their travelling officials. The following day, the Dalai Lama rode on to Yatung, where he asked for British protection at the Trade Agency. Macdonald had been given orders which allowed him to offer the Dalai Lama protection, but instructed him to remain neutral in the conflict between Tibet and China. He stretched those orders to the maximum.[12]

Macdonald sheltered the Dalai Lama in his own bedroom, and fed him chicken soup, roast mutton and baked custard pudding. He also stationed his own small escort to guard against Chinese attack. The following day, local Chinese officials arrived demanding to see the Dalai Lama, both to ensure it really was him and not a decoy, and in the hope of delaying him for long enough to allow their army to capture him. Macdonald would only admit them into the Tibetan leader's presence one at a time, after he had personally searched them for weapons. When news arrived early the next morning that a large Chinese force was soon to arrive, the Dalai Lama and his party left hurriedly for the Sikkim frontier, 12 miles away across the Jelep la.[13]

It was mid-winter, and snowing heavily. Not until long after dark did the Dalai Lama reach Gnatong, the first village in Sikkim, where two military telegraphists, Sergeants Luff and Humphreys, were stationed. The Tibetans were greatly relieved to note that the two soldiers were armed with their service rifles and the exhausted party of Tibetans slept soundly in the telegraph hut. Luff and Humphreys stayed up all night on guard and then escorted the Dalai Lama's party on towards Gangtok the following morning. Only later did Luff reveal that while they had had rifles, they hadn't had any ammunition, but by then the Dalai Lama was safely in India.[14]

A few days later Macdonald was also able to assist the young Tsarong Shapé to escape to India, disguised as a British mail-runner. In their memoirs, in order to avoid accusations of breaching neutrality, Bell and Macdonald both carefully avoid mentioning that Tsarong was given a British mail-runner's uniform for this disguise. But Macdonald's papers contain an unpublished article of his which describes Tsarong's arrival in Yatung. While giving a colourful description of how the Chinese were held off at Chaksam, the Tibetan drew his gun and

> illustrated how he had killed I forget how many Chinese. At the most exciting part of the tale the gun went off, the bullet missing my stomach by only a fraction of an inch. This incident brought the story to an abrupt end, and I very soon sent him over the pass disguised as one of my mail-runners, carrying a mail-bag the same as the others.[15]

* * *

The Dalai Lama was naturally grateful to the British officials who had aided his escape. As Bell later stated, the assistance given to the Dalai Lama was 'perhaps the chief reason why the British name stands high in Tibet'.[16] As the Political Officer Sikkim, it was Charles Bell who was responsible for dealing with the Dalai Lama during the three years in which he remained in exile in India, and Bell began to reorientate the Tibet cadre's aims to take advantage of this unexpected turn of events.

Bell understood that Whitehall would not allow Tibet to be taken into the British empire, but realised that it could still prove a viable 'buffer state' for India's northern frontier if it was strong and unified. In the British understanding this required it to be under a single central authority. Bell saw that the Dalai Lama was the one figure with the necessary authority to provide stability in Tibetan politics. Only the figure the Tibetans regarded as the earthly incarnation of Chenrezi, *bodhisattva* of comapassion, could stand above the religious and secular divisions of their society. Bell saw that the Dalai Lama's presence in India had given him the chance to ally with the Tibetan leader, and that if he could gain his trust, he could influence the Tibetan to follow policies which would further what Bell considered the Raj's interests. Thus Bell devoted himself to cultivating the Dalai Lama's friendship, a task in which he was strikingly successful.

The Dalai Lama's sudden arrival, and his immediate request for British assistance against China, created a problem for the Government of India. As he was a religious figure with a considerable following in the British Indian Himalayas, it was obviously necessary to treat the

Dalai Lama with 'respect', but it was generally felt that he had no future as a political figure. Although he was received by the Viceroy, Minto refused to offer him any assistance against China. Minto's Tibetan policy was dictated by Lord Morley at the India Office, who considered that the Dalai Lama was 'a pestilent animal... [who]... should be left to stew in his own juice.'[17]

When he realised that the only assistance the British would give him was refuge in India, the deeply disappointed Dalai Lama again tried to obtain Russian support. But Anglo-Russian understanding over Tibet had temporarily improved following the 1907 treaty between the two powers and the Dalai Lama received a sharp lesson in the new political realities. When Russia's non-committal reply was delivered to him by their Consulate-General, the Russian used Charles Bell as his interpreter.

Yet Bell continued to be an understanding host and the Dalai Lama began to suspect that British officials in India lacked the power, rather than the will to assist him. He decided to travel to London to appeal directly to King George V and he asked Bell to accompany him. Bell tried to persuade him to drop the idea but found, as he reported to his government, that 'no considerations of discomfort, danger, or loss of dignity appear to influence him'. Only when King George wrote to the Dalai Lama explaining that he was 'unable to interfere between him and his suzerain' did the Tibetan leader abandon his journey.[18]

The Tibetans began to offer major concessions in an effort to obtain British support, even to the extent of offering to give them suzerainty over Tibet. They also proved to be skilled at the diplomatic art of telling their hosts what they wanted to hear. They referred to Younghusband's mission as 'when the British officials and troops kindly came to Lhasa' and in a complete reversal of their usual policy, invited the British to send another mission to Lhasa. With Younghusband's recent involvement in mystical religion in mind, one official described the Dalai Lama's change of heart as 'a conversion...almost as remarkable as that of Sir F. Younghusband'.[19]

The Dalai Lama wanted to return to Lhasa as soon as it was safe to do so and he hoped to persuade the British to provide a military escort to ensure his safe return. Although Whitehall refused to allow him an escort they had, at least officially, no objection to his returning to Tibet. But elements of the British Indian government considered that the Dalai Lama was in some senses a British hostage, guaranteeing the safety of the Trade Agencies from Tibetan attack. Bell was instructed that a discreet watch should be kept on the Tibetan leader and that secret arrangements to be made 'to ensure that the Lama cannot recross [the] frontier without permission'. A close watch was thus kept on the Dalai Lama's movements, although Bell was concerned that 'it would be highly undesirable that he or any Tibetan should know that measures to restrain him are under consideration'.[20]

The question of a Tibetan attack on the Trade Agencies was raised by the Gyantse Agent. He reported that if the Dalai Lama returned to Tibet without British assistance, the Trade Agencies might be the 'object of their contempt and possibly attacks'. This report offered Bell the chance to engineer a particular response, which a skilful Political officer could do by relying on his authority as the government's 'man on the spot' and blurring the very fine line between fact and opinion in his reports. When Bell reported the Agent's comments, he referred to 'probable', rather than 'possible' attacks. The difference was crucial. If government ignored a warning of 'probable' attacks, and these eventuated, they would be blamed for ignoring the warning by their 'man on the spot'. Bell's exaggeration of the threat therefore demanded a response.[21]

The British government refused to allow troops to be sent into Tibet, as Bell suggested, fearing this would be interpreted internationally as British support for the Tibetans against the Chinese. But they did agree to allow a force to be posted on the border, to be ready for immediate despatch to the Agencies in the event of unrest. As Bell surely expected, even this move caused 'an immense stir' on the frontier, and was seen by the Tibetans as support for their cause. Bell's aim of assisting the Tibetans by relieving Chinese pressure was achieved whether the force crossed the border or not. The Chinese, realising their prestige would be damaged if they failed to control the Tibetans, were concerned enough to commence security patrols around the Gyantse Agency, although their efforts were largely symbolic. The patrols consisted of 'one Chinese policeman with a rifle and three rounds, one Tibetan armed with a blunt spear and two Tibetans carrying large paper lanterns'.[22]

The Dalai Lama's request for a British escort to Lhasa revived the old question of posting a British officer there, a possibility that seemed to have vanished when the Chinese established control in Tibet. This issue was also raised by Younghusband's own account of his mission to Lhasa, which first appeared in print around this time. His book, *India and Tibet*, concluded with a strong appeal for a British representative in the Tibetan capital. O'Connor's voice also re-emerged in the debate. He wrote several times from his new post in Persia to suggest that a British representative in Lhasa would be the 'simple, natural and conclusive solution to all our difficulties in Tibet'. He argued that as the Tibetans would welcome a British presence in Lhasa, and the Chinese would be unable to prevent it, the time was now right to take this step. Even the Gartok Trade Agent, who was largely peripheral to these events, suggested this policy in his reports.[23]

O'Connor's suggestions came in response to a letter he had received from the Panchen Lama, who was in an awkward position now that the Dalai Lama was in exile. The Chinese had forced him to write to the Dalai Lama, urging him to return to Tibet, although he had managed to send a secret message with that letter, warning the Dalai Lama not to return unless the British guaranteed his safety.[24]

The Chinese tried to use the Panchen Lama as a replacement for the Dalai Lama, keeping him in Lhasa for some months and offering him the Regency. That might have suited British interests after the Younghusband mission, but the Chinese efforts to get rid of the Trade Agencies had made the Tibet cadre extremely hostile to the Chinese.

The Panchen Lama eventually refused to join the Chinese, and was allowed to return to Shigatse, but many Lhasa Tibetans felt that his actions were pro-Chinese. This sowed the seeds for a dispute between the supporters of the two leading Tibetan incarnations, which eventually led to the Panchen Lama fleeing into exile in China.

During the Dalai Lama's absence in India, the Panchen Lama made a number of approaches to Bell and Macdonald, seeking their advice and support, but the replies were inevitably non-committal. In the Tibetan understanding, however, powerful individuals remained important even when their status changed. Thus, to the Panchen Lama, O'Connor remained a powerful friend and with Bell and Macdonald refusing to assist him, he turned to O'Connor.

In 1910, however, O'Connor was serving in Mashad. So the Panchen Lama despatched several emissaries to Persia, bearing bags of gold-dust and a letter requesting O'Connor's assistance. Although they only spoke Tibetan, the envoys managed to reach Bushir in the Persian Gulf, still clad in their Himalayan dress. From there they were repatriated by the British resident, with assurances that their message would be forwarded. O'Connor duly received the Panchen Lama's letter, along with

> a little bag of gold dust...two or three musk deer pods...some bundles of incense, and a small image of [the Buddha] Amitabha – a rather pathetic little reminder of the country and people of whom I was so fond.[25]

The Panchen Lama's pleas went unanswered. Now that the Dalai Lama was becoming an ally, the Panchen Lama was an embarrassment and he no longer featured in the cadre's plans. Bell was concerned with the Dalai Lama and had concluded that 'the sentiments of the [Panchen] Lama and nearly all of his court are of pro-Chinese tendency'.[26]

In addition to signalling the end of British attempts to manipulate the Panchen Lama, Bell's focus on the Dalai Lama also marked the end of any lingering ideas that Tibet might be taken into some kind of association with the Government of India. When the Dalai and Panchen Lamas each requested an invitation to attend the Delhi Coronation *durbar* in 1911, Bell recommended that they both be excluded as the *durbar* was exclusively for Indian royalty.[27]

The value of Bell's policy of support for the Dalai Lama became apparent after October 1911, when the revolution led by Sun Yat-Sen overthrew the Ch'ing dynasty. There was a mutiny by those elements of the Chinese army within Tibet who supported the revolution, and the Tibetans began to rise up against the divided Chinese forces. The Dalai Lama sent Tsarong Shapé back to Tibet to encourage this insurrection, and by November Lhasa was divided into two areas, one under Tibetan control, the other under the Chinese. Intermittent fighting and a series of negotiations lasted for nearly a year before the beleaguered Chinese garrison finally surrendered. They negotiated safe passage to India, from where they were repatriated. Macdonald, in a reversal of the events of 1910, found himself sheltering fleeing Chinese officials from attack by the Tibetans.

By this time, India had a new Viceroy, Charles Hardinge (later Lord Hardinge of Penhurst). Hardinge had previously served in the British Legation in Teheran, as Under-Secretary at the Foreign Office with responsibility for Central Asia, and as British Envoy to Russia. Although he was not in the visionary mould of Lord Curzon, his contact with the Russians had made him determined to prevent their expansion threatening British interests. While he favoured negotiated settlements such as the 1907 Anglo-Russian accord, in which he played a key role, he had also supported the Younghusband mission and as Viceroy he was soon convinced of the need for a British representative in Lhasa. Once again the Tibet cadre had a Viceroy with some sympathy for their outlook on frontier problems.[28]

With the overthrow of Chinese authority in Tibet, the Dalai Lama began preparations for his return home. He asked the Government of India to send an officer to mediate between the Tibetans and the Chinese forces still holding out in Lhasa. Hardinge, with support from Bell, devised a plan to get around Whitehall's refusal to allow a British officer to visit to Lhasa. They decided to send as mediator a British Indian Buddhist, Sirdar [later Rai Bahadur] Wangfel Laden La (1876-1937). Laden La, a nephew of Chandra Das's companion, Urgyen Gyasto, was a Sikkimese-born Police Inspector who had been responsible for the Dalai Lama's personal security during his stay in India. On 22 May 1912, it was suggested that

> On pretext of assisting Trade Agent at Gyantse, he [Laden La] might, in the first instance, be sent...[Gyanste]...and on receipt of orders then proceed to Lhasa without it being publicly known.[29]

Bell agreed and two days later Laden La was ordered to Gyantse. Hardinge then waited a week before informing Whitehall that he had sent Laden

La to Gyantse with instructions to be ready to go to Lhasa. When no immediate reply was received from Whitehall, their 'silence... [was]... interpreted...as...approval'. On 4 June, Laden La was ordered 'to proceed immediately to Lhasa', along with Norbu Dhondup, a young clerk at the Gyantse Agency of whom more will be heard later. The telegram reached Gyantse at 9am on 5 June and the two men left for Lhasa that day.

Hardinge's telegram was sent to Whitehall on Friday, 31 May 1912. Given the slow pace of communication and government at that time, Whitehall's reply was most unlikely to have reached India by the 4th and Hardinge had not made it clear that Laden La was already in Gyantse. Hardinge clearly hoped to present Whitehall with a *fait accompli*. A telegram was drafted in London on the 4th approving the mission (it is unclear if this was actually sent) but the following day the Secretary of State requested more information and, on the 6th, he ordered that Laden La should not proceed past Gyantse without permission from London. When Whitehall finally realised what was happening, a 'clear the line' telegraph [the most urgent status] was sent, ordering Laden La to halt and await orders. He and Norbu Dhondup had reached Chaksam Ferry when the message reached them that they were to halt. A few days later they were recalled to Gyantse. The plan had failed.

There were precedents for a British Political officer 'losing' a telegram for long enough to allow a traveller to reach his goal. Younghusband had 'lost' an order to stop Sven Hedin crossing from Kashmir to Tibet in 1906.[30] But the Trade Agent in Gyantse at that time was inexperienced. By following his orders he lost the opportunity to let Laden La and Norbu Dhondup reach Lhasa.

* * *

With Tibet no longer under Chinese control, the Dalai Lama was able to return to his country at the end of June 1912. En route to Lhasa he stayed in Yatung for five days with Macdonald. He considered the Agency 'a place of good luck' as it sheltered him en route to exile in 1910 and Macdonald's personal prestige and popularity with the local Tibetans was greatly enhanced by this demonstration of the Dalai Lama's favour. This had its drawbacks; the Tibetans regarded everything that had come in contact with the Dalai Lama as sanctified, and they tried to remove anything he had touched. But that was a small price to pay for such goodwill.[31]

The Dalai Lama waited until the last Chinese had been expelled from Lhasa before re-entering his capital in January 1913. He had indicated to the British on several occasions that he intended to sever all ties with China, and on reaching Lhasa he issued what the Tibetans regard as a declaration for independence.[32]

The British were not pleased when they found out that Tibet and Russian-dominated Mongolia had subsequently agreed a mutual-aid treaty in which each recognised the other's independence. Two aspects of this treaty worried the British. The first was that it raised the somewhat far-fetched possibility that Russian officers serving with the Mongolian army could enter Tibet if Mongolia came to Tibet's assistance in the event of war with China. The second problem was that the treaty was signed on behalf of Tibet by Agvan Dorzhiev. The exact status of this treaty in international law has never been fully resolved, and the question of whether it was made with the full approval of the 13th Dalai Lama remains unclear, but the treaty was another indication of the Dalai Lama's determination to fully separate from China. In fact the implicit Russian threat in this treaty was a remote one. Britain had no definite knowledge of the treaty until they were supplied with a copy by the Russians nearly a year after it was signed and Russia advised Britain that as Dorzhiev was a Russian subject, they did not regard the treaty as valid. The British eventually decided that the matter was best left alone and that, as it raised awkward questions over Tibet's unresolved status, 'it might be of advantage to H.M.'s Government to be without authoritative information on this point'.[33]

Agvan Dorzhiev had been in Yatung to greet the Dalai Lama on his return to Tibet. He introduced himself to Macdonald, who invited him to tea, but the British immediately put pressure on the Dalai Lama to expel Dorzhiev, who was forced to depart for Mongolia soon after.[34]

Dorzhiev remained a shadowy figure whose activities were always regarded with suspicion by the Tibet cadre. Although many later writers on the period have dismissed these fears, in recent years the Russian archives have opened to reveal that Dorzhiev did indeed try to bring about an alliance between Russia and Tibet. But as *Buddhism in Russia*, the late John Snelling's biography of Dorzhiev reveals, Dorzhiev's ultimate aim was not to assist Russia, but to create a Pan-Mongolian state, in which Central Asia's Buddhist followers of the Dalai Lama would come together, albeit under Russian protection.[35]

* * *

The Tibet-Mongol treaty was one of many contemporary factors which indicated that the changes in Tibet required new international agreements.[36] Thus in September 1913, Charles Bell was ordered to Simla for negotiations with China and Tibet. These eventually resulted in the Simla Convention of 1914. Bell acted as advisor to the Indian Foreign Secretary, Sir Henry McMahon, the British plenipotentiary at the Convention, whose name was given to the Indo-Tibetan boundary agreed at the Convention.

The negotiations for the Simla Convention were long and torturous, with China desperately trying to salvage something from the talks. The British were keen to make a lasting settlement at Simla and were thus prepared to make compromises to get China's agreement to the Convention. In the end however, the Chinese refused to ratify the Convention, although the question of whether their delegate could be said to have signed it is open to argument.[37]

The Convention resulted in a settlement based on the artificial concept of an 'Inner' and 'Outer' Tibet. China was granted rights in 'Outer' Tibet, but the British and Tibetan Governments agreed that her refusal to ratify the Convention precluded China from enjoying any of the rights she was granted under the Convention, while the British and Tibetans would treat the agreement as binding on themselves.

Charles Bell's influence on the final agreement was clear. Article Eight of the Convention bore the obvious imprint of the 'forward school'. It was virtually identical to the separate agreement which Younghusband had made – and Whitehall repudiated – allowing the Gyantse Trade Agent to visit Lhasa. This article was clearly at odds with the 1907 Anglo-Russian agreement forbidding British officials access to Lhasa, but that was overlooked. Furthermore, the 1893 and 1908 Trade regulations, which had imposed so many restrictions on the British Trade Agents, were cancelled. In addition to the main Convention, a separate agreement between Britain and Tibet was signed, which removed those aspects of previous treaties which the Chinese had exploited. Thus provision for the removal of the Trade Agent's escort disappeared and there were to be no restrictions on the cadre's access to Tibetan officials.

Bell did what he could to advance Tibetan interests during the negotiations; on one occasion he even represented Tibet in the absence of their delegate.[38] But while Bell had great sympathy for Tibetan aspirations, he never allowed this to stand in the way of his primary duty as a British frontier officer – to protect the security of the Raj. As we have seen, Younghusband had failed in his attempt to bring the Chumbi Valley under British authority. Now Bell managed to bring the Tawang area, an outcrop of territory bordering eastern Bhutan, inside India. His intention was that Tawang would act as a centre for British influence on the north-east frontier.[39]

Bell used the Simla Convention to annex Tawang and several smaller areas. In an exchange of notes which were attached to the Convention, Tawang was made part of India. But Tawang was unquestionably part of Tibet prior to 1914 and accepted as such by both Bell and the Government of India. As Bell advised his government, the Simla Convention meant 'the cession by Tibet to us of the Tawang district...Also...other tracts of Tibetan territory on...the north-eastern frontier'.[40]

There is no record of how Bell persuaded Lönchen Shatra, the Tibetan Chief Minister and representative at the Simla Convention, to agree to cede Tawang. Certainly it was not with the Dalai Lama's approval. Bell himself described (although without mentioning the Tawang issue) how the Tibetan leader publicly demonstrated his dissatisfaction with the results of his minister's negotiations by summoning Lönchen Shatra for an interview at 6am., then making him wait until 5pm. for the audience.[41]

Lönchen Shatra may simply have been naive. The newly independent Tibetan Government were grateful to Bell and his government for sheltering them during their exile, and were concerned with the threat from China, not India. But Bell's notes demonstrate that his plan was to absorb Tawang into India, while avoiding giving direct payments for it, which would clearly 'make us a party to interference with the integrity of Tibet'. Bell planned to give Tibet money later, 'for some supposedly unconnected purpose' and Lönchen Shatra would probably have been told this. In the event, a different currency was used. A month after Tibet signed the Convention and ceded Tawang, the Government of India supplied it with 5,000 rifles and 500,000 rounds of ammunition.[42]

It is doubtful that Whitehall understood the significance of the annexation, or even knew that Tibetan territory had been taken. Within a month of the conclusion of the Simla Conference, Britain was at war with Germany and events on the periphery of empire were given little attention. For the Tibet cadre, perhaps the biggest immediate effect was that they incurred the enmity of Lhasa's Drepung monastery, particularly its Loseling college, to which Tawang monastery had paid annual tribute.

In the wider perspective, the consequences of the Simla Convention were far-reaching. The loss of Tawang was never accepted by the Tibetans. As Tibet could only legally cede territory if it was a sovereign state, which China did not accept, the Chinese also refused to recognise its loss. While Bell presumably felt that both parties should be satisfied, Tawang's incorporation into India was never accepted by Tibet or China and became an important issue behind the 1962 Indo-China war.[43]

Officers such as Bell and Macdonald made no mention of Tawang in their memoirs. In his book *Tibet and its History*, Hugh Richardson, who headed the British mission in Lhasa in the 1930s and '40s, refers to the Tawang issue as having aroused 'some resentment from the Tibetan Government', but he does not mention its former status.[44]

The attempted annexation of the Chumbi, the commandeering of Tawang, and O'Connor's plan to divide Tibet, are all evidence that in the 1904-14 period the British did not treat Tibet as a single, geographically defined state. What they wanted was to create a Tibet which served the interests of the Raj.

In the ten years between the Younghusband mission and the Simla Convention, much had changed. The British had established a firm foothold in Tibet and, despite the Tawang issue, established good relations with the Tibetans. Bell was liked and trusted by the Dalai Lama and his own government had signalled their approval of his part in the Simla Convention by awarding him a CMG; a higher grade of knighthood than Younghusband had been given after his mission in 1903-04. Sir Charles Bell now had the frontier he wanted, Tibet was free of China and, for all practical purposes, was independent. Thus Bell had achieved as much as the 'forward school' could have hoped for, and proved himself a worthy successor to Younghusband.

Chapter Four

'I became Tibetanised'

In September 1914, Charles Bell returned to Gangtok from the Simla negotiations and resumed his duties as Political Officer Sikkim. Although the Government of India informed Bell in 1915 that they regarded the Simla Convention as invalid due to China's refusal to sign it, relations proceeded on the understanding that the Convention was valid between Britain and Tibet.[1]

Bell was now the Raj's acknowledged expert in Tibetan affairs, although Whitehall would still not permit him to take up the open invitation he had from the Dalai Lama to visit Lhasa. They continued to regard themselves as bound by the 1907 Agreement with Russia, in which both countries had agreed not to send representatives to Lhasa.

After returning to his capital, the 13th Dalai Lama had initiated a series of reforms designed to modernise Tibet. Many of these changes were suggested by Bell, who offered as much support for this reform process as was possible within the limits of British policy and finance. Aiding the modernisation process would, Bell recognised, make the Tibetans 'economically and militarily dependent on us to just that extent that is desirable'.[2]

As it was financially impossible for the British to defend Tibet, Bell's first priority was to encourage them to develop their own military forces. In 1915, Bell extended his inspection tour of the Gyantse Agency into a five month stay so as to observe the first group of Tibetan troops to be trained by the Gyantse Escort Officer. This was part of a plan to modernise the Tibetan army which was, at Bell's suggestion, to be increased in size from five to fifteen thousand men.[3]

Bell attempted to persuade his government to supply the Tibetans with additional arms and ammunition, but he had little success. War had broken out in Europe and that conflict was uppermost in the minds of India's military commanders. But Bell ensured that arms supplies to Tibet became a major issue in the 1915-20 period, one which a Secretariat official noted 'turns up in every report or comment we get about Tibet'.[4]

International restrictions on arms sales made this supply of weaponry a difficult issue, as Tibet was not recognised as an independent state. Nor, as will be seen, were Tibet's military forces able to overcome the conservative monastic powers within the country. But if Tibet was to be an effective 'buffer state' it needed to be able to defend itself and when the Tibetans defeated Chinese forces in fighting along the eastern Tibetan border in 1917, with the help of the rifles supplied by India after the Simla Convention, this appeared to be a realistic aim. But the cadre eventually abandoned their support for the Tibetan army after a damning report by Brigadier-General Neame in 1936, which concluded that

> the Tibetans are absolutely unmilitary, all their thoughts and energies are devoted to their religious life. The Tibetan Government have absolutely no idea of military organisation, administration or training...The troops are untrained, unreliable and unpopular.[5]

One other significant issue Bell was concerned with at that time was road-building. If trade and communications between India to Tibet were to be encouraged, the roads had to be improved. But the Tibetan attitude to change was ambivalent. While obliged under the terms of the 1904 Convention to maintain the roads leading to the Trade Agencies, they feared that this would hasten the introduction of foreign ideas, threatening the traditional fabric of Tibetan society. They also quoted a proverb describing the British as the 'road-builders of Tibet', with the implication that when the British had built these roads, others would use them to Tibet's detriment.[6]

In western Tibet, where roads in the modern sense were non-existent, the Trade Agents sometimes resorted to using dynamite to clear the road up to the Tibetan border. This led to the fantastic suggestion that the cheapest and most effective way of improving the route in Tibet itself is to authorise the Trade Agent to buy a good drill and to take with him a small supply of dynamite each year...No political negotiations would be necessary...and...I cannot see that anything but good would ensue.[7]

The cadre eventually downplayed the road-building issue. They realised that making Himalayan roads suitable for modern traffic was an immense undertaking and that there was little chance of obtaining the necessary funding from India or Tibet.[8] This was typical of the way in which the cadre prioritised issues and demonstrates how their concerns were liable to change over time. Aims such as road-building and arms supplies, which came to be seen as unrealistic, were put aside.

If the Dalai Lama was to transform Tibet into a modern state, as Bell hoped, there were other problems to overcome. It was clear that,

> While...there is a definite area within which Tibetan culture and religious ideas are predominant, this area does not necessarily coincide with the effective limits of Chinese and Tibetan administration at any particular time.[9]

Bell therefore encouraged the Tibetan Government to strengthen its assertion of sovereignty and state responsibility for its citizens and, in particular, to enforce its authority over outlying areas of the country. Bell, knowing that many eastern Tibetans tended to prefer Chinese administration, gave the Dalai Lama 'constant advice' that he should improve the quality of his government in that region. This, Bell stated in an implicit acknowledgement of Tibet's previous lack of unity, would mean that 'eastern Tibetans [would] add their wide territories to the rule of Lhasa and work for a large, united Tibet...strong enough to gain freedom for itself'.[10]

Unity was regarded by the British as an essential element of a strong state, and was another reason for Bell to abandon the Panchen Lama. Bell urged future cadre officers, in their dealings with the Panchen Lama, 'to avoid encouraging... [him] in any aspirations towards independence of Lhasa'.[11] Bell had realised that, historically, the Dalai Lama was the only leader acceptable to all factions of Tibetan society. While there may have been opposition to the application of some of the Dalai Lama's policies, his personal status was unchallenged. This made the 13th Dalai Lama the ideal figure for the British to befriend; by influencing him, they influenced Tibet.

Bell clearly stated that 'We want a united Tibet' and the cadre tried to encourage national unity at different social levels. When they started a school in Gyantse in the 1920s, they encouraged the children to wear Tibetan clothing and gave them photos of the Dalai Lama as prizes. As will be seen, they later created a Tibetan football team, in designated 'Tibetan colours', and played international football matches, Britain versus Tibet. These were deliberate actions, with the stated aim of 'developing the ... national consciousness of Tibet'.[12]

While the Dalai Lama was open to other foreign influences, notably Dorzhiev, Bell was the major external influence on his thinking in the 1910-20 period. To conceal the extent of his influence and avoid charges of British involvement in Tibetan internal affairs, Bell claimed he gave advice in his 'private capacity'. He stated that, 'I made it clear that my views were entirely my own, that they did not emanate from, and were in no sense inspired by, my Government'.[13]

Such qualifications were a polite fiction for public consumption. The recipients of 'advice' from an officer of the Raj clearly understood that they had to act upon this 'advice' if they wanted British support. The result, as Bell admitted, was that he did not need to interfere in the internal administration of Tibet because 'the Dalai Lama...has accepted all the opinions that I have given him, and has acted on them'.[14]

There were limitations to Bell's power to influence the Tibetan leadership because he could not impose policies which would alienate his new allies among the traditional Lhasa ruling classes. This meant that he had to support their aspirations and cultural traditions at the expense of power structures elsewhere in Tibet. Bell's lack of real authority had the advantage of enabling him to ensure that the British avoided responsibility for the reforms he initiated in Tibet – and their consequences.

An insight into Bell's thinking is provided by his *Grammar of Colloquial Tibetan*. In the section containing suitable phrases for 'Diplomatic intercourse' the first entry is 'The British Government is not responsible....'. An entry in the section concerning 'Buying supplies for troops' illustrates how he appealed to others sections of the community. It reads 'You will make a large profit, and be able to live in comfort without working'.[15]

Bell's logical approach to Tibetan affairs rarely veered from the rational. In 1912, however, he did slip into the realms of fantasy. Tibet imported its rice from India and Nepal and Bell claimed that as the 'Chinese soldiers could not live without it' they have to withdraw if the export of rice to Tibet was banned![16]

* * *

The 1914 Simla Convention removed most restraints on British activities in Tibet, but the cadre were still unable to obtain Whitehall's permission to visit Lhasa. If Bell was to continue to influence the Dalai Lama he needed a change of policy. Whitehall, however, insisted on strict adherence to the terms of the 1907 Anglo-Russian Convention and refused to allow either Tibet cadre officers or British officials serving in China to visit Lhasa.[17]

Events in eastern Tibet provided the catalyst for a change in Whitehall's policy. Fighting broke out between China and Tibet in 1917, and ended in a truce brokered by Eric Teichman, a British officer of the China Consular service who was stationed at Tachienlu (on the eastern Tibetan frontier).[18] Teichman was more sympathetic to the Tibetan cause than was usually the case with British officials in China and he was in close accord with Bell's views on the need for British access to Lhasa. When Teichman became the principal advisor on Tibetan affairs at the British Legation in Peking in 1919, his influence softened the Legation's opposition to British representation in Lhasa.

In April 1918, however, Charles Bell announced that in future he intended to devote himself to academic study of Tibet, and he went on leave prior to retirement. Bell probably retired because he had given up hope of being permitted to visit Lhasa and, in any case, the Dalai Lama had entered a religious retreat in February 1917, from which he did not emerge until October 1919.[19] Captain W.L.Campbell, the Gyantse Trade Agent, replaced Bell in Gangtok. But although Bell 'retired', he remained on the frontier, and kept in close touch with developments in Tibet.

While Campbell was Political Officer Sikkim, the flow of information from Tibet was disrupted by the death in 1919 of two of the cadre's main sources of information on events at Lhasa; the Tibetan Prime Minister, Lönchen Shatra and the half-brother of the Maharaja of Sikkim, Lhasé Kusho. The Raj's interests were also threatened at that time by a Chinese mission, nominally from the Kansu Provincial Government, which reached Lhasa. The cadre feared that this meant China would re-establish her influence in Lhasa.

The Kansu mission (which had little, if any, success) was one of a number of factors which opened the way for a British mission to Lhasa. Whitehall's principal objection to such an embassy was overcome when the new Communist government in Russia repudiated international treaties signed by its predecessor. The 1907 Anglo-Russian treaty thus became a dead letter, although Whitehall did not acknowledge this until 1920.[20]

Late in 1919, fortuitously for Bell, Campbell resigned suddenly. Bell came out of retirement on the understanding that there was a strong possibility that he would be allowed to visit Lhasa. Once back in office, Bell explored this possibility with characteristic thoroughness. He consulted frontier colleagues, British and Tibetan, as to whether he should visit Lhasa and explored ways in which his mission, if it eventuated, could be made more successful. David Macdonald, who had now spent ten years as Trade Agent in Yatung and Gyantse, was strongly in favour of Bell visiting Lhasa, and gave him particularly valuable support.[21]

Since 1908-09, Bell and Macdonald had developed great personal prestige and they were respected both by the Tibetans and their own government. Their expertise in all things Tibetan enabled them to speak with growing authority on questions of policy and their calls for a mission to Lhasa began to be heeded.

Ultimately it was Bell's mastery of the art of influencing government which was to have the crucial effect. Whereas most of his predecessors on the Tibetan frontier were censured for outspoken comments in their reports, Bell's dispatches were models of reasoned analysis, with the succinct and detached tone favoured by the Secretariat.

Before Bell established himself as the dominant figure on the frontier, the cadre had lacked the ability to present their case to an unsympathetic government 'in such a way as to ruffle as few as possible of their prejudices and enlist as many as possible of their sympathies'. Younghusband had realised the need for more discretion, claiming that British India might have kept the Chumbi Valley 'if I had known better how to handle Government'. But the early cadre officers had ignored the need for diplomatic restraint. O'Connor, for example, described one of Secretary of State Morley's decisions as 'an abject lesson to all observers on the feebleness of our policy', although he knew that Morley would read the report.[22]

Bell was the first cadre officer to master the art of influencing a hostile government. Henceforth the cadre's promotion of policy acquired a new subtlety. They learned that 'there was usually somebody...whose opinion was liable to be decisive in a particular matter' and that these decision-makers must be influenced. Then, if their recommendations were 'reasonable, and fought for until they were granted...each point gained made it easier to win the next one'.[23]

Bell succeeded by promoting a consistent course of action, a British mission to Lhasa as a solution to most, if not all, Tibetan problems.[24] Curzon and Younghusband had advanced the same strategy without success, but Bell was more effective at presenting 'forward' moves in the guise of a defensive strategy. By formulating a consistent 'party line', he effectively created an alternative Anglo-Tibetan policy. His simple and logical plans became the obvious approach for government to adopt when the existing policies failed.

Bell was also a master of the art of presenting a case to government in which minor policies, designed to buttress his main lines of argument, could be used as 'bargaining chips', to be sacrificed if necessary. Bell's expertise in this subtle art of influencing government means that we cannot necessarily accept any particular statement of his as indicating his real beliefs and aims. His proposals must be seen in the context of his long term goals. Early in 1920, for instance, when Bell was confident of being allowed to visit Lhasa, he claimed there was no point in going there unless he was allowed to offer arms supplies to the Tibetan Government. When it became apparent Whitehall would not allow this, Bell ceased stressing that issue and concentrated on obtaining permission to visit Lhasa.[25]

When Bell was recalled to service, Whitehall was considering adopting the alternative policy long advocated by the 'men on the spot'. The British Legation at Peking had softened their policy of opposing a British mission to Lhasa and the powerful Sinophile lobby in the British Foreign Office began to accept the need for a new approach.[26] Perhaps the most significant factor however, was that Lord Curzon became British Foreign Secretary in 1919. As Viceroy of India he had tried to establish British representation in Lhasa. Fifteen years later Curzon was in a position to see that goal achieved and he had the perfect representatives in Charles Bell, who provided a personal link with his own years of dealing with Tibet.

Throughout the summer of 1920, Bell anxiously awaited permission to visit Lhasa. One opportunity arose which he failed to capitalise on; the construction of a telegraph line to the Tibetan capital. The Tibetan Government (probably at Bell's instigation) had first suggested extending the Gangtok-Gyantse telegraph line on to Lhasa in 1915. Nothing came of the proposal at the time, but in 1918 there were reports that China was to open a wireless station in Batang on the eastern Tibetan frontier. The cadre feared that the wireless could be controlled by Japan, whose growing power in the east was regarded with increasing suspicion by the British.[27]

In India, the advantage of improving communications in Tibet was recognised – 'provided these communications are under our control' – and extending the telegraph line to Lhasa became the favoured response to China's plans. The Indian Army approved the proposal on the grounds that 'The existence of such a line might, under certain circumstances, become of great military value to us.'

Bell was quick to see the opportunity that the construction of the telegraph line offered him. The line had to be surveyed and when a telegraph engineer, James Fairley, was deputed from Delhi for that purpose, Bell asked 'shall I go to Lhasa at the same time? This telegraph survey affords a reason for going'. He suggested that he be allowed to go on alone if the surveyor was travelling more slowly; which inevitably he would have been. Bell clearly wanted to be the first to reach Lhasa.

Bell was not permitted to accompany the surveyor and although many accounts of the period fail to mention him, Fairley reached Lhasa around 5 October 1920. He remained there for a fortnight and was received by the Dalai Lama, but he somehow upset the Tibetans and was not employed in Tibet again.[28] The telegraph line was completed by another officer in 1922, and it was subsequently maintained by the long-serving telegraph engineer, W.P.Rosemeyer, who made seven visits to Lhasa over the next 15 years.

By late summer, Bell was becoming increasingly anxious. On 30 August, the Viceroy sent a 'clear the line' telegram to the Secretary of State, which reported that

> Bell wires that his health precludes his continuing in service much longer and I think it very important that before he retires his special experience and friendship with the Tibetans should be utilised by permitting him to visit Lhasa. The cold will make it impossible unless orders are received during the next fortnight.[29]

Bell was clearly trying to force Whitehall's hand. Although his health was generally poor there was no reason he could not travel in winter. While it was undoubtedly difficult, winter travel in Tibet was the rule, rather than the exception. The fallow winter season was when Tibetan farmers went on pilgrimage or trading expeditions.[30]

The British Government probably used Fairley's mission to test whether Bell would be safe, as it was only after Fairley had reached Lhasa that Whitehall finally approved Bell's requests. On 15 October 1920, while lingering over his annual inspection of Yatung and Gyantse, Bell was ordered to proceed to Lhasa.

Bell finally achieved his long-term ambition, arriving in Lhasa on 17 November 1920, a day he had carefully determined was an auspicious one according to the Tibetan astrological system. Bell was escorted from Gyantse by a Tibetan official and in the final miles he received many ceremonial welcomes from Lhasa's Nepalese, Bhutanese and

Ladakhi communities, as well as from the various Tibetan authorities. Then it was 'Lhasa at last', as Bell became the first European ever to arrive there with an invitation from the Dalai Lama. Bell always kept a tight grip on his emotions and the various accounts he gave of his arrival are as understated as their author. But he had been trying to get to Lhasa for more than a decade and he must have been highly satisfied at accomplishing his goal.[31]

Bell had to make a number of compromises to reach Lhasa, but he had not abandoned his 'forward' aims.[32] As Alastair Lamb notes, the Morley-Minto years had taught the cadre that they needed to be 'somewhat devious' to advance their objective.[33] Thus they couched their appeals for support in often exaggerated terms of threats to the security of India, concealed their true motives for all manner of actions, and often avoided consulting, or even deliberately misled, Whitehall.

* * *

The Bell Mission to Lhasa in 1920-21 marked a major turning point in the history of the British presence in Tibet. It effectively opened the Tibetan capital to British Indian officials. In future, at least one representative of the Raj visited Lhasa every year.[34] Ultimately, the Bell Mission paved the way for permanent representation in Lhasa, thus fulfilling the original intention behind Curzon's Tibet policy.

For Bell personally, this mission was the culmination of his career. For more than ten years he had worked to persuade his political masters to allow him to visit Lhasa. Now that he was able to remain there for a year (although his government wanted him to make only a short visit), he brought all his influence to bear on the Tibetans and cemented his friendship with the Dalai Lama.

Bell's visit to Lhasa was not welcomed by all Tibetans. He faced considerable opposition from conservative clergy. This came to a head during the annual Mönlam Chenmo ['Great Prayer Festival'] in the Tibetan New Year. The exact nature of the hostility he faced is difficult to ascertain, as Bell's own discreet account is our main source. He does record that placards were put up one night urging that he be assassinated, but Tsarong Shapé, now Commander-in-Chief of the

Tibetan army, was also a target. That suggests that the protest was really inspired by Tibet's monastic powers, who feared that they would lose their power if Bell's plans to increase the size of the army were accepted.[35]

The opposition to Bell was centered around Loseling College of Drepung monastery, which, as noted, had lost income when Tawang monastery was annexed by British India. Bell, who carefully avoided referring to Tawang in either of the books in which he describes his visit to Lhasa, was not the sole cause of this dispute however: there were wider dimensions to the conflict which pitted monastic against lay officials. But Bell was an obvious focus for discontent and he diplomatically absented himself from Lhasa when matters came to a head and the Dalai Lama sent troops who blockaded Drepung until the rebellious monks surrendered.

Bell remained in Lhasa until October 1921, although the extension of his term as Political Officer Sikkim had ended in January that year. Throughout his stay he had the company of a Medical Officer. An Anglo-Indian, Dr Dyer, travelled with him to Lhasa and after a few weeks was replaced by an old friend of Bell's, the former Gyantse Medical Officer and Acting Trade Agent, Lieutenant-Colonel Robert Kennedy DSO MC. Although his government had refused to allow his wife to accompany him, Bell did invite David Macdonald to join him in Lhasa for Christmas 1920, without asking permission from Delhi. Macdonald spent a month in Lhasa and had several meetings with the Dalai Lama. But the Government of India was reluctant to allow too many officials to visit the Tibetan capital. When they discovered where Macdonald was, he was ordered to return to Yatung.

Although Laden la and Norbu Dhondup had failed to reach Lhasa in 1912, they both joined Bell there in 1920-21. Norbu arrived with Macdonald. Laden La replaced Bell's clerk A-chuk Tsering, who fell victim to the world-wide flu epidemic soon after arriving, although his family always suspected foul play. A-chuk Tsering had been one of the cadre's most trusted sources of intelligence, a role his son was to inherit in the 1940s.[36]

One notable attainment of Bell's visit to Lhasa was that the Dalai Lama gave him permission for the British to send an expedition through

Tibetan territory to Mount Everest. In London, Younghusband was the moving force behind efforts to mount such an expedition and with Nepal refusing access to mountaineers, Bell's achievement was highly valued. It led to a series of assaults on the world's highest mountain in the 1920s and '30s.

When Bell finally left Lhasa, content that he had achieved his aims, he retired a second and final time and began to write the then definitive works on Tibetan civilisation. Before he left office, Bell submitted an extremely important and influential report to the Government of India. Virtually all of the minor proposals it contained were later adopted in some form and his major recommendations became the basis for future Anglo-Tibetan policy.[37]

Bell recommended that the British help Tibet to develop its military forces and that the Raj should allow Europeans (although not shooting parties or missionaries) to travel on the trade route to Gyantse so that Tibetans would become accustomed to European ways. Bell also advocated that if a Lhasa mission was established it should be under the control of the Indian Political Department. The Yatung Agency could then be abolished in all but name and the Gyantse Agency could be reduced to a staging-post en route to Lhasa.[38]

Bell's most significant conclusion was that the British only needed a permanent representative in Lhasa if the Chinese established a mission there. Otherwise British interests were best served by temporary missions such as his own. He argued that Lhasa's isolation and the danger from 'unruly monks' made a permanent mission inappropriate. But Bell was concealing his real motives. The Political Department maintained at least one post (Kashgar) which was much more inaccessible from India than␣Lhasa and many of its positions (particularly on the North-West Frontier) had greater security problems.[39]

Bell's recommendation that there was no need for a permanent mission in Lhasa could be seen as a reversal of the 'forward' policies on the frontier which he had always supported. But his real purpose emerged in his first book, *Tibet Past and Present*, published three years after his retirement. Bell had realised that current British interests were better served by temporary missions such as his own. A permanent

British mission would raise the prospect of China demanding the right to station a representative in Lhasa, with all the attendant risks to Tibetan security that would entail. Finally, definitively, Bell quoted Dalai Lama as saying

> If an Amban must come, I wish to have a British Representative also in Lhasa. But, until an Amban comes, it is sufficient that a British representative should visit Lhasa occasionally, as necessity arises.[40]

Thus we can see that in this important area, Bell's identification of British interests was identical to the Dalai Lama's wishes for his country. Bell clearly followed the Politicals' *Manual of Instructions*, which stated that Political officers should 'assume an identity of interest between the Imperial Government and the Durbar'.[41]

* * *

Sir Charles Bell was the most influential of the British officers who served in Tibet. During his career on the frontier he gained an unprecedented understanding of Tibet and its people. He used this understanding to develop policies which were the basis of the Anglo-Tibetan relationship for most of the first half of the 20th century.

Bell's great achievement was to mould Curzon's 'forward' policies into a contemporary idiom. He drew on his vast knowledge of Tibet and his close personal relationship with the Dalai Lama to promote policies which would achieve Curzon's aim of a secure northern frontier for India. Bell understood that the age of imperial expansion had passed and that the interests of the Raj could be better served by working with the Tibetans, rather than against them. This meant that he identified policy goals which were consistent with their aims.

Ultimately, Bell sought to protect the interests of the Raj without committing India to protecting Tibet's independence from China by military means. While reluctantly accepting that China would eventually play a role in Tibet, he realised that this could even serve British interests if it then lead to a mission in Lhasa.[42] An apparent weakness of Bell's policy was that it produced a solution to the representation in Lhasa problem which was based on a reactive policy.

But this reveals Bell's understanding of policy formation. British policy towards Tibet after 1905 was essentially reactive in nature. Bell had come to realise that anything resembling a 'forward' move on the Tibetan frontier would only be permitted by Whitehall as a defensive counter to Chinese (or other foreign) 'forward' moves in the region. The idea of a 'foreign threat' to India, real or imagined, had often been used by 19th century frontiersmen to obtain support. Bell and his successors used this ploy, but it succeeded in this period only after specific, and verifiable moves by foreign powers, such as the Kansu mission.[43]

An alternative interpretation of this process is that Whitehall only permitted 'forward' moves on the Tibetan frontier when the flow of information was disrupted. In this perspective, the Younghusband mission was sanctioned when Tibet refused to respond to British efforts to establish communications with Lhasa, the Bell mission when the principal British informants in Lhasa had died, and, as will be seen, a Lhasa mission was established in 1936-37 when the British lost the ability to monitor Chinese communications from Tibet. Maintaining the flow of information can be seen as central to British actions on the Tibetan frontier.

* * *

Bell's success was based on his understanding of the Tibetans. He was also one of the few cadre officers who studied the Chinese viewpoint and gained any insight into their perspective. Most cadre officers disliked the Chinese as a race. As one officer commented, 'Williamson hates Kashgar and the Chinks. I agree with him as regards the chinks[sic].'[44] But it was not surprising that that those who devoted themselves to Tibet failed to understand China.

Understanding Tibet was difficult enough. In 1936, the Political Officer's mission to Lhasa visited a monastery where the Abbot predicted rain, as

> the holy pig was just due to rise out of Manasarovar Lake and... three days rain usually fell on it, as this rain water was necessary to consecrate the pig.[45]

Two published accounts of this journey, by members of the mission, repeat this prediction, but neither comment on it.[46] For minds trained in the tradition of scientific enquiry, this forecast was noteworthy because it defied logical comprehension and explanation; it was inexorably 'Other'.

In 1926, the officer inspecting the Gartok Trade Agency reported that, as the local people were still 'medieval', British and Tibetan officials there had 'almost no basis on which to approach each other'. This lack of understanding is apparent in many aspects of Anglo-Tibetan relations. But the cadre were well aware of how difficult it was to understand another culture and knew that 'Asia does not think along European lines.'[47]

At the time, however, it was considered that frontier officers gained understanding of the local culture through their presence 'on the spot'. Hence Bell's claim that Tibet's atmosphere 'must be almost impenetrable to one who has not been there'. Cadre officers with the longest terms of service, such as Bell and Macdonald, were thus thought to have gained the deepest insight into Tibet.[48]

The Tibetans shared the belief that insight increased with time and preferred cadre officers to serve long terms, a principle they expressed with their proverb that 'Old devils are better than new Gods'. The Dalai Lama himself told Bailey that, 'it took the Tibetans a long time to get to know a new man and it took a British officer a long time to get to know Tibetans and their language'.[49]

The basis of understanding was, as the Raj recognised, becoming fluent in the local language. A fundamental tenet of the Politicals was that they were expected to learn the local language of their domain. In practice, few of the cadre learned Tibetan fluently. Most Political Officers mastered the necessary ceremonial phrases and relied on translators for detailed discussions. Bell, however, became fluent in Tibetan.

Bell also had another quality essential to gaining an understanding of Tibet: he had an intuitive, as well as empirical awareness of local concepts and attitudes. This was recognised by the Raj as a highly desirable quality in frontier officers. Ideal frontiersmen needed to possess an 'intuitive perception...from an Oriental as well as an English point of view'.[50]

This institution provided an insight that others, however learned, could never gain. As his fellow-officers observed of Norbu Dhondup, 'he has such an intuitive knowledge of Tibetan affairs and people that his conclusions, however fantastic they may appear, are practically always right'.[51]

Few imperial officers had this intuitive grasp of the local cultures, and many never gained any real understanding of Asian perspectives. But being a successful colonial officer did not necessarily require a particularly high level of cultural understanding, particularly in a system where officers were frequently transferred. Those who did come to understand another culture were those with a personal interest which went beyond the requirements of duty. Deep understanding was largely gained outside the formal imperial structure, and often at the expense of career advancement.

Bell immersed himself in Tibetan culture, adhering strictly to Tibetan etiquette and traditional ceremonial forms. He deliberately chose to take this to an extreme, not only arranging his dealings with Tibetans according to their system of auspicious dates, but even riding a horse of an auspicious colour. This adherence to their customs was an important aspect of his being accepted within Tibetan society. Living amongst the Tibetans, speaking their language and following their ways, Bell became, as he put it, 'in a large measure Tibetanised'.[52]

Of course some aspects of Tibetan culture remained incomprehensible, even to Bell. But there are degrees of understanding. Failure to comprehend some aspects of a culture does not preclude an overall understanding of it. Culture and society are organic and different cultures may exist within one society. Even within societies, individuals may not understand aspects of the culture they are born into. But Bell did gradually become an 'insider', accepted by his Tibetan allies as 'belonging' to their society.

The trust which the Tibetans placed in Bell (such as when they allowed him to represent them at the Simla Convention), demonstrates their recognition of him as 'belonging to' their society. This they indicated ritually by what Peter Bishop calls 'an honorary kinship designation in a religious framework'. They concluded that Bell was involved with Tibet because he had been a Tibetan in a previous incarnation and had prayed to be reborn in a more powerful country in order to help his own.[53]

In Tibet: *A Political History*, by former Government Minister, W.D.Shakabpa (the nearest we have to an official Tibetan history in the English language), Bell is referred to as 'a very close friend of the Dalai Lama'. Bell himself quotes the 13th Dalai Lama as telling him 'I have complete confidence in you, for we two are men of like mind' and he records a leading monastic official as having written to the Dalai Lama that

> When a European is with us Tibetans I feel that he is a European and we are Tibetans; but when Lönchen Bell is with us, I feel that we are all Tibetans together.[54]

Imperial understanding tended to be class-based. Imperial officers generally relied upon upper-class informants and the Tibetan behavioural forms which Bell adopted were those of his allies, the Lhasa aristocracy. When Bell became an accepted member of Tibetan society he naturally became a member of a class and consequently identified with those class interests. As Bell found his place in the highest levels of Tibetan society he identified with that class, rather than with regional or marginalised sectarian or social classes. As a result, although he had dealings with all classes of Tibetan society, Bell's identification with the ruling class inevitably resulted in his marginalising lower-class and regional 'voices'.

Although he became 'Tibetanised', Bell avoided 'going native'. In British India, that would have meant to a large extent placing himself outside the social and intellectual boundaries of the Raj. The insights of an officer who 'went native' ceased to be trusted, or accepted as 'true', by knowledge-making bodies such as the Royal Geographical Society, which only processed knowledge expressed in forms and using conventions it deemed appropriate.

Bell did not cease to identify with his own culture. In such matters as dress, bearing, religion and behaviour, he remained very much a British officer. Despite his long service among the Tibetans, he never lost sight of the interests of his government. While gaining a place in Tibetan society was beyond imperial requirements, he used his position to advance the interests of the British empire. In his reports, Bell could be sharply critical of the Tibetans and, as we have seen, he clearly stated on several occasions that he sought to make the Tibetans dependent upon the British.

Bell was able to reconcile his duty to the Government of India and his sympathy for Tibet as he believed British and Tibetan interests coincided. He felt Tibet's future prosperity and India's security were best guaranteed by an independent Tibet under British guidance. In retirement, however, Bell came to doubt that this conjunction of interests would continue. He foresaw a greater Mongolia, centered on Lhasa and including Sikkim, Bhutan and Ladakh, as a means of ensuring a strong and independent Tibet; the same idea which had occurred to Bell's Russian rival, Dorzhiev.

Aware of the great importance of religion to the Tibetans, Bell went to great lengths to avoid appearing to be of any threat to Buddhism. He gathered an extensive knowledge of the faith, and displayed a respect for its outer forms, being quite prepared to bow in a Buddhist temple when that was appropriate.[55] Nonetheless, although Bell did not emphasise his Christian beliefs, he did not become a Buddhist. Studying an indigenous religion such as Buddhism was considered a perfectly proper imperial pursuit, but to have adopted that religion would have removed an officer from the acceptable parameters of behaviour for a British official, he would have been considered to have 'gone native'.

By allying with the Buddhist leadership of the Dalai Lama, Bell effectively marginalised any religious opposition to the British presence. Through such devices as allocating him a Tibetan heritage from a previous incarnation, Bell could be given 'honorary Buddhist' status within the broad parameters of the Tibetan religious system, which was essential if he was to be accepted within Tibetan society.

Bell's career is evidence that attaining a deep understanding of a society requires a 'crossing-over' from one culture to another, and indicates his ability both to 'cross-over' and to return to his own culture. We are reminded of the 'myth of the eternal return', which as Mircea Eliade has explained, involves the quest of an archetypal hero journeying to an unknown place or culture. With the assistance of an intermediary, the hero gains the object of his quest, which may be seen as a symbol of knowledge or power, and returns with it to his own society.[56]

Bell was not unique in 'crossing over' from British to Tibetan society. Other officers followed his example. Macdonald, with his mixed background, perhaps found it easiest. Norbu Dhondup made the journey in the opposite direction and, of Hugh Richardson, cadre officer in the 1930s and '40s, it was noted in the Secretariat as early as 1939 that 'he has identified himself more closely with Tibetans and Tibetan affairs, and...gained more insight and respect, than any Englishmen[sic] since the time of Charles Bell'.[57] Bell had become the standard by which other officers were measured.

Many cadre officers were not, however, fully accepted within Tibetan society and they did not expect to be. While they established good personal relations with Tibetans and developed a love of the country, to them it remained 'Other'. This was an important part of Tibet's attraction. Politicals wanted to serve on the frontier, with all that symbolised. They did not seek the familiar. Only a few individuals such as Bell, with a particular personal interest and commitment to service in Tibet wanted to fully understand it.

While it is commonly concluded that the unequal power equations involved in colonial encounter meant that neither culture could really understand the other, this ignores the insight gained by the 'men on the spot' such as Bell. Their understanding was not dependent on the imperial context of their encounter. Imperial and career factors provided the opportunity for, and affected the transmission of, understanding, but individuals 'crossed over' from personal desire to do so, rather than as an exercise in power.

Chapter Five

Growing up 'with a profound belief in the British Empire'

The Tibet cadre was an elite order of imperial officials, and their distinctive character was no accident. It was the result of a deliberate training process designed to produce a particular type of individual, one regarded by the Raj as ideal for service on the imperial frontiers. Cadre officers were carefully selected and trained to ensure they were of this right 'type'. But the ideal officer was not considered to be the product of training alone. He also had to have certain innate qualities which were, as Curzon put it, 'an instinct rather than an acquisition.'[1]

Any officer of the Political Department could be posted to Tibet, but the Secretariat recognised that its officers were individuals; some suited Tibet, some did not. Those who were successful there had certain distinguishing aspects to their character, many of which were the result of their background and training.

The majority of cadre officers came from a middle or upper-middle class background, and had close family connections with India. The British cadre officers had all had a public school education and entered Tibetan service after a period in the Indian military or civil services. This background had a significant formative affect on the character of cadre officers, as it did on other imperial service officers.[2]

There were two primary influences which attracted young men to imperial service. The first was having family members who had served the empire. A family tradition of Indian service certainly influenced Bailey at an early age. Preserved among his papers are an 'Essay on

Choice of a Career in Life [sic]', and another on 'Outdoor Games', written when he was an 11 year old schoolboy. Bailey then favoured a naval career 'Because I like travelling'. His chosen games topic was polo, a sport which his father had presumably played while serving in India.[3]

The other major influence was literary. Young men were attracted to the empire by the books they read. Hugh Richardson, for example, was inspired by reading of George Bogle's 18th century travels in Tibet. Rudyard Kipling (who was a close friend of O'Connor), was a particularly powerful influence on those who served the Government of India. Although he was by no means an unequivocal supporter of imperialism, Kipling's romantic tales of an exotic land full of adventure had a great appeal. As one Political wrote, 'With the literary backdrop of the Jungle Books and Kim...I longed to see India.'[4]

An early taste for Kipling was common and lasting among the cadre. Bell would relax by reciting Kipling's poetry, while 1940s Political Officer Arthur Hopkinson gave his new bride a collection of Kipling's works, along with riding lessons. Both were of equal importance if a Political officer's wife was to fit into her new role.[5]

For most officers, the first step on the road to imperial service in Tibet was attending a British public school. Three cadre officers attended Marlborough, although Sir Charles Bell and Sir Basil Gould, who had both attended Winchester school, occupied the senior Gangtok post for almost half the 1904-47 period.

The role of British public schools in producing individuals with the particular qualities regarded as desirable for service in the empire was clearly recognised as part of their function. It was said that, 'Every school building is a citadel of Empire and every teacher its sentinel'. Thus young men absorbed the desired imperial values. Lord Curzon, for example, traced the origin of his imperial views to a lecture at Eton.[6]

Cadre officers thus

> grew up with a profound belief in the British...Empire...completely satisfied about the superiority of everything British, and never doubting that the British Empire would endure for ever.[7]

Public schools fostered common standards of behaviour and taught their pupils qualities which were considered necessary to run the empire. The desired qualities included self-confidence, leadership, a sense of duty and respect for tradition, along with a certain 'amateur spirit', an ideal of generalised, rather than specialised or lucrative knowledge. These were precisely the qualities sought by the Political Department. Thus a probationary report on Basil Gould states approvingly that, 'His manners are perfect, as might be expected from a Winchester and Oxford education.'[8]

Sport was an important part of the educational process as it was believed to foster both the physical virtues of strength and endurance and the moral virtues of self-discipline and duty, thus producing, 'the confidence to lead and the compulsion to follow'. The sporting milieu of the public schools created a particular code of ethics, which used symbols and metaphors derived from the Victorian amateur sporting ethos. Thus, in the imperial setting, an officer was expected to have 'a sense of fair play', and expected his fellow-officers to 'play the game'. This 'games ethic' became the moral basis of the frontier officers' sense of identity.[9]

Although a cult of 'Socratic virtues' also existed in parallel to the cult of 'Muscular Christianity',[10] those intellectual virtues were not specifically incompatible with the ideals of empire. While there was no anti-intellectual ethos in the cadre, they were generally 'outdoor types', shaped by, and adhering to, the 'games ethic'. A high standard of fitness was essential in the harsh Tibetan environment, and the keen intellect demonstrated by cadre officers such as Bell and Richardson was in addition to 'outdoor' qualities.

After public school, the military colleges and universities (particularly Oxford and Cambridge), continued the imperial training process begun by the public schools. Curzon remarked that he 'could not understand how anyone educated at Oxford in his time could fail to be an imperialist'.[11] A pro-imperial ethos naturally reigned at the military colleges. English composition exams at Sandhurst involved answering such questions as whether Polar expeditions were 'worth the hardship and sacrifice involved?' – the desired answer was obvious.[12]

Military colleges tried to bind individuals into a single unit with a shared sense of purpose. Their culture centred on the mess, where the nuances of appropriate behaviour were learned. They also emphasised equestrian skills, and 'manly sports' which were considered to enhance work performance. Hence Bailey's comment (in 1924) that 'if he [Norbu Dhondup] was not good at polo, football etc...his work would not be so good.'[13]

The military influence on the cadre was considerable and courage proved in battle was a common cadre characteristic. Ten cadre officers came from the Indian Army and two of the ex-ICS men, Frederick Williamson and Arthur Hopkinson, had served in World War One.[14] At least seven cadre officers saw active service – in Tibet, Persia or the World Wars. Hopkinson, Bailey and O'Connor were wounded in action. Williamson, Captain E.W.Fletcher and Major George Sheriff were mentioned in despatches, while Captain Alec Russell won a Military Cross in anti-Bolshevik operations in Northern Persia in 1924.

The public schools did not, of course, produce only imperial administrators. Products of the military colleges were not always 'gentlemen' who upheld the honour of their regiment, and the universities did not, despite Curzon's statement, only produce unquestioning imperialists. But the system did produce sufficient men who believed in the imperial ideal, and those who did not subscribe were not favoured for imperial service.

But times changed, and the prevailing attitudes of the Curzon era gradually became the minority view.[15] The Indian services did adapt to the changing conditions and later officers no longer expected the British empire to last forever. But the educational and selection process of the Political Department did not change with the times. In the 1930s and '40s the ideal of the desired type of Political officer was largely unchanged from that of Younghusband era. Thus Bell and the last cadre officer to leave Tibet, Hugh Richardson, were very similar 'types', despite the changes that had taken place between their periods of service.

* * *

Future cadre officers continued their training when they arrived in India. The Indian services believed that their cadets had the right character and education to make good imperial officers, but that they needed experience and training under Indian conditions before they could be given responsibility.[16]

Both civil and military recruits underwent specialised training in their duties, during which time they also absorbed the values and traditions of their service. In the Indian Army, a newcomer was attached to a regiment, where he learned the practice of his profession in the Indian context. In the ICS, a trainee was posted to a district under the supervision of an experienced ICS officer. There he learned the practical methods by which British rule was administered.

One of the most important aspects of their initial training was that newcomers, both civil and military, learned their social place and the behaviour appropriate to that status. While their education and family background (particularly if it was British Indian), had taught them much of the required behaviour pattern, the singular culture of British Indian society, with its particular codes and nuances of behaviour which were by no means always clearly articulated, imposed its own demands. For example, an ambitious Indian Army officer learned that 'you had to push to get there, but it would not be good form to push too hard'; the 'swot' was frowned upon. He learned to drink, but not too much, and to have pride in himself and his regiment, but not boast about either. The ideal officer mastered these subtle distinctions between good, and bad, 'form'.[17]

Whether it was their training in India, or 'the values they absorbed in their youth' which had the greater influence on imperial officers is debated by historians.[18] Certainly the most important factor shaping the character and mentality of the Tibet cadre was their school. An officer's school was part of his identity and it remained their most common reference point. For Arthur Hopkinson 'there was no school but Marlborough', while Bell's obituaries refer to his school, but not to the obscure district in eastern India where he began his ICS career.[19]

The imperial training process was, in the wider perspective, an established means of uniting people for a common purpose. Individuals whose personal goals benefit from their role in an organisation may be trained to internalise its values. They develop a loyalty to their institution, and act for its benefit. The group develops a shared ethos as individuals expect their fellow group-members to behave in the same manner as themselves.[20] The collective mentality which the cadre acquired as a result of this process was the result of a deliberate effort to produce the desired 'maximum degree of uniformity of intellect, education and general outlook'.[21] This ensured that their government could rely on them to act independently, but within the overall limits of British aims and policies. Trained to believe in their right to rule, the cadre were self-confident administrators, who saw themselves as loyal servants of a righteous empire.

* * *

Although the three locally-born cadre officers, Norbu Dhondup, Pemba Tsering and David Macdonald had a different background, they attended schools on the British model, and were promoted to Political Department posts only after a long period of service in lower-ranking positions on the frontier, when they had thoroughly absorbed the mentality of an officer of the Raj. They did encounter some prejudice along the way, but the Tibet cadre was essentially a meritocracy, and relied heavily on the knowledge of local employees.

These three officers were not actually members of the Political Department. They were officially classified as 'attached' to the Department, but this was an administrative matter of little practical significance which enabled the Politicals to employ specialists in areas where cultural expertise was particularly required. Four British cadre officers, including Charles Bell, also had 'attached' status. These officers received all the benefits of Political employ, such as language allowances and a pension, and identified fully with the Politicals' aims and ethos.

In 1906, the Secretary of State objected to the Politicals' use of 'attached' status officers.[22] The practice declined thereafter, but became common again in World War Two due to manpower shortages. But the Viceroy always retained the power to choose *any* officer he wished, and every officer selected for the Politicals was personally approved by him. A vital part of the admission process was lunch at the Viceregal residence, where a candidate's social abilities were closely monitored. Such meetings were not necessarily formal. Sherriff was posted to Lhasa after an interview with Lord Linlithgow which culminated in a catapult competition out of the Viceregal window; a curiously appropriate means of selecting frontier officers.[23]

Men generally joined the Politicals because they wanted a more varied and interesting career. Money was another factor, particularly for Indian Army officers who were not paid as well as ICS officers. Political service also appealed to the ambitious, the Politicals were considered, at least by themselves, as having the highest status of any Indian service, and none of the Tibet cadre ever returned to their former service after serving in the Politicals.[24]

When an officer joined the Political Department, it became the focus of his loyalty, although to a great extent the Politicals' traditions and even duties, built on those of the ICS and Indian Army. Politicals largely ceased to identify with their original service and this was often resented by their former colleagues. The Army and the ICS naturally had no wish to lose promising young officers; Younghusband noted that 'the regiment always looks side ways at men going into the Politicals and make it difficult to get leave[sic]'.[25]

Entry into the Political Department was theoretically governed by certain rules, but as Bailey noted, 'All the rules for entering [the] Political Department are made simply to keep out people they don't want'. While the specified age limit (under 26 for military entrants), was regularly used to exclude unwanted candidates, Fletcher was admitted when a year over age and Macdonald's application was accepted when he was over 50.[26]

What then were the real criteria for admission into the Politicals? Russell was too idealistic when he wrote that 'I could perhaps get some influential backing but I would infinitely prefer to get in on my own merits and I believe the latter course would be appreciated.' Admittance to the Politicals required patronage.[27]

The Secretariat admitted that, 'we do attach considerable importance to a favourable report from an officer of the Political

Department'. Thus Hopkinson had backing from O'Connor, Richardson from Gould and so on. Officers with other influential backing also stood a good chance of selection; for example, 1930s Gyantse Agent Major P.C.Hailey, who had a reference from his uncle, the Governor of the Punjab, Sir William Hailey.[28]

Lieutenant-Colonel Weir's father, a Colonel in the IMS, solicited the backing of Foreign Secretary Dane for his son's candidature. Dane had once promised him that a pay cut 'would be counted unto me for righteousness' and he successfully asked if 'the counting might take the form of the admission of my boy into Political employ?'[29]

* * *

We have seen that the influence of writers such as Kipling could lead youths to aspire to imperial service. The Political Department, recognising this, used suitable texts as training manuals for its new recruits. They were examined (at least into the 1920s) on four works; Lyall's *The Rise and Expansion of the Brtish Dominion in India*, Edwardes's *A Year on the Punjab Frontier*, Thornton's biography, *Sir Robert Sandeman*, and another text pertaining to the Middle East. It is instructive to analyse the policies and role models these textbooks present, because they clearly demonstrate aims and activities approved by the Department in terms which were not otherwise officially articulated.

The works of Edwardes and Sir Alfred Lyall, a former Indian Foreign Secretary, reflected British imperial confidence that the Raj was a 'benevolent despotism [which] is the best of all governments'. They depicted the ideal of Political officers as sent 'forth beyond our boundaries to be a pioneer of Christian civilisation'. These were views the Tibet cadre were to have a little argument with, at least until the 1940s.[30]

The ideal Political officer emerges most strongly in Thornton's work, a hagiography of Lieutenant-Colonel Sir Robert Sandeman, Chief Commissioner of Baluchistan from 1877 to 1892. According to Thornton, Sandeman displayed just the qualities desired by school and empire, 'energy, perseverance...a strong sense of duty', and so on. But trainee officers could see other qualities of Sandeman which suggested the real route to success on the frontier. Sandeman was 'no favourite with officials...In important matters, he rarely accepted an official negative as final'. He apparently delayed a telegram postponing an assault (an action described in approving tones) and he crossed the frontier without permission, but, as the trip was a success, the 'irregularity was condoned'.

Both Lyall and Lord Curzon contributed to Thornton's work. Lyall approvingly observed that Sandeman, 'continually discovered excellent reasons for advancing...and annexing fresh territory'. The ultimate seal of approval was Curzon's support for Sandeman's 'spirit of somewhat greater independence of central Government than a rigid officialism either encourages, or readily condones'.[31]

Trainee Political officers reading Sandeman's biography could be left in little doubt that rules and regulations were of secondary importance. Sandeman broke all the rules and became a hero of the British empire. Clearly it was bold action advancing British interests or frontiers that the Politicals required, whatever their role might be defined as for public consumption.

The Tibet cadre followed Sandeman's example. O'Connor made his name by an unauthorised border crossing and Younghusband delayed a negative telegram long enough to allow explorer Sven Hedin to cross into Tibet. The early Trade Agents, in the unsettled frontier conditions which made for potential expansion, all 'continually discovered excellent reasons for advancing' into Tibet.[32]

In addition to these set texts, officers naturally read other works on the empire. One particularly influential book was *The Defence of India*, a confidential report by Sir Charles Macgregor, Quartermaster-General of the Indian Army, which emphasised the Russian threat to India. This work was a great influence on the 'forward school'; Younghusband for example, studied it closely.[33]

Ambitious cadre officers also read everything they could on Tibet. Williamson's wife recalled his study 'lined with books in which...travellers described their abortive attempts to enter the forbidden city'. Bell listed 76 books on Tibet and its neighbours among his collection.[34]

Government encouraged these studies, establishing libraries at the Gangtok and Gyantse posts. Many of the books on Tibet were by former cadre officers. These works were closely studied by serving officers. Hokinson, for example, took all of Bell's books with him to Lhasa in 1945, and thoroughly absorbed their contents.[35]

There was an implicit political agenda in much of what the cadre read. These works generally reinforced imperial concepts of British rule as a 'civilising mission', bringing the many benefits of 'progress' to 'uncivilised' Asia. The ideals these works promoted were the product of an earlier age and, although their message became increasingly outdated, later cadre officers continued to read the books read, or written by, earlier cadre officers. Improved communication, increasing government centralisation and a changing climate of opinion all prevented the fulfilment of the 'forward' ideals these works promoted, yet through these texts the ideals remained with the frontiersmen into a later age.

Chapter Six

'The strange laboured breathing of men and mules'

The conditions under which the cadre lived varied depending on which post they occupied. The most congenial location was the Political Officer's Residency at Gangtok, the capital of Sikkim. This was the gateway to Tibet for most cadre officers and travellers. It was the place to begin acclimatising to the altitude and to make final arrangements for the journey to Tibet. Gangtok was then a small town of around 2,000 people, stretched along a ridge amongst densely wooded hills. A small community of European officials, missionaries and teachers resided there, although during the summer, when the rains and the ubiquitous leeches were at their worst, the Political Officer usually left for his annual inspection tour of Yatung and Gyantse.

Sikkim was ruled by a Maharaja, who was, in practice, under British control, particularly during the White era. British influence was symbolised by the concrete road which ran from the Maharaja's palace to the British Residency, home to the Sikkim Political Officers.

The Residency was, and still is, a substantial two-storey mansion, built in 1888-89 after the style of an English country house. The walls are of stone, with a red felting roof, and the interior is panelled with local timbers. Its comparative splendour was enhanced by White, who added the gardens which then, as now, surround it, and of which he was particularly proud. The overall effect was to provide all the grandeur considered necessary for the maintenance of British imperial prestige.[1]

Though it was reputedly haunted, the Residency was a 'dainty gem of a house, furnished from Oxford Street within, and without the tree ferns and orchids of this exquisite valley'. But despite the touches of England, the wilderness was close; leopards were common visitors. As late as 1925 a Miss Wiggin shot one in the Residency gardens.[2]

The 175 mile route from Gangtok to Gyantse became well-trodden and descriptions of it abound in travellers' accounts. The journey took around 11 days at normal pace, although it could be done in as little as three. Nights were spent in the *dak* bungalows along the route.

The original bungalows were sparsely furnished and provided only basic accomodation. They contained just two beds, and travellers needed their own bedding. The *chowkidars* who were employed to maintain them were permitted to run a small tea shop beside the bungalows. However, 'Natives', White originally decreed, 'are not allowed to occupy bungalows, otherwise they would be in a short time unfit for Europeans'.[3] In later years however, many of the bungalows were improved and upper-class Indians and Tibetans were permitted to stay there.

The journey from Gangtok to Yatung over the Nathu la, like that from Kalimpong over the Jelep la, was a strenuous one.

> It felt like climbing up a continuous ladder, each step higher than the one before. Up. Up. Up; right onto the roof of the world. Your head felt light and your limbs like lead, and all that could be heard was the strange laboured breathing of men and mules, with occasional fits of coughing.[4]

The layout of the Chumbi Valley was complicated by most places having more than one name. The passes into the Chumbi, the Nathu La and Jelep La, met at Pipitang, four miles to the south of the Yatung Trade Agency. The Agency was actually situated in Shasima (also known as New Chumbi) at the junction of the Phari and Kamba valleys, but this place became commonly called Yatung. The original Yatung (which became known as Old Yatung) was a small village of no importance, located in a bleak and isolated valley off the main trade route. This trade route passed through 'Yatung' Bazaar and by the British Trade Agency on the eastern side of the Amo river, on the western side of which was the Yatung *dak* bungalow.

The long, low-roofed Yatung Trade Agents' bungalow was erected during the Younghusband mission. It was originally a three-roomed shelter made of rough shingle, but was gradually improved until it consisted of seven rooms, with a glassed-in verandah at the front, surrounded by lawns and a terraced garden.

On leaving Yatung, travellers passed by the European cemetery on the edge of town, and then climbed the wild slopes of the Amo river gorge. At the head of the Chumbi Valley they passed through the infamously filthy town of Phari, a windswept hovel built on its own refuse. There the British maintained a telegraph and post office at a healthy distance from the bazaar.

There followed an almost monotonous journey across the vast, desolate plain dominated by the massive 24,000 foot peak of Mount Chomolahari. It ended with two or three days travel through more populated territory along the banks of the Nyang Chu, a tributary of the Tsangpo/Brahmaputra. Gyantse itself was visible only for the last seven miles of the journey. It was surrounded by bare sandy hills in shades of brown and grey, which were usually topped with snow. The third largest town in Tibet, although with a population of only around 4,000, Gyantse was dominated by two imposing buildings. Atop either end of a rocky spur rising up above the valley were a 14th century *dzong* (fort) and the Pekhor Chödé monastery.

'Chang lo', the original Gyantse Trade Agency, consisted of two, square-roofed two-storey blocks, around a courtyard. One block was used for offices and barracks, the other as the Trade Agent's residence, and a mess was added soon after O'Connor moved in. The house was furnished in European style by carpenters supplied by the Panchen Lama, but lack of finance for maintenance meant that the buildings soon became very run-down. The condition of the military escort's building became so bad that three sepoys died 'due to over-crowding and the insanitary state of the lines', and the soldiers moved into tents despite the cold.[5]

As part of their efforts to isolate the Trade Agency, the Chinese prevaricated endlessly when the British wanted to build new premises during the 1906-09 period. A new fort, built on the military pattern used on the north-west frontier, was finally completed in 1911. It was half a mile from the original site, and farther from the river, but the building was still frequently damaged by floods and earthquakes in the ensuing years and required more-or-less annual repairs. In contrast, the Gyantse *dak* bungalow was half a mile away, pleasantly located amongst willow and poplar trees and with a fine view of the Gyantse *dzong*.

The new fort was rectangular, with outer defensive walls of mud-brick enclosing the Agency buildings. Except for the stables and military hospital, the buildings were all two-storey, with external staircases and verandahs. The lower floor was, for defensive reasons, occupied only by storehouses. The officers' quarters, a reception room, the mess and the Trade Agent's office were all on the upper-floor, overlooking the main courtyard and parade-ground. At the bottom of the main stairs were a pair of guns used on the Younghusband mission; a reminder of the Agency's essentially military character.

By the 1940s, the Trade Agent and his fellow officers lived there in a fair degree of comfort. Lieutenant D.A.Walters, who arrived in Gyantse in 1940, described the conditions as:

> very comfortable. I had, as second-in-command, two rooms and a bathroom. The British Trade Agent had a big bedroom, bathroom and dressing room. We also had a common room where we used to dine, a mess hall where the liquor was kept and a morning room – all glass-fronted – where we had our breakfast...In each room there was a wood-burning stove...the British trade agent had the most [wood] so we usually clustered in his room and kept ourselves warm.[6]

The bitterly cold winters were a serious problem. A number of Europeans died from pneumonia at Gyantse and names like Hann and Patterson joined those buried on the Younhusband mission. The conditions were particularly difficult for the military escort, whose duties were principally outdoors. Their periods of guard duty were soon limited to 45 minutes and regulations specifying how often they should bathe were also relaxed. They were issued extra fuel and given balaclavas, tinted goggles against the snow, great-coats, fur-lined gloves and special boots. When the temperature dropped below minus 10[f] degrees they were also given an extra rum ration – poured down their throats to ensure that it was drunk, rather than sold.[7]

While the Trade Agency was comfortable, Gyantse was a hostile environment in which to serve even in summer. Situated at a breathless height of over 13,000 feet, it had freezing winters and frequent duststorms in summer. There were few visitors, particularly in the early years, and for those who loved European society, life there could be a trial. Yet the cadre officers who served there were young and fit and as frontiersmen they were accustomed to both the joys and the hardships of service in remote locations. O'Connor did complain to his government of the isolation, elevation, climate, responsibility, lack of feminine company and a house 'unfit for European habitation' where he was 'alone...among a wild and treacherous people'. But these complaints were designed to bolster his request for a pay-rise, and in his memoirs his fondness for Gyantse is clear.[8]

O'Connor was not actually 'alone'; by which he meant European company. There were always five or six other Europeans there. Nor did the Tibetans prove to be either wild or treacherous. In the years that followed, Gyantse came to be regarded as a peaceful and pleasant location by most of the British who served there. Perhaps the biggest problem was boredom; for those without a particular interest in some or other aspect of Tibet, 'life could be excessively tedious'.[9]

For F.M.Bailey life was never tedious. In an article for *Blackwoods Magazine*, entitled 'A Quiet Day In Tibet', he described his first waking thoughts in the morning as he waited for his servant to bring his tea.

What is to be done today?...The obvious answer to the question had just presented itself – Let us kill something.[10]

Bailey filled his time in Gyantse with *shikar*, polo, hockey, football and even wrestling. Such was Bailey's fondness for *shikar*, which was then considered a perfectly proper activity for an officer and a gentleman, that his diary entry on the day he marched into Lhasa with Younghusband read, in characteristically terse style;

Wednesday 3 August 1904. Marched to Lhasa morning. (fly) 34 fish.[11]

Bailey's letters and diaries record an enormous, and very mixed, bag of game, including a coolie, who was accidentally shot in the buttocks by a telegraph sergeant; a wound which proved fatal. Whether this was entered in the game book kept in the mess at Gyantse is uncertain, but in the 1940s an escort officer did hook a dead baby while fishing, and he entered that in the book – before putting his fishing-gear away for the duration.[12]

A by-product of Bailey's fondness for *shikar* was a zoo stocked with the offspring of his victims. At various times it housed monkeys, snow leopards, gazelles, wolves and a variety of other birds and animals. Bailey tried unsuccessfully to tame his animals and they invariably died. Luckily, he also collected skins and specimens of Tibetan flora and fauna, some previously unknown, for museums in Britain. This also provided a welcome supplement to his regular income.[13]

Cadre officers were rarely troubled by an excessive work-load. One noted in 1943 that the paperwork at Gyantse only took about 15 minutes a day. Even in the early years, when Gyantse was of more importance, the workload was light. But much of an officer's time was taken up with activities 'which are not exactly work, although they are apt to consume a good deal of energy and patience'.[14]

These activities included much of their socialising with the Tibetans, for as Hopkinson explained 'It may seem curious, but it is definitely part of my job to attend parties, and I shouldn't be able to do my job of I didn't'.[15] But along with their private and semi-official duties, there were a number of other matters to which considerable energy had to be devoted.

* * *

One recurring frustration concerned the telegraph line from Gangtok to Gyantse, which had been established during the Younghusband mission. Most histories of the period repeat the story that the Tibetans did not cut the telegraph wire because the British had told them it was to enable the mission to find their way back to India. That story may have been true and on several occasions travellers caught in snow-storms were only saved by following the line. But after the Younghusband mission the telegraph wire was an irresistible temptation to passing Tibetans, who either climbed the poles and stole sections of wire or used the conductors as targets for their sling-shots.

The Trade Agents were naturally annoyed by these interruptions to their communications, but the offenders generally escaped. When Bailey sought Chinese assistance in preventing this damage, they suggested nailing a man's hand to any damaged pole. Bailey declined to take up this original solution and although at least one offender in the 1940s was whipped by the Tibetan authorities as a deterrent, the problem was never solved.[16]

An immediate problem confronting the early cadre officers was Annie Taylor, a formidable Presbyterian missionary, who had made a courageous effort to reach Lhasa from China in 1892. When the 1893 Trade Regulations allowed British traders to reside in Yatung, Miss Taylor applied for permission to open a medical supplies shop there. While it was well-known that she was a missionary, it proved impossible to refuse her a trading permit. In August 1895, she arrived in Yatung and set about her self-appointed task of converting the Tibetans to Christianity.[17]

Two or three other female missionaries joined her at various times, but none stayed long, for she was clearly awkward company. The China Customs Officers in Yatung were a particular irritant to her. She argued over who had the right to first look at the weekly mailbag and protested that Captain Parr was in the habit of 'drowning his illegitimate children in my well' (an accusation which was not taken seriously). Taylor seems to have had little success in her proselytising, but the wary Tibetans ensured that her local assistant reported her activities to the Lhasa government. During the Younghusband mission her nursing skills proved of value, but when she returned to England early in 1905, the frontiersmen doubtless breathed a sigh of relief.

Unfortunately Miss Taylor returned in December of the same year. She crossed the frontier by night without a pass, and took up residence in the Yatung Customs House where she refused to pay rent on the grounds that it needed repairs. Her sanity was increasingly questioned as she wrote a series of abusive letters to government. In one such rather incoherent missive she wrote

> You are all brave enough to attack a little Englishwomen but none of you are brave enough to tackle the Chinese Customs. Has the age of chivalry ceased?

The frontiersmen were at rather a loss as to how to deal with her. They were trained to face hostile tribesmen; not hostile elderly Englishwomen.

Miss Taylor was finally removed to a 'lunatic asylum' in October 1906, probably by fellow churchpeople. Captain Campbell, then in charge of the Chumbi, duly disposed of her belongings in the traditional frontier manner; a public auction.

The cadre had to deal with others of questionable sanity who wrote to the Government of India, or to the Dalai Lama. In 1911, one correspondent to the Viceroy claimed that the Dalai Lama had agreed to follow his advice on how to regain his position at Lhasa. Another wrote claiming to be 'General of the Grand Duke's Army of Russia in Asia', and urged the Dalai Lama to summon this army to the aid of Tibet.[18]

Visitors also posed problems for the cadre. The first private traveller to visit Gyantse Trade Agency was an American, Francis Nichols from Wanston, Illinois. Although an experienced, Tibetan-speaking traveller who had spent a year on the Upper Salween river, Nichols collapsed after arriving at Gyantse. He died of pneumonia on 29 December 1904. On the same day, O'Connor and his Medical Officer had to deal with the Telegraph Superintendent, Mr E.A.Michael, who suffered a fit which left him dumb and partially paralysed.[19]

Many later travellers produced similar difficulties for the cadre, or created political troubles (as will be seen), but there were also problems with the sort of individuals who embarrassed colonial governments everywhere. One resourceful rogue was Major W.H.Cairncross, an Australian who was educated in the rough gold-mining town of Ballarat, Victoria, where his father was a mining engineer. Cairncross was commissioned in the British Army at the outbreak of World War One and served as an Intelligence Office in Mesopotamia. After being invalided to Bombay in 1917, his career record became less worthy.

Following a court-martial for dishonesty, he was dismissed from the army in October 1918. He remained in India and soon came to the attention of the police for various 'shady transactions'. In 1921, he fled to Tibet to avoid charges of deception pending against him in Calcutta.[20]

Calling himself 'Mr Brown', Cairncross reached Yatung with his 'wife' (a Miss Irwin), and their ailing, eleven-month old baby. Arriving at the Trade Agency, he told Macdonald that he had been robbed the night before and was now penniless. Having crossed the frontier without a permit, he was liable to immediate deportation, but Cairncross knew enough about the Trade Regulations governing the British presence in Tibet to claim to be a trader, and thus entitled to Trade Agent Macdonald's assistance.

Bailey, who was now Political Officer Sikkim, was then unaware of Cairncross's background. He authorised Macdonald to advance the Major 400 rupees, with Miss Irwin's jewellery as security. Cairncross then refused to leave Yatung. Macdonald arranged with the Tibetans to deny him any supplies and when the money ran out after three months Cairncross admitted defeat. He and Miss Irwin returned to India, where they were arrested. Bailey was left with the jewellery and four years later asked his superiors for permission to sell it. He was advised that legally he needed Cairncross's permission, but that 'in the circumstances you will probably be prepared to take the risk of selling it'; although, as it was noted pessimistically, the jewellery was probably fake.

That should have been the end of Cairncross's involvement in Tibet, but he was obviously a resourceful character and he put his Tibetan experience to use in Europe. In 1924 the Swiss Tourist Department enquired of the British Legation in Berne as to the *bona fides* of a 'Major W.H.Cross', who was claiming to be an agent of the Dalai Lama. The Major had conducted a lecture tour in Switzerland, receiving free hospitality and collecting funds 'for Tibetan medical institutions'. This tour brought Cairncross to the attention of the British intelligence services, although with the little apparent effect.

The following year Cairncross turned up in England, posing as the Dalai Lama's mining manager and giving public lectures which were very well received. His testimony must have been strengthened by his father's mining background, and by the fact that in the early 1920s the Dalai Lama had employed a Government of India surveyor to conduct mineral exploration in Tibet.[21]

Cairncross was last heard of in 1927, when he gave a lecture on the religions of China at University College, Swansea. This turned out to consist of slides of a trip from Calcutta to Peking via Lhasa (the source of which remains a mystery), along with scientific comments which the university staff considered 'dubious'.

Problems with travellers increased in the 1920s, when, as suggested by Bell after his visit to Lhasa, restrictions on the number of travellers allowed on the trade route to Gyantse were eased. By the 1940s, the trickle of visitors had become flood, particularly in the years immediately after the second World War, when visits to Tibet were popular with military personnel awaiting return to Britain. The numbers peaked in 1945-46, when more than 200 Europeans visited Yatung, although only a handful of them continued on to Gyantse, a journey which required more time, effort and money than most visitors could spare.

The cadre found that many of their visitors were short of cash and needed to borrow from the Trade Agents. Many were what they called 'spongers' – travellers who expected to enjoy the hospitality of officers of the Government of India at every stop. Many of these were well-connected members of the British aristocracy, carrying letters of recommendation which the cadre officers could hardly ignore. Others were well-known travel writers who used, and sometimes later abused, the cadre's hospitality. The problem was particularly acute in Sikkim, which was far easier to obtain permission to visit than Tibet, but the Political Officers learned to be fairly ruthless in dealing with these 'spongers'.

Tibetans today are accustomed to dealing understandingly with all manner of eccentric and misguided individuals seeking spiritual enlightenment, but in the early years of the Anglo-Tibetan encounter they were less diplomatic. One such eccentric character arrived at Gyantse in 1926. He was a wealthy American theosophist, Mr H.A.Carpenter, a retired engineer.

Carpenter believed that a man had followed him from America and always carried a loaded pistol in his hip pocket in case he was attacked by him. He presumed that he would be allowed to visit

Shigatse and to live with his 'master'. But, as the British expected, the Tibetan authorities refused to allow him to visit Shigatse. When Carpenter asked after his 'master', the Khenchung 'just laughed in his face'. There was no such person. Yet Carpenter was allowed to return to Gyantse in 1930, although he never reached Shigatse.[22]

It was not only private travellers who posed problems for the cadre. There were a number of difficulties with supporting personnel and even with officers at the Agency, including the escort and medical personnel. The Supply and Transport Department was renowned for corruption, always suspected and sometimes proven, while the various building contractors employed at Gyantse frequently proved dishonest.[23]

One Escort Commander proved particularly embarrassing. Lieutenant Macready, who was stationed in Gyantse in 1908-09, began surprise mock night attacks on the Gyantse Agency and nearby villages. Later he had a villager flogged on suspicion of forging invoices for transport supplies, which he had no authority to do. Soon after, a boy guarding the escort ponies let them stray onto private land. The farmer who owned the land threw the boy in the canal, which should have been the end of the matter. But Macready sent some of his soldiers to beat the farmer. Kennedy, the Medical Officer who was then acting as Trade Agent, had to pay the victim compensation, and Macready was ordered back to India.[24]

The key problem with the escort officers was one of authority. The precise responsibilities of the Trade Agent and the Escort Commander were not clearly laid down, something which O'Connor had pointed out when applying for control of the escort in July 1906. The fact that the Escort Commander could hold higher military rank than the Trade Agent further complicated the matter. The problem simmered on until 1914, when after an illicit visit to Shigatse by Captain Fenton, the Indian Army issued orders that placed the Escort Commanders under the full control of the Trade Agent. The Escort Commander remained responsible for military precautions for ensuring the safety of the Trade Agent and other personnel at the Agency.[25]

Such problems only arose when there were personal difficulties between the officers concerned, for there were usually common-sense solutions to divide authority. As one Secretariat official commented after a dispute between Trade Agent and Escort Commander in the 1930s, 'This is a stupid little dispute, no doubt attributable to the fact that the tempers of men who live at 13,000 feet are liable to be short.'[26]

Captain Cobbett, however, Escort Commander in 1923-24, kept his temper when losing it might have caused a diplomatic incident. He attended a monastic festival where he was knocked unconscious by a monk wielding a stick. Although the British party did not appreciate it, the monk was presumably one of those who kept order in monasteries, which they regularly did at festivals by means of whips or clubs. Over-eager Tibetan spectators were generally protected from injury by their thick garments. Cobbett had no such protection, but he swallowed his pride and restrained the party of soldiers with him. Cobbett accepted an apology, thereby avoiding a potentially dangerous rift between British soldiery and Tibetan monks.[27]

Several Escort Commanders performed well enough to raise questions as to whether they might be appointed to Political posts in Tibet and during World War Two the Gyantse officers acted as Trade Agents on a regular basis. But none of them ever returned to Tibet in an official capacity and in retrospect this must have been a waste of expertise. One young Escort Commander did go on to higher things, however; Lieutenant, later Field-Marshall, Claude Auchinleck, who served in Gyantse in 1906-07.

Clerical staff, who handled money, frequently caused difficulites. In 1908, Bailey was embarrassed by his Gyantse Head Clerk, Mr Pierpoint. After Bailey dismissed him for leaving his post early prior to leave and for falsifying accounts, Pierpoint attempted to blackmail Bailey. He demanded 1,000 rupees, later reduced to 500 rupees, in return for keeping silent about various irregularities in Bailey's accounting. At least one accusation was true. If he used up the money allocated for one purpose, such as *dak* bungalow repairs, Bailey would supplement it with money which had been allocated for another purpose, such as road-building. This was actually common practice throughout the empire, not least to avoid paperwork, and involved no personal gain to the officer concerned. But it was against regulations, and thus not something an ambitious young officer wanted attention drawn to.

When Bailey refused to pay, Pierpoint reported him to Bell in Sikkim and even to the Viceroy. But with his mentor, O'Connor who was then in Calcutta, acting for Bailey, the matter was dropped. Some years later, Pierpoint wrote from Canada asking for the return of his belongings from Gyantse, but by then Bailey had sold them to cover the shortfall in the accounts.[28]

Pierpoint's case was typical of the problems experienced with the Head Clerks in the early years. When his successor, Pursing Karthak, an Indian Christian, was jailed for conspiracy, it was noted that all 'the previous incumbents, whether Indian or European, have proved dishonest or incompetent'. Karthak's dishonesty had come to light in 1913, when the building contractor with whom he was conspiring tried to bribe Private John Johnson, a military telegraphist. Johnson reported the bribe and, in the absence of any other candidate of proven honesty, he was transferred from the military to the civil post. Johnson, however, found his post a lonely one and shot himself in November 1916.[29] In later years Johnson's grave was said to be haunted by a ghost who sat on the cemetery wall and begged for cigarettes![30]

* * *

After the Simla Convention of 1914 had solved the Raj's immediate problems with Tibet, the outbreak of war in Europe further reduced British concern with events in that remote corner of the empire. Tibet became something of a backwater in the minds of ambitious officers, and the wartime shortage of staff meant that the number of Europeans in Tibet was reduced. In the immediate post-war years the situation continued and the general neglect gave rise to a major scandal at Gyantse.

After more than a half a century, the exact circumstances of this affair are difficult to establish, but it caused a sensation on the frontier at the time. Travel writer Robert Byron, who visited Gyantse ten years after the events, provides a somewhat garbled account of the affair, omitting the names of those involved. But from his account, and official records, it is possible to partly reconstruct the events.[31]

When Charles Bell temporarily retired in April 1918, he was replaced by Major W.L.Campbell, Gyantse Trade Agent for the preceding two years. David Macdonald then acted as Trade Agent both in Gyantse and Yatung. As his family were in Yatung, he made only occasional visits to Gyantse. The European Medical Officer had been withdrawn in 1915, leaving only one European officer at Gyantse; the Escort Commander. Between April 1918 and July 1920, this post was filled by one of the frontier's more colourful characters, Captain Frank Perry, a former Indian Police Officer, serving with the 2/10th Jat regiment.

Although Perry was the only British officer left at Gyantse, there were other Europeans present; Martin, the Head Clerk, Luff, the telegraph sergeant and Sergeant Little, of the Supply and Transport Department. In addition, a close friend of Perry's, David Macdonald's son John, who had no official status, was a frequent visitor.

As Escort Commander, Perry was in immediate charge of the Gyantse Treasury, which he handed over to his replacement, Lieutenant Chatterjee, when his term expired. The young Chatterjee was one of the first Indians to receive a commission and was, by all accounts, well-regarded. But he apparently neglected to count the money in the treasury and when he came to hand it over to his successor in July 1921, nearly 65,000 rupees was found to be missing. (An amount approximately equivalent to ten years salary for a young Political officer.) Chatterjee was technically responsible, and took what he must have considered the only honourable step possible in the circumstances: he killed himself with an overdose of sedatives.

It emerged that Perry, along with the local Jongpon, Sergeant Luff, and others, had relieved the boredom of service in Gyantse by drinking, gambling and entertaining various local women. Perry had moved into the sergeants' mess and the furniture and fittings of the officers' mess had disappeared along with the money from the treasury. According to Byron's account, this situation came to the attention of Perry's superior, who, from the description given, must have been Campbell. He was discovered to have his own weaknesses, 'though of a different type', and when these were reported, he left the service: Campbell did in fact resign suddenly for unknown reasons in December 1919. Perry and his friends then continued as before.

What is a matter of record is that Perry, who had been transferred to Delhi after his service in Tibet, was arrested in June 1921 in connection with the loss of treasury funds. Perry then escaped from open arrest at his Delhi bungalow and fled – to Yatung. It was while he was in Tibet that Chatterjee died, and the rumour spread among the Tibetans that Perry had arranged for Luff in Gyantse to murder Chatterjee; a conclusion which British sources noted, but dismissed.

In retrospect it is very unlikely, although not impossible, that Chatterjee was murdered. The new Escort Commander, Lieutenant Andrews, was then in Gyantse and reported nothing untoward. According to Byron, Henry Martin (who was well-regarded by his superiors) had his suspicions, but it seems more probable that Perry fled to Yatung because he hoped to be sheltered by his friends there, John Macdonald and his sister Annie. That Perry was back in Yatung when Chatterjee died was probably coincidental, but perhaps Perry and Luff took the full story to their graves.

Perry was eventually taken into custody again in August 1921 at Yatung. He was sent back to Delhi, where he was court-martialled in February 1922. He faced charges of fraudulently converting public money to his own use, negligence, escaping from custody and desertion (for the period of his escape) It was impossible to prove Perry had taken the money, but he was found guilty on the charges of negligence and escaping from custody. His only punishment was dismissal from the service.

Perry promptly returned to Tibet, this time to marry David Macdonald's daughter Annie in the first, and only, European wedding ever held in Tibet. It was a popular affair on the frontier, with a number of guests arriving from India, including one old lady who walked all the way. But Perry was soon in trouble again. Firstly he overstayed his pass and in September 1923 was fined 25 rupees for the offence. Soon after, he assaulted a Chinese who failed to greet him in the accepted fashion, but the Macdonalds smoothed over the matter with a payment to the victim.

Perry then founded a trading company with another former Gyantse Escort Commander, Captain Parker, apparently in an attempt to establish residence in Yatung as a trader under the Trade regulations. Although the partnership was soon dissolved when Perry failed to provide his share of the capital, it enabled him to remain in Yatung. There he was a constant thorn in the side of F.M.Bailey, now the Political Officer Sikkim. Late in 1923, Perry became the Tibet correspondent for the London *Daily Mail*. His reports, which were frequently inaccurate, infuriated Bailey, as did Perry's refusal to admit he was the author of reports – which were by-lined 'From Our Correspondent'. The only people in Yatung who knew enough English to produce the reports were the Macdonalds, Perry and Parker. Parker quickly denied any involvement but Perry refused to comment, although it was clear he was the correspondent. [32]

Perry's problems inevitably began to involve his father-in-law, David Macdonald. News emerged that Macdonald had written to the Dalai Lama in 1923 asking him to employ Perry in the newly-formed Lhasa Police Force. Bailey, who did not hold Macdonald in high regard, protested to his government about his Trade Agent's actions.

While it was generally recognised that 'it is a pity that the real offender (...Perry) gets off unscathed', the Government of India ruled that Macdonald's pending admittance into the Political Department, which was to have been a reward for his long and valuable service, be revoked. In addition he was censured for his attempt to find Perry work with the Lhasa Police and it was decided to reintroduce the system of having separate Agents at Yatung and Gyantse, with Macdonald reverting to the lower ranked post at Yatung. All that could legally be done to Perry was to expel from Tibet and forbid him to return. Perry remained on the frontier; annoying Bailey with his newspaper articles. Eventually he became a convivial and popular host at the Himalayan Hotel in Kalimpong. But Perry's luck finally ran out; he never returned from active service in Burma in World War Two.

The final years of Macdonald's long and distinguished career in the Tibet cadre were marred by these events, which took much of his energy. In one of his final annual reports from Yatung he declared that 'Everything has been very quiet in the Chumbi Valley...and there is nothing whatever to bring to notice.'[33] This was not what his superiors wanted to hear. But

Macdonald was not the only cadre officer to hang on to his post for too long. As will be seen, this was a common cadre characteristic.

Macdonald at least retired honourably, but Gyantse was soon to see a Trade Agent whose brief career ended in disgrace. Major H.G.Rivett-Carnac was from a distinguished family which provided an early Governor of Bombay and several senior police officers in various parts of the empire. But he was totally unsuited for service in Tibet. Rivett-Carnac was married, with two young children, and was more concerned to be with his family in India than with service in Tibet. The Political Officer Sikkim privately described him as 'utterly useless' and 'more of an uxorious horticulturalist than a working political officer'. After Rivett-Carnac was transferred, the collapse of a private bank established in Gyante with Government of India assistance revealed that he had borrowed 3,000 rupees from the bank and made no attempt to repay it. To make matters worse, he had previously filed a report clearing the bank of allegations of cheating the government. When it collapsed, the allegations were shown to be true. Rivett-Carnac's failures in Tibet were followed by very unfavourable reports from his subsequent postings and, when further unpaid debts were revealed, he was forced to retire.[34]

It was these minor incidents, odd personalities and in-house problems which occupied much of the cadre's time and thoughts. Moments of crisis and danger were rare and, in such remote locations, petty irritations such as the severing of the telegraph line were apt to take on greater significance than they deserved. The ability to surmount these problems and to cope with eccentric visitors or fellow-officers was an important part of a cadre officer's duty and in the wider context, was part of their constant struggle to uphold British prestige. This could have been seriously threatened by another case in the 1920s, which centered on the charismatic figure of F.M.Bailey.

Chapter Seven

'Tom-foolery on the part of Laden La, Tsarong and others in Lhasa in 1924'

As Bell was still in Lhasa when his one-year extension of service ended in January 1921, a new Political Officer was needed at Gangtok. The man appointed was Frank O'Connor. The Panchen Lama, whose relations with Lhasa were becoming increasingly strained, hoped that the appointment of his old ally would bring him a measure of British support and he sent two ponies as a welcoming gift. But O'Connor, although he had hoped to be given the Gangtok post in 1908, now wanted the higher-ranking post of British Envoy to the Court of Nepal, which was soon to become vacant. He served in Gangtok for just three months, and with the focus in this period on Bell in Lhasa, there is almost no record of O'Connor's time there and he did not bother to mention it in his memoirs.[1]

Although he didn't want the post himself, O'Connor wanted a fellow-thinker in Gangtok and he advised Bailey to apply for the position. The vacancy occured sooner than planned, as O'Connor had to return to England in March 1921 when his mother fell seriously ill. Bailey, who was on leave in England, was appointed to replace O'Connor as Political Officer Sikkim despite being considered 'somewhat junior for the post'.[2]

As Bailey was not due to return to India until June 1921, O'Connor's sudden departure left the Sikkim post vacant for three months. David Macdonald arrived back from Lhasa to find himself appointed Acting Political Officer Sikkim, in addition to his existing positions as Trade

Agent in Yatung and in Gyantse. This was the peak of Macdonald's career. He was liked and trusted by the Tibetans and, with his mentor Charles Bell in close communication with the Dalai Lama in Lhasa, this period was the highpoint of Anglo-Tibetan relations, at least from the British perspective.

Yet within four years, relations had sunk to their lowest level since the Younghusband mission and there was no real improvement until after Bailey's departure. This raises the questions; what went wrong, and was Bailey to blame?

In the wider context, the issue is one of control. If the British were to understand, influence and rule South Asia, they needed to attract the support of indigenous elites. Thus, as we have seen in the cases of O'Connor with the Panchen Lama and Bell with the Dalai Lama, imperial officers actively tried to obtain allies amongst the ruling classes of the societies they encountered: this was a deliberate strategy by the imperial power.

This strategy was the Political Department's speciality. Its officers were specifically instructed that 'The first duty of a Political Officer is to cultivate direct, friendly, personal relations with the Ruling Chiefs with whom he works'. As one Political Officer's wife recalled, 'it was important to get to know people, and...thereby be able to exert a positive influence in Tibet.'[3]

But what were they to do when diplomacy failed, and a former ally, while not becoming actively hostile or threatening, ceased to act upon the advice he was given? This was the problem that Bailey had to face.

Bailey began his term in Sikkim under awkward circumstances. He was out of touch with both events and personalities in Tibet. In the ten years since he had been in Tibet he had had no personal contact with the Lhasa authorities; nor had he ever met the Dalai Lama. When Bailey took-over, Bell was in Lhasa dealing directly with the Dalai Lama, leaving Bailey something of a lame-duck until Bell left in October 1921.

Bell could have invited Bailey to join him in Lhasa and introduced him to the Tibetan Government, but neither officer entirely approved of the other's methods and they were not friends. Nor was Bailey keen on Bell's loyal assistant, David Macdonald, and he had apparently found it demeaning to his prestige to take over Sikkim from an Anglo-Sikkimese.[4]

Bailey inherited the Bell policy of British support for the gradual modernisation of Tibet. He had no quarrel with that policy but, unlike the scholarly Bell, Bailey's view of a Political officer's role was more orientated to command than to advice. Bailey's personality made it obvious that he would take a slightly different approach to Tibet than that taken by Charles Bell.

On paper, Bailey was the ideal choice. In the years since he had been in Gyantse, he had become one of the empire's heroes. He had explored the eastern extremities of the Brahmaputra, been ship-wrecked off the China coast, and was twice wounded at Gallipoli in World War One, before being withdrawn from war service by the Government of India. In 1918, he was sent on an intelligence mission to Tashkent, to report on the anarchic situation there as the Bolsheviks took control. A series of story-book adventures followed. Bailey was forced to disguise himself – notably as an Albanian deserter. His disguise so successful that he was hired by Russian secret police to find a British agent they knew to be in the area. The agent was Bailey himself. He lost touch with his government, who had to tell his mother that 'We can only hope Bailey is making his way across the passes to India', but so important a figure was Bailey that a party of Bolshevik officials in war-torn Persia were held as hostages until he returned safely.[5]

Bailey had little trouble establishing his authority on the Tibetan frontier, or with his own government. His mentor O'Connor was in Kathmandu and Bailey was also on very good terms with the Political officer in Assam, Captain G.A.Nevill, and the missionaries in eastern Tibet who provided the British with valuable intelligence on that sector of the frontier.[6] In England, Lord Curzon was now British Foreign Minister and, in addition, Bailey had married into the aristocratic Cozens-Hardy family and had built up contacts at many levels of the British establishment.

Bailey's career also had another dimension. He was one of Britain's most renowned intelligence agents, as his exploits in Russian Central

Asia showed. That role was behind many of his activities, such as his famous journey from Peking to Sadiya in 1911. Although officially described as private, that earned him a substantial sum from 'Secret Service' funds.[7] Bailey's experiences in Central Asia had had a great impact on his thinking. As a young Trade Agent in Gyantse he had been strongly influenced by the 'forward school' fear of imperial Russia's ambitions in Asia. Now he saw an even greater threat to British interests in the newly emerged Soviet communist system. Bell had reported from Lhasa that, despite there being a Russian agent in Lhasa's biggest monastery, Drepung, 'there is no danger of Bolshevism in Tibet', as it was unsuited to their religion and culture.[8] But Bailey took a very different view.

While it was long doubted, recently opened Russian archives show that there were attempts by the Soviet regime to gain influence in Tibet in the 1920s. Russian agents were dispatched to Lhasa among pilgrim parties from the Russian Buddhist regions and, in 1921, there was a 'sinister plot to send weapons and ferment revolution in Tibet'. Although Agvan Dorzhiev was no supporter of communism, he was still concerned with Tibet and assisted his new masters in these activities.[9]

Bailey had obtained his own informants among the Russians, in particular, the Kalmuck Buriat leader Zamba Haldenov, described as 'Chief Buddhist priest of the Astrakhan Kalmucks'.[10] The information he received from these sources must have convinced him that there was a real threat of communist influence in Tibet and, like Curzon 20 years before, he was determined to meet the challenge in Tibet before it became a challenge to India.

The Russian threat was not Bailey's only concern. He also had to face the fact that the gradual modernisation of Tibet had aroused conservative opposition from within Tibetan monastic and aristocratic circles which was proving too strong for the Dalai Lama to ignore. Although the Dalai Lama had introduced some well publicised changes – telegraph and electric installations in the Potala for instance – the majority of Tibetans showed little enthusiasm for modernisation. They opposed changes to their traditional social structures just as they had done when the Chinese had attempted to introduce similar changes in the 1907-11 period. The powerful monastic forces were particularly opposed to reform, and were strong enough to prevent the Dalai Lama from carrying through many of the changes Bell had recommended.

Economic factors also hindered reform. Tibet lacked the finance necessary for modernisation and the structural basis to obtain loans. This meant that the Lhasa Government had to either impose new taxes or divert resources from the monasteries to the reform programme. Both measures were tried and both were unpopular, with the imposition of new taxes on the Panchen Lama's estates adding to existing Lhasa-Shigatse tensions.

Within Tibet, those who rejected the reform process also tended to oppose Western influence generally, seeing it as a threat to Tibetan culture. These conservative forces objected to Europeans entering Tibet. Their views became more influential when problems arose with the first Everest expedition. The large party imposed a great strain on the local resources, and one of its members carried out unauthorised exploration off their route to Everest. After the expedition a party of monks from Gyantse were taken to Europe, where they performed religious dances without their abbot's approval.[11]

A major problem was caused by the illicit journey to Lhasa early in 1923 by an American lecturer at the School of Oriental Studies in London, William McGovern. McGovern was a member of a 'British Buddhist Mission' which was allowed to visit Gyantse in 1922, although it was refused permission to visit Lhasa. The India office had warned Bailey that the mission, mainly composed of Oxford University graduates, 'are a queer crowd...[who]...clearly show the cloven hoof'.[12]

After visiting Gyantse, McGovern returned with his fellows to India, having given his word in writing that he would do so when he applied to enter Tibet. Having freed himself from that bond of honour, he then secretly made his way back through Tibet in disguise, reaching Lhasa on 15 February 1923. He revealed his presence to the Tibetan authorities, who expelled him from Lhasa six weeks later. His subsequent book and newspaper articles, widely publicised in Britain, greatly annoyed the cadre.[13]

McGovern's worst 'crime' in their eyes was probably his assertion that there was a pro-Chinese party in Lhasa. Any evidence suggesting that any Tibetans, particularly in Lhasa, in any way favoured the Chinese rather than the British was always denigrated. To counter McGovern's claims, Bailey called on Arthur Hinks, the Secretary of the Royal Geographical Society [hereafter the RGS], who arranged for the journal of the society to publish as strong an attack on McGovern's reliability and reputation as was legally possible. The journal pronounced that 'whatever little value the story [of McGovern's journey] might have possessed is discounted by Dr. McGovern's obvious predilection for sensational journalism'. His conduct, they claimed, had done 'great disservice to good relations with Tibet', while his 'boast' that Indian frontier police were punished for failing to prevent his visit meant McGovern 'stands self-condemned'. Later references to him by cadre officers were inevitably derogatory; two decades later Bell described McGovern's book as 'a thriller' and incorrectly alleged that his disguise had been penetrated.[14]

British India's embarrassment over this affair was compounded by protests from the Tibetan government when McGovern escaped prosecution. Delhi had decided that as the available penalty was just a small fine, it was not worth enforcing, as it would only give McGovern more publicity. This led the Tibetan authorities to suspect, quite wrongly, that McGovern's journey had British support.[15]

By mid-1923, it was clear to Bailey that the existing Tibetan Government would not make the changes which British interests demanded, and that their military forces were not sufficient to resist any threat from Russia. Bailey was unable to arrange a visit to Lhasa until 1924 and, suspecting that the Dalai Lama was unwilling, or unable, to lead Tibet in the direction the interests of the Raj demanded, Bailey looked for other powerful figures in Lhasa who might support reforms.

As a military officer himself, Bailey found natural allies in Tibet's military forces. The newly emerging military power in Tibet was closely associated with Tsarong Shapé, who following his role in helping the Dalai Lama escape to India in 1910, had become the Commander-in-Chief of the Tibetan Army.

Tsarong was clearly an outstanding individual, a powerful figure in Lhasa politics who enjoyed a close relationship with the Dalai Lama. He was unusual among Tibetans at that time in having a great interest in the outside world. Tsarong enjoyed the company of foreigners and he was the kind of man the British liked to deal with. They described him as 'the one man who is really wide-awake in Lhasa', – and as one who could 'hold his drink well'.[16]

Although Bailey naturally identified Tsarong as a potential ally, Tsarong lacked a monastic or aristocratic power base and his officers, who had been trained by the Gyantse Escort Commander or at Quetta Military College, were already suspected by conservative Tibetans of having adopted European values. In addition, Whitehall was reluctant to allow Bailey to visit Lhasa, making it difficult for him to establish close ties with Tsarong.

In 1922, Bailey personally arranged, apparently without the support of the Government of India, for General George Pereira to visit Lhasa en route from Peking to India. Pereira was a former military attaché at the British Legation in Peking, where Bailey had met him in 1910. He was officially described as a 'private traveller', but David Macdonald, who was not then in Bailey's confidence, later made a curious comment on Pereira's travels. He wrote that

> Whether his...journey was inspired by motives other than exploration and the desire to be the first European to reach Lhasa from the Chinese side I do not know, nor did he tell me.[17]

Pereira sent detailed reports to Bailey on the state of Tibetan military forces throughout the country and, when he reached Lhasa in October 1922, he held talks with Tsarong. Pereira subsequently told Bailey that if the Tibetan army was to be strengthened, 'it is absolutely necessary to send a military advisor to Tsarong'. Obviously Pereira had some influence in Lhasa. The day after he left, the Tibetan Government asked the Government of India to lend them the services of the Darjeeling

Police Inspector, Laden La, to establish and train a police force in Lhasa (an innovation Bell had recommended to the Dalai Lama).[18] This request gave Bailey the chance to develop ties with Tsarong. Bailey knew that wider international considerations meant that Whitehall would not sanction posting a British military officer to Lhasa. But Laden La had recently been allowed to visit Lhasa along with Charles Bell and was a highly regarded police and intelligence officer, trusted by the Tibetan authorities. Laden La, while setting up a police force, would have access to all levels of Tibetan society, and could thus also advise Tsarong and the military. Bailey therefore persuaded his superiors that it was of 'considerable political importance' to send Laden La to Lhasa.[19]

In September 1923, Laden La reached Lhasa and established close ties with Tsarong.[20] He also recruited a 200 man police force, although relations between the ordinary Tibetan soldiers and the far-better paid policemen quickly deteriorated. On New Years Day 1924, another problem arose. News reached the Gyantse Trade Agent that Lhasa's long-simmering dispute with the Panchen Lama had culminated in the Shigatse Lama fleeing into exile in China. Tibet's ideal power balance had collapsed.

Bailey was genuinely worried that the Russians would take advantage of the confused situation in Tibet. He began planning a mission to Lhasa, which was approved early in March 1924. While Political Officers invariably exaggerated their need to go to Lhasa in order to convince a reluctant Whitehall to give them permission, Bailey warned his Government shortly before his departure that one 'Zyrianin' was undertaking a mission from Urga to Lhasa 'with a view to establish Bolshevism in Tibet'.[21]

Bailey set out for the Tibetan capital around the middle of June, accompanied by a Medical Officer, Major Hislop. Joining them, for reasons unknown, was his old friend the Assam Political Officer, Captain Nevill. They arrived in Gyantse on 3 July 1924, with events in Lhasa already overshadowing the mission.[22]

Early in May 1924, there was a fight between some police and soldiers. Tsarong had two of the soldiers punished by mutilation and one later died. The Dalai Lama had forbidden the use of mutilation as a punishment, and Tsarong's monastic and aristocratic opponents sought to use this incident to engineer his dismissal. Tsarong's supporters, including Laden La, sought to preserve his position and petitioned the Dalai Lama to pardon Tsarong. That much is definitely known. Accounts of events that followed, and who was involved, are confused.

This incident brought tensions between the 'modernising' and 'conservative' tendencies in Tibetan society to a head. Tsarong's supporters, including Laden La, began what was apparently a somewhat disorganised effort to take secular power from the Dalai Lama and transfer it to Tsarong Shapé. The atmosphere in Lhasa was tense, with rumours of conspiratorial oaths and hidden weapons.[23]

The timing of these events was such that, had the Dalai Lama been relieved of secular power by Tsarong's supporters, Bailey would have arrived in Lhasa to be greeted by a new Tibetan Government headed by Tsarong. But things quietened down and nothing dramatic happened. Bailey's reports barely mentioned the issue. Several years passed before versions of events began to emerge publicly.

Bailey's visit went ahead as normal. He remained in Lhasa between 16 July and 16 August 1924, during which time he had several meetings with the Dalai Lama. He also had a number of discussions with Tsarong, which he reported in unusual detail. Bailey noted that he had asked Tsarong what would happen if the Dalai Lama died? This was perhaps a curious question, given that the Tibetan leader then appeared to be in good health, but Bailey may simply have been considering all eventualities. When Tsarong replied that Indian troops could prevent any 'trouble', Bailey warned him that Whitehall policy made it impossible to send Indian troops to Lhasa. He did, however, advise Tsarong to deposit money in India in case he had to flee into exile.[24]

When Bailey left Lhasa, he stayed at Gyantse, where Tsarong joined him a few weeks later. Bailey left Gyantse on 26 September and Tsarong left the following day, travelling via Shigatse, seat of the now-exiled Panchen Lama. They met up again in India, when Tsarong conveniently combined an inspection of the Yatung mint with a pilgrimage to the Buddhist sacred sites of India. Bailey accompanied Tsarong on parts of this pilgrimage, which included meetings with leading officials in Nepal and India, including the Viceroy. It was all rather reminiscent of 1906 and O'Connor introducing his candidate for the leadership of Tibet to British royalty and India's highest authorities.

It was all too late for Tsarong however; he was already eclipsed. After Bailey's departure from Lhasa a series of events greatly damaged the reform movement in Tibet. The struggle between the 'conservative' and 'modernising' tendencies there culminated in the defeat of the reformers.

Laden La left Lhasa on 9 October 1924, just six weeks after Bailey,[25] and his police force went into rapid decline. Tsarong returned to find he had been dismissed as Army Commander and that his young military supporters had also been dismissed or dispersed to the provinces. There were a number of other indications that the British were out of favour with the Tibetan leadership and the final years of Bailey's term as Political Officer in Sikkim saw Anglo-Tibetan relations at a very low ebb.

This decline has been blamed on various causes; British failure to obtain Chinese agreement to the 1914 Simla Convention, their failure to supply further weaponry, the Everest expedition and the affair of the Gyantse monks, the social stresses produced by modernisation, or as part of a wider British decline in power in the East. The nearest thing to a neutral observer on the spot, a Japanese monk, blamed it partly on a more esoteric cause. According to Tada Tokan, Bell had presented the Dalai Lama with 3 ceremonial coaches, but the coach horses were not trained for riders. One of the Dalai Lama's attendants was killed when he tried to ride one of the horses, and this was seen as an omen indicating that pro-British policies were dangerous.[26]

Although it would certainly explain the downturn in Anglo-Tibetan relations, Western writers have dismissed any suggestion of British involvement in a plot to depose the Dalai Lama. But Chinese textbooks on Tibetan history do accuse 'the British' of fermenting a coup, and, in this instance, they are probably partly correct.[27]

There was no doubt that Laden La was involved in a plot against the Dalai Lama, although his role took some time to emerge. The local Gyantse administrator, the Khenchung, gave the Trade Agent there a more detailed account of the incident in 1926, at the Dalai Lama's behest. The school-teacher Frank Ludlow, who as will shortly be seen, was in Gyantse in 1923-26, was inclined to believe the Khenchung's account. Even the Government of India eventually accepted that Laden La had been involved, judging from the Indian National Archives file on this matter, which is entitled 'Indiscretion of Laden La in associating with Tibetan officers attempting to overthrow the Dalai Lama' – a file unfortunately still classified.[28]

The Government of India's treatment of Laden La is instructive. When he left Lhasa, ostensibly suffering from a nervous breakdown, he took six months leave and then resumed his post in Darjeeling. Far from being censured, he was promoted to the post of Yatung Trade Agent. The Dalai Lama, who now deeply mistrusted him, objected, stating that Laden La 'is not altogether a steady and straight-forward man and it is not known how he would serve to maintain Anglo-Tibetan amity'. The posting was cancelled, but Laden La continued to be regarded as a valuable agent and was employed by subsequent Political Officers on missions to Lhasa.[29]

Laden La, however, had plenty of critics on the frontier. He had annoyed Ludlow, while McGovern's account of his journey to Lhasa, published in 1924, mentioned in passing that Laden La used his office for profit. Macdonald later wrote to Bell that

> It is amazing to me how Laden La manages to mislead the powers that be! In Darjeeling he is liked openly only by those he can override. When McGovern published his so called libel on Laden La, if he had gone the right way about things, Laden La would not have been in power today.[30]

Bailey protected Laden La. At first he claimed that the Khenchung's account was 'inconceivable'. When he finally conceded that Laden La had indeed 'certainly committed a serious indiscretion', he added that he hoped no action would be taken against Laden La: none was. As Norbu Dhondup told Bailey, 'through your favour Laden La [was] saved, otherwise he was ruined.'[31]

Did Bailey plan to overthrow the Dalai Lama? Certainly he claimed ignorance of Laden La's activities, but Bailey was too good a secret agent to be ignorant of the activities of his own key agent at a crucial time and place. He may have been ignorant of many events at the time, for there were always gaps in the flow of information which the British received, but the weight of circumstantial evidence definitely points to a coup having been planned under Bailey's direction. We can hardly expect written evidence. An experienced intelligence officer such as Bailey would naturally conceal evidence of a failed coup attempt if he could, and at that time and place it was not unduly difficult for him to do so. The reporting of events in Tibet was largely controlled by the Political Officer in Sikkim, and Bailey took full advantage of his power to prevent any knowledge of the matter emerging. It was only when Bailey went on leave some two years after these events, that they were fully reported to the Government of India.[32] If Bailey did attempt to depose the Dalai Lama, he certainly did it without official support from either the British or British Indian governments.

Bailey's motive was unlikely to have been his disappointment at Tibet's failure to follow the path of reform. But if he believed that the new communist government in Russia was making serious attempts to gain influence in Tibet (as it apparently was), that could have been sufficient motivation for him to ferment a coup which would give Tibet's military forces secular power at Lhasa.

If that was the case, the events of this period can be seen to follow a logical sequence. Pereira's reports were a significant factor; it is clear from the way in which Bailey arranged permission for him to travel freely in areas normally closed to travellers that he had an important role. Pereira's reports must have helped convince Bailey that the only way to modernise Tibet to the extent where it would provide a secure northern border for India, and exclude Russian influence, was under Tsarong's leadership.

Laden La was the ideal agent, one whose actions could be officially disowned if he failed. Of course he may have acted on his own initiative, in the tradition his 'forward' thinking superiors had inculcated in him. But Laden La was only a provincial police officer. Had he been involved in a foreign conspiracy without significant support from British officers, it is hard to believe he could have escaped dismissal. It is equally unlikely that the British would have continued to employ a frontier officer who really had had a nervous breakdown on duty.

Bailey's plans (if such they were) for Tsarong, echo O'Connor's earlier plans for the Panchen Lama. O'Connor may even have been involved in this plan. He was then in Kathmandu and in close touch with Bailey, as was the Assam Political Officer Nevill, who accompanied him on at least part of his mission to Lhasa. Bailey's plan would have been a typical 'forward school' move, aimed at linking Tibet more closely to British India, while also serving to place Bailey in the position Bell had obtained; of being a close friend and advisor to Tibet's ruler.

Bailey would have known that he could not expect his government to approve the overthrow of Tibet's Government. But if such a plan succeeded, with British involvement concealed, his government would accept the situation. They would rely largely on the advice Bailey, O'Connor and Nevill would give; that a Tsarong-led Tibet was in Britain's best interests.

The Dalai Lama would have had no real proof of any British involvement in the events of May 1924. As more details emerged, he must have gradually come to suspect that Bailey had been involved. That would explain why he began to distance himself from the British, and turned away from British-sponsored reforms.

In the late 1920s, the Dalai Lama did explore alternative avenues of support for his regime which were less liable to arouse monastic opposition, or create a secular alternative to his rule. The conservative forces within Tibet had won the battle against reform. They were too strong for the military, or the Dalai Lama, to overcome. The conservative's victory, however, was to cost Tibet dearly in the long run.

If a government under Tsarong was Bailey's aim, his plan failed because he could offer no practical support to the 'modernising' faction, particularly military assistance, which would have been decisive. In addition, Tsarong was apparently unwilling to take the decisive step of declaring his claim for power. He owed his position to the Dalai Lama's patronage and knew that if his patron died or was overthrown he lacked sufficient support to take over Tibet without British military assistance. Tsarong was also a Tibetan patriot. His dealings with foreigners were designed to benefit Tibet, not the British, and his personal and patriotic loyalty to the Dalai Lama was too strong for him to turn against his benefactor.

Many of the events at that time remained unexplained, particularly the role played by Pedma (or Padma) Chandra. He was a Bhutanese monk who had taught Tibetan at Calcutta University c.1922-23, and was then briefly employed by the British as a translator for Tibetan troops training at the Gyantse Agency, which apparently earned him the rank of Major. Chandra then turned up in Lhasa, seemingly assisting Laden La. The Tibetan authorities later accused him of being one of the prime movers behind the alleged coup. Pedma was accused of encouraging Tibetan military officers to gather their troops in Shigatse, where there was considerable ill-feeling towards the central government since its tax-demands had driven the Panchen Lama into exile.

Chandra attempted to flee Tibet when the Dalai Lama began to dismiss military officers suspected of involvement in the plot, but he was pursued and killed by Tibetan troops. His head was brought back and exhibited in Lhasa, with a notice accusing him of embezzlement and of speaking out against the Dalai Lama. The 13th Dalai Lama had abolished the death penalty in Tibet, so executions were rare, particularly at state level, but whether Chandra was guilty of these crimes or just a convenient scapegoat, remains a mystery.[33]

In the 19th century, a plan such as Bailey apparently had might have succeeded. Now he was the right man in the right place at the wrong time. In his final years in Sikkim, Bailey had little option but to adopt a more conciliatory attitude to the Tibetan Government, and to accept that it had chosen to reject the path of modernistaion. The Raj was no longer strong enough to offer significant support to its allies, let alone force them to follow British advice if they rejected it. The era in which a Political Officer could have a decisive affect on events had passed and many of the qualities of the ideal frontiersmen of legend were no longer relevant to service on the imperial frontiers. Diplomats were needed now, not men of action.

In retrospect we can see that the rejection of modernity was to cost Tibet her freedom. Given Whitehall's refusal to allow Tibet to be taken into a closer association with the Raj, Tibet's only chance of surviving as an independent entity was to transform itself into a modern society and establish its identity on the world stage. The turning away from reform meant the survival of existing Tibetan society was ensured for a few more years, but it only postponed the inevitable collision with modernity.

The events of this period indicate that ultimately the British presence in Tibet was designed to advance British interests, just as the Chinese sought to promote their interests. The cadre had not supported the Dalai Lama until he came under Bell's influence and they were only prepared to continue supporting him as long as he served their interests, or when there was no alternative. Bailey's actions in this period must be seen in the light of this *realpolitik*.

The Bailey years greatly enhanced the cadre's understanding of the Tibetans. They did not make the mistake again of allying with one faction of Tibetan society to the exclusion of others and in the next two decades they greatly expanded their range of contacts in Tibet. A fundamental consideration in understanding Tibetan history and government was that, as Richardson later wrote

> descriptions of this or that official...as "pro-British", [or] "pro-Chinese" [are] too facile. The only thing the Tibetans have been "pro" is the preservation of their Religious State.[34]

* * *

One of the principal elements in the reform process which Tibet abandoned in the mid-1920s was the attempt to introduce Western education into Tibet. While the rejection of reforms was a setback to British aims, it was also a personal blow to Frank Ludlow, Headmaster of Gyantse School.

Traditionally, education in Tibet was solely the preserve of the monasteries. Modernisation entailed establishing an educational system which would teach a new generation the skills and modes of thought necessary to transform society on the European model. In 1913 an expensive experiment was undertaken when four Tibetan boys were sent to Rugby School in England. This brought little proportionate benefit and the Dalai Lama was persuaded that a Western-style school should be established at Gyantse to train Tibet's future administrators.[35]

So it was that Frank Ludlow of the Indian Education Department arrived in Gyantse in October 1923, holding a three year teaching contract with the Tibetan Government. Ludlow was a much admired figure, 'in every way the best possible man for the appointment'.[36] 'Lean and keen' in the frontier tradition, Ludlow was also a thoughtful and modest man, who kept a diary in which he revealed feelings otherwise concealed. While Ludlow was not in Bailey's confidence, that diary sheds much light on many other events in the period 1923-26.[37]

When he arrived in Gyantse, Ludlow was keen to start work and optimistic about the future, but it took several months to build furniture and to gather in enough pupils to begin classes. Parents were reluctant to send their children to this new innovation. When the school officially opened in December 1923 there were only 13 students, although the numbers eventually doubled.

In August 1924, Ludlow began hearing the first rumours that the school would be closed. September brought further shocks. One of his pupils turned out to be a stand-in whom the parents of the real pupil were paying to fill-in for their son. Two other pupils, aged 14 and 15, were found to be suffering from venereal diseases. When Ludlow proposed expelling them, the Tibetan authorities told him that if he did, 'other boys will voluntarily get these diseases in order to escape being sent to school.'

Ludlow did however, introduce one lesson which was popular with the pupils and which demonstrates how great plans may end in tiny successes. As imperial educators modelled their schools on British public schools, they emphasised sporting activities. Other than as a part of a basically military training, sports were virtually unknown in Tibet, but Ludlow's pupils quickly learned to love football.

Ludlow took several balls with him to Tibet, and soon had to send for more as the originals were quickly worn out. The long *chubas* normally worn by Tibetans were not suited to kicking a ball, so Ludlow ordered football uniforms, in 'Tibetan colours' of yellow and maroon. Their arrival occupied more attention in his diary than the news received that day that the Panchen Lama had fled into exile.

The school played regular matches against teams from the Gyantse Agency military and civil staff. These brought 'great excitement and plenty of enthusiasm and energy, if not science'. Rivalry between the teams produced its problems. Ludlow had to lecture the boys on 'keeping their temper when playing football and generally playing the game' and several players were sent off.

Football even attracted the attention of Tibet's ruler. The Dalai Lama telephoned the Khenchung, and

> was rather fed up because he couldn't get on quickly. The Khenchung explained that he had been watching the football match between the School and the soldiers. The Dalai Lama then asked who had won and the Khenchung said the school played well but lost 2-1.

The Dalai Lama also asked if it was true that Ludlow was fond of 'kicking the ball with my head'. Ludlow, in fact, generally refereed, finding that due to the altitude 'I couldn't run more than twenty yards without getting hopelessly out of breath'.

Amidst constant rumours that the school was to be closed, Ludlow gamely carried on teaching. Although his pupils rarely returned from their holidays on time, he cared for them and was proud of their progress. Finding the rote-learning methods of Tibetan traditional education 'utterly dull and boring' he introduced texts such as *King Arthur and the Knights of the Round Table* to keep their interest.

Along with monastic and parental opposition, Ludlow also had to contend with the Gyantse Khenchung's implacable opposition to the school. Ludlow discovered that the Tibetan administrator had good reason to want the school to fail. The Lhasa Government, lacking the funds necessary for investment in such projects, had instructed the Khenchung to pay for the school himself and he wanted it to close so he could take-over the school buildings.

A number of factors led to the school's closure. Parental and monastic opposition, the failure of the Tibetan Government to understand the importance of education, and 'tom-foolery on the part of Laden La, Tsarong and others in Lhasa in 1924' all helped to doom the school. But at the time, Ludlow placed most of the blame on the Khenchung. In his diary he described him as 'a cunning fox with pro-Chinese tendencies. He knows I hate him, I know he hates me.'

One other factor was the usual failure of the British and Indian Governments to offer any practical assistance to Tibet. Ludlow and Bailey both criticised the Indian Foreign Secretary, Sir Denys Bray, for failing to offer the school any support. Ludlow had written to Bray, asking him to

> bring all their powers of persuasion to bear on the Tibetan Government, not only in the interests of Tibet itself, but for their own political advantage as well.

But Bray, Ludlow noted in his diary, 'has not stirred a finger'.

On 29 August 1926, Ludlow was officially informed that his contract would not be renewed and that the school would close. In his diary he wrote sadly

> So that's that, in spite of my efforts. Rather bad luck that the work which has attracted me more than any other I have ever had in my life should thus be snatched away from me. I would rather have made a success of this school than reached the topmost rung of the Education ladder in India.

Shortly before the school closed, the boys played their last soccer match, a 2-2 draw; 'How the boys will miss their football' Ludlow wrote. But he would have been pleased to read Spencer Chapman's report that when he was in Lhasa in 1936-37,

> We met several old boys of Gyanste school and found that they spoke English extremely well, had perfect manners, and a fair knowledge of the game of football.[38]

The deeply disappointed Ludlow left Gyantse at the end of October 1926, presuming that his involvement in Tibet had ended, and prophetically observing that the Tibetans 'will regret this decision one day when they are Chinese slaves once more, as they assuredly will be'.

Chapter Eight

The Weir Years, and 'The right hand of every Political Officer'

In October 1928, Major Leslie Weir took over from Bailey as Political Officer Sikkim. Weir had served as Gyantse Trade Agent when the Dalai Lama was in exile in India and it was a formative period in his life. While on leave he had met a young New Zealand woman, Thyra Sommers, the daughter of a Danish gold-prospector, and married her in Rangoon in 1912. In Gyantse Weir had also come under the influence of 'his guru', Charles Bell.[1]

Weir was in the Bell mould. He was a modest and understated Scotsman, though not without ambition, whose philosophy was that there was 'too much written and not enough done'. Erudite, observant and witty, Weir was the kind of officer the Political Department could rely on in any region, but he was particularly fond of Tibet and the Himalayas and read all he could about them. Weir's father and two of his uncles had served in Kathmandu in the 19th century and when a vacancy arose in Gyantse while Weir was serving in the Secretariat, he took the opportunity for himself.[2]

At Gangtok, Weir soon found that 'our prestige...has gone back woefully since I was last here'.[3] This was brought home to him when he wanted to obtain an invitation to visit the Dalai Lama. Weir needed this invitation to persuade Whitehall to allow him to go to Lhasa and, although the Government of India's reports to Whitehall suggested these invitations were issued 'spontaneously' by the Tibetans, they were in fact, after the Bell era, solicited by the Political Officer.[4]

Only the Dalai Lama had the unquestioned power to invite a European to Lhasa, and Political Officers unofficially instructed intermediaries such as Norbu Dhondup to obtain their invitation from the Dalai Lama. The intermediaries would also indicate that such an invitation would be accepted, to ensure that neither side risked the 'loss of face' that would follow an official refusal of an invitation.

Following Bell's mission, Whitehall had not objected to the despatch of local intermediaries to Lhasa, and Laden La or Norbu Dhondup travelled there regularly. But the cadre saw their own access to the Dalai Lama as of paramount importance, both as a barometer of the state of Anglo-Tibetan relations, and as a matter of personal prestige.[5]

In 1929, however, when Norbu asked the Dalai Lama to invite Weir, the Tibetan leader requested that the visit be postponed to avoid complications with China. He feared that a British visit would provoke a Chinese response and wrote to Weir explaining that 'it is not at all an attempt to slight you...I would request you not to get disappointed by misunderstanding things'. But with Weir still establishing his authority in Gangtok, he took the refusal as a rebuff, symbolic of the poor state of Anglo-Tibetan relations.[6]

Weir also had problems with his Gyantse Trade Agents. None of those who served under him were entirely satisfactory. Consequently, he had to rely heavily on advice from Laden La and Norbu Dhondup. But he may not have been aware of Laden La's unpopularity in Tibet, or its consequences. In 1930, when Weir sent him to Lhasa, Laden La was detained by the Tibetan authorities at Chaksam ferry and told that 'no useful purpose could be served' by his visit. Laden La appealed to Tsarong, who was still an influential figure in Lhasa, and after two days he was allowed to proceed. Laden La later claimed his mission was successful and apparently did not mention his detention to Weir. But according to David Macdonald, the fact that Tsarong was demoted from Shapé rank in 1930 was due to his having assisted Laden La.[7]

In 1930, the Dalai Lama did invite Weir to visit Lhasa. Although Bell and Bailey had been refused permission to take their wives with them, the Chinese had recently sent a female envoy to Lhasa. Mrs

Thyra Weir was therefore permitted to accompany her husband. The Weirs were attended by the Gyantse Medical Officer, Lieutenant M.R.Sinclair.[8]

After the decline in relations with Tibet in the 1920s, an atmosphere of suspicion lingered when Weir arrived in Lhasa; Tsarong prudently kept his distance. But Weir was aware of the problem and made improving Anglo-Tibetan relations his priority. He carefully followed Bell's methods of diplomacy, ensuring that his actions conformed with Tibetan etiquette, while socially, the presence of his wife was a great success.

Weir had visited the Foreign Secretary shortly before his departure, to take the 'chance of saturating him so much with Tibet that I might be able to squeeze a little more money out of Foreign [sic] for presents'.[9] He was given a budget of 15,000 rupees for gifts to local officials (5,000 rupees more than Bailey had been allowed) and could thus afford to be generous to his hosts.

In his discussions with the Tibetan authorities, Weir diplomatically avoided raising several controversial issues, such as the Dalai Lama's recent contacts with China. When the talks went well, Weir announced that his government were prepared to allow them to buy supplies of cheap silver (which they could use to build up hard currency), an offer the Tibetan Government naturally appreciated.

Although it did not entirely eradicate their suspicions about British intentions, Weir's 1930 Lhasa visit was a successful bridge-building exercise. On his return journey, he was even permitted to travel via Shigatse. There, he found 'the inhabitants sullenly resent the sterner rule of the central Government, and are longing for the return of the [Panchen] Lama to his home'.[10]

Early in August 1932, Weir, on his annual inspection visit to Gyantse, heard rumors that the Dalai Lama was anxious to invite him to Lhasa again. Fighting had broken out between Tibetan and Chinese forces on the eastern border, and Tibet was now eager to obtain British support. Both parties were also concerned about the Panchen Lama. His presence in China threatened Tibetan unity, by creating pro- and anti-Panchen Lama factions. Weir was keen to go to Lhasa again, but he was due to transfer to Baroda (now in Gujarat) in November. When the Dalai Lama's invitation arrived he was unprepared for it, and urgently sent for all the items essential for a visit to the capital, such as his dress uniform and an array of presents.[11]

Weir needed Whitehall's permission to take up the invitation and their approval could not be taken for granted. Weir's wife, and their 18 year old daughter Joan-Mary, were in Gyantse with him, and they also waited anxiously, as Weir had asked permission for them to accompany him. The two women walked around a sacred *mani* wall made of stones and yak-horns inscribed with religious texts, chanting, not a Tibetan *mantra*, but "We want to go to Lhasa, we want to go to Lhasa..." On 18 August, a telegram from London gave them the go-ahead.[12]

Weir's second visit to Lhasa was notable for a number of gestures by the Tibetans which indicated that they were again turning to the British for support against China. As a mark of honour, an important religious ceremony was postponed until the Weirs' arrival, and he was given permission for the British to mount another Everest Expedition. Steps were taken towards solving the Panchen Lama problem, with the Dalai Lama agreeing to invite him to return to Shigatse. But Weir, in one of his less perceptive comments, recommended that if the Panchen Lama failed to respond to the invitation 'he deserves little further consideration at our hands'.[13]

The Dalai Lama was reluctant to let Weir and his party depart until he was sure that fighting had stopped on the eastern frontier, and the Weirs remained in Lhasa for three months. It was December when they left and the snows blocked the passes to India they day after they crossed. When Weir next wrote to the Dalai Lama and mentioned how lucky they had been with the weather, the Tibetan leader's reply informed them that 'It wasn't wonderful at all, I prayed for it.'[14]

Weir's subsequent report enthused that 'Never in the history of Anglo-Tibetan relations has our prestige stood higher or the Tibetan attitude been more friendly'.[15] This was an exaggeration, but there is no doubt that Weir's visit marked a turning-point for the better in Anglo-Tibetan relations. Weir's term in Gangtok demonstrated that a successful cadre officer did not need to have the level of understanding attained by those who were able to devote most of their careers to Tibet. He was able to repair the damage done to Anglo-Tibetan relations during the 1920s by following Bell's methods of diplomacy, in contrast to the more authoritarian attitudes of officers such as Bailey. Bell acknowledged this improvement as due to Weir's 'genial and kindly disposition', while Macdonald commented that 'Colonel Weir is better liked by the Tibetans than Colonel Bailey, being more reserved and dignified.'[16]

* * *

Weir was not, and did not intend to be, a specialist in Tibetan affairs. Because of this, and because the Gyantse Trade Agents during his term were not specialists either, Weir relied heavily on the expertise of the local employees, Norbu Dhondup and Laden La.

The cadre acknowledged that their success depended 'largely on the personality and contacts' of local employees.[17] While British officers came and went, there was a gradual build-up of experienced local staff, who carried out much of the day-to-day work and tactfully instructed new British officers in their duties. Every cadre officer learned from local employees and to understand the role of the cadre, the part played by these intermediaries between Tibet and the British Raj must be considered.

The intermediaries had an important behind-the-scenes role and the most successful of them were promoted to Political Department postings. Three can be classified as Tibet cadre officers. Norbu Dhondup and Pemba Tsering both served as Trade Agent Yatung and were then promoted to take charge of the British Mission Lhasa, and in the 1940s Sonam Tobden Kazi, 'a worthy successor to Laden La and Rai Bahadur Norbu' was groomed for a senior position with postings as Trade Agent in Gartok and Yatung.[18]

From the very beginnings of the empire, the Raj had needed local employees who could translate the language, culture and aspirations of one society to the other. In each of the different cultural and linguistic regions of the empire, a small, distinct and ultimately powerful class of intermediaries developed to fill this role.[19]

When the Tibetans were forced to open diplomatic relations with British India, the Raj needed intermediaries with the social skills necessary to deal with the Lhasa aristocracy. These people were difficult to locate in such an isolationist society as Tibet, where the ruling class appeared to present a united front against high-level foreign contact. But the punishment inflicted on the aristocratic Palhe family for assisting Chandra Das's visit to Tibet in 1881-82 (as noted in the Introduction), had alienated the Palhe family from the Lhasa ruling classes, creating an opportunity for the British to exploit their estrangement, as well as to reward the assistance they had given Chandra Das.

Kusho Palhesé, exiled scion of the Palhe family, became Bell's personal assistant. Bell relied heavily on his understanding of Tibet and the two men became close friends. Bell was, by the standards of the time, generous in his praise of the Tibetan's contribution to his knowledge and he even brought Palhesé to Britain in the 1920s to assist his research.[20]

The punishment of the Palhe family also provided O'Connor with his principal assistant, a Buriat monk, Sherab Gyatso, also known as Shabdrung Lama.[21] He had been a personal attendant of Lama Sengchen Tulku, who was executed for assisting Chandra Das. Sherab Gyatso was also imprisoned and tortured, but escaped to Darjeeling, where he was given employment as a teacher at the Bhotia school. He also worked as a British agent, gathering information in Darjeeling bazaar and he was employed by O'Connor as his personal secretary on the Younghusband mission.[22]

According to David Macdonald, Shabdrung Lama saw his service with Younghusband as an opportunity for revenge on the Tibetan Government. During the 1903-04 mission he told Tibetans the expedition was to punish them for their treatment of Sengchen Tulku. When O'Connor secured the release of two of Shabdrung Lama's colleagues, who had been imprisoned in Lhasa since Das's 1882 visit, the Tibetans must have seen the connection.[23] Certainly it carried an implicit message, that the British supported those who supported them, an essential message to convey if they were to receive loyalty in return.

Palhesé and Shabdrung Lama differed from intermediaries such as Laden La in that their primary loyalty was to a particular officer, rather than to the Raj in general. Palhesé's first loyalty was to Bell; he served on the understanding that if Bell left 'government service today, I leave tomorrow' (although Palhesé's association with the British also enabled him to restore the family estates). Later cadre officers continued to have assistants loyal to them personally, but these assistants were not politically influential. Gould's personal servant for instance, was described as 'a notorious robber who looked after Gould excellently and maltreated everyone else'.[24]

While Palhesé and Shabdrung Lama were of great personal assistance to Bell and O'Connor, they were, like Chandra Das, unpopular in Lhasa. Legally, Tibetan employees could not be given full protection from Lhasa's authority by naturalising them and Palhesé remained the only important Tibetan-born intermediary to be used by the cadre.[25]

Ideally, what the British wanted was an individual who could match the status and talents of Agvan Dorzhiev, a Russian citizen, but also a member of Lhasa's religious elite. He was a formidable opponent for the British, but they recognised that he was the ideal type of intermediary; a loyal citizen of the imperial power, but highly placed in the local society. After meeting Dorzhiev in 1912, Gould described him rather enviously as 'a man who impresses one a great deal...[by his]...frank manner and...earnest purpose...[He is] certainly respected by the Tibetan officials.'[26]

Lacking a Dorzhiev, the Government of India began to develop suitable candidates from among Tibetan-speaking peoples within India. The process began in earnest when the Younghusband mission recruited a number of these young men from Darjeeling High School to work as clerks and translators. Many of them carried on into cadre service, and this group formed the basis of an emerging class of intermediaries on the Tibetan frontier. Many of them came from marginalised communities on the periphery of Himalayan society and their lack of ties to local power elites was seen as an advantage by the British.

The intermediaries underwent a similar training process to that of British cadre officers. Their schooling was on the British model, giving them an understanding of the language, culture, and correct behaviour patterns as defined by the dominant culture. Like cadre officers, they also needed to master unwritten codes of behaviour and to study privately to improve their language skills and local knowledge. Pemba Tsering, for example, was fluent in five languages, but worked hard to improve himself, reading English literature and underlining unfamiliar words to look up later. As a result of this process, these intermediaries formed a distinct group in Himalayan society, readily identifiable by their social behaviour. They passed on these behavioural patterns to their children, thereby creating an bureaucratic 'caste' which still persists today.[27]

None of those chosen for responsible posts in Lhasa, Gyantse and Yatung were Hindu or Muslim. The cadre wanted the predominantly Buddhist, British Indian frontier peoples for Tibetan service. With their close historical, cultural, racial and linguistic ties to Tibet they could be expected to adapt most easily to that social system. Cadre officers also maintained a barely-concealed personal preference for all the hill people. This was more than the usual colonial officer's inclination towards the peoples among whom he worked. In British India, hill people were commonly seen as morally and physically superior to those of the plains.[28]

This preference for frontier peoples over 'Indians' shows that the cadre recognised 'India' as a British construction, a state made up of different peoples, some of whom had their strongest socio-cultural and economic ties with groups outside India's borders. While it was necessary for British strategic and administrative reasons to define certain areas as 'Indian', the artificial nature of the actual boundary was clear. After Indian independence, Bell even stated that Ladakh, along with Bhutan and Sikkim, had been taken from Tibet by the British and should be returned.[29]

Bell discussed appointing an 'Indian' as Yatung Trade Agent in 1909, but claimed that 'Indians are handicapped by their inability to speak Tibetan, by the difference of their religion and by their ignorance of the habits of the people.' Bell's judgement reflected the imperial assumption of superiority at the time; the British obviously had a similar 'handicap', but he assumed they could overcome it.[30]

Once the early cadre officers had established a precedent for the exclusion of Hindus and Muslims from any but menial positions in Tibet, no further consideration was given to employing them. When it became obvious that India would become independent, Richardson tried to locate suitable Indians to serve in the Gyantse Agency, but it was not until after Indian independence that any Hindu or Muslim was given a responsible post in Tibet.[31] The only exception to this was the Gyantse Escort Commander, Lieutenant Chatterjee, whose untimely death in 1921 was noted in Chapter Six.

Within British India, Anglo-Indians, those of mixed parentage were often subject to greater prejudice than Indians and were excluded from several areas of government employment.[32] In Tibet, however, Anglo-Indians were preferred to Indians. Several Anglo-Indian Medical Officers were employed in Tibet, including Dr Dyer, who accompanied Bell to Lhasa. In the 1940s, an Anglo-Indian Christian, Dr Humphreys and an Indian Christian, Captain M.V.Kurian, paved the way for the subsequent posting of Hindu Medical Officers to Gyantse.[33]

Personal relations between British cadre officers and local employees were more relaxed than in India. The physical isolation of Tibet and the more tolerant mores of the frontier, with its traditional intermingling of cultures, meant greater tolerance to those of different, or mixed, race. It was also easier to enjoy informal gatherings with Buddhists, as opposed to Hindus, who had caste restrictions on social contact. The reliance the cadre placed on their local employees' experience also created a more egalitarian atmosphere. The fact that the cadre officers' regard for their employees, particularly the lower ranking servants, was generally what Lionel Caplan termed 'paternal', rather than exploitive, has meant that the frontier people today still remember the individual officers of the Tibet cadre (as distinct from the policies which they represented) with fondness.[34]

* * *

The most popular and successful intermediary was Norbu Dhondup, a colourful character with considerable personal charm. Born in Kalimpong, he had no aristocratic connections, and is described variously as being Sherpa or Tibetan. Taken from Darjeeling High School by O'Connor to serve as a translator on the Younghusband mission, he was then given a clerical post at Gyantse, and worked his way to the top. Although originally recruited by O'Connor, Norbu was not associated with any particular British officer, but he became

> the absolute right-hand of every Political Officer. He knew the ways of everybody, how to speak to them, what to say, what not to say, [and] how to be diplomatic.[35]

Norbu's character fitted the British ideal of the frontiersman. Gould described him as having 'lots of common sense, a ready laugh and infinite guts'. General Neame, who accompanied Gould to Lhasa in 1936, observed approvingly that Norbu was 'one of the few Oriental officials...who will tell one his real opinion, palatable or not, and strong and decisive opinions too'.[36]

As Norbu was a Buddhist, some doubted that he could 'put things bluntly' to the Dalai Lama. But Norbu satisfied his superiors that he could take a firm line where necessary. In the late 1920s he even argued that the cadre were too 'polite' to the Tibetans and should employ officers who would 'deal with the Tibetans more strongly'.[37]

Norbu visited Lhasa on 15 occasions prior to the establishment of a British mission there in 1936, and developed excellent ties with the Tibetan leadership. He had automatic access to the Dalai Lama and was given Tibetan aristocratic rank, as a *dzasa* of the fourth grade. He also charmed Lhasa's aristocratic ladies, who provided him with considerable 'inside' information. Tibetan women were otherwise a potential source which the cadre neglected until Mrs Sherriff and later Mrs Guthrie took up residence in Lhasa with their husbands in the 1940s.[38]

The presence of other foreign agents at Lhasa meant that Norbu's career was not without its dangers. His life was, he reported, threatened on several occasions by Russian or Chinese agents. His reports may have been exaggerated, but whereas it was unlikely that foreign agents would have risked the international complications involved in killing a British officer, they may not have had such scruples about killing Norbu. But Norbu pledged that 'I...shall not die before I murder at least two, as I have my rifles and pistols...always loaded'.[39]

By the 1930s, Norbu had become a trusted cadre 'insider', and was given appropriate honours. He was appointed Yatung Trade Agent in 1936 and subsequently headed the Lhasa Mission, where he was treated with all the ceremony considered necessary to uphold the prestige of a British officer; for example on his arrival at Gyantse from Lhasa in 1941, the Trade Agent, Captain Saker, rode out with 25 troops to escort Norbu into the Agency.[40]

Norbu's acceptance by the cadre was not only due to the manner in which he performed his duty; it owed much to his adoption of British forms of behaviour. He played football, rode well, and acted with the necessary 'tact and common-sense'. Yet Norbu remained proud of his Tibetan rank and heritage. Off-duty, he aspired to the lifestyle of a Tibetan aristocrat, rather than a British officer, and wore particularly colourful Tibetan clothing. Weir's daughter remembered one such outfit – a yellow brocade gown, royal blue brocade coat, red boots and a gold hat with a red tassel: even his pony had a red and yellow saddle with tassels![41]

Dress was a significant issue. Adopting European dress was an indication that the wearers identified themselves with modern society. Yet the leading intermediaries wore traditional dress even in the late 1940s, when European dress had become common among the frontier peoples. They were encouraged to do this by their employer's belief that local people should not be 'dressing like third-rate Europeans... they must...wear their national dress'.[42]

Just as cadre officers did not adhere to Tibetan forms of behaviour in their private life, they did not require, or want, local officials to abandon their own traditions. In presenting Laden La's uncle, Urgyen Gyatso, with the title Rai Bahadur in 1893, the Lieutenant-Governor of Bengal noted approvingly that, while rendering valuable service to the British, 'he has not forgotten the traditions of his ancestors, nor failed in his reverence for, and duty towards, his religion'.[43]

The cadre did not need its local employees to 'become British'. They needed intermediaries able to understand and express themselves in British forms, to translate their understanding of the local culture to the cadre. Just as the British in India deeply mistrusted any European who 'went native', so the reverse applied. The result was that successful employees were those able to function as 'insiders' in both cultures, while retaining their own cultural identity. Successful intermediaries learned British frontier codes of behaviour and patterns of thinking; they 'understood' the British. But while these men 'behaved just like *sahibs*' in carrying out their duties, they maintained their own cultural identity. A long-serving local such as medical assistant Bo Tsering, might speak of "we British", but he remained a Buddhist, and wore local dress off-duty.

Norbu represented the ideal type the British hoped would emerge from a modern Tibet; one who had retained what they considered were the best features of his own culture, while adopting the necessary British officers' modes of thought and behaviour. As Norbu was also liked and respected in Lhasa, his career represents evidence that an individual could understand, and be accepted by, both imperial and local societies.

Another example was Pemba Tsering, who was from a Tibetan family which had settled near Darjeeling. His uncle had served as Head Clerk at Yatung under Macdonald and, after he matriculated from Darjeeling High School, Pemba was recruited by Bailey. His character matched the British ideal; he was 'straightforward', a man of integrity, with a good sense of humour, punctual, meticulous and disciplined. In the British fashion he relaxed with theatricals, tennis, music and billiards, but at home he retained his cultural identity and wore local clothing.[44]

* * *

Norbu's contemporary, Laden La, was a very different individual. Having worked his way up in the Indian Police, he became a powerful figure on the frontier, and was active in frontier politics in opposition to the growing power of the Nepali community.[45] Unlike Norbu, he made many enemies in India and Tibet and we have seen that although he claimed to be popular in Lhasa, the Dalai Lama personally intervened to prevent his appointment as Trade Agent Yatung. Despite that, Laden La remained of great value to the cadre because of his intelligence skills. As one officer commented, 'Laden La is very full of himself, but is very interesting regarding events and personalities in Lhasa.'[46]

Laden La also differed from Norbu in that he adopted British dress and social customs, and aspired to a British lifestyle.[47] But the British generally did not regard him as warmly as Norbu Dhondup and he did not get a Political post. He was also less successful than Norbu in cultivating the friendship of the Tibetan leadership. Ultimately Laden La failed to achieve the desired balance of British and Tibetan understanding and forms of behaviour, and was not trusted by the Tibetan Government after his involvement in the events of 1923-24.

Norbu Dhondup and Laden La always had their critics. Following service tradition, Macdonald complimented Laden La in his memoirs, but was extremely critical of both him and Norbu in private correspondence. Macdonald considered that both men were responsible for the downturn in Anglo-Tibetan relations in the 1920s. He accused them of working for their own ends, and even of giving political information to the Tibetans. Macdonald's negative view of Norbu Dhondup was supported by Rosemeyer, the telegraph officer who supervised the Gangtok to Lhasa line (and himself an Anglo-Indian).[48]

Norbu and Laden La, however, were of great value to the cadre because they could be sent to Lhasa at short notice, whereas missions by Political Officers involved considerable preparation and permission from Whitehall. The extent to which the cadre relied on their information is difficult to assess, but Political Officers were aware of their difficult position, and exercised their own judgement in assessing the worth of the intermediaries's reports.[49]

Intermediaries worked for the British because salaries were two or three times higher than in any comparable position, conditions were good, and government employees, even in menial positions, gained great prestige in the local community. While relationship to a serving government employee was an advantage in recruitment, promotion was on merit, and there was a clear ladder of opportunity available in serving the Raj.

The selection of recruits related to a serving government employee was common in British India, particularly in Army recruitment, and it inevitably continued in Tibet. In the frontier districts there was only a very small body of educated people suitable for government service and most of these were related in some way, or became related through marriage. Thus the family tradition of service became the predominant mode among cadre employees.[50]

The intermediaries, particularly those from Sikkim, did not then have a sense of loyalty to an independent India, although loyalty problems did arise for the Tibetan-born Palhesé. Bell recorded that Palhesé 'was known in Tibet as "two-headed" because he had to serve two masters'. But, again according to Bell, Palhesé was able to reconcile any divided loyalties because 'on most of the main issues the interests of the two countries lay very close together'.[51]

There was, for some local employees, an added advantage to employment with the British. Cadre officers were aware of 'what masses of money...[we] could make if we wanted to be corrupt', but with the exception of White, Rivett-Carnac and possibly Campbell, cadre officers maintained high standards of financial honesty. Yet they applied somewhat different standards to the intermediaries. In 1944, Trade Agent Frederick Mainprice found corruption among local staff, but noted that 'sacking anyone from the [Gyantse] Agency had been almost unheard of'.[52]

Early in his career Norbu was implicated in a case where a building contractor bribed Gyantse Trade Agency staff to win a contract. Norbu (who denied the accusations) was not charged on the curious grounds that he was absent at the time charges were preferred, and the matter does not appear to have been raised again. Similarly there was no investigation into the charges of dishonesty levelled against Laden La by McGovern. Clearly, some cadre officers were prepared to turn a blind eye to a certain level of corruption if the persons concerned were sufficiently valuable to them.[53]

British service offered both Norbu and Laden La the chance to ensure future prosperity for their families and they competed for British favour. The contest was won by Norbu, as his promotion to cadre posts indicates. While his son died young, Norbu's daughter now works for the Tibetan Government-in-exile. Laden La failed to gain government employment for his family, but acquired considerable wealth and while he died early, his family, like the Macdonalds, established a successful hotel business.[54]

While memoirs by colonial officials usually pay them a brief tribute, the contribution of the intermediaries has been largely forgotten by history. In common with other marginalised groups or social classes in the imperial process – including British subordinates – their 'voice' has been historically submerged beneath those of both imperial and indigenous empowered social classes. This process has partly been due to the needs of Indian nationalist historians, who have preferred to emphasise those who engaged in indigenous resistance to the Raj and to highlight the oppositional nature of the imperial process. Those who had given great service to the imperial power, such as Norbu Dhondup, were viewed with less enthusiasm in independent India. But the imperial mistrust of locals who abandoned their own culture led to the creation of a body of sophisticated and cosmopolitan individuals, at home in both imperial and indigenous societies. Many of their families continue to serve the Indian and Tibetan Governments today.

Chapter Nine

'Passed to the Heavenly Fields'

Early in May 1924, 'Derrick' Williamson arrived in Gyantse to replace the long-serving David Macdonald, who was retiring. But six weeks passed before Macdonald could hand-over to his successor, who was suffering from a near-fatal fever. Williamson's health remained poor during his two-year term at Gyantse, but his performance was good enough to establish him as a candidate for promotion.

Williamson was something of an outsider, who single-mindedly worked his way to the top. Even his friends found his ambition made him 'self-centered'.[1] But he had a more varied and less privileged background than his cadre contemporaries, which must have affected his outlook. In contrast to those whose early life were spent in India, Williamson spent five years in Australia as a child. He attended a minor public school, noted for its low fees, but he was intelligent and hard-working and won a scholarship to Cambridge. He then joined the ICS, arriving in India shortly before World War One. During the war he saw active service in Mesopotamia, where he was wounded in action and received a 'mentioned-in-dispatches'.

Gyantse was Williamson's first Political posting, and as there was a shortage of young officers with Tibetan experience, he saw the opportunity for rapid promotion. He actively canvassed his claims to succeed Weir, and strengthened his chances by gaining as much experience as possible in Tibetan affairs. In 1927, he used his leave to travel to China where he met the Panchen Lama, then in exile in a monastery in Manchuria. In 1932 he spent his leave in western Tibet, along with Frank Ludlow, a friend since their Gyantse days together. These journeys were theoretically private, but on both occasions

Williamson reported to the Government of India, because, as he put it, 'Although I was on leave I was doing official business'.[2]

In 1926 and 1931, Williamson acted as Political Officer Sikkim, relieving Bailey and Weir respectively while they were on leave. When Weir's term ended in January 1933, Williamson was the obvious choice to replace him. While awaiting a permanent vacancy at Gangtok, Williamson had served as Consul-General in Kashgar from 1927-30. Though in China, this post was so remote from Peking, and so vital to the security of India (in that it was theoretically a likely invasion route for Russian troops), that it was under the control of the Government of India, rather than being a China Consulate posting. Kashgar was a centre for the 'Great Game', with the British and Russian consuls fighting for power and influence in what was nominally Chinese territory. The Consuls' duties were

> mainly for intelligence work, including military intelligence, the supervision of Intelligence agents and the collection of military intelligence by means of touring.[3]

Williamson's assistant at Kashgar was Major George Sherriff, an energetic and determined army officer, very much the outdoor type. Sherriff's family were Scottish whisky distillers, and he was of independent means. Although he was promoted to Consul-General when Williamson left, he resigned his post in 1932 to devote himself to collecting plants.

It was at Kashgar that Sherriff met Frank Ludlow, now a full-time naturalist, after Williamson invited the former Gyantse schoolmaster to Kashgar in the winter of 1929-30. Although Ludlow and Sherriff were disparate characters they became close friends and subsequently went on a number of botanical expeditions together in the Himalayas. All three men loved Tibet, and as Williamson was ear-marked for the Gangtok post, it was a frequent topic of conversation at Kashgar,[4] and all of the trio were eventually to reach Lhasa.

When Williamson succeeded Weir at Gangtok, he wrote the usual formal letter advising the Dalai Lama of the change-over. The reply included an apparently unsolicited invitation for him to visit Lhasa and, in May 1933, Whitehall approved acceptance of the invitation.[5]

A visit to Lhasa was the perfect opportunity for Williamson to establish his credentials, as his authority was under some threat from an unexpected quarter; Sir Charles Bell's return to the frontier. Although retired, Bell had an open invitation from the Dalai Lama to visit Lhasa again and he had now returned to the frontier to take up the invitation. This created a problem for his successors. Such was the prestige Bell had acquired that Tibetan officials continued to view him as having great influence at the highest levels of British policy making. As Weir had foreseen, any Political Officer visiting Lhasa at the same time as Bell would be 'considered [a] nonentity'. Hence, in urging his government to allow him to accept the Dalai Lama's invitation, Williamson noted that

> Sir Charles Bell will probably be going to Lhasa next year. If I visit Lhasa at the same time as he does, I shall be entirely eclipsed.[6]

The cadre's love of Tibet and their role there made it difficult for them to detach themselves from Tibetan affairs when they left. Most of the Sikkim Political Officers attempted to return to the frontier in some capacity. O'Connor, after failing in a new career in business, worked as tour guide on the frontier in the 1930s. Bailey, posted to the Central Indian Princely State of Baghelkhand after leaving Sikkim, soon tried to persuade the Political Department to return him to Gangtok. Instead he was made Resident at Baroda, then given the 'plum' job of Resident in the delightfully scenic state of Kashmir. But he did return to the Himalayas as Envoy to the Court of Nepal before retiring to England in 1938. Macdonald, whose Kalimpong hotel was a meeting place for Tibetans and European Tibetophiles, made several attempts in the 1930s and '40s to return to Tibet in an official capacity. He even made totally unrealistic attempts to persuade Bell to return to service and lead another mission to Lhasa.[7]

Serving Political Officers displayed little sympathy for their predecessors' travel plans. Macdonald recalled that in 1931, when he asked for permission to visit Gyantse, Weir replied that 'in view of my firm friendship with the Tibetans and long stay in Tibet, he could not see his way to giving me permission.'[8]

Bell posed more of problem because as a private individual with a personal invitation from the Dalai Lama, it was difficult for government to prevent him visiting Lhasa. In retirement, Bell had pursued an independent line, refusing to allow serving officials to read his correspondence with the Dalai Lama and continuing to give private advice to the Tibetans. While Weir and Williamson both held Bell in the highest regard, they needed to establish their own authority, and naturally feared that with Bell's high status in Lhasa, his advice would be more valued than their own.[9]

It was, therefore, important for Williamson to establish good ties with the Tibetan leadership. This was the primary purpose behind his 1933 mission, which left for Lhasa via Bhutan within weeks of obtaining Whitehall's approval.

Before leaving, Williamson had personal matters to attend to. He married Margaret Marshall, the sister of a Gyantse Escort Commander, at the John Claude White Memorial Hall; which still stands in Gangtok today. There was a gathering of 'Tibet hands' for the celebration, including Bell and Macdonald. George Sherriff was best man, and he and Ludlow then accompanied the Williamsons on the Bhutanese leg of the journey.

The Williamsons, along with Norbu Dhondup and Captain Tennant, the Gyantse Medical Officer, visited the Tibetan capital from 14 August to 4 October 1933. British Lhasa missions were now taking on an almost routine character, deliberately following precedents established by Bell's mission. They all stayed at Dekyi Lingka, a square-roofed, two-storey building, owned by Kundeling monastery, which had been home to British visitors since Charles Bell. In intervals between official duties, they occupied their time visiting the same sights of Lhasa as their predecessors. Apart from the time-consuming business of encoding and decoding reports to and from India, most official business involved socialising with lay and monastic authorities.

A strong stomach was needed to cope with the enormous banquets in the Chinese fashion, which were given in their honour. But as Weir's daughter recalled, there were usually little Lhasa terriers running around under the tables who 'helped out' with such items as sea-slugs. A great deal of patience was also needed by even the keenest Tibetophiles to endure the lengthy dances and musical performances provided. For officers such as Williamson, who smoked, these could be particularly trying. Following Bell's example, the British in Lhasa did not smoke in public as it was against Tibetan custom.[10]

While the highlight of a visit to Lhasa was inevitably meeting the Dalai Lama, the most relaxing social events were those at Tsarong Shapé's estate. Although no longer at the forefront of Tibetan politics in the 1930s, Tsarong remained Finance Minister. While he didn't speak English, he was a fine host, who knew British likes and dislikes. His 'lunch' parties went on long into the night, and it was considered very poor form to remain sober.

Many of the guests at Tsarong's parties were officials who had been educated by the British, whether at Rugby, in India, or at Ludlow's school. They formed a growing circle of generally progressive thinkers, in whose company European visitors felt comfortable. Naturally, when they befriended this group, the cadre hoped to induce them to exert a friendly influence on the Tibetan government. They recognised that 'the pupils from these schools...constitute a major propaganda channel'. Despite this ulterior motive, however, there were many genuine friendships between cadre officers and these Tibetans.[11]

Williamson's 1933 visit to Lhasa built on the goodwill developed by Weir's mission the previous year. Mrs Williamson was present at two of her husband's meetings with the Dalai Lama, who showed his knowledge of the comings and goings of British officers. To Mrs. Williamson's delight, he asked her if it were true that Captain Marshall, who had been training Tibetan troops at Gyantse, was her brother.[12]

The problem with the Panchen Lama remained unresolved, but this was not a point of dispute between Tibet and the Raj, and it appeared that if the Lama could be persuaded to return to Shigatse without a Chinese escort, Tibet would indeed be a stable frontier for India. It seemed, as Williamson and his party returned to Gangtok, that Anglo-Tibetan relations had recovered their former warmth.

But late in 1933, while Williamson was putting the final touches to his Lhasa mission report and Bell was having tea with the Macdonald family in Kalimpong, grave news arrived. The 13th Dalai Lama, the architect of independent Tibet, had 'passed to the heavenly fields' on 17 December.

* * *

Although there was a great difference between the view of Tibet held at Whitehall and the view held by the cadre, there was no such division between Chinese frontier officials and their central government. Their perspective was consistent; Tibet was a part of China; irrespective of the wishes of its people. Although her officials had been expelled in 1912-13, China had subsequently made several informal attempts to re-establish a presence in Lhasa.[13] The death of the Dalai Lama provided an opportunity for a full-scale response.

A 'condolence mission' to Lhasa was organised under the command of General Huang Mu-sung, a member of Chiang Kai-shek's General Staff. The mission was preceded by two envoys who reached Lhasa in May 1934. When Huang Mu-sung's mission eventually arrived in August 1934, the envoys ensured that it was received by the Tibetans with the ceremony due to a consular mission.

Under the incarnation system, a Dalai Lama's death meant a period of rule by Regent until the new incarnation came to maturity. There was a great deal of jockeying for power in Lhasa in 1934 until, in what must have been a compromise, the diffident young abbot of Reting monastery was chosen as Regent. But the real power struggle continued behind the scenes.[14]

In the spring of 1934, Williamson sent Norbu Dhondup to Lhasa. His reports on Huang's mission alarmed the Government of India as Huang proved an able diplomat who used his large reservoir of funds to win support. When Huang departed on 28 November, he left behind the nucleus of a permanent Chinese mission, including a radio operator with a transmitter. The British were particularly troubled by the radio; it freed the Chinese from reliance on India's telegraph system, where their communications were routinely monitored. Chinese intentions were now much harder to ascertain.

The Government of India had already concluded that it needed a British officer in Lhasa to ensure its influence was paramount. In

1. Sir Charles Bell: The Architect of British policy in Tibet.
Source: Bell Collection: Copyright, Pitt Rivers Museum, Oxford.

2. David Macdonald with Gurkha escort at Yatung, c1911. The original of this photograph identifies the figure standing to the right as 'Enchung a travelling curio dealer who was one of Macdonald's informants'.
Source: Macdonald Collection: Copyright, Pitt Rivers Museum, Oxford.

3. Lt-Colonel & Lady F.M.Bailey, with Lt-Colonel Sir W.F.T.O'Connor [to Bailey's left] and ubitquitous dogs: c1924.
Source: Bailey Collection: Copyright, Oriental and India Office Library and Records.

4. The British Residency, Gangtok, c1934. Home to the Sikkim Political Officers.
Source: Bell Collection: Copyright Pitt Rivers Museum, Oxford.

5. Interior of the Gyantse Trade Agency, c 1940. The protruding glassed-in room was part of the Trade Agent's quarters. The small canon at the foot of the stairs were left behind by the Younghusband mission; a reminder of the fort's 'essentially military character'.

Source: Walters' Collection: Copyright R.Mouland.

6. Yatung Trade Agency, c1927. Where Macdonald's favourite hour was "when everyone was settled down and he could sit out on the verandah with the Bible beside him and contemplate the scenery". [Macdonald papers]
Source: Hopkinson Collection: Copyright British Museum.

7. Bell and party, Lhasa 1921. Seated to Bell's right are Lt-Colonel R.Kennedy, Rai Bahadur Laden La, and Dewan Bahadur Kusho Palhesé. Standing between Bell and Kennedy is Rai Bahadur Norbu Dhondup. The seven members of the party with hat feathers are Sikkimese employees.

Source: Bell Collection: Copyright Pitt Rivers Museum, Oxford.

8. Frank Ludlow, standing [with characteristic hat], Major George Sherriff, and Frederick Williamson, with onlookers at the Residency, c1933.

Source: Williamson Collection: Copyright, Cambridge University Museum of Archaeology and Anthropology.

9. "Lords of half the earth". Arthur Hopkinson, the last British Political Officer Sikkim, in travelling wear, c1927.
Source: Hopkinson Collection: Copyright British Museum.

10. The 1936 British Lhasa mission lunch with the Taring family near Gyantse. Gould is seated with pith helmet.
Copyright: The Estate of Lt. General Sir Philip Neame VC.

September 1934, the Indian Foreign Secretary wrote to Williamson asking him to assemble all the arguments necessary to convince Whitehall that influence at the Tibetan capital was vital to their interests. What he meant was that he wanted Williamson to apply for permission to visit Lhasa, and the Political Officer took the hint. He filed a report concluding that he needed to go to Lhasa and for good measure he asked for an increased budget for presents. The point of Williamson's mission was to ascertain whether the Chinese were now permanently ensconced. Charles Bell's 1921 report was not directly mentioned, but the policy it had recommended was that if the Chinese established a permanent mission, the British should do the same.[15]

* * *

Charles Bell remained in Kalimpong with the Macdonalds for several months after he heard the news of the Dalai Lama's death. Although he had gently dismissed Macdonald's idea that he return to service, and was content that 'the younger men' deal with Tibet, Bell had hoped to meet the Dalai Lama once more.[16] But now his old associate was gone and the country to which he had devoted most of his life was at a turning point.

Although Bell was regularly asked by the Tibetan Government for his advice, he was uncertain whether to make another journey to Lhasa. He had Macdonald's support, but he also, with characteristic thoroughness, obtained Laden La's assurance that he would be welcomed back. Bell had no desire to be an embarassment to either the Raj or the Tibetans, but he eventually concluded that if he could still help Tibet plan for the future, it was his duty to do so.[17]

In July 1934, Bell travelled to Gyantse, along with a former Sikkim Medical Officer, Lieutenant-Colonel Harnett. Bell wrote to the Tibetan Government for permission to visit Tibet's capital once more, and waited in Gyantse for the reply. Williamson, on his annual inspection of the Gyantse Trade Agency, was an interested spectator to the events that followed. The Kashag sent back a polite refusal, sweetened with a pass allowing Bell to visit Shigatse. The pass stated that

> the Great Minister...[Bell]...established relations between Britain and Tibet which were good in every way. Others therefore, cannot

ask for this permission that we are giving him. The Regent, Chief Minister and Kasha[g] are granting this permission to Sir Charles Bell alone.[18]

Before Bell left for Shigatse, he tried again, writing a personal letter to the Regent in which he stated that

> he was an old man and wished to visit Lhasa once more and that, as he was a former close friend of the Dalai Lama, he hoped his request would not be refused.[19]

Bell arrived in Shigatse on 22 August, but there was no reply from Lhasa awaiting him, 'a fact which disappointed and hurt him greatly'. Instead the Kashag wrote asking for his advice on relations with China. In his reply, Bell stressed that he needed a personal meeting with the Tibetan Government to fully explain his views. Early in October, he sent the Kashag an ultimatum; a 6 day deadline for receipt of an invitation to Lhasa. The deadline passed without a response.

Bell waited for three days after the deadline expired before setting off on the return journey to India. En route he heard a rumour that the permission would soon arrive. Although Harnett was anxious to escape the encroaching winter, Bell halted for one more day. But he was no longer a young man, his hair had turned white, his health was failing, and the dream of Lhasa was fading. To travel to the capital and return across the passes to India in winter was too risky for a man of his age. Bell sadly set off to return to India on 21 October. Two days later, the longed-for pass to Lhasa finally arrived. But it was too late. Sir Charles Bell was leaving Tibet for the last time.

Bell spent the winter in Gangtok and Kalimpong, annoying the Raj by sending further advice to the Tibetan Government and warning them that 'Bit by bit, Britain is giving more power to India, who will hardly show the same friendship...or have the same power to help Tibet.'[20]

When the Government of India objected to him offering advice to the Tibetans, Bell replied that it would have been discourteous to refuse their requests. He denied any intention of upstaging Williamson, adding waspishly that 'It appears that our Government does not understand Tibetan mentality'.[21]

Bell left the Tibetan frontier for the last time late in 1935. He took his family through Manchuria and bandit-ridden Mongolia, where he intended to study the local Buddhism. But Bell's wife Cashie died of meningitis in Peking. Bell upset officials one last time by defending Tibetan rights to the Chinese Foreign Minister while an uninvited guest at the British Embassy. Then he left the East forever.[22]

Bell retired to Canada, anticipating the outbreak of war in Europe. There he devoted the last years of his life to writing a biography of the 13th Dalai Lama, the man with whom his own destiny had been so entwined. Bell died shortly before the book was published. The news of his death took some time to reach India and although Gould wrote an obituary, it was submitted too late for the London *Times* to print it. The death of Sir Charles Bell, the architect of Anglo-Tibetan policy and friendship, passed almost unnoticed outside the corner of the world he had shaped.

Bell had at least made a final visit to Tibet. His old rival for the Dalai Lama's favour, Agvan Dorzhiev, was less fortunate. Dorzhiev had made his final appearance in British records in the mid-1920s. In the 1930s, Stalin's purges began to decimate the Russian Buddhist community. Dorzhiev escaped arrest until November 1937, when he was charged with various crimes, including treason. His interrogation was interrupted when his health failed, probably under torture, and he died in a prison hospital on 29 January 1938. His dream of a Russian-sponsored Buddhist empire had long since vanished, but there was an echo of it in his interrogation report. It claimed that he 'showed that he was one of the leaders of the counter-revolutionary Pan-Mongolian insurrectionary terrorist organization'.[23]

* * *

Bell's final reappearance on the Tibetan frontier had put the Political Officer Sikkim in an awkward position. Early in April 1935, Williamson had received a private letter from the Regent, suggesting he apply for permission to make another visit to Lhasa, with the understanding that his request would be accepted. Bell's intervention had threatened Williamson's authority and the Indian Foreign Secretary, Olaf Caroe, advised him to explain to the Tibetan Government that Bell no longer had any official status. Williamson, fearing that they would not believe him, asked his government for a written statement to that effect.[24]

With the Chinese mission now firmly ensconced in Lhasa, the main purpose of Williamson's second mission was to ascertain whether the Tibetans would accept a permanent British mission. Of almost equal importance was the continuing problem of the Panchen Lama. Although he still contacted Macdonald occasionally in the hope of obtaining British support, he had come under increasing Chinese influence. His threat to return to Shigatse with a large escort of Chinese troops was being taken very seriously in Lhasa when Williamson was preparing to visit in 1935.

Williamson's mission was of crucial importance to the British. The cadre had always stressed the importance of having a Political Officer in personal contact with the Tibetan leadership. Williamson was expected to ensure that British interests in Tibet would be protected in the face of the Chinese threat. But fate now took a hand.

We have seen that successful cadre officers put duty above personal considerations; this was never more clear than in Williamson's case. Shortly before his departure for Lhasa his doctor in Gangtok found that he was suffering from uraemia, a kidney disease for which there was no known cure. Mrs. Williamson recalled that

> even though we now knew that he was very ill, Derrick insisted on going...to Lhasa. Derrick's position was that there could be no debate about it. He had to go. The service always comes first...I too understood the needs of the service and it would never have occured to me to try and deflect him from any course of action that he felt to be his duty.[25]

The Williamsons were accompanied to Lhasa by the Gyantse Medical Officer, Captain James Guthrie, and Captain Keith Battye, the new Gyantse Trade Agent, along with Norbu Dhondup. They reached Lhasa on 26 August, but the Regent was away on the search for the new incarnation of the Dalai Lama and time began to hang heavily on their hands. They filled the days until his return with the obligatory rounds of socialising. This included a rather strained 28 course dinner with the Chinese representatives, for despite their rivalry, the diplomatic niceties had to be observed.

Williamson's health slowly worsened. Guthrie repeatedly advised him to leave Lhasa, but he insisted on waiting to negotiate with the Regent. Williamon's party had hoped to leave Lhasa on October 20th, to catch the best time for duck-shooting on their return, but the Regent did not arrive until that day. They found him

> an anaemic looking youth of about 24. Large head, protruding ears, no chin, weak mouth but responsible expression. Seems a bit shy but very friendly.[26]

In talks with the Regent, progress was made on the Panchen Lama question and it also became clear that the Chinese mission had no intention of leaving, although its exact status was undefined. Unofficial enquiries were made as to the Tibetan Government's attitude to a permanent British mission and plans were then made for the party to return to India. But on 1 November, Williamson collapsed and Battye had to take over. Within a week Williamson was 'very pale, voice almost whispering'.[27]

Battye asked the Tibetan Government if it would permit an RAF plane to fly in from India to evacuate Williamson. The Tibetans, fearing that this would create a precedent which could be exploited by China, and worried that the proposed airstrip beside Sera monastery would be attacked by monks angry at such modern innovations, refused. The request was pointless anyway; the RAF did not have aircraft with the technical capability to take-off at Lhasa's altitude.

Williamson showed signs of recovery for a few days, but on the night of 16 November his condition suddenly worsened, and he died the following evening, aged just 44.

Captain Battye, after only five months in Tibet, became Acting Political Officer Sikkim. Life in Lhasa had been rather difficult for him. Like Williamson he found the prohibition on smoking hard to bear and he had little in common with Guthrie, a man of eccentric humour, though well-liked by Tibetans. Mrs Williamson even mentioned the tensions within the party in her memoirs. But while he was inexperienced, Battye was from a long and distinguished line of empire builders, his forefathers had filled the ranks of Generals, and fought in the Raj's great battles.[28]

With the pressure on, Keith Battye, it was noted approvingly in the Secretariat, 'kept his head'. He organised the mission's departure from Lhasa and the funeral march back to Gyantse, where Williamson was buried on 25 November, alongside the graves from the Younghusband mission. Battye read the funeral service, and the coffin was lowered into the ground. Then, as Mrs Williamson described

> three volleys were fired into the air and the buglers sounded the Last Post - always very haunting, but never more so than up there in that remote outpost on the Roof of the World.[29]

Williamson's death delayed a response to the Chinese presence in Lhasa and the British feared it had damaged their prestige with the Tibetans. Some Tibetans, however, reportedly considered his death had a more esoteric cause. They regarded it as punishment for his having photographed images of powerful deities at a Lhasa shrine.[30]

The British Government wanted as little publicity as possible given to Political Officers' missions to Lhasa, to avoid international complications. But Williamson's death gained unwelcome attention, with questions raised in the British parliament. In February 1936, William Gallacher, who had won fame by punching Glasgow's Chief Constable on the nose during a dockyard strike, asked the House of Commons what Williamson had been doing in Lhasa, and whether the Government of India was intending to appoint a permanent representative there. This question may well have been asked on behalf of the Russians; Gallacher was a Communist MP and his party were in receipt of Russian funds. But the Minister concerned played down the visit, claiming it was a routine one. He blithely denied that India was considering a permanent representative in Lhasa.[31] But the denial was some way away from the truth, for the appointment was now being actively considered.

Chapter Ten

'One distinct forward move'

In December 1935, as Basil Gould returned from home leave, he stepped off the boat at Bombay to be given a telegram appointing him Political Officer Sikkim. Gould had already served a year at Gangtok in 1913-14, when he relieved Charles Bell during the talks which culminated in the Simla Convention. Prior to that he had served as Trade Agent in Gyantse for eight months, and he subsequently escorted the four Tibetan boys to Rugby School in 1914. Charles Bell was his mentor; he closely followed Bell's policy recommendations and general approach to Tibetan affairs.

Gould had got on particularly well with the Dalai Lama, and had unofficially accompanied him on his return from exile in India. Along the way they had caught tadpoles and examined flowers together and, at the Dalai Lama's request, Gould arranged an 'international' polo match between 'India' and 'Tibet' when they arrived in Gyantse. As the winning captain, Gould had been presented with a white scarf by the Tibetan leader[1]

Gould was a tall, imposing figure, and not one to suffer fools gladly. He was a man of restless energy, prone to adopting an idea with great enthusiasm and just as suddenly dropping it to take up another cause. At one point he devoted his attention to promoting the widespread planting of *kikuya* grass. Then he wanted sun-rooms in all the Agencies and *dak* bungalows. Yet in the sphere of politics and diplomacy, Gould's actions, until he became ill, were logical, methodical and entirely focused.

Gould was conscious of his status and deliberately maintained the aloof aura of imperial power and self-control so easily parodied. When, for example, he visited Gyantse, he insisted on being received at the precise distance of several miles as dictated by Tibetan etiquette. If he reached the designated spot before his reception party, Gould would sit and wait until the escort arrived to conduct him into the Agency.[2]

The British in India believed that maintaining status was crucial to their rule. Prestige was, as Younghusband put it, 'little understood in England, but...of immense practical value in the East'. Prestige was a potent weapon because it was believed that if the Raj's power was seen as invincible, resistance to it would be considered futile. It served as an almost tangible tool of government, a symbol of power which became increasingly important as the British sought to avoid the political and economic cost of using military force as an instrument of policy in India. As Secretary of State Lord George Hamilton wrote in a letter to Curzon, 'our power in India [is] largely based on prestige'.[3]

Prestige, in the British understanding, involved creating an impression of personal and national superiority over the local peoples and power structures. Superior status was demonstrated through both individual and national behaviour, and through outward forms and symbols. In assuming this superior status, the Raj could claim to be following local custom; the precedent of *izzat*, the charismatic authority of the Mughal rulers. To this they added aspects which were quintessentially British; Gould dined at eight every evening, and always donned formal dress for dinner, even in camp.[4]

In the wider context, British prestige was a part of the prestige of European civilisation; there was a solidarity of purpose among Europeans generally to demonstrate and uphold the superiority of their culture. Thus Madame Alexandra David-Neel, the French traveller, wrote to Bell when he had her deported from Sikkim, complaining that 'It is not good that Europeans appears[sic] to be quarrelling before natives who do not like them.'[5]

The belief that 'natives' were essentially hostile contributed to the social segregation which became a feature of the British Indian social system. Imperial distinctness was preserved by both physical separation, expressed in architecture and living space, and social separation, which was enforced by rules and customs. Again, the Raj claimed local precedents for this, with indigenous religiously-sanctioned social divisions providing the precedent for the British to remain a distinct 'caste'. This concern for social distinctness predominated in British India despite the existence of a counter trend towards lessening the distance between the races.

There was considerably less social separation from the local people in Tibet than in British India, but the concepts of correct behaviour and appropriate action associated with the maintenance of status were equally assiduously followed by the cadre. After the Younghusband mission had demonstrated British military power to the Tibetans, the cadre followed the strategy used in India. They sought to create an impression of power which would instil in the Tibetans a respect for the British, and persuade them to support imperial interests. As Curzon had stated,

> What I want is that our present intolerable and humiliating relationship with the Tibetans shall not continue, and that they shall be sufficiently impressed with our power as to realise that they cannot look to any other quarter for protection.[6]

Considerations of status were manifest in most imperial actions, from personal dress and bearing to government policy, and the Raj's concept of prestige was constantly re-evaluated and refined, just like weapons of military power. The symbols of distinction were an important part of an individual officer's self-esteem. Macdonald proudly recalled how, in 1911, when he was inadvertently caught up in a battle between Chinese and Tibetan forces, both sides recognised him by his white *topee* and stopped firing to allow him to leave the battle-field. He and other officers enjoyed this eminence. They realised that 'As a British Trade Agent a man was something. There was the prestige and pomp of the empire to be maintained and this meant one reflected the glory'.[7]

The Escort and Medical Officers played an important part in this process. The Medical Officers' concern with personal status 'matched that of the Politicals'. While the advantages of modern medicine, and its free application to all classes of Tibetans naturally enhanced the British reputation, the 'right type' of doctor was also considered to do 'a tremendous lot for British prestige'.[8]

The Trade Agent's escort symbolised British military power. Attempts to withdraw the escort for political or financial reasons were successfully resisted by the cadre on the grounds that 'it would leave the Trade Agents divested of the needed symbols of authority'.[9] A Gyantse Escort Commander recalled how, when the Trade Agent paid official calls, they 'showed the flag'.

> We rode out in great pomp and style. Liveried scouts riding on ahead, then the Mounted Infantry with the bugler, and the men carrying a huge Union Jack, and finally the B.T.A. and Officers. I feel sure the locals found this an imposing sight.[10]

The cadre claimed the highest possible status for themselves *vis-à-vis* the Tibetan officials with whom they dealt. Bell arranged that the Political Officer Sikkim rank with the Tibetan Chief Minister. This meant that, although within British India the Sikkim post was never more than a second-class Residency, in Tibet the Political Officer could justly claim, 'You couldn't get any higher'.[11]

The social status cadre officers held in the empire was much higher than that to which they might have aspired had they remained in Britain. There, they had been from professional middle class backgrounds, yet in the empire they became the ruling class. When they returned to Britain, however, they reverted to their previous status; obviously a factor in many Political Officers' reluctance to retire from Sikkim.

Individual cadre officers were keenly concerned with maintaining and increasing their own personal status. Even when the Tibetans were not directly involved, no detail of protocol was ignored. For example, when Campbell was Trade Agent in Yatung, he objected to receiving orders from the Political Officer Sikkim signed by the Gangtok clerk; his personal honour demanded that he take orders only from his (British) superior.[12]

However 'tiresome' these matters seemed to witnesses, the Raj always supported the principle involved. Bell reported that Campbell, then in charge of the Chumbi Valley, 'insists and perhaps rightly so on the local people dismounting from their ponies and removing their hats whenever they see him'. Bell was not personally given to demanding such public deference, but he clearly supported the all-important principle of maintaining the highest possible status. If the British 'were to represent a superior race, they had to act the part'.[13]

By the 1930s, frontier officers had little real power outside their own district. Yet, like Gould, they continued to act as if they had the power enjoyed by predecessors such as Younghusband. The Tibetans, however, were actually much less impressed by the symbols of British prestige than the cadre hoped. They valued their own ceremonial forms, and British adherence to these was undoubtedly contrasted favourably with the approach of the Chinese. But the waxing and waning of Tibetan fondness for the Raj was not related to British prestige.

Certainly outer forms of prestige such as dress were of little consequence to them. After seeing a picture of the 'Trooping of the Colour', an official commented, 'You are just like us when you are at home. Why don't you wear bright colours like this when you come to Tibet?' Nor do the cadre appear to have created such a deep impression on the ordinary Tibetans as British accounts suggest. Many of the people, even monks in Lhasa, were actually unaware that the Government of India's representatives were there.[14]

Several studies have shown how architecture was an important weapon in establishing imperial prestige, with Residencies acting as symbols of the Raj in the context of British Indian power.[15] Thus cadre officers described the inadequate Trade Agency buildings as 'incompatible with dignity' or 'a disgrace to the name and prestige of the British Government'. The Tibetan view was expressed to Bailey regarding the building of the English school in Gyantse in the 1920s. Bailey reported that 'They said our houses were always badly made and required repairs so they wanted to build the school themselves'.[16]

Despite the evidence that British prestige was interpreted in a very different form from that intended, its effectiveness as a weapon went largely unquestioned. It was taken for granted, for reasons which reflect the imperial confidence. During the 1940s however, while there was no decline in the cadre's use of the symbols of prestige, there was an increasing emphasis on an apparently more successful means of impressing the Tibetans. There was an increasing use of financial support to key elements of the local power structure, a point we will return to. It was a move from outdated modes of cultural expression to a more cynical *realpolitik*.

* * *

When Basil Gould took over in Sikkim he considered that the Chinese presence in Lhasa, and in particular their radio capability, demanded a strong response, along the lines suggested by Bell. Gould had firm support from the Indian Foreign Secretary, Olaf Caroe,[17] for a more actively interventionist policy in response to the Chinese moves. Gould began the response by strengthening his positions. The experienced Norbu Dhondup was appointed to the reactivated Yatung Trade Agency, which had been combined with Gyantse since 1918, and a new Gyantse Trade Agent was appointed: Hugh Richardson.

Richardson was a Scot who had become interested in Tibet at Oxford. His grandfather had been an ICS officer at the time of the 'Indian Mutiny', and Richardson was firmly in the mould of the 'lean and keen' frontiersman. Though he served only briefly as Political Officer Sikkim, relieving Gould for six months in 1937, he was to spend 8 years in Tibet, including 6 years in total as Head of Mission Lhasa (for both the British Indian and Indian Governments). With his keen intellect and empathy with the Tibetans, Richardson was to become one of the cadre's outstanding officers.

Battye's report on the Williamson mission concluded that the attitude of the *kashag* to a permanent British mission in Lhasa was one of 'distaste'. Yet they were prepared to give it 'favourable consideration' if they were forced to accept a Chinese embassy. By 1936 it was clear that General Huang's 'condolence mission' had become just that.[18]

Gould of course, wanted to visit Lhasa, which still required permission from Whitehall. Each succeeding Political Officer's arguements for a Lhasa mission built on the arguements raised successfully by his predecessors. Gould mustered most of them in his application but claimed his primary purpose would be to arrange for the Panchen Lama's return from exile. Whitehall approved, subject to an invitation, which Norbu Dhondup was duly sent to obtain. Gould then made preparations on a far more lavish scale than for any previous such mission.[19]

Gould's hopes that his mission would become a permanent one were supported by the Government of India, following Bell's policy of responding to Chinese moves. But Whitehall was more hesitant. They instructed Gould to 'be cautious in sounding Tibetan Government regarding permanent representation.'[20]

Gould arrived in Lhasa on 24 August 1936. He was accompanied by six British officers, the largest contingent since the Younghusband mission. Joining him were Hugh Richardson, along with a Medical Officer, Captain Morgan IMS, a Secretary, F.Spencer Chapman, two telegraph sergeants, S.Dagg and E.Nepean, and Brigadier-General P.Neame VC., who was to report on the Tibetan military forces. They had needed 145 pack-animals to carry their supplies to Gyantse, including 25 pony loads of wireless equipment. At Gyantse, another 55 pack-animal loads were added. Gould had hoped to bolster the mission's popularity by calling David Macdonald out of retirement to act as their Tibetan language instructor; a symbolic affirmation of his identification with the Bell-Macdonald approach. Macdonald was keen to go, but illness prevented him making the journey.[21]

From the outset, Gould intended the 1936-37 mission to become permanent. He extended his own stay as long as possible and had little difficulty in finding arguments for the mission itself remaining. The search for the Dalai Lama's new incarnation was underway and the fragile unity of the Lhasa government was still threatened by the Panchen Lama's plan to return with a Chinese military escort. Gould claimed that his presence in the capital was strengthening the Tibetan Government's determination to resist such a force. But he covered his bets by proposing that if the Panchen Lama did return with an escort, he should negotiate for a permanent British presence in Lhasa.[22]

In correspondence with Whitehall, Delhi now argued forthrightly that 'The real solution for our difficulties would...appear to be some kind of permanent representation at Lhasa'. They noted that while Gould had to return to his duties in Sikkim, Norbu and Richardson could remain after he left. Whitehall accepted that a change of policy was needed and agreed to the mission remaining for another year. But they cautiously asked that Norbu remain there, rather than a British officer.[23]

Given this permission, Gould's 'chief aim was to produce the impression of normality and immobility' about the British presence.[24] His understanding of the importance of symbolic gestures is revealed in the use of the mission football team's regular matches as one means of appearing 'permanent'. As his reports from Lhasa made clear, the team was an important part of their efforts to gain closer relations with the Tibetans, in addition to giving members of the mission exercise and an outside interest. Gould reported that

> many personal contacts and even friendships were formed by the younger members of the mission, particularly in pursuance of their specialised occupations or hobbies, and football matches particularly against local teams showed that the Tibetans play [a] hard clean sporting game.

Gould's team, the 'Mission Marmots' (with Gould as goalkeeper) went unbeaten in the first season, without conceding a goal. But they had the advantage of playing in boots. This led one opposing team to request that they play bare-foot, and desist

> from wearing fearful boots, which some of you used last time, because we are not able to buy such boots in the market and because we fear if you use those fearful boots.

The Marmots' opponents consisted of the Nepalese mission in Lhasa, the Nepalese school team and a team made up from the Lhasa Muslim community, which 'ranged from a bearded shaven headed goal-keeper to a crowd of boys who closely followed the ball in a breathless pack'.

These teams were soon joined by a Tibetan team made up of members of the Trapchi regiment, soldiers specially chosen for their size and robust appearance, who served as the Dalai Lama's personal bodyguard. They were captained by one Yutok Dapön, and provided the best opposition for the mission, drawing two matches with them. The first Lhasa season were becoming more competitive when it was brought to a premature end on 26 November 1936 when the goalposts were stolen for firewood.

Football increasingly penetrated Tibetan society. Eventually there were 14 teams in Lhasa and it was reported that 'officials have a practice match twice a week; while it is a common sight to see street urchins playing football with a ball composed mainly of paper and string'. Football boots were even reported to be on sale in the market. The Reting Regent followed the fashion. He borrowed a ball from the British, and Spencer Chapman wrote, half-seriously, that 'this alone seemed to justify the Mission!' The Regent, who never enjoyed good health, was a regular patient of the British Medical Officers in Lhasa, and as late as August 1944 he was reported to be taking 'daily exercise, including football'.

By 1944 however, football in Tibet had been dealt a mortal blow. Tibetans were banned from playing by their government. Monastic opposition to football, and the passions it generated, was behind the ban, as it was behind most opposition to modernisation. The Tibetans' paramount values were religious; sporting values in the European sense were alien. Monastic officials regarded football as a threat to social and cultural stability. This became a decisive argument when during a game there was a hailstorm; an event considered inauspicious, in addition to the damage it caused to crops.

Gould delayed his departure from Lhasa as long as possible, claiming that it would be a 'grave discourtesy' to leave before the Tibetan New Year celebrations. When Gould finally departed on 17 February 1937, there was no formal statement that the British mission was now permanent. After ascertaining in private talks with leading Tibetans that it would be acceptable, Gould simply informed the Kashag just before he left that as various matters were outstanding, Richardson would remain to discuss them. The Tibetans, as Gould put it, 'swallowed this', and the cadre had their Lhasa mission.[25]

The exact legal position of the Lhasa post was never defined, nor was it covered by any agreement. No official notification of any intention to create a permanent position was given, then or later, to the Tibetan Government; or to Whitehall. The post of Head of British Mission Lhasa always remained under the command of the Political Officer Sikkim. The mission continued until August 1947, when it became the Indian mission, although Hugh Richardson continued to command the post until 1950. Theoretically it remained temporary, but the officers there were determined not to depart, at least while the Chinese remained in Lhasa. The Tibetans never asked the British to leave, and made the most of the mission as a channel of contact with the outside world.[26]

In December 1937, the exiled Panchen Lama died. In many ways this was a convenient death for the Tibetan Government, giving it a respite from the threat of Chinese troops accompanying his return. Yet the Panchen Lama was an integral element of the Tibetan system and despite his exile status, he had been consulted in the search for the new incarnation of the Dalai Lama.

This death removed much of the supposed basis for the British presence in Lhasa. Gould was asked by his government presumably pre-empting Whitehall's enquiry, if there was 'any reason why the Lhasa Mission should not be withdrawn entirely as soon as possible?'[27]

Gould responded along predictable lines. He argued that the mission had prevented the Chinese from establishing a stronger presence, and claimed that if the mission was withdrawn it might prove impossible to return, and would mean the loss of influence and reliable information. He cited the rising threat from Japan and even raised the prospect of a withdrawal being used as a bargaining chip if China agreed to negotiations over the status of Tibet, a prospect Whitehall always hoped might eventuate. In summary, he recommended that the mission remain until 'we are able to estimate the present intentions of the Chinese and also of the Japanese'; a time which could clearly be postponed indefinitely. Gould's arguments were accepted, with the post sanctioned until September 1938.[28]

As the Lhasa mission was theoretically temporary, Gould had to justify its value every year to obtain an extension. He was not alone; there was a united effort by the various cadre officers to stress its value. The reports of Richardson and Norbu in Lhasa, and the Trade Agent in Gyantse, frequently referred to the advantages of having a representative in the capital.[29] The cadre had fought for too long to have its Lhasa mission; it would not easily give it up.

In August 1938, Gould sought a further extension of the position, citing all the usual reasons, adding that the British should be present at the forthcoming installation of the new Dalai Lama. Sanction was duly given for the Lhasa mission to continue for another year.[30]

Gould subsequently suggested that a Residency be built in Lhasa, capable of conveying both British prestige and 'the impression of stability and permanence which it would be politic to convey.' He added, presumably for Whitehall's consumption, the rather peculiar suggestion that with a Residency to symbolise the British presence, an actual representative would not be needed. But Whitehall would only sanction a new Residency if the Tibetans could be persuaded to pay for it.[31]

During World War Two, Gould's annual requests to maintain the Lhasa mission and government's subsequent approvals became increasingly routine. The Allies' need to consult the Tibetan Government on various war-related issues brought home to Whitehall the advantages of a representative in Lhasa and the closure of the post ceased to be a consideration. Gould had finally succeeded in his, and his predecessors, 'major preoccupation' by establishing a permanent representative in Lhasa.[32] For the Raj to have relations with a neighbouring state without representation in its capital had always been an obvious anomaly, whatever Tibet's status. Yet it had taken the cadre more than 30 years to convince Whitehall of this.

Gould had achieved his primary aim by following the policy espoused by his 'guru', Charles Bell, and 'brought about de facto permanent representation...at Lhasa under the name of a "temporary" Mission'.[33] Secure in the knowledge that he enjoyed the complete support of the Foreign Secretary, Olaf Caroe (a fellow Wykemist), Gould expressed the realistic view that the

> prime need is to admit to ourselves that our aims are not ALTRUISTIC[sic]...[British interests were best served by] a friendly and sufficiently strong and independent Tibet...[Thus he had] concentrated on one main objective viz. the establishment of our mission at Lhasa. Round this one distinct forward move I have endeavoured to throw a *purdah* of conservatism and of help in such matters as trade and medical work.[34]

The Lhasa mission became the focus of Anglo-Tibetan relations, with a body of men experienced in Tibetan affairs having unrestricted access to all levels of society. As Bell had suggested should happen, the Gyantse Agency became less important and was primarily a staging post for Lhasa. It was often controlled by the Escort Commanders, who had little significant input in policy matters and who successfully concentrated on maintaining smooth relations with the local populace. Only Captain Saker, Trade Agent in 1941-43, served a full term there.

Saker, a tall, blue-eyed extrovert, keen on *shikar*, was very much in the cadre 'mould'. His father had been killed at Gallipoli, serving with the ANZAC forces, and as a youth Saker had been inspired with an interest in Tibet by a near neighbour, Lieutenant-Colonel Rivett-Carnac. Given Rivett-Carnac's poor record in Tibet, he was not the ideal mentor, but his pupil proved a more than able officer. In India Saker served under Weir, who had been made Resident in Baroda after his term in Gantok. He then joined the Politicals to 'move around a bit' in search of interest and adventure. Like Weir, he was at the Secretariat when a vacancy arose at Gyantse, and he took the job.

In a break with previous practice, Saker's wife Angela was allowed to spend six months in Gyantse during his term there, although their child had to be left cared for in India. Mrs Saker started a women's spinning and weaving scheme during her stay, producing woollen sea boot stockings for the British war effort and enjoying the mixture of monotonous days when 'one lived for the post', interspersed with all-day parties on local estates and the 'terrific bustle' when the Political Officer passed through.

During his term at Gyantse, Captain Saker was sent with the Lhasa Medical Officer, Dr Terry, to inspect the Gartok Trade Agency. Like Williamson and Ludlow, they took the opportunity to join the pilgrims on the circuit around the awesome Kailas, the sacred mountain near the source of the Brahmaputra, Indus, Sutlej and Karnali rivers. Mrs Saker set out from Almora to greet her returning husband. Wartime restrictions meant the only food she was able to bring was a plumcake, but Saker had some wild honey and when they met on the trail they stopped and shared the meal among the hills. Such incidental memories, far removed from politics, often remained most strongly in the minds of those who served the empire.[35]

* * *

When the cadre settled into their new base at Lhasa, they were able to expand their influence and their knowledge of the country. Richardson developed new contacts in the monastic power structure, such as the State Oracle, an influential figure in local politics. Richardson proved an expert at those aspects of his duty 'which are not exactly work, although they are apt to consume a good deal of energy and patience'. These new contacts meant that he and Gould were soon regarded by their government as having developed a greater understanding of Tibetan society than any cadre officers since Bell and Macdonald.[36]

The purpose of these contacts was of course to persuade influential Tibetans to support British interests. At the same time, China's agents were seeking support for their interests. Both sides tried to combat the other's impact in a constant struggle for influence, quite at odds with Britain and China's status as World War Two allies.

Although they did co-operate in some matters relating to the war, the normal state of relations between the two powers was summed up by Radio Officer Robert Ford. When he reached Lhasa in 1945, he

> was shocked at the mutual mistrust and hostility between British and Chinese...[who] I had thought of as gallant allies...I could hardly believe we had been waging a cold war with them in Lhasa all the time.[37]

The Anglo-Chinese rivalry was often carried to extremes. Each country's initiatives quickly drew a response from the other; if one country found a new means to impress the Tibetan, the other followed suit. This meant that although the cadre succeeded in gaining the friendship of many Tibetans, China too had its friends. In the search for the upper-hand, the cadre increasingly turned to the simplest method of obtaining support; money.

The British had always followed the local custom of presenting gifts when visiting important Tibetans. The offering of gifts to a host, or social superior, was part of Tibetan tradition. This gift-giving was highly ritualised, with objects retaining gift status, being received and then passed on. The British quickly adapted to this system, offering gifts to their supporters. White was so generous in giving modern weapons to various Tibetan officials that he was censured for failing to consider the potential threat these weapons offered to the British.[38]

Even in the Younghusband era the British recognised that judicious distribution of cash won them friends. A contemporary street song recorded that:

> At first they speak of 'Foes of our True Faith';
> And next the cry is 'Foreign Devildom';
> But when they see the foreign money bags,
> We hear of 'Honourable Englishmen'.[39]

Charles Bell, finding that his efforts to persuade his government to supply arms to Tibet were unsuccessful, took 30,000 rupees with him to Lhasa to present to various influential groups and individuals.[40] The extent to which Bell's generosity assisted his success is difficult to gauge. He naturally downplayed this aspect and in 1935 he did caution the Government of India against giving the Tibetans too many presents, pointing out that they would know why it was done. But Bell had always recognised the possibility of buying support. In 1914 he had promoted arms sales partly because they would 'give us a good hold over the Government of Tibet'.[41]

Charles Bell was a strong influence on Gould's policies. Gould, who had been away from Tibet for more than twenty years when he was posted to Gangtok, went to considerable trouble to obtain private advice from Bell without the knowledge of his government, routing correspondence through one of Macdonald's daughters in Kalimpong.[42] Under Gould, direct financial payment to influential individuals became an increasingly important aspect of the cadre's efforts to influence the Tibetans.

The Chinese had traditionally made large donations to Tibetan monasteries as part of their religious policy (although those payments had clear political implications). But the cash payments or benefits to individuals in the 1930s and '40s, whether by the Chinese or the British, greatly exceeded the traditional ethical limits of this system. After the arrival of the General Huang's mission in 1934 there was an increasing emphasis on paying influential elements of Lhasa society in return for their support. This policy was implicit rather than articulated, but its basic aim was clear: 'to keep the Tibetans happy'.[43]

In 1936-37, Gould frequently gave cash payments to Lhasa monasteries and 'certain of the officials'. By the 1940s, Lhasa mission reports detail regular payments to Tibetan officials and institutions. These proved effective, at least in the short term. When the Drepung Abbots called on the British mission for the first time in November 1942, the Lhasa Mission Head was in no doubt as to the reason for their visit, 'All this of course' he wrote, 'is due to the sum of money that has recently been placed at my disposal for distribution among monasteries.' His successor not surprisingly found his reception at Sera monastery was 'markedly friendly' after he had given the Abbots 700 rupees.[44]

The long term results were less certain. Richardson, in 1946, reported that 'Drepung is still aloof' and that 'the monasteries...have always been comparitively inaccessible to social contacts and impervious to the small contacts that are possible'. But a Drepung monastic college did claim to be the British 'protecting college', charged with providing the necessary prayers for their well-being, for which the cadre duly made necessary payment. At Sera monastery, two colleges claimed this privilege: both were given a 'a special present'.[45]

It was clearly stated that the continuance of these gifts 'depends on the maintenance of a friendly attitude on the part of the Tibetan Government', and payments were withheld when this was in doubt. After conservative elements forced the closure of an English school established in Lhasa in 1944, Gould vetoed the Lhasa mission's plan to donate 20,000 rupees to the monasteries at the annual Mönlam festival.[46]

In the absence of any other effective policy weapon, payments to individual Tibetans became the central pillar of the cadre's policy. This was never officially stated and has passed largely unnoticed by historians. The policy was essentially reactive, following the Chinese use of much greater amounts of money for the same purpose, but its great weakness was that it was not foreign aid in the official sense. Individuals profited, but the Tibetan state remained starved of funds. As Richardson later observed (although in the context of funding from wartime trade and profiteering), 'A good deal of money flowed into

Tibet during the war years, but it fell into individual hands and did not do any good to the country.'[47]

The payments which the cadre made are placed in perspective by the fact that the Chinese made similar, and larger payments. British sources record that they gave the Lhasa monasteries 80,000 rupees in December 1943. But in the later war years the British were able to supply items like kerosene and sugar which neither Chinese nor Tibetans could obtain. They also offered customs exemptions on goods imported through India, a significant saving for Lhasa aristocrats, whose lifestyle relied on imports from China and India.[48]

After the installation of the 14th (and current) Dalai Lama in 1940, cadre officers proved to be adept at selecting gifts which would appeal to the young Lama. The Chinese representatives gave him traditional gifts; carpets, silks, and so on. But the British brought him toys, such as a pedal-car, picture books and a bicycle, and these naturally found greater favour with the young boy. Consequently, as the Dalai Lama recalled with a smile when interviewed, as a boy he was 'always excited and happy' when he heard that British officials were coming to visit him.[49]

Chapter Eleven

Gartok: Edge of Empire

Despite the focus of events in the 1904-47 period being on central Tibet, the British maintained the Gartok Trade Agency throughout that period. The Agency was established largely due to Louis Dane's concern with that area. As a young Political officer he had planned to travel to Gartok in 1884, but the Punjab government refused him permission. Dane continued to devote attention to the area when he served in Kashmir, which shared a border with western Tibet.[1]

Dane and other British Indian strategists saw western Tibet as a potential route into India for Russian influence. During the Younghuband mission Dane proposed meeting this threat by extending the Indian frontier across western Tibet to the Kunlun range. This would have involved a massive financial and military commitment and Dane must have known the proposal would be rejected. But he used a common 'forward school' policy-making tactic; suggesting an extreme policy in order to obtain a lesser aim by compromise. When the Acting Viceroy, Lord Ampthill, duly replied that 'HM Government would have a fit if we proposed anything of the kind', Dane promptly made a successful follow-up proposal for a Trade Agency at Gartok.[2]

One reason Dane's proposal attracted support was that western Tibet contained gold mines. Their existence was probably the source for early Greek reports of 'gold-digging ants'. Soon after Curzon arrived in India there were rumours that the Rothschilds, among others, were interested in investing in these mines. This lead the Government of India to obtain information on the area. But it soon became clear that although mine shafts were sunk by local miners, and nuggets of up to 350 grams had been found, the harsh conditions and lack of infrastructure made European investment impractical.[3]

Despite Dane's fears, neither Russia, nor China, ever established any significant influence in western Tibet. As only local intelligence was to be obtained, Gartok was of little interest to the cadre and the Agency remained largely peripheral to Anglo-Tibetan relations. British officers were not posted there and the early Gartok Agents had neither personal knowledge of, nor influence on, policy and events in Central Tibet. Until 1932, the Agents were not even in direct contact with the Political Officer Sikkim.

Ironically, Gartok came closest to Whitehall's ideal of a Trade Agency as the Agents' duties principally involved assisting Indian traders. But the neglect of this Agency again shows that the cadre's primary role in Tibet was political and diplomatic, and that cadre officers considered trade a low priority which could be dealt with by local employees.

The Gartok Agency was created without adequate thought for its location. At the turn of the century western Tibet was thinly populated by only 10-15,000 mainly nomadic people. It is still a forbiddingly remote area today. Purang, the regional administrative centre, was several days' journey from Gartok and the local administrators, the Jongpons, had their summer headquarters at Gargunsa, 34 miles from Gartok. Even recent maps often confuse these two towns and they were probably confused when the Agency site was chosen.[4]

Gartok was a hardship posting, probably the most remote outpost of the British Empire. The 'town', in a desolate valley, 14,240 feet above sea level, consisted of 'some fifteen squalid mud huts huddled together on damp ground in the middle of a bleak and isolated plain perpetually swept by cold winds'.[5]

The early Gartok Trade Agents lived in extreme isolation and discomfort in a three-roomed, seven foot high, mud hut, with only a medical assistant and a clerk for company. In the harsh winters they lived, as one observer put it, 'the existence of prehistoric cave men'.[6]

Gartok was also an unpopular posting with the Tibetan officials, most of whom came from Lhasa. Some feigned illness to avoid going there; others sent their servants to act for them. But they had one compensation available; there was plenty of opportunity to make money from official and unofficial taxes on traders. Free trade, which the British wanted, would have removed even that compensation and so the Jongpons tried to ignore British demands for change. As one report noted, while the Jongpon was friendly, he 'gave me the impression that he would not be inconsolable if he never saw a white man again in his life'. Two years after the 1904 treaty was signed between Britain and Tibet, the Jongpons claimed they had still not received an official copy and they used this as an excuse for refusing to comply with its terms.[7]

* * *

When the Government of India decided against posting a British officer at Gartok, it instructed the Government of the United Provinces to staff the Agency. (In 1911 it passed to the control of the Punjab Government.) But the Political Department did influence the selection of Thakur Jai Chand as the first Trade Agent at Gartok. Before the former local government employee in Lahoul was appointed in December 1904, he was interviewed by Younghusband in Simla.[8]

When Chand took up his position, a mail courier service was established to communicate with him. Gartok was so remote that his weekly reports took at least three weeks to reach Simla and as Gartok was virtually deserted, they were, of necessity, brief. Chand wrote in Urdu, but something was lost in the translation and his reports must have been received more with amusement than with interest. The medical assistant opened a dispensary which was said to be 'very popular...the daily average is about 2 patients'! Another entry noted that 'The Hospital Assistant has performed a successful eye operation. The patient can now walk'.[9]

The posting of Indian provincial officers to Gartok raised the question of whether the necessary British prestige could be maintained by local employees. One observer suggested that a British officer should make an annual visit to Gartok, 'as such a visit would improve, in the eyes of the Tibetans, the status of Thakur Jai Chand'.[10]

The first inspection visit was in 1905, by Charles Sherring, District Commissioner at Almora (accompanied by the mountaineer, Tom

Longstaff). Sherring reported optimistically that it was 'impossible to imagine a more successful visit'. But whatever merits Sherring may have had, modesty was not among them. Sherring praised his mission as an indication of how 'in dealing with ignorant barbarians the personal equation far outweighs all others'. In reality, the Jongpons had simply agreed with everything he proposed and then ignored the arrangements completely when he had left. It became clear that western Tibetan officials considered the Government of India 'a shadowy and far-off power, agreements with which can be safely ignored'.[11]

H.Calvert and W.S.Cassels, Assistant Commissioners at Kulu, visited Gartok in August 1906 and 1907, respectively. Cassel's report had a pessimistic tone; it was already apparent that Gartok was a 'dead end'. In January 1910, the abolition of the Agency was proposed, as it cost nearly 14,000 rupees per annum and brought little benefit in return. But a report arrived soon after of Chinese surveyors in Gartok. The 'Chinese threat' (and optimistic predictions for the tea trade), was used to support the need for the Agency. As this was the only report of a Chinese presence ever sent from Gartok, Chand probably invented the threat to ensure the Agency was maintained. If he did, it was certainly an act in the tradition of imperial frontiersmen.[12]

Financial and logistical problems meant that inspections of Gartok by British officers became infrequent and the inspecting officers were from the ICS, not the Political Department. In the absence of any controlling influence from the Politicals, the behaviour of the Gartok Trade Agents began to seriously threaten British prestige in this remote region.

In 1911 the Indian Bhotia traders officially complained of Chand's 'apathy and indifference to their interests'. N.C.Stiffe, District Commissioner at Almora, inspected the Agency soon after, but concluded that these traders were constantly feuding among themselves. He reported that 'I do not think the Bhotias deserve much consideration'[13]

Although the Bhotias' complaints were ignored, other problems with Chand arose. Government had discovered in 1910 that he had kept the proceeds from the sale of tea sent to Gartok to test the market for the Indian brew. He had also withheld two months wages from the *dak* runners. Ordered to Simla to explain his conduct, Chand went on leave, and then postponed his return until he was due to leave for Gartok. He was allowed to return there for the winter, but ordered to Simla as soon as the passes opened again in 1911.[14]

The government concluded that 'our Trade Agent at Gartok is a thoroughly hopeless person and quite unsuited for his appointment'. In October 1911 they appointed a new Agent, Lala Devi Das, in the hope that 'this new man will prove a better Trade Agent...He could not possibly be worse'.[15]

After Chand was dismissed, his accounts were found wanting and early in 1912, Mackworth Young ICS was sent to investigate the matter. He found that the Agent, who received a monthly salary of only 200 rupees, had appropriated various unspent allowances totalling 9,000 rupees, which he had invested in land and cattle. Chand, however, had invested shrewdly and was willing and able to repay the missing sums. Young's report displayed some sympathy for the Agent. It acknowledged the extreme discomfort of the post and recommended that the Agency be closed during the winter.[16]

Later in 1912, C.M.Collett, Deputy Commissioner Garwhal, visited Gartok. He concluded that the conditions there were 'dangerous to health and sanity and directly contributed to such irregularity as occured at the time of the late T.A.'. Collett added his support to Young's proposal, urging that 'until proper accomodation can be provided it is only common humanity to withdraw the miserable officials during the winter'.[17]

The recommendation that the Agency should be seasonal was not accepted immediately as the Punjab Government were concerned at the reported presence of Russian agents in Khotan and Kashgar. Not until 1925 was the Gartok Agent finally permitted to return to India during the winters.[18]

Lala Devi Das served from 1912-1925. While marginally more efficient than Chand, he made the fullest possible use of his travelling and personal allowances and also carried on a money-lending business. Devi Das's successor, Pala Ram, while effective in negotiating observance of the Trade Regulations, unnecessarily antagonised local officials, and was found to have 'little tact and less discrimination...an exaggerated sense of his own importance and...a petulance and lack of dignity which were unworthy of one in his position.'

Pala Ram's successor, Thakur Hyatt Singh, served a brief and unhappy term. Appointed in 1928, he gained such a bad reputation for profiteering that after his dismissal he was banned from entering Tibet. His term ended when a Tibetan official took the unusual step of writing directly to the Government of India to complain about Singh's part in a drunken brawl with local officials after they argued over a women. The Tibetan official (who was killed soon after by lightning), pointed out the threat posed to bilateral relations by the poor choice of Agents.[19]

* * *

After Collett's visit in 1912, 14 years passed before another European officer inspected the Gartok Agency. Hugh Ruttledge ICS, who later lead the 1933 Everest expedition, was accompanied by his wife, the first European women to travel in the region. Ruttledge's report was forwarded to N.C.Stiffe, by now Commissioner at Kumaon, who noted that 'the situation is exactly the same as when I was there 15 years ago; and [as] it has probably has been for several hundred years'.[20]

In 1929, E.W.Wakefield ICS was sent to inspect Gartok. His journey was not without incident. There were numerous bandits in western Tibet and Dr Kanshi Ram, the Agency Medical Officer, was fired on by a would-be robber while riding ahead of Wakefield. By the time Wakefield arrived the doctor, who was armed with a revolver, had doubled back and captured the bandit (who later received 100 lashes from the local authorities). Apart from impressing Wakefield, who recommended that Dr Ram be made Trade Agent, this also convinced him to support the requests of Indian traders for permission to carry guns with them into Tibet.[21]

Wakefield was delighted to find that one of the Jongpons was the English-speaking Mondo, one of the four Tibetans who had attended Rugby school. But Mondo, he reported, while considerate to Indian traders, was considered by his Tibetan subjects to be

> the most oppressive of a long series of tyrannical Jongpons...No means of extracting money from impoverished subjects is neglected by this avaricious Jongpon'.[22]

Wakefield, who sent off a successful application to join the Politicals during his journey, had a wide remit from the Government of India to report on the future of the Agency. He was a conscientious and sensitive observer, whose reports were far more thorough than those previously submitted. His findings were a damning indictment of the Gartok Agents. He pointed out that as the Agents were residents of the Hill States bordering western Tibet, they were invariably open to accusations of bias in favour of traders from their own clan. In addition, the neglected and poorly paid Agents had numerous opportunities to take financial advantage of their post, and most of them had done so.

Although Wakefield blamed the Agent's poor pay and conditions for their failures, his reports led the Government of India to conclude that the Agents had failed because they were not 'of the right class'. Ultimately, although the Raj needed local employees, they felt that with the rare exception of a particularly talented individual such as David Macdonald, their prestige could only be properly upheld by British officers. Local officers not trained to command at British public schools could not be expected to understand and maintain public school codes of behaviour. Consequently, when a local officer failed to maintain the required status and standards of behaviour, his failure was blamed on his race or class, whereas if a British officer failed, it was the individual who was blamed, not their class or system of training. As one Indian Foreign Secretary wrote, 'A man who does not play the game at the outposts is a traitor to our order.'[23]

Following Wakefield's report it was decided to select candidates of a higher caste than previously and to increase their pay and rank in order to enhance the prestige of the Gartok Agents. The reforms instituted were temporarily successful at least. Dr Ram was given command of the Gartok Agency and he reported that following Wakefield's visit, Tibetan officials 'understood the status of the Trade Agent'. In 1932, when Derrick Williamson made a 'demi-official' visit to western Tibet, he reported that Dr Kanshi Ram was 'an efficient, energetic and tactful officer, popular alike with British subjects and Tibetans'.[24]

Williamson was the first serving officer of the Political Department to visit Gartok and his journey marked the first step towards incorporating the Agency within the wider scheme of the cadre's plans. At Williamson's suggestion, the Gartok Agent's reports were subsequently copied directly to the Political Officer in Sikkim.[25]

Further steps were taken ten years later, when Pemba Tsering was appointed to replace Dr Ram. Basil Gould sought to link the Gartok Agency more closely with the main Agencies, and Pemba was the first Gartok Agent with experience of working in the other Trade Agencies. When he was withdrawn from Gartok during the winters he returned to Gangtok and in the winter of 1943-44 he served as Trade Agent Yatung.

In 1942, the Gartok Agency was finally brought under the control of the Political Officer Sikkim and the Gyantse Trade Agent, Captain Ken Saker, was sent to inspect the Agency (suggesting that Saker was seen as a potential Sikkim Political Officer).[26] Saker's report, however, suggests that the improvements that had been made had not lasted long. He found that 'the position of the British Trade Agent has gradually deteriorated'.[27]

The Gartok Agency was never of any real importance to the Raj. It was of value only in the sense that the British had obtained the right to maintain a Trade Agency in western Tibet and were determined to exercise that right in order to maintain British prestige in the Himalayas.[28] Yet financial economies, the poor choice of Agents and the failure to support the better Agents meant that Gartok did little for the Raj's prestige.

In retrospect, it is clear that a reasoned analysis of the 'Russian threat' – the original justification for the creation of the Agency – would have seen the British reject the idea of a representative in western Tibet. Had there been a more conscientious effort by Rawling's mission to investigate condition there, they would have realised that the Agency would be of little use. Even with better information and planning the Agency might have been located at the picturesque and certainly more hospitable town of Purang. Instead, a series of local employees suffered a miserable existence on the edge of empire for the sake of prestige.

Chapter Twelve

'Keeping the Tibetans happy'

The British Mission Lhasa was housed at Dekyi Lingka, where the Union Jack flew above the building. When the Gould mission departed in February 1937, Richardson and Radio Officer Dagg remained there. Dagg was soon replaced by 'Reggie' Fox, whose call sign AC4YN became a popular target for amateur radio operators around the world.

Richardson was relieved in July 1937 by Norbu Dhondup, later returning for a year in 1938-39. Gould made a second visit to Lhasa in 1940 to attend the installation of the 14th Dalai Lama and there were occasional visits by other British officials such as the Gyantse Agents, Thornburgh and Saker. While even the most world-weary officers were initially excited at reaching the fabled city of Lhasa, they soon found that 'one grows blasé re ordinary sights'. There was, as Richardson reported, 'not much work and plenty of time for reading, walking and the occasional swim in the river'.[1]

In the 1940s, World War Two seemed remote. In 1914 both the Dalai and Panchen Lamas had offered prayers for a British victory, and the Dalai Lama had offered the British a thousand Tibetan troops, but now the young 14th Dalai Lama prayed for world peace generally. The course of the war was actually 'a matter of more or less indifference' to the Tibetans, although they appreciated that the Sino-Japanese conflict prevented China from devoting her attention to Tibet.[2]

Tibet remained neutral throughout the war, but despite her determination to chart an independent course in foreign policy, came under considerable pressure from Britain, China and America to assist their cause. The Allies wanted to send supplies from India to China via

Tibet, but the Tibetans saw that this offered opportunities for China to station officials in their territory, and they initially refused to co-operate.

Norbu Dhondup negotiated this issue for the British, but he shared the Tibetans' fear that it would increase access to Tibet. Whereas he had always supported 'forward' policies in the past, this time his heart was not in it. As Gould recalled, until he was ordered to obtain permission for this 'Trans-Tibet Transport' scheme, Norbu, 'brought up in the straight-minded school of Bell, had never...attempted to persuade the Tibetans to believe anything of which he was not himself convinced'. Norbu's failure to gain approval for the opening of this supply route led to his being replaced in Lhasa in April 1942 by the former Gyantse Headmaster, Frank Ludlow.[3] Norbu was then close to retirement age and reverted to being Trade Agent Yatung for six months before retiring. He died of tuberculosis just over a year later.

Ludlow was appointed to Lhasa because of war-time manpower shortages in the Political Department. While he had no administrative experience, his background was typical of Politicals and as Gyantse school-teacher his sensitive and tactful approach to Tibetan matters had made him *persona grata* at Lhasa. Ludlow, by a 'judicious blend of bribes and threats of economic sanctions',[4] persuaded the Regent to allow the passage of non-military supplies to China. The Tibetans controlled the transport of these supplies, and their traders were able to make vast profits from the system.

This politicking was not to Ludlow's taste, however, and after a year he was replaced as Head of Mission by his old friend from the Kashgar Consulate, Major George Sherriff, whose wife Betty accompanied him. Although he often found Tibetan ways frustrating, Sherriff's open and straightforward character won him many friends in Lhasa. Having private means, he could afford to take a more independent line than most of his contemporaries, and earlier in his career he had resigned from the Political Department, only returning during the war to 'do his bit'. Sherriff served in Lhasa for two years (with Hugh Richardson relieving him for three months mid-term) before failing a medical, whereupon Pemba Tsering took over the mission.

A Medical Officer, officially termed the Civil Surgeon Bhutan and Tibet, was based at the Lhasa mission after 1940. As in Gyantse and Yatung, most of his work involved treating local people for venereal diseases and bites by the ubiquitous Tibetan guard dogs. The Civil Surgeons were a mixed bunch. Lieutenant-Colonel Hislop, who had accompanied Bailey to Lhasa in 1924, 'survived drinking more at high altitude than was previously thought possible'. But Major James Guthrie, though inclined to use his command of Tibetan to say what his superiors considered 'the most stupid and senseless things', had a great empathy with the Tibetans. Guthrie was given considerable responsibility as the only senior British officer in Lhasa during Pemba Tsering's first months in charge of the mission.[5]

Among Gurthrie's varied tasks in Lhasa was an operation to remove a cyst from the eye of one of the Dalai Lama's peacocks. The worried young Dalai Lama watched the operation and he remembers that Guthrie assured him, in the three forms of Tibetan speech, inferior, regular, and honorific, 'Don't worry, it will not die.'[6]

Conditions were far from ideal for medical work, but a new hospital was built in Lhasa in the 1940s. This replaced the converted barn which Weir's Medical Officer had described as 'an "Aviary"... though why the sparrows should choose such dark and insanitary quarters I cannot imagine'.[7]

The new hospital was designed by the British, but paid for by the Tibetans, whose attitude to Western medical practice had undergone a sea change since 1904. Originally there had been considerable opposition to Western medicine, particularly from monastic medical practitioners, who lost much of their custom, and hence fees. But the greater efficiency of modern science won over the general populace, not least because the British provided treatment free of charge. That was a deliberate strategy. In November 1904, Younghusband had observed that the Gyantse dispensary, 'is extremely desirable on political grounds' and this point was regularly made by the cadre in their reports on the Medical Officers.[8]

Modern medicine was a means by which the imperial power could gain goodwill among all social classes, and generate a positive attitude to modernity. It also became part of the struggle for influence in Tibet after China opened a hospital in Lhasa in 1944. Gould warned that 'Chinese competition in medical work calls for a high standard of work from us'.[9]

Despite the presence of the Civil Surgeons at Lhasa, the Gyantse Medical Officer continued to accompany Political Officers on visits to the capital. Thus Gould, in 1944, and Hopkinson in 1946, were both accompanied by Dr M.V.Kurian from the Gyantse Agency. Kurian was another who enjoyed Tibetan service, and he was offered the post of Trade Agent Gartok by Indian Foreign Minister K.P.S.Menon in the 1950s, but his married status forced him to decline.[10]

An increasing number of Gyantse Trade Agency staff were able to visit Lhasa; Captain Allen Robins, for example, Escort Commander and Acting Trade Agent Gyantse, accompanied Hopkinson's mission in 1945. A kindly and generous man, his attitude to Tibet was typical of most of his contemporaries, 'my sympathies', he recalled, 'were entirely with the people'.[11]

Robins' attitude matched that of Arthur Hopkinson, who replaced Gould as Political Officer Sikkim in June 1945, having previously served as Gyantse Trade Agent for 15 months in 1927-28. Gould had been permitted to extend his term at Gangtok on a number of occasions because of war-time shortages of staff, but remained at his post for too long. In 1944-45, he suffered a mental and physical decline; although he later recovered. Hopkinson was brought to Gangtok to train as his replacement in 1943 and waited patiently for promotion. He managed to avoid upsetting his increasingly temperamental superior and when Gould finally departed, Hopkinson wrote with characteristic humility

> I think BJ [Gould] was a great man with big ideas, who stayed on just a little too long, and if I could do half of what he did here, I should be well pleased.[12]

Gould's decline was symptomatic of a wider malaise. In 1946-47, the Chinese communist threat had yet to emerge fully, and the cadre were primarily concerned to train their Indian successors for the usual struggle for influence vis-à-vis the Chinese in Lhasa. By then it was obvious that there was little future for the imperial presence in the East. While Richardson was young and energetic, older officers who had not had leave during the war were 'worn out'. Hopkinson wrote that

> Everything seems to be held together by a boot-lace, and all the people I should normally rely on are either going potty or taking to drink or opium or [are] otherwise incapacitated.[13]

During his visit to Lhasa in 1945-46, Hopkinson did have a well-regarded assistant in Gangtok, Stephen (later Sir Stephen) Olver, one of the last British entrants into the Political Department, but the cadre had to cope with the fact that many of their government officials were 'moribund...intent on their next jobs'. Within Tibet they faced a 'get-rich-quick' atmosphere, as well as renewed threat from China.[14]

Some observers found; Hopkinson a less commanding figure than a Political Officer was generally expected to be, but his reports were incisive and his vision extended beyond the immediate concerns of cadre and empire. With British power in the East rapidly declining, Hopkinson was an appropriately thoughtful, even philosophical figure. One observer recalls him as a man 'with a vast calm and humble vision...the kind of calm that a Chinese sage might have' and quotes him as soliloquising.

> Just look at what we are reduced to, after being lords of half the earth...that's how it is. You come into the world, you dance according to the music, and then the time comes for you to go. That applies to empires and individuals.[15]

With Lhasa becoming less-and-less a 'forbidden city', and communications improved, the conditions the cadre faced were a little easier than they had been in the days of White and O'Connor. There was still no electricity, roads remained appallingly bad and the food was monotonous. But women were now permitted to reside in Gyantse, although Gould drew the line at allowing women more than visiting rights to the Mess.

Another woman who attracted considerable attention on the frontier at that time was the Maharaja of Sikkim's daughter, Princess Pema Tsudeun, better known as Coo-Coo la. She was a women of beauty, charm, intelligence, vitality...long lashes...[who] slowly exhaled the smoke of a cigarette...[and had] a low clear musical voice...[She was] subtly devastating.[16]

The cosmopolitan Coo-Coo la charmed a generation of frontiersmen and she proved to have courage as well as charm. During civil strife in Sikkim in the 1970s she stood guard at the Maharaja's palace, cradling a machine-gun.[17]

* * *

The establishment of a permanent British mission in Lhasa inevitably opened the Tibetan capital to the outside world. No Europeans had visited Lhasa for 15 years after Younghusband's mission and between 1920 and 1935 there were only 25 such visitors. But from 1936-1950, 57 Europeans made their first visit to Lhasa, and many returned.[18]

All but a handful of these visitors were British officials. The cadre generally favoured excluding others, but to an extent they were caught between the conflicting desires of Tibet's isolationist conservative class and the outside world, which wanted access to the 'Forbidden City'.

Unauthorised visits to Tibet had been formally banned in 1873, with the introduction of the Bengal Eastern Frontier Regulations. While permitting the continuance of traditional local cross-border travel, this law barred non-official travellers from entering Tibetan territory. Travellers required government permission to cross designated 'Inner Lines' set back from the border. But restricting access to Tibet only increased its allure to Western travellers.

Individuals and institutions such as the Royal Geographical Society hoped that the Younghusband mission signalled the opening of Tibet to foreign travellers. But the cadre, aware of the strength of Tibetan opposition to this, and fearing Russians could then enter the country, continued to discourage most individuals who sought to go there.

Following Bell's recommendation that the restrictions be gradually eased, the cadre implemented a compromise. Visitors would be permitted to travel on the trade route to Gyantse, but the number and type of visitors would be controlled. The Tibetan Government continued to object to the number of Europeans admitted, but the

Government of India was always sensitive to criticism that it encouraged Tibet's isolation. Consequently they tried to control, rather than to totally prevent, access.

Right of entry to Lhasa, or places away from the trade route, such as Shigatse, remained tightly controlled. Tibetan approval was required for these visits, and the Governments of India and Tibet regularly played out an elaborate charade, in which each claimed the other was refusing access. In fact, apart from a handful of visitors who obtained an invitation directly from the Tibetan authorities, permission to visit Lhasa was obtained through unofficial representations by the cadre to the Tibetan Government. They usually admitted travellers whose applications were supported by the cadre, and always gave permission for British officers. This system enabled the cadre to ensure that travellers who came in contact with the Lhasa authorities were of the 'right type'.[19]

The Government of India had legitimate reasons for seeking some control over European entry to Tibet. They wanted to keep out known criminals and those seeking to exploit Tibetan ignorance of the outside world. Unauthorised individuals could create incidents such as that involving an American 'adventurer' in 1907, who shot a tribesman in eastern Tibet in a dispute over money.[20]

In addition to the criminal element, however, there was another class of visitor the cadre opposed. The usually perceptive Teichman supported the opening of Tibet to visitors and concluded that 'once the novelty of the thing had worn off none would want to go there but Indian traders and wool buyers'. But Teichman greatly underestimated Tibet's appeal.[21]

Tibet attracted large numbers of Europeans who were outside the mainstream of their own culture, the culture which the cadre were attempting to present in the most positive light. Large numbers of religious seekers (particularly Theosophists), eccentrics, adventurers, and even the mentally disturbed, sought to enter Tibet. Such individuals were unlikely to present the image of Europeans which the cadre sought to project and were thus seen as a threat. This 'threat' grew as the number of visitors in the 1920s and '30s increased.

The cadre were particularly concerned with travellers' dress and mode of travel. They strongly objected to a Swiss traveller with 'only' two coolies who borrowed bedding from the *dak* bungalow *chowkidars* as 'Such conduct...lowers the prestige of foreigners'.[22] Even in the 1930s they felt that,

> while nowadays no one expects to see a Curzonian frock coat in the middle of a desert, it is a pity that occasionally even Englishmen should travel...looking like sweeps.[23]

Again, prestige was a very important factor in the cadre's attitude. For them, the ideal visitor was of a particular type, whose bearing and behaviour emulated that of cadre officers. Such travellers were considered of 'a type which many other tourists would do well to emulate'.[24]

From the perspective of officers whose contact with women was restricted throughout school, university and colonial posting, female travellers were a particular threat to British prestige. Ludlow, noting the visit of one 'weird lady', wrote that 'we do get some funny people as visitors. All the women seem to be only too glad of an excuse to wear puttees and breeches all day long.' Richardson considered it 'particularly undesirable that European ladies should live in the servants quarters of *dak* bungalows'. To counter this problem, Gould decreed that female travellers were not permitted to travel in Tibet without a male escort. This was even applied to cadre officers' wives, although, in the case of the Politicals, they had been socially assessed by the Viceroy, along with their husbands.[25]

These restrictions were of dubious value. There is no evidence that the Tibetan authorities were likely to think less of the British when women travelled cheaply or alone. Both were common within Tibetan society. They were far more concerned that European women, like men, would affect their culture; as shown by the ban on 'bobbed hair and foreign style shoes' which the Tibetan Government sought to impose on women in 1946.[26]

The cadre's attitude to religious seekers in Tibet was ambivalent. Travellers who were sympathetic and respectful to Buddhism were less liable to upset local sentiments. Many of the cadre officers themselves were also personally, as well as professionally, interested in Tibetan religion, and were not untouched by the attractions of the wider shores of Tibetan mysticism. Nonetheless they were brought up with a belief in scientific lines of enquiry. When a traveller such as the American, Theos Bernard, visited Lhasa in 1937 as a student of Buddhism, his exotic dress and manner were not unacceptable. But when he claimed to be the incarnation of an important religious figure and to have participated in 'secret ceremonies', British (and Tibetan) support for him vanished.[27]

The crucial issue, however, was political. The dress and bearing of religious seekers could be distinct from that of other Europeans without threatening British prestige, for such distinctness was characteristic within local society. Those whose actions did not alienate the Tibetans, and whose later writings and speeches were likely to avoid discussing Himalayan politics, were considered acceptable.[28] But if these seekers became at all involved in political issues, they became *persona non grata* with the British, and generally with the Tibetans also.

For the cadre, the ideal traveller was one whose character and behaviour were of the type thought necessary to uphold European prestige, and one whose visit would further British interests in Tibet in some way. Although non-British travellers were generally discouraged, the epitome of the ideal traveller was considered to be the Italian, Professor Giuseppe Tucci, a colourful character who made a number of visits to Tibet.

Tucci, already an eminent scholar when he first applied to visit Tibet in the 1920s, cultivated good relations with important British officials such as Basil Gould and the Indian Foreign Secretary, E.B.Howell. He gave them detailed reports of his travels, including maps and copies of his books, and he took care not to transgress the frontier travel regulations. He also had considerable personal funds. This, together with his professed Buddhism, ensured that he established good relations with the Tibetans. The Government of India supported Tucci's travels throughout the 1930s, even after another Tibetologist, Marco Pallis, had written to Delhi criticising Tucci's removal of large numbers of artifacts from Tibet. Tucci responded to Pallis's criticism by advising the Tibetan Government to set up a Department of Antiquities which would, among other duties, prevent the removal of artifacts from Tibet! The Government of India was inclined to accept that, until that happened, the artifacts were better off in Tucci's keeping.[29]

In 1946, Britain and Italy were still technically at war and Tucci had lost his chair at Rome University for supporting Mussolini. In the circumstances, cadre support for him was more circumspect. When he applied to visit Lhasa, Richardson was not prepared to support the Italian officially. But he suggested to Tucci that he send eight copies of his latest book, 'for distribution as ground bait' to Tibetan officials. Tucci did so and duly got approval for another expedition. As the cadre acknowledged, Tucci's researches were 'a valuable contribution towards...our main aim of policy viz. that Tibet always has had, and continues to have, a separate national existence'.[30]

Although they supported Tucci, the cadre were generally reluctant to allow non-British travellers into Tibet. They saw foreign travellers as representatives of their native government. As the interests of Japan, France, Germany, America, Russia and China (who provided the bulk of non-British travellers), were not normally synonymous with those of the British in Tibet, foreign visitors were viewed with great suspicion. Non-British travellers with sufficient backing in official circles, along with a few wealthy individuals who obtained an invitation directly from the Tibetans, did reach Lhasa, but a close watch was kept on those who entered from India. Travellers needed to employ local caravan personnel, such as guides and syces, and the cadre could generally arrange for some of these men to provide information on their employers.[31]

After McGovern's clandestine visit in 1923, the greatest problem posed to the cadre by visitors to Lhasa occured in 1938-39. A five-man German expedition, under the command of Dr Ernst Schäfer, applied to the British for permission to visit Tibet. Schäfer had previously travelled in the eastern Tibetan border regions and was a respected zoologist and botanist. Lord Astor acted as the German's contact in London, and assured Whitehall that their visit was for purely scientific purposes. The British Ambassador in Berlin, however, reported that the German press were describing it in different terms. They reported it as an expedition under the patronage of SS leader Himmler, which would be carried through 'entirely on SS principles'.[32]

Nazi German attitudes to Tibet were ambivalent. While some considered the country and its religion part of a 'yellow conspiracy' aimed at world domination, other Nazi theorists saw Tibetans as part of the Aryan peoples, albeit much degraded. Schäfer belonged in the latter camp and obtained support as the establishment of contacts with Tibet generally furthered Nazi German aims because it threatened the interests of British India.[33]

When Schäfer's party applied to the Government of India for permission to visit Lhasa, Gould simply informed them that Tibet refused to allow them entry. But this was the time of 'appeasement'. Gould was told that it was considered 'politically desirable to do anything possible to remove any impression that we have put obstacles in Schäfer's way'. Gould arranged permission for the expedition to travel in Sikkim and Nepal, in the hope that would satisfy them. Admiral Sir Barry Domville, a Nazi sympathizer, then wrote to British Prime Minister Neville Chamberlain, claiming to be a friend of Himmler's. He forwarded a letter in which Himmler suggested that British failure to support Schäfer's visit to Lhasa had

> given rise to the thought that...there is no point in treating British subjects in Germany in a comradely way, since on the other side such treatment has not the slightest echo.

Schäfer's party was given permission to visit Gyantse and Gould referred their request to visit Lhasa to the Tibetans. He asked his government if the request should be left 'to the free discretion of the Tibetan Government' or whether the Lhasa mission 'should be instructed to exert influence, if necessary, to obtain the desired permission'.

In Lhasa, Hugh Richardson strongly objected to asking permission for Schäfer's party to visit. The Government of India sympathised but this was obviously a matter beyond their control. The Viceroy, uniquely, sent Richardson a personal telegram stating

I have to ask you to do what you are asked because the Foreign Office have been approached by Himmler, and it is his special wish that the mission should go ahead.[34]

The cadre duly arranged permission for Schäfer's party to visit Lhasa for a fortnight. They arrived on 19 January 1939 and were able to extend their stay for several months. They found natural allies in the Chinese mission, which allowed the Germans to use their wireless. Richardson reported that Schäfer's party were denigrating the British and telling the Tibetans that Germany was the most powerful nation on earth. Gould, increasingly suspicious of their intentions, arranged that Schäfer's permission to visit Nepal after Tibet be rescinded. The Nepalese did so on the pretext that there was no accomodation available!

The cadre kept as close a watch on the Germans as possible. Some of their servants were reporting back to the cadre, and as they had to use the British-Indian postal system for all their mail, the British were able to read it. One discovery was a letter from Himmler to Schäfer which referred to 'this expedition by SS men', and ended with the postscript 'I think of you often'.

Although they initially saw them as a great threat, the cadre soon found that Schäfer was not winning many friends. His party were stoned by monks at the *Mönlam* festival for taking photos too blatantly and it emerged that they had upset communities along the road to Lhasa by openly killing wildlife and ill-treating their local servants.

The German expedition was also seriously affected by Schäfer's personal problems. He had accidentally shot and killed his wife shortly before he left Germany and was 'affected mentally'. He formed a relationship with one of his local servants, a youth referred to in the files as 'Kaiser', the son of the Political Officer Sikkim's Head Clerk. Schäfer wanted to take him back to Germany and on his return to India made a series of emotional pleas to various British officials to allow Kaiser to accompany him. Gould concluded that Schäfer was

> forceful, volatile, scholarly, vain, disrespectful of social convention... and the feelings of others...almost a high priest of Nazism...Schäfer's habit with his employees is to pay them well and beat them often... We are all inclined to think that the gentle Kaiser had some sort of special appeal for the dominant Schäfer.

As the Government of India feared that Kaiser could become a Nazi sympathiser, he was not permitted to leave Sikkim and Schäfer and his party returned home without him. A little over a month later, Britain and Germany were at war and Schäfer's mission was largely forgotten. Richardson was delighted to be able to report that the visit had unexpectedly brought 'results of lasting value to us...they created an unfavourable impression in Lhasa...and by contrast heightened our prestige.'[35]

World War Two brought unexpected visitors to Lhasa. On the night of 30 November 1943, a plane was heard flying over Lhasa. This had never happened before and monks had predicted a grim fate for anyone breaching the prohibition on looking down on the Dalai Lama. The monks were right in this instance; news followed that the plane had crashed near Samye monastery, south-east of Lhasa. The British mission sent medical assistant Bo Tsering to investigate.

The aircraft turned out to be a US Airforce B-24 bomber, which had lost its way en route from China to India. The pilot, Lieutenant Robert E.Crozier of Waco, Texas, along with his four crew members, had survived the crash. They were brought to Lhasa and welcomed at the British mission by George and Betty Sherriff, before being sent on to India. A popular account of their adventures was later published, and revealed that in Lhasa they were stoned by a local mob, angry that they had overflown the Tibetan capital. But as Tibet was a British ally, that news was censored at the time.[36]

In January 1946, two Austrians, Henrich Harrer and Peter Aufschnaiter, reached Lhasa after escaping from a wartime internment camp in India and making an exhausting journey through western Tibet. The cadre were initially suspicious, but eventually concluded that they were politically harmless. They gave up their attempts to persuade the Tibetans to deport them to India, and the two escapees remained until 1950. They found work with the Tibetan Government and Harrer later wrote a best-selling account of his experiences, entitled *Seven Years in Tibet*.[37]

* * *

The search for information had remained a priority for the cadre since the days of Younghusband and O'Connor. Although there are no breakdowns of Secret Service expenditure in official records after 1909, private papers show that Secret Service funds continued to be used to pay local informants. In 1944, for example, Gyantse Trade Agent Mainprice refers to giving a 'Secret Service' payment of 450 rupees. In addition, Indian archives confirm that what the Government of India itself termed 'Secret Agent(s)' were still used to report on Tibet in the 1940s.[38]

Governments are naturally reluctant to admit they spy on their allies. British sources claim that the open nature of Tibetan aristocratic society meant information was freely obtainable in Lhasa.[39] Nevertheless, there was an ongoing use of 'secret agents' by the British throughout the period of their involvement in Tibet; but once the system had been established there was no further need to articulate it.

There was, however, a reorganisation of intelligence gathering in the 1936-37 period, soon after Gould and Richardson took up their posts. The relevant archives remain classified, but it is possible to reconstruct the effect of these changes from scattered references to intelligence on the north-eastern frontier.[40] Much of the responsibility for collecting information in the region apparently shifted from the Political Officer Sikkim to the Central Intelligence Officer in Shillong (Assam).

The Central Intelligence Bureau was created by Lord Curzon in April 1904 and placed under the Home Affairs Department of the Government of India. It liased closely with the Political Department; after 1944 all telegrams concerning Tibetan affairs were copied to the CIB's Shillong office. That post was headed during the 1940s by an Irish police officer, Eric Lambert, who had travelled extensively in north-east India. After 1946, Lambert was given an assistant based in Kalimpong, specifically to deal with Tibetan affairs. Lambert's chosen assistant was Lieutenant Lha Tsering, the son of Bell's early confidant, A-chuk Tsering.[41]

Lambert's office became an important influence on Tibetan policy in the 1940s, and the close links between Lambert and the Political

Officer Sikkim show that they shared similar aims. In September 1944, for example, Lambert recommended an increase in government contributions to Tibetan monasteries, a policy which the cadre strongly supported.[42]

To increase support to the monasteries, however, the cadre needed more money, which they could not get from their government. Arthur Hopkinson found the means to finance the increased payments recommended in Lambert's 1944 proposal. He formed a syndicate for the procurement of cotton cloth in Bombay and sold it under license. The licenses to procure cloth under this system were allocated to Tibetans 'on account of...[their]...supposed position or supposed political usefulness past or future'.[43]

The licenses were transferable, meaning the recipients could immediately sell them to established traders at a considerable profit. Richardson, in Lhasa, was 'constantly being besieged by people who wanted a quota'. He recalls that

> Hopkinson also quite unofficially took a proportion of the profits somehow... and established a Tibetan 'cess' fund...and then we used that 'cess' fund for keeping the Tibetans happy.[44]

The 'cess' fund was not normally referred to in official records, except when it was ended in 1947. The balance of the fund, 11,398 rupees, was deposited with the Tibetan Government so that an annual payment of one *trangka* per monk could be made from the interest.[45]

Hopkinson's explanation of the purpose of the quota system policy was that

> through the system of cloth procurement...we have deliberately set out to demonstrate to the Tibetans the economic and commercial advantages of the connection with India; in order that, when changes should come, the economic and commercial bonds should hold firm.[46]

The 'cess' fund was a significant step. The generation of revenue by officials in any empire enables them to act outside government policy and hence outside their control. The cadre had finally taken this step in the complete absence of any support from Whitehall for the policies they favoured.

Although the British were withdrawing from government in India, Hopkinson's aims were fundamentally consistent with those of Curzon and Younghusband; to draw Tibet into a closer relationship with India. But Hopkinson introduced a note of moral caution. He observed that

> The Trans-Tibet Transport system (which we imposed on [an] at first unwilling Tibet at the instance of China)...created a get-rich-quick atmosphere that tended to debauch and demoralise Tibetans.[47]

This was not the only reference to a decline in the moral climate of Tibet at that time. It may have been typical of their system that, in the absence of a ruling Dalai Lama, there would be a decline in the spiritual emphasis in society, but in the 1940s this decline was greatly accentuated by Anglo-Chinese rivalry. The Two Regents in the 1933-48 period were themselves open to bribery and, as Richardson reported, 'govt.[sic] here is rather uncouth...most of them heavily involved in trade...under pressure of Chinese bribery'.[48]

British sources describing the colourful social life of the Tibetan aristocracy in the 1933-47 period can be read as a discourse on spiritual decline and aristocratic decadence which offers a strong contrast to the expected image of a theocratic society. The British certainly contributed to this decline through their policy of profiting individuals, as did the Chinese, to the ultimate benefit of the Chinese Communists.

Tibet's religious identity implied and articulated the privileging of certain ethical and humanitarian qualities. The 13th Dalai Lama, on his accession to power in 1895, proclaimed that the Tibetans' Buddhist character gave them such virtues as 'compassionate hospitality'.[49] There may have been an idealisation of these virtues, but later cadre officers, such as Richardson and Hopkinson, saw in the social structure they observed, a system with genuine merits. That system deeply challenged the value of their own society, and they regretted that Tibet's encounter with modernity threatened the survival of the qualities which both parties defined as essential aspects of 'Tibet' and 'Tibetan'.

Hopkinson was particularly concerned that the encounter with modern culture had brought 'the worst aspects of capitalism' to Tibet. He realised that reforms had often had consequences very different from those intended by the cadre. When they encouraged education, for example, they intended it to strengthen Tibetan identity. Frank Ludlow had been determined to ensure that pupils at his Gyantse school 'adhere to their own customs'. But when British-style schools in Tibet failed to survive conservative opposition, some Tibetans began sending their children to schools in India. Those schools, however, gave them ideas which had been

> founded on the underlying idea of [the] racial, religious or cultural superiority of the Vatican or Salt Lake City to the Potala.

Hopkinson considered these schools 'set out, with the kindliest of motives, ultimately to demoralise [the Tibetan pupils and to teach them]...to despise their own country'.[50]

In addition to his concern with the political implications of this issue, Hopkinson also began to question the accepted ethical values underlying the imperial process. Noting, 'the happiness, contentment, self-sufficiency, and liberty' of its people, he concluded that 'the modern world has more to learn from Tibet than to teach [it]'. There were always imperial elements which believed that contact with Western civilisation would be beneficial. White had argued that 'the more Tibetans come into contact with Europeans the better' and in the late 1940s, Hopkinson noted how 'One important diplomatic lady in Delhi said to me "Of course I'm going [to Tibet]; it is good for them".' But, he concluded, 'The Tibetans take a different view.'[51]

Hopkinson's comments, on the eve of the British departure from Tibet, reflect his own values, as well as the characteristic identification of imperial officials with the peoples among whom they lived and worked. His conclusion was also a significant development, representing a view diametrically opposed to that of the prevailing ethos at the time of the foundation of the Trade Agencies. The British encounter with Tibet, begun in hostility, had ended in respect, and even esteem, for the indigenous culture.

The cadre had grown up with the idea that British imperial expansion was a 'civilising mission'. Consequently they had a genuine desire to help Tibet progress and made personal as well as official attempts to help the country and its people. In the 1920s, for instance, Ludlow (whose wages from the Tibetan Government did not cover his expenses there) personally paid the fees of Tibetan boys studying telegraphy in Kalimpong. After his departure, Williamson and later Bailey continued to meet these costs from their own pocket.[52]

Later cadre officers did not oppose change *per se*, but they understood that the majority of Tibetans were conservative and resistant to innovation, so deliberately 'adopted a conservative policy of making haste slowly'.[53] By excluding missionaries and other agents of change, the cadre tried to preserve the country's stability. Through their opposition to the introduction of European dress and modes of thinking, they also attempted to preserve existing Tibetan identity. But they could not control the pace of change, and Tibet's exposure to the modern world increasingly destroyed their hopes.

The cadre's concern partly reflected a similar attitude within Tibetan society. The alliance of interests between the cadre and their local supporters naturally meant that threats to one group were regarded with concern by the other. This was a two-way process, the Lhasa ruling classes also identified with British aspirations. They feared, for example, Gandhi's influence and the possible resulting instability in India.[54]

As the empire came to an end and the cadre looked back, they began to have doubts as to which was the superior society. When the 'men on the spot' had been able to influence policy they had identified more closely with the goals of their government. Now that power had been taken by Whitehall, the frontiersmen identified less closely with those aims, and increasingly questioned Whitehall's policies and their results.

The cadre did not publicly express their concern over Tibet's moral climate until after they had left. That concern did not support the image of Tibet which the British were trying to project, nor did it reflect well on their influence. When a concern for morality did emerge into the public sphere, it was for a political purpose: a concern to gain the moral high ground vis-a-vis Communist China.

This was a deliberate strategy. After the Communists took power in China, Richardson was aware that

> It is merely a question of when the Communists choose to come... The only possible line I can recommend for the government to pursue is to arouse moral feelings for Tibet.

China's subsequent military invasion enabled the Tibetan Government-in-exile to appeal to morality and justice. They have never relinquished that claim and it has become the primary weapon of the Tibetan independence movement.[55]

Sympathy for Tibetan aspirations left the cadre 'unspeakably sad' when it became obvious that Tibet was unlikely to be accepted as an independent nation-state in the post-war community of nations.[56] This concern was genuine. The survivors of the British period in Tibet, such as Hugh Richardson and Radio Officer Robert Ford, remain active in the Tibetan cause.

Chapter Thirteen

'They've all got something special about them'

The distinct character of the Tibet cadre has long been recognised. Alastair Lamb refers to an 'apostolic succession' of Sikkim Political Officers. Premen Addy exalted this 'band of intrepid political officers...schooled in the certainties of Victorian values...who served their country with distinction'. Robert Ford, a first-hand observer, described cadre officers as being 'in the mould'; while some outsiders thought 'they've all got something odd about them', those involved with Tibet felt that 'they've all got something special about them'.[1]

We have seen that the collective character of the cadre was deliberately cultivated by the educational process they went through.[2] These formative influences remained with them, but once they were in Tibet other factors affected their character and outlook; particular types of personality thrived, or failed. What then were those characteristics and what factors shaped their thinking?

Theoretically, any Political officer could be sent to Tibet, but in practice the Secretariat usually sent officers who wanted to serve there and who had been recommended by the Political Officer Sikkim. Gould, for example, asked for Richardson to be posted to Gyantse, knowing he was interested in Tibet. Thus just as patronage governed entry to the Political Department, it governed entry to Tibet. Several Political officers who wanted to serve there were not selected because they lacked any backing from a cadre officer.[3]

This selection system was designed to ensure a continuity of attitude and hence of policy among cadre officers. It was also necessary to ensure that suitable trained candidates were available for the senior post in Sikkim. As early as 1905, in recommending that Bailey relieve him while he was on leave, O'Connor pointed out the 'extreme importance of training one or more young officers as experts in Tibetan affairs'. This point continued to be made by the cadre. As late as 1948 Hopkinson recommended 'the training of a succession of officer-Cadets[sic] to form a future supply'.[4]

In 1912, government agreed that

> If we keep Gyantse as a training ground, we should generally have an officer who has sufficient experience of the Border and knowledge of the language to be appointed Political Agent[sic] Sikkim and Bhutan.[5]

All of the officers subsequently appointed to the Sikkim post were former Gyantse Trade Agents.

The most successful and influential cadre officers were those who wanted to serve there; officers who preferred the Indian States to the frontier were less likely to succeed in Tibet. Surviving letters indicating posting preferences show that Bailey, Gould and Williamson (who was 'keenly interested in Central Asia and Tibet') were among those who specifically wanted a post in Tibet. In 1928 Hokinson, about to get married, asked for a post suitable for a couple, such as Mysore or Kashmir. But he noted how happy he had been in Gyantse, and how he hoped with seniority to aspire to Gangtok or Kabul.[6]

Two Gyantse Agents whose careers were less than successful, Majors Rivett-Carnac and M.C.Sinclair, both preferred service in the Indian states. Russell and Battye favoured respectively the Persian Gulf and Baluchistan to service in Tibet. The cadre's belief that they needed men keen to serve in Tibet was correct.

* * *

Cadre officers and frontiersmen generally, believed that the frontiers of India were a zone requiring particular personal qualities from those who served there. They drew a distinction between the type of person best suited for service in India and those best suited for service in Tibet. Administration in India was associated with bureaucracy; service on the frontier had a tradition of freedom of action. As Bell wrote, 'A man, efficient in administrative work in India...is not always the best for Tibet, and Hopkinson repeated this 'truism uttered by Bell' in his final report from Gangtok. Tibetan frontiersmen could not, they believed, be bound by 'rules and regulations framed to meet...Indian conditions'.[7]

There was, however, a significant element of expediency in postings to Tibet, particularly in the case of Agency technical and support staff. But the Politicals also faced problems with wartime manpower shortages, officers on leave, getting married, falling ill, or being deputed on special missions; such as Bailey's surveying expedition in Assam in 1913, which precluded his return to Gyantse. Last-minute changes of posting were also commonplace. Richardson was sent to Lhasa instead of Kashgar in 1945, while Mainprice was diverted from Gangtok to Lohit (Assam) ten days after his first appointment as Trade Agent Gyantse in 1943.[8]

In the early years, personnel shortages were solved by doubling up control of the Gyantse and Yatung Agencies; between 1918 and 1936 they were under joint command. But the distance between them generally meant one or other position was neglected, although the system was popular with the Agents as they received 300 rupees a month extra pay.[9] A more successful alternative seems to have been to appoint as Acting Trade Agent Gyantse, either the Medical Officer (as in 1909 and 1926), or the Escort Commander (in 1929 and on six occasions in the 1940s).

Particularly careful consideration was given to the appointment of the Political Officer Sikkim; officers were earmarked for that position some time in advance. For career-minded officers with an interest in Tibet, but an eye on their pension, the Gangtok post offered a stepping stone to a higher position. Career prospects were an important factor in a Political officer's thinking, when Weir accepted the post of Political Officer Sikkim, he was planning for his retirement. As a Second-class Residency would add 100 rupees a month to his pension and a First-class Residency would add 200 rupees, he accepted Sikkim only 'on the understanding that by doing so I would not forfeit my chances of getting a Residency'.[10]

Cadre officers who were not actually members of the Political Department, such as Bell and Macdonald, could remain in Tibet throughout their careers. There can be no doubt that these officers with 'attached' status, wanted to serve in Tibet. Ludlow, for example, wrote that, 'If they wanted me I would come back from the ends of earth to Tibet.'[11]

It was possible for members of the Political Department to stay for long periods. Gould, for example, used wartime shortages of manpower as an excuse to remain at Gangtok an extra five years. That Politicals such as Gould and Richardson served such lengthy terms in cadre posts demonstrates their attachment to Tibetan service. But other career Political officers, such as Russell, Worth and Hailey, had no desire to remain or to return. Not everyone liked Tibet; some regarded it as 'the ends of the earth'. As Macdonald recalled

> I have known men posted to the Agencies who did nothing but bemoan their luck in being stationed in such an out-of-the-way place, and who passed most of their time devising some scheme which would obtain them a transfer. Others did all they could to get an extension of their term of duty.[12]

Macdonald's comments must relate to escort and technical personnel, as his Political contemporaries had all sought service in Tibet. Even then the number of those who did not appreciate the posting was probably small. Several technical staff in Macdonald's time remained in Tibet for long periods and later Escort Commanders such as Lieutenant D.A.Walters and Captain Allen Robins greatly enjoyed Tibetan service. Another Escort Commander, Captain Robert Grist, was so keen to stay that he had Gyantse monks perform (unsuccessful) ceremonies aimed at ensuring that his term would be extended. While many of the technical and support staff were initially attracted to Tibet by a sense of adventure, ultimately it was their fondness for the country which kept them there.[13]

For various reasons a number of officers did fail to make a success of Tibetan service. Failure to adapt to the altitude was common. It was a problem which posed a serious health risk; several deaths occured among Agency or Escort personnel en route to Gyantse. Lieutenant Warren, for example, appointed to the Gyantse Escort, died at Yatung in September 1939 en route to his new post. The basic requirement that officers be fit for life at altitude also ruined the career of 1929 Gyantse Agent Captain D.R.Smith. He had been keen to serve in Gyantse, and was showing promise, but soon found he could not adjust to the altitude. His failure lead to the introduction of medical examinations before officers were posted to Tibet. Nevertheless, a Major Laughton fell ill at Gangtok en route to take over as Trade Agent Gyantse in 1940. His replacement, Major Sinclair, also suffered badly from the altitude and, as he proved unsuitable for Tibet in a number of ways, he also returned early to India.[14]

To be a successful cadre officer and to enjoy a posting to Tibet, required an empathy with the local people. An officer could be a good frontiersman, but not suited to the cadre because he failed to achieve this empathy. Frederick Mainprice was the perfect example of the 'lean and keen' frontiersman, efficient and hard-working, who failed to satisfy that requirement.

Mainprice was of a new generation. He had driven overland from England to India in 1939 to join the ICS; but his sense of duty and moral standards reflected the ideals of an earlier age. Taking over at Gyantse after an unsettled period, he reorganised the local staff, dismissing several for corruption and inefficiency, and he had the Agency cleaned and painted. His performance certainly matched the Politicals' standards, but Mainprice did not appreciate the Tibetans or their government and he was transferred when a more suitable post became vacant.[15]

Officers such as Mainprice were quickly relocated, and were often successful elsewhere. Those who remained in Tibet more than a year were generally successful, although the long-serving J.C.White had an appalling record and several Gyantse Trade Agents in the early 1930s made little impression on Anglo-Tibetan affairs.

Captain E.W.Fletcher, though certainly the 'lean and keen' type, fell out with local Tibetan officials over hunting and fishing trips on which he demanded the free transport to which Tibetan officials and guests on official duties were entitled. Other 1930s Gyantse Agents, such as Russell, simply found life in Tibet not to their taste, or regarded it as just another posting in a long imperial career.[16]

Such a reaction was only to be expected. A 'generalist' tradition, developed from the 'amateur ideal' inculcated in the public schools, was originally an important part of the imperial ethos. It was felt that a good frontiersman should be able to work in any location. By the late 19th century, however, an expert knowledge of local cultures and conditions was increasingly seen as essential for decision-making by government. 'Generalists', such as Weir, were still valued in the 20th century, but the growing realisation that policies had differing effects in different locations meant that the Raj needed its 'men on the spot' to become experts in the particular culture in which they operated.[17]

One hindrance to gaining expertise was the frequency with which Political officers were transferred. Officers became more influential the longer they remained in Tibet. Their expertise, particularly in language, naturally increased, and personal relations with the local peoples generally improved with time.

Political officers were, however, theoretically posted to Gyantse for only two years and to Gangtok for five; although their actual terms varied. Isolation was a factor in this restriction, particularly in regard to Gyantse. But the Political Department also considered that lengthy terms of service in Tibet (and elsewhere) produced a general staleness reducing an officer's effectiveness; while frequent postings 'removed the temptation of corruption'.[18] There was also concern that long-serving officers would form too close an attachment to their host-state to function with the necessary detachment. Most importantly, however, the Departmental career structure required officers to regularly relocate to gain experience and promotion. That was the advantage of using 'attached' status officers such as Bell, who could remain in one region throughout their career.[19]

Although the frequent transfers of personnel did reduce the cadre's efficiency, there were always local experts to advise new officers and to provide continuity at a post. Officers made their successors aware of the reliability, or otherwise, of these local experts, with their advice being perceived accordingly.[20]

The need for expertise led to another distinguishing characteristic of the Tibet cadre; their scholarship. While later research has naturally reduced the value of some of their earlier works, the cadre's books and reports remain essential references today. In particular, Bell and Richardson established themselves as Tibetologists. This scholarly aspect of their character manifested in various other ways, such as Bell's taste for classical Greek writings. The judgement of one academic, that the Politicals were 'a byword for intellectual mediocrity', cannot be applied to the Tibet cadre.[21]

Along with scholarship, another quality emerges. O'Connor was described as 'having a touch of the recluse' and this quality emerges, explicitly or implicitly, in most cadre officers, particularly in their early, bachelor years. A fondness for separation from Western society, and in some cases any society, was a significant element of their mentality. This quality predisposed them to the isolation of Tibet. Service in the Politicals naturally appealed to those attracted to the more remote locations and, while by education and background well-trained in contemporary social skills, many officers were happiest with the simplicity of life in the wide-open spaces of Central Asia. This is most obvious in the case of Ludlow, who clearly favoured 'the stony bridle path in preference to the tarred road'. After serving as a schoolteacher in Gyantse in 1923-26, he dreaded 'the hurry and hustle of the west after the hinterlands of Tibet'. When he served under the Political Department as Head of Mission Lhasa in 1942-43, he found even that limited society too crowded, and he was not unhappy to leave.[22]

Cadre officers also had a strong sense of duty. The case of Rivett-Carnac, torn between duty and family, shows that successful officers, and their wives, always put duty first. The extreme example of this was Williamson, who knew that his last journey to Lhasa posed a serious risk to his health, but chose to go anyway, a decision his wife accepted.[23]

* * *

Most of the successful cadre officers came from a civilian background. While there is little evidence of the tension between ex-ICS and ex-Indian Army Politicals which existed elsewhere, the less successful officers were all, with the exception of White, ex-Indian Army Politicals.[24] Those with a strong military background had greater difficulty understanding Tibet and its people, perhaps because the practical focus of their training precluded sympathetic insight into a contemplative society. George Sherriff, for example, failed to understand Tibetan concepts of good behaviour. He held gun classes in Lhasa, which commenced at 10 a.m. That meant '10 a.m. sharp in the military mind'. When the Tibetan trainees arrived at least an hour late, Sherriff was not impressed; but the Tibetans considered it was good behaviour to arrive late, so as not to appear 'too keen'. Lhasa did not, in any case, have a reliable system for telling the exact time, nor any particular reason for wanting to. Some said Lhasa time came from a sundial in the Potala, others that it came from a clock which was liable to 'jump back suddenly' and make everyone late.[25]

Most military Politicals, however, as well as the Escort Commanders and Medical Officers, were keenly interested in Tibet and had successful careers there. O'Connor gained a particularly deep empathy with the Tibetans. Other military men such as Saker, Robins, Ford, Kennedy and Guthrie liked Tibet, were sympathetic to the Tibetans' cause and were highly-rated by the cadre. They genuinely felt, like Mrs.Saker, that 'it was special, a great experience...a privilege to be there'. But as their careers took them elsewhere, their involvement was more limited, whereas officers such as Bell and Richardson could devote much of their life to Tibet.[26]

Although the cadre shared aims, traditions and mentality, they did not necessarily get on well with each other. While O'Connor and Bailey, or Ludlow and Sherriff, were close friends, there were actually few opportunities for cadre officers to meet and their relations were often 'fairly superficial'.[27] They judged their fellow officers mainly on the basis of their reputation, and the views they expressed in their reports.

There was certainly ill-feeling occasionally between some individuals. Altitude contributed to shortness of temper and those stationed together in such isolated posts as Gyantse could find that 'pressure built up and nerves became frayed'. Yet evidence of such ill-feeling does not appear in the published works of the Politicals, although there are frequent references to ill-feeling in diaries and personal correspondence. It was an unwritten part of their code, deriving from the public school code of 'no snitching', that such disputes were not aired in public. Younghusband, for example, wrote a laudatory obituary of White, although privately he detested him.[28]

The only specific published remarks concerning personal differences are those published years later by a female observer, Williamson's widow. Officers wives' could also cause problems, a series of petty complaints by Mrs Bailey against her successor in the Gangtok Residency cannot have helped their husbands' relationship.[29]

For those 'in the mould', however, personal differences were of little consequence in the long term. Service in Tibet had special attractions apart from the unique culture and environment. There were none of the communal troubles increasingly common in India, no caste barriers to communication with the local people, and the frontiersmen enjoyed great independence. Those 'in the mould', whether posted to Tibet by choice or circumstance, liked the country and its people and immersed themselves in various aspects of its culture.[30]

* * *

An important element of the attraction of service on the frontiers of India, and in particular in Tibet, was that they occupied a special place in the British imagination. Myth and legend generally require a placement outside normal constraints of time and space, so it was no coincidence that the frontier, the zone with the weakest area of definition and administration, was the strongest realm of Indian indigenous and imperial myth. Just as the frontiers were the setting for much of India's indigenous mythology, so they were the setting for a powerful mythology of empire. This was popularly portrayed in newspapers and magazines, imperial memoirs, novels such as Kipling's *Kim* and more subtly in Political Department textbooks such as Thornton's *Sir Robert Sandeman*.

The frontiersman occupied the hero's role in this discourse. Portrayed as strong, self-reliant, courageous and upright, he was a pioneer of European civilisation. By gaining the trust of the 'unruly' indigenous peoples and imposing the British concept of good order and civilisation he acted for the greater benefit of all. This frontiersmen of legend thus mirrored the qualities the public schools sought to produce and the Political Department sought to recruit. The ideal was the legend.

Imperial heroes, officers such as Cecil Rhodes in Africa, Sandeman in India and Younghusband in Tibet, took on legendary status. So too did martyrs, like General Gordon at Khartoum and Captain Cavignari at Kabul. As Peter Bishop states, 'Tales of explorers' hardships and deaths were utterly essential for the Victorian British...imaginative associations with the region.'[31]

In 19th century India, this imperial mythology focused on the ethos of the North-West Frontier Province, although it included elements of regional traditions, particularly the Punjab, and service traditions such as those of the Politicals. In the 20th century, it embraced the new Tibetan frontier. Competition with Russia saw the cadre drawn into the last phases of the 'Great Game'. They came to be seen as players in this romantic struggle, and they had an added mystique because of their association with Tibet, itself an often mythical place in the Western imagination.

At school, cadre officers had absorbed these imperial legends from magazines such as *Boys Own Paper, Magnet* or *Gem*. Those born in India had learned them first-hand.[32] The cadre were thus predisposed to service in the frontier zone that was the setting for the heroes of empire.

Cadre officers were aware of their legendary status; it was part of their identity. They played a large part in creating it, and attempted to live up to it. Hence their identification with 'forward' policies. That was an integral part of their sense of cadre identity rather than a reasoned analysis of potential means to protect the security of India. Had the cadre portrayed themselves as bureaucrats or civil servants, they would have lost much of their proud mystique.

Cadre 'founding fathers', Curzon and Younghusband, were role models for would-be 'Great Gamers'. Both were legendary figures following their 19th century exploits in Russian and Chinese Central Asia, with Younghusband an active 'Great Gamer' and Curzon providing the ideological impetus. Their inspiration remained strong throughout the 1904-47 period and their protégés, O'Connor and

Bailey, saw their role as continuing the traditions which those two pioneers had established. They in turn selected officers who would carry on the ideas. The result was that just as 'the first generation of frontiersmen in the Punjab had become legendary by the end of the 19th century', so too had the founding officers of the Tibet cadre became legends 30 years later, when they were seen as ideal types to emulate.[33]

Younghusband also gave the cadre an open-minded attitude to spiritual matters, very much accentuated by their location. In the final pages of his book *India and Tibet*, he attributes the source of British 'forward' policy in Tibet, not to individual, geo-political or economic causes, but to a 'great world-force, energizing through Nature'. Younghusband explains that this world-force guided the affairs of men, and had guided the British to Tibet. Characteristically, he concluded that this spiritual force would be best served in the Tibetan sphere by a British agent in Lhasa![34]

The Tibet cadre were imperial administrators, schooled in the ideals of positivist enquiry; they took a pragmatic approach to their duty. Ultimately they placed that duty above any consideration for the Tibetans. To describe them as mystics would be an obvious misconception. But Younghusband established an ethos in which a place in imperial mythology was a part of the cadre's tradition and prestige, and interest in spiritual matters was regarded as an acceptable indication of intellect, vision, and even character.

While Younghusband, O'Connor and Bailey were more colourful figures, and are consequently better known outside academic circles, the greatest influence on succeeding officers in Tibet was Sir Charles Bell. A quiet man, he was 'disposed to let a newcomer see things for himself and form his own conclusions',[35] but Weir, Macdonald, Williamson, Gould and Hopkinson all acknowledged a great debt to him, and their written work contains constant echoes of Bell's influence, both acknowledged and unconscious. Like Bell, they passed on their enthusiasm and sense of mission to their successors.

In-service traditions were deliberately passed on to newcomers by serving cadre officers. Serving officers selected promising individuals with an interest in Tibet, supervised their training, and instilled in them the history and traditions of the Anglo-Tibetan encounter. Ludlow, for example, describes how Bailey had taken him and another young officer and 'pointed out the old haunts of the mission in 1904-05[sic]'[36] This was a deliberate policy, and the cadre sought to hand down these traditions to their Indian successors after 1947. Hopkinson wrote that he wanted

> to get some Indians genuinely interested and sympathetic, who would help to continue the ideas on which British officers, in succession, had tried to work...and try to bring the Indians up to the right idea.[37]

Richardson too, hoped that he might encourage his successor to work 'along the right lines'.[38]

Officers naturally took an interest in the careers of those they had promoted as their own judgement would be considered at fault if their protégés failed. As Younghusband told Bailey's father, 'tell him [Bailey] to be sure and do me credit for I am responsible for him and I want any man I recommend to be a credit to me'.[39]

Most officers actively solicited their predecessors' advice. For example, Bailey profited from O'Connor and Younghusband's counsel throughout much of his career, and Gould wrote to Bell in 1936, noting he had tried to meet Bailey and 'pick his brains', and now sought his old superior's advice.[40]

The cadre, and those associated with them, guarded their reputation. In 1934, when Professor Tucci claimed to have been the first European to visit Rabgyeling monastery in western Tibet, H.Calvert ICS, who had been there en route to inspect the Gartok Agency in 1906, promptly sent a correction to the London *Times*. More recently, officers such as Richardson have also been quick to respond to any criticism of their role.[41]

Other British Indian services, such as the ICS, also had a distinctive group identity maintained through selection and training. But critics have accused their officers of being narrow careerists.[42] The cadre, however, had a more complex motivation, including purely compassionate concerns. They were not dominated by careerists. Certainly there was ambition, but there was also a strong sense of 'mission', which emerges clearly throughout the period under consideration. Even ambitious officers promoted to other positions, such as O'Connor, continued to work for what they saw as the Tibetan's benefit and they continued to do so when the British empire ended.

The romantic image of the Politicals has also been criticised, but it was an important part of an officers' sense of identity and purpose, although it could also produce an inflated sense of self-worth. Officers such as Bell and Macdonald, with 'attached' status, were noticeably less egocentric than most Politicals. But a certain amount of pride and self-confidence was usually an integral part of the ambition to attain higher rank in the empire. If the self-effacing Ludlow deplored the ego of some of his Political Department contemporaries, Gould enjoyed this proud stance; 'To a jealous outside world "a Political" might be a term of abuse. To us it was a term of glory.'[43]

The early officers such as Bell and Bailey, modest though they were by nature, learned that advancing their careers and the policies they favoured required judicious self-promotion, and the obscuring of their failures. Yet a fine line was drawn in the 'gentlemanly codes' they had learned in school, between quiet self-promotion and immodesty. Bailey defined this when he wrote of Sven Hedin, 'I think he did a great deal but it is a pity he did not let other people praise it instead of praising it himself.'[44]

As Edward Shils observes, traditions are defined by insiders, not the observers.[45] The cadre saw themselves as frontiersmen of the Raj, protecting India against Russian influence and bringing progress to local societies. They identified themselves as diplomats,[46] not as administrators and they considered freedom of judgement and action an essential requirement for their role. They had a romantic image, but the image was partly created by the officers themselves; therefore it was largely self-descriptive. Officers who failed to live up to the image were not considered 'in the mould' and were not re-employed in Tibet. Those who remained there were naturally those who lived up to the ideal image.

Chapter Forteen

'We want a united Tibet'

As the first Europeans to reside in Tibet in the modern era, the cadre had a unique opportunity to shape our knowledge of that land. They became its main interpreters to the outside world and the historical image of Tibet held in the West today is largely based on the information they obtained and propagated. Seven cadre officers wrote books wholly or partly about Tibet, with another by Younghusband, the cadre's 'founding father'. These were influential works, which reached a wide audience and left a lasting impression on European scholarship.[1]

Despite this scholarship, the word 'Tibet' still conjures up a series of images of a 'Shangri-La'; images which are more mythical than historical. Whereas mythical images of other unknown lands, such as Australia or Africa, faded as those places became known to European science, an image of Tibet as a spiritual realm beyond precise empirical understanding has survived to this day.

The continued existence of both historical and mystical images is largely due to the political circumstances surrounding the British presence in Tibet. Ideas and images were weapons in the political battles the cadre fought. They were used not to construct an accurate portrait, but one which served various Anglo-Tibetan interests. This resulted in the survival of two images; historical Tibet, and the Tibet of the imagination, a fantasy land of magic and mystery.

That the British sought to produce an image of Tibet was originally implicit in the search for contact and meaning. After Younghusband, it became explicit, with the cadre specifically stating that they sought to propagate ideas and images for a political purpose. This was part of a battle to establish a view of Tibet on the international stage, and the cadre used images as tools to develop a strong Tibetan 'buffer' state. They saw, 'in the case of Tibet...[little or no]...difference between propaganda and policy'.[2]

Although the immediate cause of the Younghusband mission was the determination to exclude Russian influence from Tibet, a significant underlying cause was the need for more information about India's northern neighbour. In the 19th century, the Tibetans had largely succeeded in preventing Europeans from entering the main centres of Tibetan culture and the Government of India had only limited knowledge of their government and leading personalities. None of the 19th century pioneers of European Tibetan scholarship had had access to the centres of Tibetan culture. There were reports from *pandits* and agents such as Chandra Das, but at the turn of the century, there was a great shortage of up-to-date political and strategic intelligence.

The British could not allow this situation to continue. Imperial power relied on the continuing flow of information, including that from their spheres of interest beyond the frontiers. This need for intelligence made the Younghusband mission a logical imperial response to their enforced ignorance about their northern neighbour.

Defining the Tibetan state which British forces entered in 1903-04 is difficult. There was then a fundamental difference between European and Asian understandings of statehood. The European model was the nation-state; a territorial entity, within defined borders, in which a single government was sovereign and enjoyed a monopoly of force. Citizens of a nation-state were assumed to be predominantly from a single ethnic group, or composed of ethnic groups sharing certain aims and assumptions and coming together in a single state for mutual benefit, as with the United Kingdom. The assumption that citizens of such a state shared common interests and perceptions meant that their indentity was defined as characterised by certain shared qualities and symbols; language, culture, collective history and so on.[3]

Tibet in 1904 was not a nation-state in the European understanding. Despite centralising structures, it included a variety of political and administrative formations, in which a single central power did not consistently maintain authority throughout a fixed territory. Tibet even included enclaves under the jurisdiction of Bhutan and Sikkim and, at various times in its history, power centres such as Shigatse conducted dealings with foreign powers without reference to Lhasa.[4]

The principalities which made up eastern Tibet were particularly reluctant to allow Lhasa to exercise secular authority in their domain. Lhasa was often, in their perspective, a remote and largely nominal authority. Even the religious authority of Lhasa vested in the Gelugpa sect was not necessarily acknowledged in these areas, where the prevailing sectarian orientation was towards the Bön faith, or other Buddhist sects such as the Nyingma.

Yet Tibet clearly existed as a distinguishable historical entity. Tibetans were recognised as a distinct ethnic group, even by the Chinese. They maintained a unique social system, free of the religiously-sanctioned social divisions of Hindu India, with aspects such as fraternal polyandry which were absent from Han Chinese society. Similarly, Tibetan language, landscape, art, architecture, dress and diet, as well as their economic and gender relations, were all clearly distinguished from those of neighbouring cultures. These socio-cultural elements of their identity can be traced back to the earliest recorded periods of Tibetan history around the 7th century AD and some are clearly older.[5]

These shared socio-cultural values contributed to a strong sense of collective identity among the peoples of the region, which persisted despite changing institutional loyalties. The key element of this collective identity was their Buddhist faith, which had been an integral part of their social and political systems since at least the 14th century.[6]

The Tibetans defined their own identity by the term *nangpa*, meaning a Buddhist, or an 'insider'. Non-Buddhists, even those of Tibetan race such as the minority Muslim community, were termed *chipa* or 'outsiders'.[7] The indigenous construction of Tibetan identity was, therefore, primarily religious. It was this religious orientation which gave a fundamental historical unity to their community, particularly when outside threats to their religion arose. Their unity then largely subsumed regional and factional divisions within that society.

Their conception of themselves as a political entity was of Tibet as a religious territory, the ideal home of Buddhism. This understanding had governed their foreign relations with countries such as China. The Tibetan Government officially described their state in such terms as 'a purely religious country' and 'dedicated to the well-being of humanity...the religious land of Tibet'. They demonstrated that this was not purely rhetoric by such actions as banning, on moral grounds, the export of live animals for slaughter in India.[8]

There is considerable academic discussion today about how best to describe the Tibetan polity which the British encountered. Certainly it resembled models of pre-modern states, in which polities were 'defined by centres, borders were porous and indistinct, and sovereignties faded imperceptibly into one another'.[9]

* * *

If Tibet was to act as a 'buffer state' for India, the British needed it to be transformed into a strong, united and clearly defined entity, on the nation-state model. But as it lacked many of the preconditions of statehood, the British had to persuade the Tibetan Government to create or develop the essential elements of national identity: state structures (those aspects of centralised authority such as government, law, and boundaries) and social processes (those aspects of society with a shared consciousness of unified or related indentity, such as traditions, values, and belief systems).

British India provided a precedent for this process. The gradual expansion of British sovereignty there contributed to the creation of Indian national structures and processes which had a considerable influence upon the creation of an Indian identity and nationhood. By establishing India's boundaries and claiming sovereignty within them, and by taking responsibility for the welfare of the peoples therein, the British helped to create India as a single, defined entity, peopled by 'Indians'. They then devised strategies of 'improvement' designed to appeal to various social groups to persuade them to support, and identify with, the new state. [10] The cadre sought to repeat that process in Tibet.

In imposing an Indo-Tibetan border at the Simla Convention, the British helped define Tibet as a geographical state. But the border was drawn as a line of defence for India, not to divide India and Tibet along racial, socio-cultural or religious lines. With time, this boundary acquired a definitive character despite the absence of formal demarcation in some areas. India and Tibet were thus created by their border; the border was not separating pre-existing states.[11]

The British twice attempted to define as 'Indian', areas which were clearly Tibetan territory. As we have seen, Younghusband tried to annex the Chumbi Valley to India, and Bell succeeded in taking Tawang. When Whitehall prevented India from absorbing the Chumbi it was a significant step towards imposing central control over frontier policy. Instead of being absorbed into India, and subjected to a process of 'Indianisation', the British defined the Chumbi as Tibetan and consequently encouraged Lhasa to exert its authority there.[12]

In the 19th century, moves such as Younghusband's had almost invariably resulted in an extension of British imperial frontiers. But in the 20th century, Whitehall called a halt to expansion and the frontiersmen were generally forced to accept central authority. Tawang was an anomaly; Bell succeeded there largely because Britain had other concerns at the time and the annexation escaped notice.

Chumbi, Tawang, and O'Connor's plan to set-up a state under the Panchen Lama's rule all showed that the British did not originally regard Tibet as having a single, geographically defined identity. But, after the Simla Convention, the cadre began to promote just such an identity for Tibet.

* * *

Towards the end of the 19th century, Tibet's policy of isolation had paradoxically led to considerable public interest in this 'forbidden land'. There was considerable competition among European and Russian explorers to be the 'first' to reach Lhasa until, as Curzon declared to Sven Hedin, the Younghusband mission 'destroyed the virginity of the bride to whom you aspired.'[13]

The allure of the unknown meant that not only the government but also the British public wanted to know more about Tibet. This demand was temporarily filled by a number of books about the Younghusband mission written by army officers or journalists who accompanied Younghusband.[14] Not unexpectedly, these writers sought to justify the mission, which had attracted considerable criticism in anti-imperialist circles.

These works presented the Tibetan Government and the religious system surrounding it in a negative light. They defended such controversial matters as the devastating death-toll inflicted by trained troops with modern weapons on primitively-armed, irregular forces. Their descriptions of Tibet and its people at that time were typical of the discourse of war. The London *Times* correspondent, for example, described Tibetans as a 'stunted and dirty little people'.[15]

Even frontier officers who were later to describe the Tibetans in laudatory terms, then joined in condemning them; Bell was associated with a military report which described the Tibetans as 'untruthful and faithless, deceitful and insincere' and Tibetan Buddhism as 'a disastrous parasitic disease'.[16] But this discourse must be seen in its context. It was produced during a period of Anglo-Tibetan conflict, and these negative images were, in general, characteristic only of that period, although echoes of them did survive into a later era.

Following Foucault and Edward Said, it is commonly argued that knowledge is constructed in a form determined by dominant power structures, and that dominant knowledge was used by the imperial powers to denigrate local knowledge, social structures and power systems, ultimately preventing an objective understanding of one society by the other. Yet in the case of Tibet, the images produced were, after the initial period of conflict, largely positive ones, although there was a sound political motive behind this construction, as will be seen.

In 1909-1911, the publication of books by White and Younghusband and an article by Bailey in *Blackwoods* magazine, signalled the replacement of the discourse of war by a more sympathetic approach, which became pronounced in the later works of Bell and Macdonald.[17] Tibet was no longer portrayed as hostile; indeed in Bailey's article it was simply an exotic location for *shikar*. In later years officers such as Bell and Macdonald explained Tibet and its culture in sympathetic and comparative terms designed to portray it as 'familiar'. Thereafter, writings by cadre officers assumed the readers' understanding of this transformation.

A comparison of two descriptions of the 13th Dalai Lama's early period of rule, both by cadre officers whom the Tibetans remember as sympathetic to them, clearly demonstrates the change in approach. In 1905, O'Connor described how the young Dalai Lama had acted.

> in accordance with the dictates of his own untrammelled will. No person or party of the State dared for a moment to oppose him. His brief rule was signalised by numerous proscriptions, banishments, imprisonings and torturings. Neither life nor property was safe for a moment.[18]

Forty years later, Sir Charles Bell described the young Tibetan leader's actions in that period in very different terms:

> His courage and energy were inexhaustible; he recoiled from nothing...[By]...skill, tinged with humour...he surmounted the obstacles...He was young and strong, and he worked continously.[19]

This change in perspective was initially due to the cessation of hostilities and became more pronounced in the new era of Anglo-Tibetan relations which followed Bell's establishment of friendship with the Dalai Lama. In return for following Bell's 'advice', the Dalai Lama received British support for his regime. Apart from the material aspect of support, the cadre produced an image of Tibet which was designed to serve the interests of both parties. The resulting image portrayed an ideal Tibet, an ideal which their policies were also designed to create.

* * *

When the cadre officers began gathering information in Tibet, their earliest concern was with matters of strategic and military value; the strength of Tibet's army, the state of the passes into India, etc. Their earliest collations of information were in internal government reports which built up knowledge within the system, so that Secretariat officials such as Louis Dane gained an expertise in Tibetan matters based on the knowledge acquired by the cadre.

After 1910, books and articles by cadre officers reached the general reading public, who read them in the expectation of receiving an accurate account of the country and its people – and cadre officers did try to discover 'the truth' about their subject. They wanted to learn as much as they could about the country and its people because it attracted them personally. If it did not, it was very easy for them to get a transfer back to India. But they understood 'truth' as being knowledge in empirical and scientifically ascertainable form.

Cadre officers therefore made considerable efforts to establish accurate records of Tibet. In most cases where their information was unreliable, they noted that in their reports, as we have seen in the case of trade figures. The search for 'truth' was seen, in the ethos of the time, as a morally higher purpose behind an official's day-to-day activities. Increasing the existing body of knowledge was considered to be part of the 'civilising mission' of the imperial nations. Lord Curzon was in no doubt that increasing the body of knowledge was part of the wider function of an Indian official. 'It is' he proclaimed, 'equally our duty to dig and discover, to classify, reproduce and describe, to copy and decipher, and to cherish and conserve'.[20]

However, while the cadre often qualified the information they supplied, there were other factors which affected the 'truth' as they gave it. Officers could, by selectively presenting opinion as 'truth', use their status as experts 'on the spot' to present information in a form designed to promote particular policies and actions by Delhi and Whitehall.

The cadre also told their superiors what they wanted to hear, as in reports containing praises for fellow cadre officers – 'Mr Macdonald has as usual managed his work tactfully and efficiently' – and even self-praise: 'by tact and influence I kept them in bounds'. Annual reports from the Trade Agencies always contained a line such as 'Relations with all officials continue to be friendly', and when this was omitted by the Yatung Agent in 1940, this subjective judgement was added to the report by the Political Officer before he submitted it to government.[21]

Generally the cadre were more subtle than this, however. When Charles Bell tried to persuade his government to accept the Dalai Lama's offer of British control of Tibet's foreign relations, he reported that the Tibetans' character, 'though in many ways admirable is permeated by a vein of impracticability, which prevents them from coming to a final decision' – implying that Tibet would not be capable of conducting its own foreign relations. Such attempts to justify British command by presenting the indigenous culture as inferior were a common imperial tactic.[22] Bell's statements were also an example of how some knowledge could be 'true', but of interest only to positivist science, while other information could be both 'true' and politically useful.

That the Tibetan Government were 'naive', became an article of faith among the cadre and, while this description was appropriate in some instances, after the British departed they admitted that although the Tibetans 'played at being a very simple people...they were shrewd diplomatic operators'.[23]

Cadre officers' reports also reflected their own inherent perceptions. These perceptions did change with time, and vary with the individual. For example, when the Gyantse Trade Agency was opened, O'Connor hired a Tibetan Buddhist exorcist, who 'kindly expelled all the devils and spirits from the new stables' in what O'Connor found a 'very interesting' ceremony. Yet in the 1940s, George Sheriff described similar religious rites as 'dreadful examples of the backwardness of Tibet...[and a]... complete waste of money'.[24]

But these individual variations in perception were largely submerged in a collective approach to, and understanding of, Tibet. This was deliberately inculcated in the cadre by their imperial training process. Of course this process was not designed to produce detached observers and social scientists. It was designed to produce imperial frontier officers who could be relied upon to follow the general trends of Government of India policy. This meant that while cadre officers gained a great understanding of Tibet and made genuine efforts to encourage what they considered to be improvements there, they never forgot that their first duty was to the British Government of India. Their perspective was governed by that sense of duty.

* * *

Perhaps the most obvious characteristic of the cadre's perspective was its very narrow class-base. Just as the British imperial process marginalised the voice of the indigenous service class, so too was the voice of the British service class ignored. The clearest example of this was in the way in which the longest-serving Europeans in Tibet have left almost no historical trace.

Long-service in Tibet was part of an officer's personal prestige. In their memoirs, they tended to exaggerate the length of time they served there. Yet the men who spent the longest time in Tibet were not officers, but two Telegraph Sergeants, Henry Martin and W.H.Luff, and the longest time spent in Lhasa was the term served by Radio Officer Reginald Fox. However, none of these three Londoners published any work, or left personal papers.

Sergeant Henry Martin was a former labourer, who served with Younghusband. He remained in Gyantse as a Telegraphist, and later Head Clerk, from 1904 until he retired in 1931. He was twice married to Tibetan women. Martin died soon after retiring, having found that despite 'his record of long faithful service...hard to beat in the annals of a Government office', his government were unwilling to correct an anomaly which reduced his pension by a third. Luff, the sergeant who escorted the Dalai Lama into India in 1910, also remained in Tibet from the Younghusband mission until he retired in the late 1920s. A colourful character, in contrast to the 'always straight' Martin, Luff then had a brief, unsuccessful career as a gardener in Weir's Gangtok Residency and died in Darjeeling in 1942. Reginald Fox served as Lhasa mission Radio Officer from March 1937 until 1950 and similarly died soon after retiring. While he and his Tibetan wife were frequently mentioned by travellers, there is almost no trace of him in surviving official records.[25]

The absence of these voices is significant in emphasising that the historical image of Tibet was constructed by a very small group of the British officer class. As Fox, Luff and Martin all sought to remain in Tibet after retirement, their involvement in the country must have been as committed as any cadre officer; but the understanding they gained was not utilised, or at least not acknowledged, by the cadre. They were not normally included in meetings with the Tibetan ruling class and the perspectives gained from their social contacts with lower levels of Tibetan society were not reflected in the dominant image created. The Tibet cadre did not admit British 'lower ranks', no matter how experienced or knowledgeable, to the ranks of opinion and image makers.

Another important factor was the cadre officer's need to balance their personal impressions of Tibet with their career ambitions. In the early years, when Anglo-Tibetan policy was being constructed by negotiation between various strands of British opinion, an officer such as O'Connor could risk being outspoken. As he told Bailey, 'I think in the long run one will not suffer from having opinions'[26] But once general trends of policy had been established, an officer expressing a radical criticism of the status quo was liable to be regarded as having poor judgement or unsound opinions. While the Politicals included a number of men of legendary eccentricity, such characters were not used on the politically sensitive Tibetan frontier and ambitious officers generally tailored their opinions to please their superiors.

This can be clearly seen in two cases where Politicals posted to Gyantse formed views which differed significantly from the usual cadre perception. It is notable that neither officer remained in Tibet for a full term and that they had little or no effect on Anglo-Tibetan relations.

The recorded memories of 1933 Gyantse Agent Meredith Worth suggest an image of Tibet closer to that presented by Communist Chinese sources than that offered in British sources. Interviewed in 1980, Worth recalled that

> My memories are of many cheerful parties in the Fort and in the homes of wealthy families, the dominance and brutality of the Lamas and officials towards the serf population and the prevalence of venereal diseases...It was, therefore, for me a relief to read recently in Han Suyin's book 'Lhasa, the Open City' [which promotes a polemically positive view of Communist rule in Tibet] that those conditions no longer exist.[27]

Paul Mainprice confided to his 1944 diary that

> I have serious doubts whether Tibet is at all fit for independence and whether the present system of Government should be bolstered up. Would China in control of Tibet really be a very serious menace to India? As we don't seem to do much developing of Tibet, I question

whether the Chinese would not be able to do it to our own mutual advantage. Of course the Tibetan aristocracy and officials would not like it, but the peasants preferred the Chinese regime in Eastern Tibet in the early years of this century.[28]

The doubts which Mainprice expressed over British policy in Tibet do reflect a different perspective from that of other cadre officers. Mainprice 'was always concerned for the underdog'. He was one of the few imperial officers to gain good relations with the warlike Mishmi tribe during service in Assam and after Indian Independence he travelled to Kashmir. His diaries of that journey record his sympathy and support for the Muslim populace, which led to his being arrested, beaten, and then expelled by the new Indian government.[29]

Neither Worth nor Mainprice appear to have expressed these views publicly during their imperial service. This self-censorship helped to ensure that the dominant image of Tibet was not affected by alternative views, even those of members of the Political Department. The cadre spoke with one voice and that unity was a part of its strength. They became the dominant voice from Tibet because they deliberately suppressed alternative perspectives.

* * *

There was one factor influencing the image of Tibet which the cadre could not control. That was the commercial element, which had a very significant effect. Human nature meant and still means, that the reading public were interested in the sensational and colourful aspects of that land.

During the 1920s, books about General Pereira's and Alexandra David-Neel's journeys to Lhasa were published. The late General's diary was a positivist account of Tibet, the journey legitimised by its catalogue of dates, places and scientific observations. David-Neel's account, in contrast, provided few precise facts, but gave a colourful and entertaining description of Tibet's people and culture. Pereira's book was never reprinted; David-Neel's has remained in print for nearly seventy years.[30]

The cadre's books were published by commercial publishers who needed to take account of public taste. Thus when Bailey submitted draft chapters of his memoirs of Tibet, the publisher's reader returned it with suggestions on how to make it more interesting for the general public. The reader advised Bailey that while his writing was

> all right for the Journal of the R.G.S...the general reader wants something more *human* – a hint of the authors[sic] physical and spiritual reaction to his disappointments and to his successes...A little description too of the peoples...the scenery also...which must be colourful...[and have]...a thrill in the telling.[31]

The result of this economic demand was that cadre officers' books contained the commercially necessary amount of 'colourful' and 'thrilling' images. Bell and Richardson's books, aimed at a more academic audience, contain the minimum of such matter. But the memoirs of other officers and official visitors contain numerous descriptions of sky burials, religious dances, hermit's retreats, aristocratic pageantry, oracle's trances and the lengthy and (in European eyes) peculiar menus at banquets; themes which recur in virtually every book. Thus while cadre officers personally had a more balanced view of Tibet, popular demand led to an emphasis on more colourful images. This commercial factor has been largely ignored in the debate over Orientalism, which ascribes political motives to the human attraction to and desire for, 'exotic' images.

The principal competition to the historical image produced by the cadre was and still is, the 'mystical' image; Tibet as a sacred land in which the paranormal was commonplace.[32] Himalayan Tibet, in particular the Mount Kailas-Lake Manasarovar region, has held sacred associations for Indian religions since the pre-Christian era. But although this representation of a sacred land predates the encounter with the West, it has been greatly enhanced by European writings.[33]

European writings on 'mystical' Tibet were directed at other Europeans: much of it was regarded with bemusement by the Tibetans. Yet while it used the language of myth, not science, the mystical image did appear to contradict the more prosaic views of those in regular contact with the Tibetans. As the cadre also appealed to a European audience, they were forced to confront this alternative image.

Yet the cadre did not try to destroy this exotic representation. Instead, they tactily encouraged it, as they found that the idea of

Tibet's separate identity was reinforced by these colourful images, which reached a wide audience. They also provided a positive moral image for Tibet, and claiming the moral high-ground became of great importance after the Chinese take-over in the 1950s.

The cadre realised that there was no inherent conflict between the image they sought to present, and the image of 'Mystic Tibet'. Nor was that popular image a political issue in the sense that neither the Chinese, nor the Russians, sought political benefit by emphasising Tibet's mystical aura. The image was, and still is, a weapon against which China has no effective response.

In their published writings the cadre implicitly encouraged the mystical image of Tibet. Their books did seem to contradict the more fantastic accounts of Tibet because they had not observed any scientifically inexplicable events there. But they used metaphors and symbols of remote space, isolation and timelessness to maintain the implicit sense that Tibet was exotic. For example, the introduction to Younghusband's account of his mission to Lhasa describes Tibet as 'a mysterious, secluded country in the remote hinterland of the Himalayas'. That they did not observe any scientifically inexplicable events was even a matter of regret to the British. Gould's secretary observed that the Tibetans 'may believe implicitly in various psychic phenomena' but that 'I was never fortunate enough to witness these myself'.[34]

There were limits to the cardre's endorsement of Tibetan mysticism. In practice they were reluctant to accept incidents which the Tibetans regarded as miraculous. Macdonald described seeing the 'corpse' of a Chumbi Valley monastery oracle, only to hear that it had revived four days later. 'I suppose' wrote Macdonald 'this must have been a case of suspended animation, for no other explanation would fit the circumstances'. On the other hand, Bell, in an unpublished manuscript, observed without comment that Gangtok Residency was haunted. There was an 'apparition of an old women, also a boy and girl' which were harmless, but there was also a ghost described as having 'the body of a red mule and the head of tiger'. Bell wrote that 'whenever one of my police orderlies saw it he fired a shot at it immediately'.[35]

The mystical image was part of the attraction of service in Tibet. Younghusband in particular understood Lhasa as having a wider, symbolic significance and underwent powerful spiritual experiences there leading him to pursue this path at the expense of his career in government service. Significantly, this in no way damaged his prestige within the Tibet cadre, and the last British Political Officer Sikkim, Arthur Hopkinson, also retired to a spiritual life, albeit in more conventional form as an Anglican clergyman.

Tibetan religion was of genuine interest to most cadre officers and remained a part of the allure of service there. One consequence of this was that as long as travellers avoided referring to political matters and maintained British prestige, the cadre had no particular objection to their seeking spiritual enlightenment in Tibet. But the cadre sought to exclude even renowned scholars whom they considered politically unreliable.[36]

Alexandra David-Neel, who made an illicit visit to Lhasa in 1924, trod a fine line here. She was an elderly women, and, as she travelled disguised as a Tibetan, her actions did not lower imperial prestige. The British did object to her ignoring India's frontier travel regulations and commenting on the British policy of excluding travellers from Tibet, but her works were immensely popular. As they emphasised Tibet's separate identity, they served British Indian interests.

David-Neel also studied Tibetan mysticism while generally remaining within the Western academic tradition; a synthesis the cadre could admire. By presenting herself as a pro-British European with a similar class background and attitudes to the cadre's own, she gained their acceptance as a harmless, even admirable, traveller from within the tradition of aristocratic European eccentrics.[37]

* * *

The British role in the construction of Tibet's historical image is important today because, in the absence of a viable alternative, their construction became the dominant historical image. That image remains dominant, yet it is an image which reflects the political realities of the 1904-47 period.

The cadre needed to create a historical image of Tibet which served the political interests of the British and their Lhasa allies. This was the most significant element in shaping the information they obtained. What mattered was to create an image of Tibet as a strong, united nation-state and friendly neighbour to India. This meant projecting Tibet's historical ties with India at the expense of those with China. As one Political Officer wrote

> One of our main political aims [was] showing that Tibet had its own art etc. and that in some ways Tibet is more closely allied to India than to China.[38]

The main focus of the cadre's historical image was what we might call the 'core' image; one of Tibet about to become a modern nation-state, united under a single government, sovereign within its borders and existing as a friendly, and indeed admirable, neighbour to British India. The core image was most clearly articulated by Charles Bell, who wove the key ingredients together. As Bell described it

> Modern Tibet...rejects...Chinese suzerainty and claims the status of an independent nation, [one in which]...national sentiment...is now a growing force. The Dalai Lama is determined to free Tibet as far as possible from Chinese rule [and in this he has the support of] the majority of the Tibetan race...[who]...see in him...the only means of attaining their goal...[Anglo-Tibetan relations are of] cordial friendship [as] they are both religious peoples, [in contrast to the Chinese]...Tibet [would] at length secure...recognition of the integrity and autonomy of her territory.[39]

Charles Bell and his successors designed this image of the new Tibet to suit both the cadre and Dalai Lama's government. Both parties thus co-operated in presenting this picture of a united and progressive Tibetan state and they have continued to do so. Since the 1950s the Tibetan Government-in-exile has generally carried on using that image to promote their interests, continuing, for example, to recommend books by Bell, and by Richardson, who, in the 1960s wrote what remains probably the most authoritative history of Tibet.[40]

One effect of this alliance was that the British privileged the Lhasa perspective. They did not, for example, articulate the interests of the eastern Tibetan principalities which aspired to autonomy, or even to closer ties with China. The result was a Lhasa-centric historical image.

Yet the predominantly empirical basis of the British construction means that any major revisions of the received historical image of Tibet will be primarily due to the acceptance of a more balanced view of the aspirations of marginalised groups in Tibetan society. The British construction, however, perhaps tells us as much about British imperial history as it does about the Tibetans. While historically, Tibet clearly had a distinct identity and culture which they understood in Asian religious terms, these were translated into Western political terms in the light of British imperial concerns.

Later cadre officers and their support system followed Bell's definitions and assumed their readers' familiarity with his works. For example, Spencer Chapman suggested that his readers might compare an illustration in his book with the same scene in an earlier work of Bell's, while Arthur Hopkinson, lecturing in 1950, stated that 'I do not wish to waste your time by repeating facts of ancient history with which you are already familiar from books and articles, such as Sir Charles Bell's.'[41]

There was a skilful manipulation of the information presented to the public. The Dalai Lama's supreme authority was certainly undemocratic in Western eyes, but Gould's secretary, in best 'spin-doctor' mode, presented this in positive terms. He wrote that

> Naturally there will always be some who from jealousy or other motives criticize one who has the strength of character to assume such autocratic power.[42]

These descriptions of a well-ruled society – the common people, for example, were described in such terms as 'extraordinarily friendly... always cheery'[43] – had a specific purpose. They created an impression of the Tibetans as worthy allies of the British.

The survival of these images has not, however, only been due to political factors. The affectionate descriptions of the Tibetan people did generally represent the cadre's real opinions, and their impressions have been confirmed by more recent travellers to Tibet. Few Europeans who have been there would dispute Hugh Richardson's statement that 'all agree in describing the Tibetans as kind, gentle, honest, open and cheerful.'[44] Thus an image may be both 'true' and politically valuable.

The mystical image of Tibet also survives today largely as it serves Tibetan interests by emphasising the separate and unique nature of their civilisation. To an extent, it compensates for the fact that the Anglo-Tibetan alliance left the (now-exiled) Tibetan Government to rely on a historical image which they consider 'incomplete' particularly in the area of Tibet's political status.[45]

In recent times, however, there has been a reaction against this mystical image by a younger generation of Tibetans and its benefits have been called into question. Increasingly, Tibetans from the Dalai Lama down have emphasised the long-term value of 'truth' over 'image'.[46]

The crucial difference between the image of Tibet presented by the cadre and the Tibetan Government-in-exile's view of themselves, is in the matter of independence. Bell's ultimate aim may well have been an independent Tibet, but as a very shrewd and far-sighted diplomat he stopped short of advocating Tibetan independence, while leading policy in a direction which could have made that result inevitable. The political requirements of wider British policy meant that the cadre could not present the 'truth' about independence as they understood it. By any practical definition, Tibet functioned as an independent state in the period 1913-1950. Cadre officers, who dealt with its government on a day-to-day basis, accepted that, 'Tibet is just as much entitled to her freedom as India'.[47]

Whitehall's refusal to recognise Tibet as independent created a fundamental gap between the cadre's knowledge and the image which they were allowed to construct, but the cadre found that defining Tibet's status was an issue which could usually be avoided. Ultimately, although the cadre disagreed with Whitehall's views, they were government employees, and were duty-bound to follow orders. Clear statements of support for Tibetan independence were generally given only after an officer had retired and was able to speak as an individual, rather than an official. As Hugh Richardson recently wrote,

> In all practical matters the Tibetans were independent...[but]... The British Government...sold the Tibetans down the river...I was profoundly ashamed of the government.[48]

Competing power structures produce different images, the ascendancy of which obviously depends upon subsequent political and social events. We cannot assume that the records of the subordinate powers involved in this process are 'true', and in opposition to dominant 'false' images. Each image contains elements of truth. There was no one, true, image of Tibet to be understood or 'discovered'. Each encounter produced different results, and different constructions by the powers involved.

Chapter Fifteen

'Nothing left to which objection could be taken'

The influx of European visitors greatly increased the publicity Tibet received. Today around 30 books are available in which visitors to Lhasa in the 1904-50 period describe their experiences; even by 1945 there were more than a dozen available in English. The cadre were determined to keep this flow of information under their own control as much as possible so as to present information in such a way as to influence British public opinion in favour of the policies they promoted.

As early as 1910, Younghusband, speaking in London, had argued that 'our line of action in Tibet is entirely dependent on the state of opinion in this country'.[1] The cadre's early press releases carefully avoided commenting on policy and deliberately included little of popular interest. Although Bell's first book recommended that 'We should do more than is done at present towards putting before the public the Tibetan side of incidents that arise', press communiqués continued to be given in the officially approved 'vague and general terms' until the 1930s. When the Dalai Lama came to India in 1910, Bell was instructed 'to assist the Press Correspondent with news while of course saying nothing as to the policy'. Bell ordered Laden La to supply 'such items of news, as are likely to soon afterwards in any case become known to the public'.[2]

As was so often the case, Gould was responsible for fully implementing Bell's policy suggestions, and his efforts became increasingly sophisticated. He recognised the public 'demand for "copy" which always appears to exist in regard to Tibet' and used this demand to advance Anglo-Tibetan interests. Where previous missions to Lhasa had sought anonymity, Gould arranged for generous publicity for his visit to Lhasa in 1936. Sections of the mission's reports were released to the press and these 'somewhat bald and colourless' excerpts were supplemented by descriptive articles written by Gould or his secretary.[3]

When the original reports are compared with those released to the press we can see the image of Tibet which Gould sought to project. Reference to the 'bizarre' appearance of the Tibetan army was tactfully deleted, as was the description of the 'in some cases imbecile faces' of the villagers. The original phrase 'The old world courtesy, politness, bowing and compliments of the Tibetans, officials as well as servants, is charming', was altered to avoid reference to politeness, bowing and compliments.[4]

In the 1940s, Gould made publicity for Tibet a priority. He arranged subsidies for a Tibetan language newspaper, published in Kalimpong by the Anglophile nationalist, Mr (later Reverend) Tharchin. Foreign newspaper correspondents with influence in America were also invited to Tibet 'in the hope that the U.S. public will be led to appreciate the Tibetan position vis-a-vis China'. Archie Steele was the first such journalist. He had come to the attention of Hugh Richardson (then serving in China's war-time capital, Chungking) by travelling to the 14th Dalai Lama's birthplace and becoming the first foreigner to meet the new incarnation. Steele's visit was followed by others in the late 1940s, but their writings had little effect on the political situation.[5]

Part of Gould's publicity campaign was to ensure that British publications reflected the desired view of Tibet. In the 1920s Bailey had unsuccessfully tried to get the British film censor to remove parts of the official film of an Everest expedition which the Tibetans found offensive (in particular a sequence in which a Tibetan was shown removing lice from his clothing). Gould was more successful in obtaining the co-operation of the editor of Whitaker's Almanack, who agreed to send the proofs of an article on Tibet to the India Office for 'correction'. Richardson revised the article, although the India Office cautiously noted that 'we must be careful not to appear to be *telling* Whitakers what to publish'.[6]

In response to the Chinese establishment of a library in Lhasa in the 1940s, the British mission built up their collection of books on Tibet. They used these to impress influential Tibetans, who were given books by writers such as Bell and Tucci which demonstrated European interest in and concern for, Tibet. Bell clearly expressed his intent when he told the Dalai Lama that he hoped for his first book would 'do good for Tibet by causing British and Americans to understand Tibet better'. Gould and Richardson compiled a dictionary which was also seen in this context. It was observed that 'Perhaps its greatest propaganda value will be the fact that the Political Officer is sufficiently interested in Tibetan to write a book about it'.[7]

An important addition to this process came in the early 1930s when the cadre found that film shows were extremely popular with the Tibetans. They concluded that 'the cinema...can be made into the most powerful of all our propaganda weapons'. The Lhasa mission put on regular shows which were attended by both lay officials and monks. Many of the films were silent comedies, particularly Charlie Chaplin's, as very few in the audience would have understood English. These films were carefully selected by intermediaries such as Norbu Dhondup. Apart from those chosen purely for entertainment, the cadre wanted films such as one on St Paul's cathedral, considered particularly suitable for Tibet due to its 'religious flavour', or those which projected 'the right impression of British power and purpose'.[8]

Although when journalist Archie Steele asked a Tibetan official why there were no newspapers in Tibet and was told that was because 'Nothing ever happens in this country', the Tibetans gradually became aware of the importance of outside opinion. One indication of this came in 1937, when, after allegations by an American journalist that the Panchen Lama had been involved in commercial schemes in China, the exiled Lama denied the allegations in a letter published in the Journal of the Royal Central Asian Society.[9]

In the late '40s, the Tibetans hesitantly began actively seeking publicity. J.E.Reid, an electrical engineer who was the last British Indian official to be invited to Lhasa, reported in January 1950 that

The Tibetan Government had suddenly awoken to the reality of the dangers which threatened it and is now regretting its past policy of keeping aloof from outside contact.

The Tibetans, he reported, 'were now anxious that full world publicity should be given to their plight and to the country itself'.[10]

* * *

While the Government of India expected to be able to trust the judgement of its officers as to what information to present to the public, they were required, by both civil and military regulations additional to the Official Secrets Act, to submit anything they wrote for censorship. The cadre generally accepted the need for such a system. For example when Macdonald wrote his memoirs, the India Office noted that he was 'anxious that we should strike out anything that is considered objectionable'.[11]

In the early years, officers, or their publishers, were not always aware of these regulations and some material was published without censorship. The official attitude to these works was inconsistent. White did not submit his memoirs to the censor and when he sent the Government of India a copy of *Sikhim and Bhutan* in an attempt to solicit sales, the book was judged to be 'vindictive to the Government he served'. Secretariat officials considered White 'guilty of a grave act of insubordination and even impertinence' for including such comments (in regard to Bhutan) as 'It is neither a pleasant nor an easy task to have to deliberately deceive people who trusted you, as I had to do'. Despite this, no action was taken against White. Although Minto's policies were heavily criticised in the book, the Viceroy generously took the view that 'The publication of a few home truths is not altogether disagreeable reading'.[12]

In practice, little could be done to prevent retired officers from writing what they wished. Bell reluctantly agreed to submit his first book for censorship, after being threatened with action under the Official Secrets Act. When officials heard he was writing another book he was asked to submit the proofs. Finding he was no longer bound by the Act, having been out of service for more than six years, Bell refused to submit them. Consideration was given to threatening his pension, but when this was found to be legally impossible, officialdom had to 'acquiesce gracefully' to Bell's refusal. All that could be done was for the India Office to press the Government of India to emphasise to the Political Officer Sikkim that as his post was 'closely connected with the affairs of foreign countries, the...Regulations governing publication apply with particular force'.[13]

Official censorship therefore depended largely on the cadre's co-operation and was ultimately unenforceable. Furthermore, what was censored in one era could be valuable propaganda in another. Bell's uncensored works were soon accepted as his ideas were supported by his successors and because the passages objected to were principally indications of British support for Tibet, which were eventually found useful to show to the Tibetan Government. White's self-serving memoirs was also subject to a positive reinterpretation, but in his case because the passage of time removed the memory of his failures and mythologised the early Tibetan frontiersmen.

Officers such as White sent their books to the Government of India because it purchased works it approved of and distributed them to departmental and Residency libraries. In effect, these orders acted as a means of subsidising publication costs. Government did not always share the authors' enthusiasm for their work. Charles Sherring, for example, who had inspected the Gartok Trade Agency in 1905, hoped to sell them at least 600 copies of his book. But after an extraordinarily lengthy process of soliciting orders from every department and Provincial government, it took only 58 copies.[14]

Most officers did submit their writings for censorship, however, and government did generally succeed in exercising its power to control information about Tibet. The Government of India even claimed the power to restrict private conversations. Not wishing to publicise the existence of goldfields in western Tibet (to avoid encouraging prospectors) they instructed Captain Rawling after his 1904 journey, 'to avoid all reference in conversation to information...regarding the goldfields'.[15]

One particularly sensitive issue with which the censors were concerned was that India occasionally supplied arms to Tibet, because this implied recognition of Tibet as an independent state. Macdonald's references to these arms supplies were removed from his manuscript by the censors. He was told that it was 'most important that nothing should be said which could tend to damage relations with Tibet or any other foreign power'. Similarly, when writing his first book, Bell referred to Tibetan troops being 'armed with the new rifles' but the next sentence, which explained that the British had supplied these weapons, was removed by the censor: although, as is so often the case with censorship, the facts were obvious to anyone interested.[16]

As we have seen, the Government of India's control over access to Tibet enabled it to favour travellers of similar background and outlook to its officials, on the assumption that their discretion could then be relied upon. Although McGovern's journey to Lhasa was made without official permission, it was followed by a tightening of this informal process. Government added a further rule to the frontier pass visitors had to sign. Travellers had to agree

> not to publish, without the previous consent of the Government of India, any statement, whether in the press or otherwise, regarding his visit to Tibet or based on material obtained during the visit.[17]

Government was not the only censor. Organisations such as the Royal Geographical Society and the London *Times*, functioned unofficially as imperial support structures, by adding a further level of censorship. These bodies acted in close association with the Government of India, in return for which their leaders could expect to be given privileged access to information, events and places. Government even gave direct 'subsidies' to the Reuters news agency in India.[18]

Arthur Hinks, the long-serving RGS Secretary, had close links with many of the Tibet cadre and played an important role in this process; as we have seen in Chapter Seven, he assisted Bailey's attack on McGovern's reputation. Hinks censored information both before, and after, it was officially censored. When Spencer Chapman submitted a paper to the RGS, Hinks forwarded it to the India Office for censorship after 'cutting out a number of things which I am sure you would not like'. There was, he hoped, 'nothing left to which objection could be taken'. When the India Office made further deletions, Hinks obsequiously agreed these were 'very properly removed'.[19]

Government maintained a close relationship with official knowledge-disseminating bodies because articles they published carried great authority, and formed part of the body of 'dominant knowledge'. Although the intended audience for the historical image produced by the cadre was never clearly specified, it certainly included the sort of audience which would read the *Times* and join the RGS. The information they published was understood by its readers to be 'true' because it was based on empirical evidence and written by persons of similar outlook, class and perspective. It represented the 'official' knowledge of their readers' society.

When the *Journal of the Royal Geographical Society* heavily criticised McGovern's book and praised those of Bell and Macdonald, readers generally accepted that McGovern's perspectives and truths could not be trusted, while Bell and Macdonald's could be. These judgements have had a lasting effect. Today Bell and Macdonald's books are still recommended by the Tibetan Government-in-exile and are frequently reprinted, whereas McGovern's book gathers dust in specialist libraries.

Epilogue

'Today we are no longer masters of the Residency'

On 15 August 1947, India became independent and the British ceased to be represented in Tibet. The UK High Commission in Delhi did propose establishing a British medical dispensary in Lhasa to represent British interests and Major Guthrie, the Lhasa mission doctor, offered to remain there, but the Foreign Office decreed it unnecessary, and formal Anglo-Tibetan ties ended.[1]

Anglo-Tibetan relations were of such low priority within Whitehall that Tibet was not officially notified that India was being given independence until less than three weeks before the event. The Tibetans were informed that the new Indian Government would inherit the rights and obligations of existing treaties previously held by the Government of India in regard to Tibet.[2]

Although the new Indian flag was raised in place of the Union Jack, there were no immediate changes in the cadre posts, not least because there were no Indians trained to replace the British. Richardson remained in Lhasa until September 1950, but an Indian was given control of the Tibet posts on 1 September 1948, when Arthur Hopkinson handed over to the new Political Officer Sikkim, Harish Dayal ICS. The entry in Mrs Hopkinson's diary on that date reads as an epitaph for the British Raj – 'Today we are no longer masters of the Residency'.[3]

When Hopkinson departed, the cadre were optimistic that India would follow the Tibetan policies established by the British. Harish Dayal was considered sympathetic to the Tibetans and in December

1949 Hopkinson wrote to Bailey that, 'At first the Congress were showing signs of completely selling out the Tibs[sic], but we persistently combated this'.[4]

The cadre's optimism was misplaced. Tibet was to be an exception to the general continuity of foreign policy by India after the transfer of power. In January 1950, India recognised the new Communist Government in China, which in August that year officially advised India of their intention to 'liberate' Tibet. On 7 October 1950, Chinese forces invaded Tibet from the east. The last Europeans left Lhasa around that time. But former Lhasa Radio Officer Robert Ford, then employed by the Tibetan Government in Chamdo, was caught out by the swift collapse of the Tibetan forces and was captured by the invading Chinese. Ford was treated as a spy. He languished in a Chinese prison, cut-off from the outside world and subjected to attempts at what was then known as 'brain-washing'. It was a symbol of the decline of British power and influence in Asia that he was not released until 1955.[5]

In April 1954, the Indian Government concluded an Agreement with the Chinese in which they recognised Tibet as part of China. This agreement allowed the 'establishment' (i.e.continuance) of three Indian Trade Agencies in Tibet. By an exchange of notes following the Agreement, however, India agreed to withdraw the Agency military escort, and to give control of the telegraph and communication systems and the *dak* bungalows along the trade route, to China.[6]

There were other events symbolic of the changes in Tibet in 1954. On 17 July, floods destroyed the Gyantse Trade Agency, killing several hundred people in the area. Trade Agent Pemba Tsering and his wife were among those drowned while the graves of Williamson and other Europeans who had died in Tibet were washed away.[7] Then, on 25 December, Lhasa's isolation ended forever with the arrival of the first motor convoy from Chengdu.

The Chinese take-over of Tibet happened in two phases. Their attempts to absorb it peacefully lasted until 1959, when increasing Tibetan opposition to China's attempts to destroy their culture caused the situation to deteriorate and the 14th Dalai Lama fled to India as Chinese forces shelled Lhasa. Three years later, the Sino-Indian conflict broke out, and the Lhasa mission and the Trade Agencies were closed. The official Indian presence in Tibet was ended.*

Independent India's policy towards Tibet differed from that of British India for a number of reasons, not least that Prime Minister Jawaharlal Nehru's idealism gave him to a naive view of Communist Chinese intentions and policies.[8] But Whitehall's refusal to recognise Tibet as an independent state had left it with an ambiguous status in international law. Tibet certainly claimed, and demonstrated, that it was independent in status. Following the British example, however, no country recognised it as such.

India had to face the legacy of the Raj's annexation of Tawang. The Simla Convention was the legal basis for this and the legal status of that Convention was, due to China's refusal to recognise it, 'at best questionable, at worst null and void'.[9] India was left in an awkward position, from which she apparently hoped to extricate herself by recognising Chinese authority over Tibet in the hope that China would accept Indian rule over Tawang.

Newly independent India was not, for reasons of prestige, nation-building and domestic politics, prepared to give up areas which it had inherited as Indian territory from the British. But Tawang was undoubtedly a 'skeleton' which India wished to keep in the cupboard; even today files relating to the area remain classified. The British annexation of Tawang has overshadowed India's Tibetan policy ever since.

Despite their struggle against the Chinese, the Tibet cadre, in the tradition of their 'Great Game' heritage, had always tended to regard Russia as the greatest threat to the security of both Tibet and India. Even in 1948, Hopkinson reported that 'in spite of changes within India, the same dangers threaten without, only more intensified, with increased Russian expansion'. Also around that time the former Gyantse Trade Agent, Major Ken Saker, submitted a report to the new Government of Pakistan (by whom he was then employed) in which he concluded that western Tibet 'was liable to be taken over by the Russians, possibly for the sake of its mineral wealth'.[10]

---

* The Nepalese however, have maintained their mission in Lhasa until the present day.

The Indian Army had considered the possibility of a Chinese Communist threat to Burma and India as far back as the 1920s. But they had concluded, in passing, that there was no real threat to Tibet from that source. When the British left India, China, although in the throes of a civil war, was still remembered as a war-time ally. Warnings of the likely collapse of Chang Kai-chek's government were not heeded. Not until early 1949 did British officials accept that the Communists would gain the victory formally signified by the inauguration of the Peoples Republic of China on 1 October 1949.[11]

Understandably, the cadre failed to foresee the Communist victory. They, and the Tibetans, were aware that China, whatever her government, would attempt to control Tibet, which could not resist a full-scale military attack. But on the frontier at the time, 'no one had seriously thought that the Chinese would take military action...The milieu was shattered by the Chinese invasion'.[12]

The cadre's basic duty was to protect the security of British India's northern border. In August 1947 they could, by this narrow definition look back and claim to have carried out their duty successfully. The cadre were not assigned to protect or advance Tibetan interests and never had enough power to direct Tibet's future in the direction which they thought best; that power was held by Whitehall, which was totally indifferent to Tibetan interests. But the cadre did identify strongly with Tibet, and they did not leave it in a virtually helpless state without deep personal regrets.

In retrospect, we may consider that had Curzon and Younghusband's 'forward' policies been carried though to their logical conclusion, Tibet, or at least part of it, would have been taken into a close association with India. It might have had a status similar to that of Bhutan, whose defence and foreign relations were controlled by India, but which was otherwise autonomous, and has remained so to this day. We may now judge that this could have prevented the cultural genocide that followed the Chinese take-over, saved more than a million Tibetan lives, and that the policies advanced by the cadre were therefore correct and that the policies of the British Government were tragically wrong.

Epilogue 251

Yet as Bell recognied, the Raj lacked the resources necessary to protect such far-flung borders.[13] That commitment was simply impractical. By 1947 there was no longer the means or the will to protect what was only ever a peripheral consideration in imperial affairs. Yet diplomatic recognition of Tibet as independent would have been an action of great significance to its future. Diplomatic recognition would have been made in 1949-50, when Anglo-Chinese relations were already poor. It was a gesture Whitehall ought to have made.

But Tibet was one of many unresolved issues the British left when they hurriedly abandoned their Indian empire. It was Tibet's misfortune that, having been released from the influence of a fundamentally benign imperial power, she was promptly conquered by a ruthless and barbaric imperialist dictatorship, whose exploitation and oppression of Tibet and its people still continues.

When the cadre left Tibet, they could look back and conclude honestly that, as individuals, 'on balance we had done more good than harm...We could look back without shame, and with some pride.'[14] But that sentiment can only be applied to the relationship of individual officers (including the military, medical, and technical staff) with the Tibetans, and not to the encounter as a whole.

* * *

In the 1950s, cadre officers such as Richardson and Sir Basil Gould, along with the former Indian Foreign Secretary, Sir Olaf Caroe, kept in touch with events in Tibet. Concern at the situation there eventually led to the formation of the Tibet Society of the UK in 1959, which aimed to draw attention to Tibet's plight and to preserve and promote Tibetan culture. This was followed by the formation of other societies, in Britain and abroad, dedicated to supporting the Tibetan cause. Thus the alliance of interests between the cadre officers and their allies in the pre-1947 period continued into the modern period.

In retirement, cadre officers did not forget Tibet. They wrote about it and played host to Tibetans visiting Britain. Thus Pemba Tsering's son, who attended medical school in England, recalls Bailey as a 'charming old gent' in his country house full of butterflies and Tibetan memorabilia. Sherriff took him grouse-shooting and Hopkinson showed him around Kew Gardens. Ludlow and Gould were similarly glad to see him; he was 'a reminder of the old days'.[15]

Today, a dwindling band of survivors of the pre-1947 Anglo-Tibetan encounter are scattered throughout Britain and India. Weir's daughter, Joan-Mary Jehu, the last surviving European to have met the 13th Dalai Lama, died during the writing of this book. She left the author with the abiding memory of a charming and dignified lady, seated in her modest English country house with a smattering of Tibetan decorations, patiently explaining what had once been obvious: "Our status?" she answered quizzically – "We were the top of the heap!"[16]

Of those 20 officers classified here as Tibet cadre, only Hugh Richardson remains alive, his posture still erect and a commanding air still apparent. After leaving Lhasa he devoted his life to the study of Tibet and became the greatest living authority on the subject, 'the father of modern Tibetan studies'. A constant stream of correspondents have benefited from his carefully considered replies and been inspired by his enthusiasm. He remains in close contact with the Dalai Lama and the Tibetan authorities, who consider his life 'very precious to us'.[17]

The harsh conditions on the frontier must have contributed to the early deaths of many cadre officers, but David Macdonald survived into his nineties. He is still fondly remembered around Kalimpong district, where his grandson Tim Macdonald, with wife Nilam, continue to maintain the atmospheric Himalayan Hotel. One of his granddaughters married Dr Keith Sprigg, an engaging specialist in Tibetan linguistics, with a wide knowledge of frontier history and culture, whose study visit to Gyantse in 1950 made him the last British visitor to enter pre-communist Tibet. The Spriggs live in retirement in Kalimpong, alert and hospitable, probably the last in a long line of frontier characters produced by the Raj.

Younghusband and O'Connor died during the Second World War and Bell shortly after. Their main supporter in Peking, Eric Teichman, was shot dead in 1944 by an American serviceman, apparently poaching on his Norfolk property. Arthur Hopkinson was ordained as an Anglican minister but died shortly after he began practising.

Gyantse Escort Commander, Captain Allen Robins, became a probation officer at the Old Bailey and recalls such famous criminals as Ruth Ellis, the last woman to be hung in England. He still corresponds with his friend and contemporary, Dr Kurian, who lives in comfortable retirement in South India. Robert Ford entered the diplomatic service after his release from a Chinese prison camp, and became Charge d'Affaires in Switzerland before he retired. A thoroughly decent and unpretentious man, he remains active in the Tibetan cause and fit enough to go bush-walking in New Zealand.

Major Saker stayed on in Pakistan for nine years, before joining the Foreign and Commonwealth Office, where his last posting was to Tonga. He died in 1979. Major Battye also remained in colonial service, latterly in what is now Tanzania. Recently Battye's grandson, Tom, found his way to Lhasa, not on a Political Officer's horse, but by hitch-hiking.

The Chinese continue to occupy and exploit their Tibetan colony and the British Government continue to ignore its plight. His Holiness the 14th Dalai Lama of Tibet now lives in exile in the village of McLeod Gang, above Dharamsala, in north India. Awarded the Nobel Peace Prize in 1989, he is an inspirational figure, who travels constantly throughout the world, preaching a message of non-violence and seeking justice for the Tibetan people. He remains in close touch with the survivors of the Anglo-Tibetan encounter.

Tsarong Shapé visited India in 1956 for the 2500th anniversary of the Buddha celebrations. But in 1958, against the advice and pleadings of his family and friends, he returned to Tibet. He intended to help the Dalai Lama into exile, and took the warm khaki clothing which His Holiness wore when he escaped. In his last ten days in India, Tsarong stayed with Laden La's family in Darjeeling and when he left for Tibet he walked so fast his son could not keep up with him, and stood and watched until his father vanished into the hills.[18] In the summer of 1959, Tsarong died in a Chinese military prison. Bailey, in retirement very much the country squire, lived until 1967. Of him, it could truly be said that few men ever enjoyed such a varied and exciting life. But if he did try to organise a coup in Tibet in 1924, he never admitted it.

Bailey represented one of the two approaches the cadre took to Tibet. He believed that if the existing Tibetan leadership could not be persuaded to reform their system along the lines required by British interests, then the cadre should find a Tibetan leadership which would do that. In contrast, Charles Bell, while equally concerned to protect British interests, believed that by understanding and befriending the existing Tibetan leadership, a strong, united modern Tibet could be created. Bell's humane and sympathetic approach succeeded in establishing a unique alliance of interests between Tibet and the British Raj.

Ultimately, Bell's ideas predominated throughout most of the 1904-47 period. But it meant that the conservative forces within Tibet refused to confront the realities of modernity, and this was eventually to cost them their freedom. It is one of the ironies of history that if Bailey and his old-fashioned imperial 'forward school' of frontier policy had predominated, Tibet and its people might have been better off today.

Appendix One

The Tibet Cadre

Lieutenant-Colonel Frederick Marsham BAILEY CIE. (1882-1967)
Born: India; son of Indian Army officer.
Educated: Wellington, Edinburgh Academy, Sandhurst.
Indian Army; Indian Political Department.

Major Richmond Keith Molesworth BATTYE. (1905-1958)
Born: Mashad Residency (Persia); son of Indian Army officer.
Educated: Marlborough, RMA Woolwich.
Indian Army; Indian Political Department.

Sir Charles Alfred BELL KCIE CMG CIE. (1870-1945)
Born: India; son of an ICS officer.
Educated: Winchester, Oxford.
Indian Civil Service.

Major William Lachlan CAMPBELL CIE. (1880-1937)
Born: Scotland; son of a 'gentleman'.
Educated: Edinburgh Academy, RMA Woolwich.
Indian Army, Indian Political Department.

Lieutenant-Colonel Edward Walter FLETCHER CBE. (1899-1958)
Born: England; son of an Army Officer.
Educated: Marlborough, RMA Woolwich.
Indian Army, Indian Political Department.

Sir Basil GOULD CMG CIE. (1883-1956)
Born: England; son of a lawyer.
Educated: Winchester, Oxford.
Indian Civil Service, Indian Political Department.

Major Philip Coates HAILEY. (1903-1980)
Born: England, son of an ICS officer.
Educated: Clifton College, Sandhurst.
Indian Army, Indian Political Department.

Reverend Arthur John HOPKINSON. (1894-1953)
Born: England, son of a Minister.
Educated: Marlborough, Oxford.
Indian Civil Service, Indian Political Department.

Frank LUDLOW. (1885-1972)
Born: England, son of a Cambridge lecturer in Botany.
Educated: Chelsea, Cambridge.
Indian Education Department.

David MACDONALD. (1870-1962)
Born: India, son of Scottish tea planter.
Educated: Bhotia School, Darjeeling.

Rai Sahib Norbu Dhondup OBE CBE. (1884-1944)
Born: India, son of Tibetan trader.
Educated: Government High School, Darjeeling.

Lieutenant-Colonel Sir William Frederick Travis O'CONNOR CSI CIE CVO (1870-1943)
Born: Ireland, son of landowner.
Educated: Charterhouse, RMA Woolwich.
Indian Army, Indian Political Department.

Rai Sahib Pemba Tsering. (1905-1954)
Born: India.
Educated: Government High School Darjeeling.

Hugh Edward RICHARDSON OBE CIE. (1905-)
Born: Scotland, grandson of an ICS officer.
Educated: Glenalmond, Oxford.
Indian Civil Service, Indian Political Department.

Major Alexander Alfred RUSSELL MC. (1898-1967)
Born: England, son of ICS officer.
Educated: Gordon Watson's Public School, Edinburgh, Quetta Cadet College.
Indian Army, Indian Political Department.

Major Richard Kenneth Molesworth SAKER CBE. (1908-1979)
Born: England, son of Army officer.
Educated: Aldenham, Sandhurst.
Indian Army, Indian Political Department.

Major George SHERRIFF. (1898-1967)
Born: Scotland, son of distiller.
Educated: Sedbergh, RMA Woolwich.
Indian Army, Indian Political Department.

Lieutenant-Colonel James Leslie Rose WEIR CIE. (1883-1950)
Born: India, son of IMS officer.
Educated: Wellingborough, RMA Woolwich.
Indian Army, Indian Political Department.

John Claude WHITE CIE. (1853-1918)
Born: India.
Educated: Bonn, Coopers Hill College of Engineering.
Indian Public Works Department.

Frederick WILLIAMSON. (1891-1935)
Born: England, son of a technician.
Educated: Bedford Modern, Cambridge.
Indian Civil Service, Indian Political Department.

The background of the 'founding father' of the cadre was very similar. **Colonel Sir Francis Edward YOUNGHUSBAND** KCIE. (1863-1943) was an Indian Army officer and a member of the Indian Political Department. Born in India, the son of a Major-General in the Indian Army, he had attended Clifton College and Sandhurst.

Appendix Two

The Government of India's Officers in Tibet

This appendix lists the officials who served in the principal Indian Political Department posts concerned with Tibet. This list, in addition to providing a source for future research, can be used to trace the careers of the principal cadre officers, as they followed a career path culminating in the positions in Gangtok or Lhasa. In addition, the sheer number of these officials – over one hundred – provides a counterweight to the generally projected image of Tibet as a land rarely visited by Europeans. In this sense it adds to Percival Landon's list of officers on the Younghusband Mission and James Cooper's list of European visitors to Lhasa.*

The lists have been compiled by a comparative review of primary sources (as noted in the bibliography), in particular, it relies on the records of the Oriental and India Office Collection [formerly known as the India Office Library], in London. Where the sources conflict, reliance has been placed on the record of the 'men on the spot' compiled nearest to the date of the event.

The principal positions were:-

1 The Political Officer Sikkim
2 The Head of British Mission Lhasa
3 The British Trade Agent Gyantse
4 The British Trade Agent Yatung
5 The British Trade Agent Gartok
6 The Officer Commanding Trade Agent's Escort Gyantse

---

* See Landon 1988, pp. 364-67; Cooper, J. 'Western Visitors to Lhasa: A Chronological List'; document available from The Tibet Society U.K.

7 The Medical Officer Gyantse
8 The Civil Surgeon Bhutan and Tibet

The Political Officer Sikkim was stationed in Gangtok (Sikkim), while the other positions listed were all located inside Tibet.

Due to transport difficulties, leave requirements, and personal arrangements between officers, the official date of posting often varies widely from the actual hand-over date. In order to indicate the actual dates of service in a particular position, the dates given are, with one exception which will be noted, those of the actual hand-over, rather than the official posting date.

Due to the complexity of events involving the Gyantse Trade Agents in the earlier years, such as the flight and return of the 13th Dalai Lama, I have given the actual day of hand-over for this position as an aid to other scholars in this area.

In a number of cases, officers were relieved temporarily during their absence on leave, or on other duties elsewhere in Tibet or India. In these cases I have indicated that the officer officiating 'relieves', and that the serving officer 'resumes'.

British personnel also served in other subordinate positions in Tibet. The early Gyantse and Yatung Head Clerks were European and the telegraph and supply posts were occupied by British non-commissioned officers. After 1936 a British Radio Officer served at Lhasa. These positions are however, outside the scope of this study.

1. THE POLITICAL OFFICER SIKKIM, BHUTAN AND TIBET

With the exception of White, whose post predated the creation of the positions in Tibet, these officers had all previously served as British Trade Agent Gyantse. The three temporary officers were all serving at the Gyantse post at the time of their appointment.

J.C. White takes up newly created post	May 1889
C.Bell relieves	May 1904
White resumes	Nov. 1904
Bell relieves	Sept. 1906

White resumes	Jan. 1907
Bell relieves (White on leave prior to his retirement in October 1908, when Bell was appointed permanently)	Mar. 1908
Capt. J.L.R. Weir relieves	Aug. 1911
Bell resumes	Oct. 1911
B.Gould relieves	Oct. 1913
Bell resumes	Sept. 1914
Major W.L. Campbell relieves (Bell on leave prior to his retirement in March 1919 when Campbell was appointed permanently)	Apr. 1918
Bell reappointed for one year after Campbell resigns	Jan. 1920
Lt-Colonel W.F. O'Connor takes up post (Bell in Lhasa until October 1921)	Jan. 1921
D. Macdonald relieves	Mar. 1921
Major F.M. Bailey takes up post	June 1921
F. Williamson relieves	May 1926
Bailey resumes	Dec. 1926
Major J.L.R. Weir takes up post	Oct. 1928
F.Williamson relieves	Apr. 1931
Weir resumes	Aug. 1931
F. Williamson takes up post	Jan. 1933
Capt. R.K.M. Battye relieves (after death of Williamson in Lhasa.)	Nov. 1935
B. Gould takes up post	Dec. 1935
H. Richardson relieves	May 1937
B. Gould resumes	Nov. 1937
A.J. Hopkinson takes up post	Jun. 1945

2. THE HEAD OF BRITISH MISSION LHASA

Of the five officers who occupied this post, only George Sherriff, a wartime appointee, had not previously served in Tibet, although Ludlow had been employed by the Tibetan Government, not the Government of India.

262 *Tibet and the British Raj*

H. Richardson remained in Lhasa after the departure of the Gould mission	Feb. 1937
Norbu Dhondup takes up post	July 1937
H. Richardson resumes	Oct. 1938
Norbu Dhondup resumes	Oct. 1939
F.Ludlow takes up post	Apr. 1942
G. Sherriff takes up post	Apr. 1943
H. Richardson relieves	Jun. 1944
G. Sherriff resumes	Sept. 1944
Pemba Tsering takes up post	Apr. 1945
H. Richardson resumes	Apr. 1946
Pemba Tsering relieves	Sept. 1947
H. Richardson resumes	Dec. 1947

3. THE BRITISH TRADE AGENT GYANTSE

After 1944 this post was nominally held by an officer stationed in Gangtok (Gould), or Lhasa (Richardson). The Escort Commanding Officer in Gyantse then acted as Trade Agent in addition to his military post, except during visits by the appointed Trade Agent.

Capt. W.F. O'Connor takes up newly created post	01.10.1904
Lt. F.M. Bailey relieves,	23.12.1905
O'Connor resumes (Hand-over at Gangtok)	15.12.1906
Bailey relieves,	18.07.1907
O'Connor resumes	27.07.1907
Bailey takes up post	01.08.1907
Capt. R.S. Kennedy {IMS} relieves (at Yatung)	05.06.1909
Capt. J.L.R. Weir takes up post	13.12.1909
D.Macdonald relieves (at Yatung)	23.01.1911
Weir resumes	01.04.1911
Macdonald relieves	10.08.1911
Weir resumes	30.12.1911
Macdonald relieves	15.02.1912
B.Gould takes up post	04.05.1912
Macdonald relieves	31.03.1913

Major W.L. Campbell takes up post (at Yatung)	24.02.1916
Macdonald takes up post	31.03.1918
F. Williamson takes up post	20.06.1924
Capt. R.L. Vance {IMS} relieves	31.05.1926
A.J.Hopkinson takes up post	03.01.1927
Major H.G. Rivett-Carnac takes up post	30.04.1928
Lt. W.J.L. Neal {IA} relieves	01-03-1929
Rivett-Carnac resumes	18.05.1929
Capt. D.R. Smith takes up post	18.09.1929
Capt. E.W. Fletcher takes up post	19.11.1929
Capt. A.A. Russell takes up post	19.11.1931
M. Worth takes up post	18.04.1933
Capt. P.C. Hailey takes up post	01.12.1933
Capt. R.K.M. Battye takes up post	20.06.1935
H. Richardson takes up post	20.07.1936
Capt. D.G. Thornburgh takes up post	03.02.1940
Major M.C. Sinclair takes up post (at Gangtok)	20.07.1940
Capt. R.K.M. Saker takes up post	15.06.1941
Major R.W.D. Gloyne {IA} relieves	12.05.1942
Saker resumes	15.01.1943
Gould reappointed, stationed at Gangtok, Capt. J.H. Davis {IA} relieves (at Gyantse)	28.09.1943
F.H. Mainprice takes up post	19.05.1944
Gould reappointed, stationed at Gangtok, the following act in Gyantse:-	12.08.1944
Capt. C. Finch {IA}	
Capt. A.G.H. Robins {IA}	
Lt. R. Grist {IA}	
Lt. T.R.W. Dark {IA}	
Richardson reappointed	12.02.1946

4. THE BRITISH TRADE AGENT YATUNG

Although provision was made in the 1893 Anglo-Chinese Convention for this post to open on 1 May 1894, it was left vacant until

November 1903, when E.C.H. Walsh was posted to the Chumbi Valley as Assistant Political Officer attached to the Tibetan Frontier Commission (which became known as the Younghusband mission). C.Bell relieved Walsh in May 1904, and was replaced by Captain W.L. Campbell in November 1905, who, following the occupation of the Chumbi Valley, was in effective administrative charge of the Chumbi. Campbell was relieved by Lieutenant F.M.Bailey between December 1906 and January 1908, when the Chumbi Valley was returned to Tibetan control, and Campbell took up the post which now became that of British Trade Agent Yatung. At intervals in 1907-09, and from October 1924 to July 1936, this post was combined with that of the British Trade Agent Gyantse.

Capt. W.L. Campbell takes up post	Jan. 1908
Lt. F.M. Bailey relieves	July 1908
Lt. R.S. Kennedy {IMS} relieves	June 1909
D. Macdonald takes up post	July 1909

(Macdonald then served at Yatung, without official leave, until his retirement in October 1924. The post then combined with that of the British Trade Agent Gyantse until 1936, for details see separate listing for Gyantse.)

Norbu Dhondup takes up post (position combined with Head of British Mission Lhasa when Norbu Dhondup stationed in Lhasa)	July 1936
Sonam Tobden Kazi took up post	Sept. 1942
Pemba Tsering relieves	Aug. 1943
Sonam Tobden Kazi resumes	Mar. 1944

5. THE BRITISH TRADE AGENT GARTOK

The post was originally full-time, but from 1925 onwards the Gartok Agent visited the Agency during the summer months only. The posting is thus shown on an annual basis from that time. This post was never occupied by a European.

Thakur Jai Chand took up newly created post	Nov. 1904
Lala Devi Das took up post	Jan. 1912
Cha. Pala Ram took up post	Mar. 1925
Thakur Hayat Singh took up post	1928
Dr Kanshi Ram took up post	1929
Pemba Tsering took up post	1941
Lakshman Singh took up post	1946

6. OFFICER COMMANDING TRADE AGENT'S ESCORT GYANTSE

At intervals after 1916, a second, junior, officer was posted as Second-in-command. This officer often succeeded to the position of Escort Commander, but ten officers served only in the junior position. Major Pearson's dates are uncertain. The officer(s) being relieved returned to India within a few days of handing over, except in the case of Captain Marshall, who remained for a month in 1932 to assist in training Tibetan troops. The Escort officers were all members of the Indian Army, and, as far as can be ascertained, were all Europeans except for Lieutenant G.N.Chatterjee. The position was commonly known as the Escort Commander.

Lt. W.L. Hogg, 3rd Brahmins relieves	Nov. 1905
Lt. C.J. Auchinleck, 62nd Punjabis relieves	Sept. 1906
Major W.R. Walker took command of the 62nd	July 1907
Lt. M.H.L. Morgan took command of the 62nd	Dec. 1907
Lt. R.B. Langrishe took command of the 62nd	Feb. 1908
Lt. W. Macready, 120th Rajputs relieves	Sept. 1908
Lt. A.O. Creagh took command of the 120th	Sept. 1909
Lt. J.Turner, 114th Maharattas, relieves	May. 1911
Lt. H.R. Wilson took command of the 114th	June 1913
Capt. L.S. Fenton, 113th Infantry, relieves	Sept. 1913
Capt. L.F. Bodkin 2nd in command from	Sept. 1914
Capt Bodkin took command of the 113th	Sept. 1915
Lt. W. de la Passy 2-i-c from	Sept. 1915
(Departed May 1916, not replaced)	

266 *Tibet and the British Raj*

Lt. M.R. Roberts took command of the 113th	Aug. 1916
Capt. F. Perry, 2/10th Jats, relieves	Apr. 1918
Lt. G.N. Chatterjee took command of the 113th	July 1920
Lt. J.A. Andrews took command of the 113th	July 1921
Capt. E. Parker, 90th Punjabis, relieves	Oct. 1921
Capt. G.B. Williams, 4/8th Rajputs, relieves	Sept. 1922
Capt. J.E. Cobbett took command of the 4/7th	Sept. 1923
Capt. E.A. Evanson, 3/17th Dogras, relieves	Sept. 1924
Lt. R.P. Taylor 2-i-c from	Nov. 1925
Lt. H.M. de V. Moss, 3/12th Sikhs, relieves	Sept. 1926
Lt. R.A.K. Sangster 2-i-c from	Sept. 1926
Capt. W.E. Dean took command of the 3/12th	Sept. 1927
Capt. H.W. Mulligan took command of the 3/12th	Sept. 1928
Capt. J.A. Blood took command of the 3/12th	Dec. 1929
Lt. A.J.W. Macleod 2-i-c from	Dec. 1929
Capt. H.R. Officer took command of the 3/12th	Mar. 1930
Capt. F.C. Goddard, 1/5th Maharatta Light Infantry relieves	Sept. 1930
Capt. A.J. Crozier 2-i-c from	Sept. 1930
Capt. N.M. Anderson took command of the 1/5th	June 1931
Capt. W.D. Marshall 2-i-c from	June 1931
Capt. Marshall took command of the the 1/5th (no 2-i-c)	Sept. 1931
Capt. E.S.E. Rennie took command of the 1/5th	Sept. 1932
Capt. H.W. Huelin, 2/7th Rajputs, relieves	Sept. 1933
Lt. G.E.P. Cable 2-i-c from	Sept. 1933
Major A.C. Bronham took command of the 2/7th	Sept. 1934
Lt. J.W. Pease 2-i-c from	Sept. 1934
Capt. J.A. Salomons took command of the 2/7th (no 2-i-c)	Sept. 1935
Major P.W. Finch took command of the 2/7th	Nov. 1936
Cable (now Capt.) took command of the 2/7th	Mar. 1937
Major W.A. Colbourne, 1/15th Punjabis relieves	Sept. 1937
Lt. H.B. Hudson 2-i-c from	Sept. 1937
Lt. Hudson took command of the 1/15th (no 2-i-c)	Jun. 1938

Major F. MacKenzie took command of the 1/15th	Sept. 1938
Capt. C.V. Clifford 2-i-c from	Sept. 1938
Major J.G. Innes-Keys took command of the 1/15th (no 2-i-c)	Sept. 1939
Major J.L. Widdicombe, 20th Garrison Company, relieves	June 1940
Lt. D.A. Walters 2-i-c from	June 1940
Walters (now Capt.) took command of the 20th (no 2-i-c)	Oct. 1940
Lt. E.F. Croyle 2-i-c from	Feb. 1941
Major R.W.D. Gloyne takes command of the 20th	May 1941
Lt. C. Finch 2-i-c from	Feb 1943
Capt. J.H. Davies takes command of the 20th	Mar. 1943
Finch (now Capt.) took command of the 20th	July 1944
Capt A.G.H. Robins Rajput Regiment, relieves	July. 1944
(originally acting Trade Agent, took command)	Oct. 1944
Lt. R.F. Grist 2-i-c from	Oct. 1944
Grist (now Capt.) took command of the 20th	Oct. 1945
Lt. T.W.R. Dark 2-i-c from	Nov. 1945
Major D.H. Pailthorpe, 1/1st Punjabis, relieves	Oct. 1946
Lt N.J. Campbell 2-i-c from	Oct. 1946
(Campbell left Feb. 1947 and not replaced)	
Major Pearson took command of the 1/1st	May? 1947

7. THE MEDICAL OFFICER GYANTSE

After the establishment of the senior post of Civil Surgeon Bhutan and Tibet, this position was, for administrative purposes, officially referred to as the Officer in Charge Indian Military Hospital Gyantse. Aside from war-time appointee Dr Humphreys, the 23 officers who served in Gyantse were all members of the Indian Medical Service. Following the appointment of the Anglo-Indian, Dr Humphreys, the position was occupied by Indian officers.

Lt. R. Steen takes up newly created post	Oct. 1904
Lt. F.H. Stewart takes up post	Oct. 1906

Lt. R.S. Kennedy takes up post	Oct. 1907
Capt. D.M.C. Church takes up post	Mar. 1910
Lt. R.F.D. MacGregor takes up post	Jun. 1911
Capt. G.B. Harland takes up post	Oct. 1912

Captain Harland departed in December 1915, the position was then vacant, with Sub-Assistant Surgeon Bo Tsering in charge of the Gyantse dispensary until September 1922.

Capt. R. Lee takes up post	Sept. 1922
Major J.H. Hislop takes up post	July 1923
Capt. R.L. Vance takes up post	Sept. 1924
Capt. D.N. Bhaduri relieves	Jan. 1926
Vance resumes	Apr. 1926
Capt. H.W. Mulligan takes up post	Sept. 1927
Lt. W.J.L. Neal takes up post	Apr. 1928
Lt. M.R. Sinclair takes up post	May. 1931

Lieutenant Sinclair accompanied the Political Officer to Lhasa in August 1932 towards the end of his term of service; Bo Tsering relieved until Captain Tennant arrived.

Capt D. Tennant takes up post	Sept. 1932
Capt. J. Guthrie takes up post	Sept. 1934
Capt. W.S. Morgan takes up post	Nov. 1936

Captain Morgan took over the post while in Lhasa with the Gould Mission. Sub-Assistant Surgeon Rai Sahib Tonyot Tsering relieved at Gyantse until Morgan arrived in February 1937.

Capt. A.H.O. O'Malley takes up post	July 1938
Capt. C.W.A. Searle takes up post	July 1940
Dr. G.F. Humphreys takes up post	Oct. 1940
Capt. M.V. Kurian takes up post	Mar. 1944

Captain Kurian was in Lhasa from November 1944 until September 1945 with Bo Tsering relieving at Gyantse.

Capt. S.B. Bhattacharjee takes up post	Nov. 1945
Capt. S. Sanyal relieves	Sept. 1946
Bhattacharjee resumes	Oct. 1946
Lt. B.B. Patnaik takes up post	Oct. 1947

8. THE CIVIL SURGEON BHUTAN AND TIBET

This position was created in August 1940 to oversee medical arrangements in Bhutan and Tibet. Although the official headquarters of the post was at Gyantse, it became, in effect, that of Medical Officer to the British Mission Lhasa, with the officers concerned increasingly spending much of their time in Lhasa. In this instance, due to the varied locations involved, the dates given are those of appointment to the post. Two of the four officers appointed to this post, Lt-Colonel Hislop and Major Guthrie, had previously served as Medical Officer Gyantse.

Capt. W.H.D. Staunton takes up newly created post	Aug. 1940
Lt-Col. J.H. Hislop takes up post	Jan. 1942
Dr. G.S. Terry takes up post	Jun. 1944
Major J. Guthrie takes up post	Mar. 1945

Notes

The following abbreviations are used:

fn	Footnote.
FD	Foreign Department
FO	Foreign Office.
ICS	Indian Civil Service.
IMS	Indian Medical Service.
OIOC	Oriental and India Office Collection and Records.
NAI	National Archives of India, New Delhi.
RGS	Royal Geographical Society.

FOREWORD TO THE SECOND EDITION

1. My thanks are due to Lobsang Shastri and Tsering Namgyal for their assistance in producing this edition. Thanks also to Scott Berry for his efforts.
2. At the time of writing (February 2009) just four Europeans who visited Lhasa before the communist Chinese invasion in 1950 are known to survive; Robert Ford, Frank Bessac, Lowell Thomas jnr, and Bruno Beger.
3. See, Alexandre Andreyev, *Soviet Russia and Tibet: the debacle of secret diplomacy, 1918-1930s,* Brill, Leiden, 2003; Tatiana Shaumian, *Tibet: The Great Game and Tsarist Russia,* New Delhi, 2000.
4. Michael Carrington, 'Officers, Gentlemen and Thieves: The Looting of the Monasteries during the 1903-04 Younghusband Mission to Tibet', *Modern Asian Studies,* 37.1, 2003, pp.81-109.

    Also see the forthcoming volume edited by Hildegard Diemberger, which will discuss the character and fate of the material objects collected – or looted - by the Younghusband mission.
5. Charles Allen, *Duel in the Snows: The True Story of the Younghusband Mission to Lhasa,* John Murray, London, 2004.

6 Michael Rank, "Frank Ludlow and the English School in Tibet, 1923-1926", *Asian Affairs*, 34.1, 2003, pp.33-45; Michael Rank, "King Arthur comes to Tibet: Frank Ludlow and the English school in Gyantse, 1923-26", *Bulletin of Tibetology* (Gangtok) 40.2, 2004, pp.49-78.

7 Isrun Engelhardt (ed.), *Tibet in 1938-39: Photographs from the Ernst Schäfer Expedition to Tibet*, Serindia, Chicago, 2007; also see Isrun Engelhardt, 'Tibetan Triangle: German, Tibetan and British Relations in the Context of Ernst Schäfer's Expedition, 1938-39', *Asiatische Studien*, 58, 004, pp.57-113; Isrun Engelhardt, 'Mishandled Mail: The Strange Case of the Reting Regent's Letters to Hitler', *Zentralasiatische Studien* (ZAS) 37, 2008, pp.77-106.

8 The last surviving member of that expedition, Bruno Beger, has also written an account entitled *Mit der deutschen Tibetexpedition Ernst Schäfer 1938/39 nach Lhasa;* privately published in Wiesbaden, 1998.

9 Julie G. Marshall, *Britain and Tibet: A select annotated bibliography of British relations with Tibet and the Himalayan states including Nepal, Sikkim and Bhutan,* revised edition, RoutledgeCurzon, London/N.Y. 2005; (first published; 1977, University of La Trobe, Melbourne).

10 James Cooper, 'Western and Japanese Visitors to Lhasa: 1900-1950', *The Tibet Journal,* 28.4, 2003, pp.91-94.

11 William Stanley Morgan, *Amchi Sahib: A British Doctor in Tibet 1936-37,* Verena Morgan Rybicki (ed.), privately printed, Charlestown (MA), 2007.

12 Martin Brauen (ed.), *Peter Aufschnaiter's Eight Years in Tibet,* Bangkok, Orchid Press, 2002, (first published in German, 1983).

13 Richard Starks and Miriam Murcutt, *Lost in Tibet: The Untold Story of Five American Airmen, a Doomed Plane, and the Will to Survive,* Lyons Press, Guilford (Connecticut), 2004; there is also an enjoyable earlier private publication by one of the crew, H.J. (Mac) McCallum, *Tibet: One Second to Live (A Pilot's Story),* Emlenton, PA., 1995.

14 Dundul Namgyal Tsarong, *In the Service of His Country. The Biography of Dasang Damdul Tsarong, Commander General of Tibet,* Snow Lion Publications, Ithaca, N.Y., 2000

15 See, for example, Sumner Carnahan, (with Lama Kunga Rinpoche, Nor Thartse Shadtrung), *In the Presence of My Enemies: Memoirs of Tibetan Nobleman Tsipon Shuguba,* Clearlight publishers, Santa Fe, 1995; Jamyang Sakya & Julie Emery, *Princess in the Land of Snows: The Life of Jamyang Sakya in Tibet,* Shambala, Boston & Shaftsbury, 1990.

16 Peter Richardus, (ed.), *Tibetan Lives: Three Himalayan Autobiographies,* Curzon Press, London, 1998; also of interest is Sonam B. Wangyal, *Footprints in the Himalayas: People, Places and Practices,* Bhutan,

Darjeeling, Nepal, Sikkim and Tibet, KMT Press, Phuentsoling (Bhutan), 2006.
17 Herbert L. Fader, *Called from Obscurity: The Life and Times of a True Son of Tibet, Gergan Dorje Tharchin,* Kalimpong, Mirror Press, vol.1, 2002; vol.2, 2004; vol.3 is forthcoming (2009).
18 See, for example, Douglas A. Wissing, *Pioneer in Tibet: The Life and Perils of Dr. Albert Shelton,* New York, Palgrave, 2004; Cindy Perry, *Nepali around the World: Emphasizing Nepali Christians of the Himalayas,* Ekta, Kathmandhu, 1997.
19 Wim van Spengen, *Tibetan Border Worlds: A Geohistorical Analysis of Trade and Traders,* Kegan Paul International, London/N.Y., 2000; Rinzin Thargyal, *Nomads of Eastern Tibet: Social Organization and Economy of a Pastoral Estate in the Kingdom of Dege,* (Toni Huber: ed.), Brill, Leiden, 2007.
20 Tsering Shakya, *The Dragon in the Land of Snows: A history of modern Tibet since 1947,* Pimlico, London, 1999 (USA: Columbia University Press, 1999); Melvyn C. Goldstein, *A History of Modern Tibet: volume 2. The Calm before the Storm,* University of California Press, Berkeley/London, 2007.
21 Alex McKay 'Sikkim: The British Period, 1817-1947', forthcoming in a volume edited by Anna Balikci, (Serindia, 2010?).
22 See, Alex McKay, '19th century British Expansion on the Indo-Tibetan Frontier: A Forward Perspective', in *The Tibet Journal,* 28.4, 2003, pp.1-16.
23 See, Alex McKay, "Tracing lines upon the unknown areas of the earth": Reflections on the Indo-Tibetan Frontier', in Sameetah Agha & Elizabeth Kolsky (eds.), *Fringes of Empire: Peoples, Places and Spaces at the Margins of British Colonial India,* forthcoming (OUP, Delhi, 2009).
24 Alex McKay, *Footprints Remain: Biomedical beginnings across the Indo-Tibetan frontier 1870-1970;* University of Amsterdam/IIAS, Amsterdam 2007 [U.S. publisher; University of Chicago Press; 2008]; see the bibliography for the author's articles in that field.
25 See for example, Roger Croston, (obituary) 'Hugh Richardson. Resident British diplomat in Lhasa, Tibet. Scholar and author', in *European Bulletin of Himalayan Research,* 19, Autumn 2000, pp.127-131; (obituary), 'Sir Evan Nepean, Bt. Amateur radio enthusiast and Army officer who went to Tibet as part of the British Mission', in *The Times,* 6 April 2002, p.44; 'The story of AC4YN - A Radio Adventure in Tibet, 1936', *RadCom* [sic], *The Radio Society of Great Britain Member's Magazine,* Potters Bar, Hertfordshire, England, June 2002, pp.39-40; 'The story of AC4YN

- A Radio Adventure in Tibet, 1936', *The Journal of the Royal Signals Institution*, Vol. XXIV.5, Autumn 2002, pp.166-68.
26 Information courtesy Zara Fleming and a family descendant in the UK.
27 Deki & Nicholas Rhodes, 'Sonam Wangfel Laden La – Tibet 1924 and 1930', *The Tibet Journal*, 28.4, 2003, pp.77-90.
28 Nicholas and Deki Rhodes, *A Man of the Frontier: S.W. Laden La (1876-1936). His Life and Times in Darjeeling and Tibet*, Mira Bose (Library of Numismatic Studies), Kolkata, 2006.
29 See for example, O'Connor's role as discussed in, Alex McKay, "'That he may take due pride in the empire to which he belongs": the education of Maharajah Kumar Sidkeong Namgyal Tulku', *Bulletin of Tibetology*, (Gangtok, Sikkim), 39.2., 2003, pp.27-52.

ACKNOWLEDGEMENTS

1 OIOC R/1/4/1091, personal file of W.F.O'Connor, file note by S.H. Butler, 23 January 1908.

PROLOGUE

1 Younghusband 1985, pp. 326-27.
2 Lord Curzon (1859-1925) Eton & Oxford. Coservative MP from 1886. Viceroy of India 1899-1905. British Foreign Secretary 1919-24.
3 French 1994, p. 243, quoting OIOC MSS Eur F197, Younghusband to his wife.
4 For an excellent biography of Younghusband, see French 1994; also see Seaver 1952; Verrier 1992.
5 OIOC MSS Eur F197-145, Younghusband to his father, 19 July 1903.
6 O'Connor 1931, p. 3.
7 Ibid, pp. 1-8.
8 In 1891 Bower made an important exploratory journey through north-western Tibet; see Bower 1976.
9 OIOC R/1/4/1091, various correspondence; O'Connor 1940, pp. 50-51. Sir Louis Dane GCIE CSI. (1856-1946) Kingstown School, Ireland. Indian Political Department. Chief Secretary to the Punjab Government 1898-1901, Resident in Kashmir 1901-03, Indian Foreign Secretary 1903-07. Later Lieutenant-Governor of the Punjab.
10 Mehra 1967, p. 12.
11 O'Connor 1931, p. 46; French 1994, pp. 208-09, 212-13.
12 OIOC MSS Eur F157-319, Bailey typescript autobiography, p. 18.

13 Swinson 1971, pp. 42-43, 46.
14 OIOC MSS Eur F157-199, Bailey's mission diary; also see Rawling 1905.

INTRODUCTION

1 Anderson 1992.
2 Although I refer throughout to the Political Department, the service underwent several name changes which reflected its twin fields of operation. At the beginning of our period (1904), it was known as the Political and Secret Department; the Political branch dealt with relations with Indian states, and the Secret Department with external territories. In 1914 it was renamed the Foreign and Political Department, and in 1937 it was divided into the External Affairs Department and the Political Department.
3 See Kaminsky 1986, pp. 151, 201; Yapp 1990, pp. 587-88.
4 Coen 1971, pp. 35, 54.
5 Trench 1987, p. 13.
6 Coen 1971, pp. 4-6.
7 Re the *pandits*, see Waller 1990; He classifies Chandra Das and his companion Urgyen Gyatso as *pandits*, but the two men were of a very different social class to other *pandits*.
8 Rai Bahadur S.C.Das CIE. (1849-1917). Sandberg 1987, p. 163; Waller 1990, p. 193 (quoting NAI FD, Secret January 1882, 722-725, Sir Alfred Croft to A.C.Lyall, 12 April 1879), pp. 194 fn.8, p. 292. In 1891 the Bhotia school merged with Darjeeling school to become Darjeeling High School
9 Macdonald 1991, pp. 138-40; Bell 1992, p. 59; Waller 1990, pp. 196, 206. For Das's account of his journey, see Das 1902.
10 Waller 1990, p. 201.
11 Das 1902, pp. 80, 101; Johnson 1994, pp. 191-206; Waller 1990, pp. 193-213.
12 For other examples of this process, see, re Bhutan, Collister 1987; re north-east India, Robb 1994, esp. pp. 7-23; also see Ludden 1993, p. 253.; also see, Dirks 1994, pp. 279-313.
13 Re the aborted (Macualay) mission; see Lamb 1960, pp. 124-137.
14 Lamb 1960, pp. 239-41; Richardson 1984, pp. 78-82.
15 Dorzhiev's role in Tibet has attracted a great deal of comment, much of it inaccurate. A recent work, which uses a number of hitherto unavailable Russian sources, provides the first reliable account of his life; see Snelling 1993.

16　The Japanese monk, Kawaguchi Ekai, who visited Lhasa in 1901, was one apparently neutral source who reported that Russian arms supplies were reaching Lhasa; Berry 1991, pp. 304-05; Kawaguchi 1979, pp. 505-06.
17　Younghusband 1985, p. 333.
18　Curzon 1907, *passim*; Lyall 1973, pp. 334-49; Prasad 1979, pp. 577-78; Verrier 1992, p. 36.
19　Quoted in Edwardes 1975, p.93.
20　Yapp 1980, p. 588.
21　Re 'suzerainty', see Lamb 1989, esp. pp. 320-26; Praag 1987, esp. pp. 101-39.
22　Fleming 1984, p. 285; also see Younghusband 1985, p. 340; Lamb 1966, pp. 13-14, quoting FO 535/5, No.83, encs. 2 and 3, Broderick to India, 2 February 1904.
23　OIOC L/P&S/12/187-4682, Foreign Secretary, India, to the Under Secretary of State, India Office, 28 June 1935.
24　RGS. Bailey correspondence, 1921-30; Mrs Irma Bailey to Arthur Hinks (RGS Secretary), 9 October 1924; OIOC MSS Eur F157-259, Richardson to Bailey, 25 February 1949; MSS Eur F157-258, Hopkinson to Bailey, 26 November 1949.
25　The major difference between British and Chinese plans for Tibet concerned the Tibetan army. While the cadre sought to strengthen Tibet's military capacity to enable Tibet to defend themselves against the Chinese, China naturally sought to weaken Tibet's military forces. Chinese plans are noted in; NAI FD, 1908 Secret E September 113-134, various correspondence; FD, 1908 Secret E February 467-482, W.Cassels to Government of United Provinces, 23 September 1907 (re western Tibet); OIOC L/P&S/7/220-1625, Gyantse Annual Report 1907-08, enclosed in Bell to India, 28 May 1908.
26　For example, OIOC L/P&S/7/251-1466, Gyantse diary of June 1911, notes that the Chinese had enquired if a British officer was to be posted to Gartok, in which case the Chinese would station an officer there, also see McKay 1994a, p. 381.
27　Re trade in Tibet, see van Spengen1992.

CHAPTER ONE

1　OIOC L/P&S/7/173-360; Government of India to Government of the Punjab, 9 September 1904.
2　NAI FD, External B March 19-31, file note by Lord Ampthill, 5 November 1904.

3 Singh 1988a, p. 29.
4 Snelling 1993, p. 101; re the Khutukhtus, see Bawden, C., *The Jetsundampa Khutukhtu of Urga*, Weisbaden 1961.
5 Snelling 1993, pp. 119
6 Younghusband 1985, p. 325.
7 OIOC L/P&S/10/1113-8573, Weir report, 18 November 1930; L/P&S/7/183-168, O'Connor to White, 23 November 1905.
8 Included in O'Connor's party was Vernon Magniac, Younghusband's private secretary and brother-in-law. He returned to India when O'Connor returned to Gyantse, and presumably gave Younghusband details of the talks with the Panchen Lama.
9 OIOC L/P&S/7/196-2152, O'Connor to India, 27 April 1906; McKay 1992a pp. 416.
10 Bell 1987, pp. 71-72.
11 NAI FD, 1905 Secret E March 295-308, various correspondence; FD, 1907 Secret E January 538-541, file note by Louis Dane, 2 December 1906. The issue of Yatung as a Treaty Port had apparently first been mentioned in 1894; see Louis 1894, p. 38. The British China Customs officers who were appointed to Yatung were J.H.Hart, W.R.M'd Parr, V.C.Henderson, F.E.Taylor and Messrs Holison and Montgomery.
12 NAI FD, 1905 Secret E March 294-308; various correspondence; FD, 1907 Secret E February 295-353, O'Connor to India, 26 December 1906.
13 Lamb 1966, pp. 39-40, quoting Foreign Office 17/1754, India Office to Foreign Office, 14 February 1905, and 23 May 1905; NAI FD, 1905 Secret E March 294-308, Younghusband to Dane, 27 August 1904.
14 NAI FD, 1905 Secret E March 294-308, various correspondence; FD, 1913 Secret E August 276-291, various correspondence; FD, Secret E June 502-511, Mr Chang to Government of Bengal, 3 May 1907; re the China Customs Service, see Wright 1950.
15 A number of these reports may be found in the OIOC L/P&S/7 series.
16 OIOC L/P&S/10/149-3807, Muir to W.H.Wilkinson, British Consul at Chengdu, 28 May 1910; also see Muir's lengthy report on military affairs in L/P&S/10/149-4076, Muir to Wilkinson 5 April 1910; L/P&S/7/251-1435, Edgar to Wilkinson, 31 May 1911, enclsosure in Wilkinson to Sir J.Jordan, 15 June 1911.
17 OIOC L/P&S/7/241-1058, Gyantse Annual Report, 1909-10; MSS Eur F157-304, Gyantse diary entry, 23 May 1909.
18 OIOC R/1/1/303, Government of India proceedings, August 1904, numbers 1-2.
19 OIOC L/P&S/11/47, Foreign Office minute, 13 March 1913, Viceroy to India Office, 6 March 1913, & Foreign Office to India Office, 4

278 *Tibet and the British Raj*

February 1913; re mail see NAI FD, 1913 Secret E April 364-401, various correspondence.
20 OIOC L/P&S/7/179-1214, Viceroy to the Secretary of State, 29 July 1905; L/P&S/7/180-1344, Gyantse diary entry, 3 July 1905; Berry 1995; pp. 65-70.
21 OIOC L/P&S/7/183, O'Connor to White, 23 November 1905. Personal correspondence with H.Richardson, October 1990.
22 NAI FD, 1906 External B August 180-181, White to India, 25 July 1906; also see FD, 1908 Establishment B December 165-195, Bell's Secret Service accounts, 1907-1908.
23 OIOC MSS Eur F157-197, Gyantse diary entry, 10 March 1908; L/P&S/7/180-1439, Gyantse diary entry, 25 July 1905; L/P&S/7/183-1868,Gyantse diary entry, 15 October 1905; re slate letters, see Bell 1987, pp. 229-30.
24 OIOC MSS Eur F 157-304, Gyantse diary entry, 24 November 1908; Interview with Mrs J-M.Jehu, March 1993.
25 Lamb 1966, pp. 22-24; O'Connor 1931, pp. 86-87.
26 O'Connor 1931, pp. 90-92.
27 NAI FD, 1906 Secret E March 45-46, various correspondence.
28 Imperial policy formation, in the words of South Asian historian Clive Dewey, 'veered between [the] two clusters of axioms'; Dewey 1993, p. V11.
29 McGovern 1924, p. 39; NAI FD, 1906 Secret E, March 45-46, White to India, 20 December 1905.
30 NAI FD, 1906 Secret E March 45-46, file note by R.E.Holland, 5 December 1905; O'Connor 1931, pp. 97-106.
31 NAI FD, 1906 Secret E March 228-245, file notes by Dane, 2 December 1905 & 30 December 1905; FD, 1906 Secret E March 154-191, India to Secretary of State, 23 January 1906, & file note by Dane, 12 January 1906.

CHAPTER TWO

1 OIOC MSS Eur F157, various correspondence.
2 OIOC MSS Eur F157-144, Younghusband to Bailey snr., 6 February 1906 (original emphasis); Swinson 1971, pp. 47-50
3 Swinson 1971, p. 42.
4 OIOC MSS Eur D510-14, Vol. XXXVI, Curzon to Hamilton, 4 June 1903.

5 OIOC MSS Eur F157-166, Bailey to his parents, 23 April 1906; L/P&S/7/196-2152, India to White, 26 May 1906; L/P&S/7/198-543, Gyantse Quarterly Trade Report, 31 December 1906.
6 OIOC; L/P&S/7/214-652, Gyantse Quarterly Trade Report, 31 January 1908; L/P&S/7/222-1910, India to Bell, 18 September 1908.
7 OIOC L/Mil/17/14-92, Military Report on Tibet; MSS Eur F157-304, Gyantse diary, 20 April 1909; L/P&S/7/197-336, Campbell to India, 18 May 1906.
8 OIOC L/P&S/7/183-1940, Bell report, 17 November 1905.
9 McKay 1992a, pp. 413-16.
10 OIOC MSS Eur F157-166, Bailey to his parents, 11 August 1906.
11 OIOC L/P&S/7/205-1574 and L/P&S/7/207-1872, de Righi to India, 12 August 1907, and 26 September 1907; L/P&S/7/205-1534, M.S.Bhatt, petition to O'Connor, 13 July 1907.
12 Bell 1987, pp. 71-72.
13 Swinson 1971, p. 49.
14 Bell 1987, p. 145.
15 NAI FD, 1908 Secret E September 113-134, various correspondence; FD 1908 Secret E February 467-82, W.Cassels to Government of United Provinces, 23 September 1907; OIOC L/P&S/7/241-1089, Gyantse diary entry, 27 June 1910.
16 OIOC MSS Eur F157-304b, Gyantse diary entry, 21 November 1906; L/P&S/7/203-1162, Gyanste Annual Report, 1906-07; MSS Eur F157-166, Bailey to his parents, 25 November 1906.
17 OIOC L/P&S/7/203-1113, Gyantse diary entry, 23 May 1907; O'Connor 1931, pp. 109-10.
18 OIOC L/P&S/7/203-1162, Gyantse Annual Report, 1906-07. The Panchen Lama finally received his car in 1909; OIOC MSS Eur F157-304b, Gyantse reports, May-June 1909.
19 O'Connor 1931, pp. 112-13; Lamb 1966, pp. 133, 136.
20 Lamb 1966, pp. 134-37 Lamb's reference (PEF 1908/22, No.1226, O'Connor to India, 3 February 1907) is no longer used.
21 Richardson 1985, p. 15.
22 OIOC R/1/4/1091, White to India, 1 May 1907.
23 OIOC MSS Eur F197-145, Younghusband to his father, 19 July 1903.
24 Swinson 1971, p. 48.
25 White 1909; NAI FD, 1910 General B April 156, file note by Viceroy Minto, 25 March 1910.
26 Re pension, see OIOC L/P&S/11/1919-2191; also see NAI FD, 1908 External A April 33-34, various correspondence

280 *Tibet and the British Raj*

27 The following section relies upon OIOC R/1/4/1091, file note by E.H.S.Clarke, 23 June 1907, and related correspondence.
28 Ibid.
29 OIOC L/P&S/7/201-901, Gyantse diary entries, 4 & 5 April 1907. Goldstein 1989, discusses these songs and gives examples and further references.
30 OIOC L/P&S/7/203-1203, Gyantse diary entry, 31 May 1907.
31 O'Connor 1931, pp. 114-16.
32 Younghusband 1985, p. 260; NAI FD, 1905 Secret E February 1398-1445, Younghusband to Dane, 30 May 1904.
33 OIOC MSS Eur F157-166, Bailey to his parents, 20 October 1907; L/P&S/7/173-388, Foreign Department margin note, 18 January 1906.
34 OIOC L/P&S/7/210-602, Frontier Confidential report, 14 February 1908.
35 OIOC L/P&S/7/210-182, Viceroy to Secretary of State, 15 January 1908, Secretary of State to the Viceroy, 31 January 1908.
36 These treaties are most accessible in, Richardson 1985, pp.268-80.
37 Addy 1985, p. 192, quoting OIOC D573-3, Morley to Minto, 19 February 1908.
38 OIOC MSS Eur F157-166, Bailey to his parents, 24 January 1909.

CHAPTER THREE

1 The report is contained in OIOC MSS Eur F80, 5a 6-7.
2 OIOC MSS Eur F157-166, Bailey to his parents, 3 January 1909.
3 McKay 1992c; Macdonald papers, 'A Himalayan Biography' unpublished manuscript by D.Macdonald jnr., Interview with Dr K.Sprigg, January 1992.
4 OIOC L/P&S/7/231-1447, Gyantse diary, August 1909, various entries.
5 O'Connor 1931, p. 124.
6 Ibid, pp. 124-26.
7 Re this 'patron-priest' relationship (*Choyon*) see, Praag 1987, pp. 10-13 & 127.
8 OIOC L/P&S/10/150-4049, anonymous contemporary file note.
9 Richardson 1984, p. 98.
10 OIOC L/P&S/10/147-401, Gyantse diary entry, 31 January 1910; Bell 1992, p. 97; King 1927, p. 59.
11 Spence 1991, p. 35; Bell 1987, pp. 94-95.

12 These orders were repeated in OIOC L/P&S/10/147-307, Viceroy to Secretary of State, 19 February 1910. *Dak* bungalows were built at Champethang, Chumbi (Yatung), Gautsa, Phari, Tuna, Dochen, Kala Tso, Samada, Kangma, Saugang, and Gyantse.
13 Macdonald papers, draft autobiography; Macdonald 1991, pp. 65-71.
14 Bell 1987, pp. 97-100; Macdonald 1991, pp. 70-72.
15 Macdonald papers; unpublished[?] article entitled 'Where a Lama leads the Way'.
16 Bell 1992, p. 111.
17 Lamb 1966, p. 212, quoting Morley to Minto, 30 June 1910, D573-5, Morley papers OIOC.
18 OIOC L/P&S/7/245-1868, Bell to India, 26 November 1910; L/P&S/10/147-2848, Under Secretary of State to the Dalai Lama, 14 January 1911.
19 OIOC L/P&S/11/38-4515, Tibetan Chief Minister to Viceroy, 14 October 1912; L/P&S/7/244-1608, Bell to India, 28 September 1910; L/P&S/7/244-1608, Dalai Lama to Bell, enclosed in Bell to India, 28 September 1910, unsigned/undated contemporary margin note.
20 OIOC L/P&S/10/149-974 India to Government of Bengal. 21 July 1910 & related correspondence; L/P&S/7/242-1212/13 & L/P&S/10/147-3802, various correspondence.
21 OIOC L/P&S/7/243-1456, Gyantse report, August 1910, cover note by Bell.
22 OIOC L/P&S/7/243-1436, unsigned/undated India Office margin note; Tibetan view reported by Colonel Manners-Smith (British representative in Kathmandu), in L/P&S/7/243-1485, Manners-Smith to India, 16 September 1910; also see L/P&S/10/149-834, 926 & 964, various correspondence.
23 OIOC L/P&S/7/243-1485, O'Connor to India, 5 August 1910; L/P&S/10/149-647, O'Connor to India, 20 March 1910; L/P&S/11/54-1872, Gartok Annual Report, 1912.
24 OIOC L/P&S/7/243-1485, Viceroy to the Secretary of State, 16 September 1910.
25 OIOC L/P&S/10/218-1778, Gyantse diary entry, 15 March 1912; O'Connor 1931, pp. 164-65.
26 NAI FD, Secret E September 1-27, Bell to India, 18 June 1913.
27 OIOC L/P&S/10/ 218, Gyantse Annual Report, 1911-12.
28 Busch 1980, *passim;* Klein 1971a, p. 103, quoting Hardinge papers, Hardinge to Lord Crewe, 14 December 1913.
29 This section relies on OIOC L/P&S/11/20-232, various correspondence; L/P&S/11/22-2595 various correspondence; L/P&S/11/21-2479, cover

282 *Tibet and the British Raj*

      note, 17 June 1912; L/P&S/11/25-2865, India to Trade Agent Gyantse, 4 June 1912.
30 Allen 1982, p. 203.
31 OIOC L/P&S/10/218-2216, Macdonald to India, 20 May 1912; Macdonald papers, draft autobiography.
32 OIOC L/P&S/11/26-2967, various correspondence; L/P&S/11/54-1873, Dalai Lama to the Viceroy, c.December 1912.
33 OIOC L/P&S/11/46-723, various correspondence; also see Mehra 1969, pp. 1-22; Snelling 1993, pp. 148-152.
34 Snelling 1993, p. 148.
35 Ibid, pp. 249 & *passim*.
36 Richardson 1984, p. 106.
37 There is considerable literature concerning the Simla Convention, see, in particular, Lamb 1966, pp. 457-590.
38 OIOC L/P&S/10/344-1602, report of 7 April 1914.
39 Lamb 1989, p. 24 fn.21.
40 OIOC L/P&S/10/344-3609, Bell to India, 6 August 1914; also see, MSS Eur F80 5d8, notes by Bell, 25 November 1913, & 1 December 1913.
41 Bell 1987, p. 232.
42 OIOC L/P&S/11/81, India to Secretary of State, 25 March 1915; L/P&S/10/218-2190, Gyantse Annual Report, 1914-15, cover note by Bell; Lamb 1989, p. 25, fn.29.
43 Tawang, and the wider issue of the validity of the McMahon Line has been subject to a considerable amount of analysis. A valuable summary may be found in Woodman 1969, pp. 196-209. For a thorough examination of the matter, see Lamb 1989, pp. 12-21, 279-80 & 401-76. The issue remains a sensitive one; the present Indian government refuses access to all files classified as relating to Tibet and this frontier, dated after 31 December 1913.
44 Richardson 1984, pp. 149-50.

CHAPTER FOUR

1 Lamb 1989, p. 20; quoting FO 535/18, Bell to India, 6 August 1915, India to Bell, 3 September 1915.
2 OIOC MSS Eur F80 5e(c) 21, Bell to India, 21 February 1921.
3 Bell 1992, p. 184-85.
4 OIOC L/P&S/10/218-4442, Gyantse Annual Report, 1919-20, unsigned contemporary margin note.

5 OIOC L/P&S/12/4193, Gould mission diary appendix, 31 August 1936.
6 British Museum, Bell Collection, Notebook No.1, p. 22, entry dated 11 February 1913.
7 OIOC L/P&S/12/4163, report No.10, by G.Worsley, Superintendent, Punjab Hill States, c.1930.
8 See, for example, OIOC L/P&S/12/4163, India to Government of the Punjab, 12 June 1931.
9 OIOC L/P&S/12/4179, report by B.J.Gould, May 1941
10 British Museum, Bell collection, Notebook No.2, p. 18; Bell 1992, p. 142.
11 Bell 1992, p. 259.
12 Ibid; re football, see McKay 1994a; OIOC MSS Eur D979, Ludlow diary entry, 1 February 1924; L/P&S/12/4197-3864, Lhasa mission report by B.J.Gould, 30 April 1937.
13 Bell 1992, p. 185.
14 Bell 1987, p. 381; also see p. 410.
15 Bell 1996, pp. 182, 160.
16 NAI FD, 1912 Secret E October 12-45, Bell to India, 27 February 1912.
17 Lamb 1989, pp. 43-46; Singh 1988a, p. 76.
18 Sir Eric Teichman KCMG GCMG (1884-1944), Charterhouse and Cambridge. From 1924-1936, he was Head of the China Consular Service in his capacity as China Secretary at the Peking Legation.
19 OIOC L/P&S/218-1606, Gyantse News report, 22 February 1917; L/P&S/10/218-8154, Yatung News report No.2, 1919; Although consulted on major issues during this retreat, the Dalai Lama was clearly not in a position to receive Bell.
20 Richardson 1945, p. 101.
21 MacDonald papers, Bell to Macdonald, 16 April 1920, Macdonald to Bell, 24 April 1920; see McKay 1992b, p. 132.
22 NAI FD, 1907 Secret E September 238-250, O'Connor to India, 13 May 1907, & India to O'Connor, 4 June 1907 & 15 June 1907; OIOC MSS Eur F157-219, Younghusaband to Bailey, 4 December 1913.
23 Gould 1957, pp. 21, 192-93.
24 Clive Dewey has described how 'the crucial factor, clinching most policy decisions, was the constant repetition of simple axioms by large numbers of comparatively obscure officials'. Dewey 1993, p. 9.
25 OIOC L/P&S/10/716-344, Bell to India, 13 March 1920; For more detail on this period, see Christie 1976, esp. p. 500; Chrisite 1977; Lamb 1989, pp. 110-113.

26 For more detail on the views of Peking and Whitehall, see Lamb 1989, pp. 39, 52-53, 73, 75, & 79; also see McKay 1992b, pp. 130-33.
27 Where not otherwise noted, this section relies on OIOC L/P&S/11/152-2647, various correspondence.
28 See, for example, King 1924. Richardson 1945, p. 25 wrongly describes him as being in the Bell party. NAI FD, Index, 1921 Secret E March 3-4, Part B.
29 Mehra 1974, p. 357, quoting NAI Proceedings, 1-102, correspondence, November 1920.
30 Fletcher 1975, p. 256.
31 Bell 1987, pp. 249-53; 1992, pp. 178-83; also see Bell 1924b.
32 Here I differ from the excellent studies of Christie, who did not, however, have access to the Macdonald papers; see Christie 1976, 1977.
33 Lamb 1966, p. 124.
34 1931 may be an exception to this, but it seems probable that Norbu Dhondup visited Lhasa that year.
35 This period is described in Bell 1987, pp. 258-384.
36 Interview with Namgyal Tsering, February 1994; Bell 1992, pp. 94, 177, 184.
37 The report, dated 9 May 1921, is contained within OIOC L/P&S/10/1011-1286, Viceroy to Secretary of State, 16 May 1921.
38 Ibid; also see Bell 1987, p. 383.
39 In the 1920s, telgerams took between 11 and 19 days from Delhi to Kashgar, compared with one to two days to Gyantse, while the journey from Gilgit to Kashgar took up to 30 days, more than twice the time taken from Gangtok to Gyantse. An indication of its security problem was that in 1934 the Consulate-General's wife was wounded by a stray bullet in local fighting, and in 1936 there was an apparent attempt to assasinate the Consul. For details, see Kashgar reports in the OIOC L/P&S/12/2383 & 2384; also see Everest-Phillips, 1991.
40 Bell 1992, p. 250; also see pp. 71-72 & 194-95.
41 OIOC L/P&S/7/237-526, 'Introduction to the Manual of Instructions to Officers of the Political Department of the Government of India', by S.H.Butler, 15 June 1909.
42 It was later noted that the Chinese Mission provided an excuse for the British presence in Lhasa; OIOC L/P&S/12/4165-7795, Gould to India, 24 October 1939, enclosing Richardson's Lhasa mission report for October 1938-Ocotober 1939.
43 Yapp 1980, esp. pp. 10-15.
44 OIOC MSS Eur F157-241, Ludlow to Bailey, 5 January 1930.
45 OIOC L/P&S/12/4193-6590, Gould mission diary, 3 August 1936.

Notes 285

46 Chapman 1992, p. 26; Neame 1939, p. 237.
47 OIOC L/P&S/12/4163-490, Report of H.Ruttledge, enclosed in Chief Secretary, Punjab Hill States, to Government of United Provinces, 10 November 1926; Bell 1949, p. 35; also see O'Connor 1931, pp. 21-22.
48 OIOC L/P&S/10/1113-1402, India to Under-Secretary of State, 6 March 1924, quoting Bell's view. Re empirical understanding, see, for example, OIOC IOLR L/P&S/11/123-2400, Yatung Annual Report 1916-17, cover note by Bell.
49 OIOC MSS Eur F157-290, Bailey's Lhasa mission report, 28 October 1924, quoting the Dalai Lama; MSS Eur F157-236, Laden La to Bailey, 18 September 1930.
50 Thornton 1895, p. 313.
51 Chapman 1992, p. 232.
52 Bell 1987, p. 29; Interview with Mrs R.Collett, March 1993.
53 Bishop 1989, p. 229. Bell's account is consistent with Tibetan beliefs, and other Europeans have claimed this status was also endowed on them; see, for example, Bernard 1939, p. 1.
54 Bell 1987, p. 29; Bell 1992, p. 206. Familiarity with Bell's dispatches suggests that in personal matters he is a reliable source, not overly given to self-praise for personal, as opposed to policy, reasons. These tributes are not the flattering platitudes routinely given by local rulers to retiring imperial officers, some of whom took them seriously enough to repeat in their memoirs. The Tibetans whom Bell quotes refer not to his abilities and achievements, but to his affinity with the Tibetans.
55 See, for example, Bell 1931; Interview with Mrs. R.Collett, March 1993.
56 See, Eliade 1955.
57 OIOC L/P&S/12/4165, Lhasa mission report, October 1938-October 1939, anonymous undated cover note.

CHAPTER FIVE

1 Coen 1971, pp. 42-43, quoting a speech by Curzon in Simla on 5 September 1905.
2 See Beaglehole 1977, pp. 237-55; Crawford 1930, pp. 650-51; Dewey 1973, pp. 283-85; Heathcote 1974, p. 140; Potter 1986, pp. 57-58; Razzell 1963, pp. 248-60; Spangenberg 1976, p. 19.
3 OIOC MSS Eur F157-142, Bailey's school and college reports.
4 OIOC MSS Eur F 203-84, Caroe Papers, draft autobiography (untitled), Chapter Two, pp. 4-5; Interview with H.Richardson, November 1990.
5 Interview with Mrs R.Collett, March 1993; Interview with Mrs E.Hopkinson, April 1993.

6 Symonds 1991, p. 47, quoting H.Edgerton, (Beit Professor of Colonial History at Oxford), c1910; Moore 1993, p. 722.
7 Hilton 1955, p. 12.
8 Potter 1986, pp. 58-59, 71-75; Symonds 1991, pp. 31-32; Girouard 1981, pp.164-67; OIOC R/1/4/1035, personal file of B.Gould, report by H.R.Cobb, 15 January 1910.
9 Mangan 1986, p. 18; McKay 1994, pp. 373-74; Hyam 1990, p. 73; Potter 1986, pp. 73-75.
10 See Dewey 1995.
11 Symonds 1991, pp. 300-301; also see Madden & Fieldhouse 1982; Symonds *ibid.* p. 36, quoting Lord Curzon, from Lord Ronaldshay, *Life of Curzon*, London 1928, (1) p. 49.
12 OIOC MSS Eur F157-272, various papers of F.M.Bailey.
13 Mason 1974, pp. 365, 386; Shepperd 1980, p. 9; Heathcote 1974, p. 168; OIOC MSS Eur F157-214, Bailey's mission diary entry, 1 August 1924.
14 Margaret Ewing has found that 'something of the military mind lingered' and affected the world view of those ICS men who had seen active service in World War one; Ewing 1980, pp. 120-21.
15 Regarding this change, see Ewing 1980, p. 206; Symonds 1991, p. 116.
16 Potter 1977, p. 875; also see Potter 1986, p. 112; Simon 1961, p. 15.
17 Mason 1974, pp. 363-66; Potter 1977, pp. 876-77; Potter 1986, pp. 101, 109.
18 Dewey 1993, p. VII; also see Dewey 1973, p. 262; Potter 1977, pp. 875-89; 1986, pp. 72.
19 Walsh 1945, p. 112; Sykes 1945, p. 134; Interview with Mrs E.Hopkinson, April 1993.
20 Simon 1961, pp. 11, 100, 110, 198.
21 Beaglehole 1977, p. 249, quoting A.R.Cornelius ICS, 15 October 1928, in OIOC L/S&G/6/351 Collection 3-16a; Ewing 1980, p. 200; Simon 1961, p. 100.
22 NAI FD, 1906 General A December 56-59, Morley to India, 6 July 1906.
23 Trench 1987, p. 13; Fletcher 1975, p. 228.
24 Morgan 1973, p. 58; Trench 1987, p. 11; Interview with Mrs A.Saker, April 1993; OIOC MSS Eur F157-319, Bailey typescript autobiography (untitled), p. 18.
25 OIOC MSS Eur F157-144, Younghusband to Bailey snr., 12 March 1905.
26 OIOC MSS Eur F157-166, Bailey to his parents, 11 January 1906; R/1/4/1236, Personal file of E.W.Fletcher; NAI FD, 1923 Establishment

B 39(1), Macdonald's Political Department entry application, various correspondence.
27 OIOC R/1/4/1297, Personal file of A.A.Russell, Russell to India, 15 February 1924.
28 OIOC R/1/4/1261, Personal file of A.J.Hopkinson, P.S.Lock to Hopkinson, 16 March 1923; MSS Eur R/1/4/2003, Personal file of P.C.Hailey, various correspondence.
29 NAI FD, 1906 General B, October 14-15, Lieutenant-Colonel P.G.Weir IMS, to Dane, 1 September 1906.
30 Edwardes 1851, pp. 1 & 722-23; Lyall 1973, pp. 334-36 & *passim*.
31 Thornton 1895, pp. 24, 36, 290-91, 294-295, 306, 314-316, 320-21 & *passim*.
32 For more detail of these incidents see, McKay 1992a, & McKay 1992b; Allen 1982, p. 203.
33 French 1994, p. 35-37.
34 Williamson 1987, p. 90; Bell's collection is listed in OIOC MSS Eur F80 5a 27.
35 OIOC MSS Eur D998-17, Hopkinson to Mrs Hopkinson, 14 October 1945; In his 'Report on Tibet August 1945 to August 1948', MSS Eur D 998-39, Hopkinson repeats unacknowledged Bell's description of Tibet as the 'cinderella [sic] of the Indian Foreign Service'.

CHAPTER SIX

1 Regarding architecture as an aspect of imperial prestige, see R.L.Jones, *A Fatal friendship*, New Delhi 1985.
2 Landon 1988, (Vol.1), p. 64. OIOC MSS Eur D979, Ludlow diary entry, 5-6 February 1925.
3 OIOC L/P&S/7/203-1164, White to India, 15 June 1907.
4 Walters papers, manuscript description of a march from Gangtok to Gyantse.
5 OIOC MSS Eur F157-304b, Bailey to his parents, 1 March 1908.
6 Walters papers, copy of an undated talk given by Lieutenant-Colonel Walters.
7 Ibid; Macdonald 1991, pp. 118-19; 'Mugger' 1936, p. 182.
8 OIOC L/P&S/7/186-886, O'Connor to India.
9 Interview with Mrs J-M.Jehu, March 1993.
10 Bailey 1911, pp. 271.
11 OIOC MSS Eur F157-97, Bailey's personal diary, entry of 3 August 1904.

288 Tibet and the British Raj

12 MSS Eur F157-304b, Gyantse diary entry, March 1906; Walter's papers, unpublished[?] article entitled 'An Unusual Fishing Experience'.
13 Bailey has several specimens named after him; e.g. *Aporia baileyi, Halpe. baileyi*.
14 Mainprice papers, Mainprice diary entry, 15-19 October 1943; OIOC L/P&S/12/ 4178-2137, Gould to Caroe, 1 March 1940.
15 OIOC MSS Eur D998-18, Hopkinson to Mrs Hopkinson.
16 Bailey 1945, p. 72; OIOC L/P&S/12/4166-3633, Gyantse Annual Report, 1945-46.
17 Re Annie Taylor see OIOC L/P&S/7/210-182, Frontier Confidential report, 3 February 1908; L/P&S/7/714, various correspondence; L/P&S/7/188-1078, various correspondence; Virk 1989, p. 103; NAI FD, 1907 External B February 18-42, Chumbi News reports, 20 September 1906 & 5 October 1906. Re Taylor's travels in Tibet, see Carey, 1900.
18 NAI FD, 1912 Deposit E June 4, anonymous file note, 28 May 1912; FD, 1911 Deposit November 14, various correspondence.
19 OIOC L/P&S/7/180, Gyantse diary entry, 29 December 1904.
20 OIOC L/P&S/11/250, various correspondence; NAI FD, 1925 F-339-X; Macdonald papers, 'A Himalayan Biography' unpublished manuscript by D.Macdonald jnr., pp. 74-75; also see McKay 1994b, p. 16
21 Re mining, see Hayden & Cosson, 1927; also see Cooper 1986b.
22 OIOC MSS Eur D979, Ludlow diary entries, July-August 1926; L/P&S/12/4166-3129, Gyantse Annual Report, 1930-31.
23 See, for example, Mainprice papers, Mainprice diary entries. 14 & 23-25, July 1944.
24 NAI FD, Secret E August 440, various correspondence;
25 NAI FD, 1914, Index, Establishment March 213-14, Part B; OIOC L/P&S/12/4166, Trade Agent Gyantse to Political Officer Sikkim, 27 March 1934 & attached 1914 'Standing Orders for the Detachments in Sikkim and Tibet'.
26 OIOC L/P&S/12/4166-6423, file cover note by A.Rumbold, 23 October 1934.
27 OIOC MSS Eur D979, Ludlow diary entry, 8 December 1923
28 OIOC MSS Eur F157-166, Bailey to his parents, 24 September 1908; NAI FD, 1912 Establishment B August 226-227, various correspondence.
29 NAI FD, 1912 External B December 208-244, various correspondence; FD, 1913 Establishment B September 136-138, various correspondence.
30 Macdonald 1991, p. 154. This is one of a number of dates in this work where Macdonald errs. Williamson 1987, p. 39.
31 Where not otherwise noted, this section relies on OIOC L/P&S/11/235-2906, various correspondence; also see Byron 1933, pp. 209-10

32 OIOC L/P&S/11/235-2906, Bailey to India, 29 December 1923.
33 OIOC L/P&S/10/218-2156, Yatung Annual Report, 1923-24.
34 Mainprice papers, diary entry, 15-19 October 1943; Weir papers, Weir to Mrs Weir, 4 June 1929 & 1 October 1929; NAI FD, 1935 Establishment B 32 (54) E, various correspondence.

CHAPTER SEVEN

1 NAI FD, Index 1921, External April (2), Part B.
2 NAI FD, 1921 Establishment B November 199-223, various correspondence.
3 OIOC L/P&S/7/237-526, 'Manual of Instructions for Political Officers', by S.H.Butler, 1909; Williamson 1987; p. 104.
4 Interview with Dr K.Sprigg, January 1992.
5 NAI FD, 1919 Secret War, November 1-248, General Malcolm to Chief of Staff, Simla, 25 October 1918; also see Bailey 1946; Hopkirk 1984, pp. 7-96; McKay 1992a.
6 Bailey had served as Intelligence Officer in 1912-13 under Nevill on the Dibong Survey mission into hostile Abor country in Assam. Nevill had subsequently turned a blind eye to Bailey's evasion of bureaucratic obstacles to his exploration of the Tsangpo/Brahmaputra; see Bailey 1957, pp. 31-40.
7 Re Bailey's journey to Sadiya, see NAI FD, 1912 Secret E January 65-92. This file is classified as it contains a map, but the 'Index for Foreign Proceedings for the Year 1912', lists this file in two entries, one of which is obviously a misprint, giving the amount involved as 1,000 and 10,000 rupees respectively. Access to the Indian archives has led me to reassess my view that Bailey was not an intelligence officer in 1911; see McKay 1992a, p. 417. Given that the Government of India curtailed Bailey's Assam exploration in 1911, and considered that he had spent too long in Russian Central Asia, [NAI FD, 1929 External 178-X, various correspondence.] it appears that Bailey's intelligence activities were not solely on behalf of the Government of India, whose interests by no means always coincided with those of Whitehall. 'British intelligence', of course, need not imply a formal organisation, much information seems to have been passed on the 'old boy network'.
8 OIOC L/P&S/11/195-1468, Bell to India, 6 February 1921.
9 Snelling 1993, pp. 212; Alex Andreyev of the St. Petersburg Cultural Foundation is currently finalising a book on the Soviet activities in Tibet during this period; also see 'The Bolshevik Intrigue in Tibet', paper

290 *Tibet and the British Raj*

delivered at the 7th Seminar of the International Association for Tibetan Studies, Graz, 1994.

10 Re Haldinov [Hodenof/Haldinoff], see OIOC MSS Eur D979, Ludlow diary entry, 13 November 1924; MSS Eur F157-214 Bailey's mission diary, various entries; NAI FD, Index 1922-23, F.No 619-X; Foreign Office, 371-10291-4178 (1924), Bailey to India, 2 September 1924.

11 Re these problems, see Unsworth 1981; Hansen 1996.

12 OIOC MSS Eur F157-221, Hirtzell to Bailey, 15 November 1922.

13 For McGovern's account, see McGovern 1924.

14 OIOC MSS Eur F157-269, Bailey's letter of 12 October [1923?], apparently to Mrs. I.Bailey; RGS, Bailey Correspondence, 1921-30, Bailey to Hinks, 8 April 1924, Hinks to Bailey, 28 April 1924, Mrs I.Bailey to Hinks, 6 December 1923; Bell 1987, p. 355; Journal of the Royal Geographical Society, 1924 (2) pp. 170-71. McGovern 1924, pp. 407-08.

15 OIOC MSS Eur F157-238, General Pereira to Bailey, 21 May 1923; MSS Eur F157-290, Bailey report, 28 October 1924; L/P&S/10/1011-3605, Viceroy to the Secretary of State, 5 September 1923.

16 OIOC MSS Eur D979, Ludlow diary entry, 22 September 1924; Re Tsarong, see in particular, Spence 1991.

17 Macdonald 1991, p. 303; Foreign Office 1842-1842-10, draft letter, Bailey to W.M.Hardy [a missionary on the Eastern Tibetan frontier], undated, c.December 1923.

18 OIOC MSS Eur F157-238, Pereira to Bailey, 13 December 1922; L/P&S/11/235-2906, Kashag to Bailey, 29 October 1922.

19 NAI Home Department 1923, File No 42 (v) Part B, File note by E.B.Howell, 9 March 1923; so keen were the Government of India to use him that the ambitious Laden La was able to demand promotion to Superintendent as a condition of acceptance.

20 OIOC L/P&S/10/218-2418, Gyantse Annual Report, 1923-24, NAI Home Department 1923, File No. 42 (V) Part B, India to Government of Bengal, 31 August 1923.

21 Foreign Office, 371-10233-2275 (1924), Bailey to India, 28 May 1924. I am indebted to Alex Andreyev for this reference.

22 Bailey's Lhasa mission diary can be read as implying that Nevill accompanied him to Lhasa, although no other evidence for this has emerged; see OIOC MSS Eur F157-214, Bailey's mission diary entry, 18 July 1924.

23 The best account of these events is by Goldstein, but despite his best efforts, the accounts given of the various actions and motives remain contradictory, and there is little point in detailing them here; See Goldstein 1989, pp. 121-137.

24 OIOC MSS Eur F157-214, Bailey's mission diary, various entries; MSS Eur D979, Ludlow diary, various entries, September 1924.
25 OIOC L/P&S/10/1088-1417, Copy of press communiqué dated 14 October 1924.
26 See, for example, Klein 1971; also see Spence 1991, p. 48; Tada 1965, pp. 70-72.
27 See for example, Richardson 1984, p. 137, in regard to a suggestion of similar events in the 1930s; Lamb 1989, pp. 162, 175; Goldstein 1989, pp. 133-34; Singh 1988a, p. 94. I am indebted to Dr Michel Hockx (IIAS, Leiden), and his wife Yu Hong, who recalled that at school in China she had been taught that the British attempted a coup in Tibet in the 1920s. This led me to examine Wung Furen and Suo Wenqing, *Highlights of Tibetan History,* (Beijing, 1984), pp. 159-60. Although their brief account does not give source references, it is reasonably consistent with this interpretation of events except in ascribing a coup attempt to the 'British' in general, rather than specifically to Bailey.
28 OIOC MSS Eur D979, Ludlow diary entry, 19 September 1926; NAI FD, Index 1924-27, File No. 38 (2)-X. A request to the Indian Department of External Affairs for access to this file was refused in 1994.
29 OIOC MSS F157-240, Dalai Lama to Norbu Dhondup, cited in Norbu to Bailey, 7 October 1924; MSS Eur F80 5a 97, Laden La to Bell, 5 September 1925.
30 OIOC MSS Eur F80 5a 92, Macdonald to Bell, 3 February 1930.
31 OIOC L/P&S/10/1088, Bailey to India, 31 July 1927 and related correspondence; MSS Eur F157-240, Norbu Dhondup to Bailey, 2 October 1931.
32 OIOC MSS Eur F157-240, Norbu Dhondup to Bailey, 1 September 1927. John Noel, photographer on the early Everest expeditions, wrote in another context that 'the opinions which Major Bailey quotes as coming from the Tibetans are entirely from himself...Government refers all matters to him and he practically dictates any answer he wishes'; Royal Geographical Society, Everest Collection, EE 27/6/13, Noel to Arthur Hinks, 22 May 1925.
33 OIOC L/P&S/10/1088-2679, Bailey to India, 18 July 1925, & 4-6 October 1925, Goldstein 1989, pp. 126-30; Richardus 1989, p. 35-38, a photo of Padma Chandra appears on Plate Vb of this work.
34 Richardson 1984, p. 129.
35 Re the Rugby school experiment, see Shakya 1986; also see Lamb 1966, pp. 599-603.
36 OIOC L/P&S/12/4166, Gyantse Annual Report, 1925-26.

292 *Tibet and the British Raj*

37 Ludlow's diary is in OIOC MSS Eur D979; unless otherwise noted, this section relies on that source.
38 Chapman 1940, p. 109.

CHAPTER EIGHT

1 Interview with Mrs J-M.Jehu, March 1993.
2 Ibid.
3 Weir papers, Weir to Mrs Weir, 4 June 1929.
4 OIOC L/P&S/12/4175-898; this file contains a list of Political Officer's visits to Lhasa, and [falsely] indicates they were all 'spontaneous' invitations, although it admits they were prepared to solicit an invitation in Bailey's case.
5 See, for example, OIOC L/P&S/12/4166-3129, Gyantse Annual Report, various comments.
6 OIOC L/P&S/10/1113-5738, cover note by J.Walton, 7 September 1929; Dalai Lama to Weir, 20 July 1929; also see 1113-5170, Weir to India, 22 July 1929; Richardson 1945, p. 38.
7 OIOC MSS Eur F80 5a92, Macdonald to Bell, 8 July 1930; MSS Eur F80 5a93, 'Private letter from Kalimpong to Macdonald', dated 9 September 1930, forwarded by Macdonald to Bell, 24 October 1930; MSS Eur F157-236, Laden La to Bailey, 18 September 1930; also see Goldstein 1989, p. 136.
8 OIOC L/P&S/10/1113-2954, various correspondence.
9 Weir Papers, Weir to Weir snr., 17 June 1930.
10 OIOC L/P&S/10/1113-8573, Weir report, 18 November 1930; 1113-2725, Weir to India, 7 March 1929.
11 Weir papers, Weir to Mrs Weir, 4 & 11 August 1932.
12 Interview with Mrs J-M.Jehu, 26 March 1993.
13 OIOC L/P&S/12/4175-1922, Weir report, 1 March 1933.
14 Ibid; Interview with Mrs J-M.Jehu, 26 March 1993.
15 OIOC L/P&S/12/4175-1922, Weir report, 1 March 1933.
16 Bell 1987, p. 419; OIOC MSS Eur F80.5a92, Macdonald report, 7 December 1930.
17 OIOC L/P&S/12/4197-6072, 'Report on 1946 Mission to Lhasa', by H.Richardson.
18 Personal correspondence with R.Ford, November 1994.
19 Robb 1984, p. 16; For the missionary use of intermediaries, see Bray 1992, pp. 371-375, 1995, pp. 68-80. Re intermediaries in British

India and the Princely States, see Fisher 1987, 1990; Frykenberg 1965; Rudolph 1984.
20 British Museum, Bell Collection, Bell diaries, various entries; OIOC L/P&S/12/4166, Gyantse Annual Report, 1926-27.
21 Later, Rai Sahib Sherab Gyatso; d.1909.
22 Macdonald 1991, pp. 137-140; Snelling 1993, p. 68.
23 Macdonald 1991, pp. 139-40; Younghusband 1985, p. 307.
24 Bell 1987, pp. 25-26; OIOC MSS Eur D998/17, Hopkinson's Lhasa diary/ letter, 27 September 1945. Regarding these two patterns of service among intermediaries in the Indian Princely States, see Fisher 1991, pp. 332, 344.
25 NAI FD, 1909 External A April 3-4, File note by L.W.Reynolds, 10 March 1909, following an enquiry by F.M.Bailey. As noted, Shabdrung Lama was a Buriat, his actual citizenship is not recorded.
26 Snelling 1993, pp. 26-35; NAI FD, 1912 Secret E October 59-82, Gould to India, 16 July 1912; Whether Dorzhiev is best seen as primarily representing Russian or Tibetan interests is a matter of debate; see for example, Kuleshov 1992.
27 Interview with Dr T.W.Pemba, March 1994. Where not otherwise credited, information in this section was obtained during fieldwork in Gangtok in March 1994, from serving officials of the Government of Sikkim, who must remain anonymous.
28 Bishop 1989, passim, esp. pp. 46-49. Also see, for example, Younghusband 1949, pp. 131-32, 141-42.
29 Bell 1949, p. 55; Ladakh had in fact been outside Lhasa's authority since the 17th century.
30 OIOC L/P&S/7/229-923, Gyantse Annual Report, 1908-09, cover note by Bell, 11 May 1909; NAI FD, 1909 Establishment B December 318-321, Bell to India, 29 July 1909. Re this ethos; see Ballhatchet 1980, p.8.
31 OIOC L/P&S/12/4197-6072, 'Report on 1946 Mission to Lhasa', by H.Richardson; personal correspondence with R.Ford, November 1994; This policy also recognised the reluctance of local rulers to accept Indian rather than the British representatives of the Raj; See Hogben 1981, esp., pp. 767-769; also see Copland 1982, p. 75; Potter 1986, pp. 119-20. The prejudice against using Hindus or Muslims in Tibet can be traced back to the first British visitor there, George Bogle. He reported that caste restrictions meant it was 'inconvenient carrying Hindu servants into foreign parts'; Woodcock 1971, p. 96, quoting Bogle's journal.
32 Ballhatchet 1980, pp. 4, 164-65.

33 Interview with Dr. M.V.Kurian, January 1994; Ballhatchet 1980, pp. 164-65, records the prejudice against Anglo-Indian Medical Officers in India as being due particularly to the question of their examining British women. When British women were in Lhasa, a British Medical Officer was available there.
34 Macdonald 1991, p. 147; Personal correspondence with R.Ford, November 1994; Caplan 1991, *passim*, esp. p. 590.
35 Interview with Mrs J-M.Jehu, March 1993.
36 Gould 1957, p. 206; Neame 1939, p. 237.
37 OIOC L/P&S/10/1113-1758, India to Weir, 7 February 1929; L/P&S/10/1113-5170, Weir to India, 22 July 1929; MSS Eur F157-240, Norbu Dhondup to Bailey, 30 August 1927.
38 OIOC L/P&S/12/4197-3864, Gould report, 30 April 1937; Interview with Mrs J-M.Jehu, March 1993.
39 OIOC MSS Eur F157-240, Norbu Dhondup to Bailey, 12 August 1925; also see MSS Eur F80 5a130, Norbu Dhondup to Bell, 17 August 1937, reporting how Chinese officers drew their guns on him when he reported the fall of Nanking.
40 Saker papers, Saker to Mrs Saker, 5 September 1941.
41 Interview with Dr T.W.Pemba, March 1994; Interview with Mrs J-M.Jehu, March 1994; Interview with Mrs A.Saker, April 1993; Gould 1957, p. 206.
42 Sangharakshita 1991, p. 73; OIOC MSS Eur D979, Ludlow diary entry, 1 February 1924.
43 Interview with A.Robins, April 1993; Interview with Dr. T.W.Pemba, March 1994; Gyatso papers, address by Sir Antony Macdonald, 30 October 1893.
44 Interview with Dr T.W.Pemba, March 1994
45 Information on Laden La's political activities from local sources courtesy of Dr Michael Hutt, (SOAS), from a forthcoming paper.
46 Weir papers, letter of 25 May 1930.
47 Goldstein 1989, p. 122; Interview with Dr K.Sprigg, January 1992.
48 OIOC MSS Eur F80 5a92 & 5a 93, various letters 1930, Macdonald to Bell. See Macdonald 1991, pp. 21, 297-98, in contrast to OIOC MSS Eur F80 5a92, Macdonald to Bell, 3 February 1930; MSS Eur F80 5a 105, Rosemeyer to Bell, 26 May 1934.
49 Interview with R.Ford, March 1993.
50 Interview with Namgyal Tsering, February 1994; Interview with Dr T.W.Pemba, March 1994; personal information regarding Norbu Dhondup courtesy of his daughter, Mrs Dekyi Khedrub.
51 Bell 1987, p. 247.

52 OIOC MSS Eur D998/18, Hopkinson to Mrs Hopkinson, 19 May 1946; Mainprice papers, Mainprice diary entry, 13 July 1944.
53 NAI FD, 1912 External B December 208-244, various correspondence; for other work on local corruption in India, see Dewey 1978, Dewey 1993, pp. 207, Frykenberg 1965, pp. 126, 234-42.
54 Such competing lineages were common under the Raj; Rudolph, 1984, p. 84.

CHAPTER NINE

1 OIOC MSS Eur F157-241, Ludlow to Bailey, 26 November 1934.
2 OIOC L/P&S/12/4163-1165, Williamson report, 14 December 1932.
3 OIOC L/P&S/12/2345, Political Department memo 6985, 1932.
4 Williamson 1987, pp. 46-47; re Ludlow and Sherriff's careers as naturalists, see Fletcher 1975.
5 OIOC L/P&S/12/4175-1981, Williamson to India, 16 March 1933; 4175-2734, draft telegram, India Office to India, 13 May 1933.
6 OIOC L/P&S/12/4175-1981, Williamson to India, 16 March 1933; L/P&S/12/4295-5572,India to India Office, 14 September 1932.
7 Weir papers, Weir to Mrs Weir, 10 November 1932; NAI FD, 1930 Establishment B 214 E, Bailey to E.Howell, 3 November 1930 & related correspondence; OIOC MSS Eur F80, 5a92 & 5a93, various correspondence, Macdonald to Bell.
8 OIOC MSS Eur F80 5a 93, Macdonald to Bell, 20 March 1931.
9 OIOC MSS Eur F157-240, Bailey to Norbu, 29 August 1927; L/P&S/12/3982, various correspondence, 1923-27.
10 Interview with Mrs J-M.Jehu, March 1993; Williamson 1987, pp. 113.
11 OIOC L/P&S/12/4605, British Embassy Chungking to Ministry of Information London, 21 May 1942; See Taring 1970, *passim*.
12 Williamson 1987, p. 101.
13 Lamb 1989, is the best source on these attempts; also of interest is Xeirab Nyima, 'A Special Envoy of the Nanking Regime', *China's Tibet*, 2.4. 1991 (Peking) pp. 39-42.
14 Regarding the Lhasa power struggle in this period, see Lamb, 1989; Goldstein, 1989; Dhondup, 1986.
15 OIOC L/P&S/12/4175-6262, Metcalfe to Williamson, 17 September 1934 & (898) Williamson to Metcalfe, 20 January 1935.
16 OIOC MSS Eur F80 5a92, Bell to Macdonald, 26 December 1930.
17 OIOC MSS Eur F80 5a 97, Bell to Laden La, 6 June 1930; also see F80 5a 92 & 5a 93, various correspondence.

18 OIOC MSS Eur F80 5a 113, translation of a passport to Shigatse, dated 17 July 1934.
19 The account that follows is taken from OIOC L/P&S/12/4178; L/P&S/12/4295; MSS Eur F80 5a; British Museum, Bell Collection, Tibet Notebook 1934, No.1.
20 OIOC MSS Eur F80 5a 124, Bell to Kashag, 26 November 1934.
21 OIOC L/P&S/12/4295-4341, Bell to Sir John Walton, 3 June 1935.
22 OIOC L/P&S/12/4295-6209, Peking to India, 3 July 1935.
23 Snelling 1993, pp. 247-52.
24 OIOC L/P&S/12/4175-2573, India to Secretary of State, 11 April 1935; L/P&S/12/4295-5238, Caroe to Williamson, 4 July 1935, India to Secretary of State, 10 August 1935, and reply, 21 August 1935.
25 Williamson 1987, pp. 186-87.
26 Battye papers, personal diary entry, 21 October 1935.
27 Where not otherwise noted, this section relies on Williamson 1987, pp. 186-87, 207, 217-24; OIOC L/P&S/12/4175, various correspondence; Battye papers, diary of Captain Battye.
28 Re the Battye history, see Battye 1984.
29 Williamson 1987, p. 222; OIOC L/P&S/12/4175-1175, Lhasa mission report, 18 November 1935, cover note by B.Gould.
30 Maraini 1952, p. 97; Maraini visited Lhasa with Tucci in 1948, his source was an ex-British employee.
31 OIOC L/P&S/12/4175-885, copy of Hansard entry of 6 February 1936.

CHAPTER TEN

1 Gould 1957, p. 24; NAI FD, 1912 Secret E Proceedings 59-282, Gould to India, 16 July 1912.
2 Mainprice papers, Mainprice diary entry, 5 August 1944.
3 Younghusband 1910, p. 11; Addy 1985, p. 94, quoting OIOC MSS Eur F111-162, Curzon papers, Hamilton to Curzon, 19 February 1903; Nilsson 1968, p. 115; Yapp 1980, p. 12.
4 Cohn 1983, pp. 165-209; Robb 1992, pp. 39, 43, 385; Interview with Dr M.V.Kurian, January 1994.
5 Sikkim State Archives, General 1916, (7) 10/3 (XX11)/1916, David-Neel to Bell, 31 August 1916.
6 Prasad 1979, p. 506, quoting Curzon to Secretary of State John Broderick, 7 November 1903.

7   Macdonald 1991, p. 84; Macdonald papers, 'A Himalayan Biography', unpublished manuscript by D.Macdonald jnr., p. 57.
8   OIOC MSS Eur F157-241, Ludlow to Bailey, 19 November 1944; Interview with Dr M.V.Kurian, January 1994.
9   OIOC L/P&S/12/4217-4253, Gould mission report; also see L/P&S/12/4166-2754, India to Gould, 12 September 1939.
10 Walters papers, unpublished[?] article entitled 'Gyantse to Lhasa 1940/1'.
11 Bell 1987, p. 455; Interview with Mrs J-M.Jehu, March 1993.
12 NAI FD, 1916 Index, Estimate May 109-110, Part B.
13 NAI FD, 1929 External Secret 178-X, File note by Sir Denys Bray, 23 June 1929: FD, 1908 Secret E, August 226-229, Bell to India, 16 June 1908; Robb 1992, p. 43.
14 Ford 1990, p. 91; Richardson & Skorupski 1986, p. V11.
15 See Nilsson 1968, pp. 105 & 111-115; also see Jones 1985, esp., p. 53; Robb 1992, p. 174.
16 OIOC L/P&S/12/4197-2781, Gould to India, 22 February 1939; L/P&S/12/4166, Gyantse Annual Report, 1929-30; MSS Eur F157-214, Bailey's mission diary entry, 14 August 1924.
17 Sir Olaf Caroe KCSI KCIE (1892-1981), Winchester & Oxford, ICS. Deputy Secretary Foreign Department 1934-37, Indian Foreign Secretary, 1939-45.
18 OIOC L/P&S/12/4175-1175, Lhasa mission report by Captain Battye, 29 December 1935.
19 OIOC L/P&S/12/4197-5041, various correspondence.
20 OIOC L/P&S/12/4197-5304, India to Secretary of State, 22 July 1936, & reply, 30 July 1936.
21 OIOC L/P&S/12/4197-5041, various correspondence; Neame 1939, pp. 236, 238.
22 OIOC L/P&S/12/4197-7301, India to Secretary of State, 10 October 1936, repeating Gould to India, 7 October 1936.
23 OIOC L/P&S/12/4197-8904, India to Secretary of State, 12 December 1936, and draft reply.
24 OIOC L/P&S/12/4197-3864, Gould's report, 30 April 1937; The following section is based on McKay 1994a.
25 Richardson 1984, pp. 147-48, 312,fn.; Gould 1957, p. 208; OIOC L/P&S/12/4197-514, India to Secretary of State, 22 January 1937. Norbu Dhondup needed dental treatment in Calcutta, and Richardson remained in Lhasa until Norbu was fit to return.
26 Interview with H.Richardson, November 1990; Richardson 1984, pp. 147-48.

27 OIOC L/P&S/12/4197-8380, India to Gould, 9 December 1937.
28 OIOC L/P&S/12/4197-8380, Gould to India, 23 December 1937, copying Norbu Dhondup to Gould, 18 December 1937, & India to Gould, 11 March 1938.
29 OIOC L/P&S/12/4166-3792, Gyantse Annual Report, 1937-38; L/P&S/12/4165-7795, various Lhasa mission reports.
30 OIOC L/P&S/12/4197-6859, Gould to India, 8 August 1938.
31 OIOC L/P&S/12/4197-2781, Gould to India, 22 February 1939, & India to Gould, 25 April 1939.
32 OIOC L/P&S/12/4197-3864, Cover note by H.A.F.Rumbold, 26 June 1937.
33 Caroe 1960, p. 9; OIOC MSS Eur F157-259, Richardson to Bailey, 30 March 1957.
34 OIOC L/P&S/12/4206-4380, Gould to India, 23 September 1944.
35 Interview with Mrs A.Saker, April 1993.
36 OIOC L/P&S/12/4178-2137, Gould to Caroe, 1 March 1940.
37 Ford 1990, p. 215.
38 NAI FD, 1906 External B July 236-247, India to White, 12 July 1906.
39 Bell 1992, p. 70.
40 OIOC MSS Eur D979, Ludlow diary entry, 3 June 1924.
41 OIOC L/P&S/12/4295-1664, Bell to H.A.F.Metcalfe, 1 February 1935; MSS Eur F80 5d8, 'Notes on our future policy in Tibet and on the North Eastern Frontier generally', by Bell [for Foreign Secretary McMahon] c.1914.
42 OIOC MSS Eur F80 5a127, Gould to Bell, 23 March 1936.
43 Interview with H.Richardson, November 1990.
44 OIOC L/P&S/12/4193, Gould mission diary, 30 March 1937; L/P&S/12/4201, Lhasa mission reports, weeks ending 11 July 1943 & 8 November 1942.
45 OIOC L/P&S/12/4197-6072, 'Report on 1946 Mission to Lhasa' by H.Richardson; L/P&S/12/4202, Lhasa mission report, week ending 30 March 1947.
46 OIOC L/P&S/10/1113-8573, Weir report, 18 November 1930; L/P&S/12/4216-982, Gould to Sherriff, 21 January 1945. For details of the English school in Lhasa, see OIOC L/P&S/12/4201, Lhasa mission reports, 1942-45, various entries; also see Dhondup 1986, pp. 155-62.
47 Richardson 1951, p. 114.
48 OIOC L/P&S/12/4201-410, Lhasa mission report, week ending 19 December 1943; MSS Eur D998-17, Hopkinson's Lhasa diary/letters, 25 November 1945.
49 Interview with H.H. the Dalai Lama, March 1994.

CHAPTER ELEVEN

1 Lamb 1986, p. 247-48; NAI FD, 1906 Secret E February 98-109, file note by Louis Dane, 24 November 1905.
2 NAI FD, 1905 Secret E February 1398-1445, reports by Louis Dane, 21 May 1904, & 13 June 1904; file note by Viceroy Ampthill, 11 June 1904. Sir John Ardagh, Director of Military Intelligence 1896-1901, supported the extension of the Indian border to the Kunlun range; Lamb 1989, p. 356.
3 OIOC L/P&S/10/139-826, various correspondence; re Greek reports, see Herodotus, (Rev.W.Beloe, trans.) Vol.2, p. 91, London, 1830.
4 Bailey's diary records the mission's difficulty in ascertaining place names in western Tibet; OIOC MSS Eur F157-199, diary of F.M.Bailey, notes.
5 OIOC L/P&S/12/4163, report of E.W.Wakefield. When the author visited Gartok in 1986 the description still applied.
6 OIOC L/P&S/11/56-2339, report of C.M.Collett, 10 August 1912.
7 OIOC L/P&S/7/207-1873, report of H.Calvert, 6 November 1906; report of W.S.Cassels, 23 September 1907.
8 NAI FD, Secret E, February 1398-1445, file note by Younghusband, 4 November 1904.
9 OIOC L/P&S/7/173-360, Government of India to Government of Punjab, 9 December 1904; L/P&S/195-2014, Gartok weekly reports, 1 & 8 October 1906.
10 OIOC L/P&S/10/186, Captain Rawling to Dane, 2 November 1905.
11 OIOC L/P&S/7/182-1656, report of C.Sherring 3 September 1905; L/P&S/7/190-1240, Sherring to Government of United Provinces, 9 March 1906; NAI FD, 1911, Chief Secretary, Government of the Punjab to India, 17 May 1911.
12 NAI FD, Establishment B May 221, File note by J.B.Wood, 2 January 1910, File note by S.H.Butler, 28 January 1910; FD, Secret E February 753-55, T.J.Chand to India, 31 December 1909 (this report would have arrived in India at least 3 weeks later); The Cassels' report is in OIOC L/P&S/7/207-1873.
13 NAI FD, 1911 Secret E June 170-72, Chief Secretary Government of the Punjab to India, 17 May 1911; OIOC L/P&S/11/21, report of N.C.Stiffe, 16 August 1911.
14 Various correspondence, NAI FD, 1911 Establishment B May 307-08; FD, 1911 External B May 20-22; FD, 1911 Establishment B February 212-13.

15 NAI FD, 1911 External B October 286-87, file note by E.H.S.Clarke. 6 October 1911; FD, 1911 Secret E June 170-72, file note by E.H.S.Clarke, 25 May 1911, and related correspondence.
16 NAI FD, 1913 Secret E January 79-81, report of M.Young, 29 July 1912
17 OIOC L/P&S/11/56, report of C.M.Collett, 10 August 1912.
18 NAI FD, 1913 Secret E January 82-86, Chief Secretary Government of the Punjab to India, 25 September 1912; OIOC L/P&S/12/4163, Wakefield report No.4. Wakefield's report, in six parts with appendices, is, where not otherwise indicated, the source of information in this section.
19 OIOC L/P&S/12/4163, Barkha Tanjum to India, 15 November 1928, contained within Appendix 'D' to Wakefield report, No.2.
20 OIOC L/P&S/12/4163, report of H.Ruttledge, 30 September 1926, enclosed in Chief Secretary Government of the Punjab to Government of United Provinces, 10 November 1926, cover note by N.C.Stiffe.
21 Wakefield 1966, p. 60.
22 Ibid, pp. 38-39, 181.
23 Stewart 1989, p. 108, quoting E.W.Howell to Claremont Skrine, c.1923.
24 OIOC L/P&S/12/4163, Government of Punjab to India, 3 July 1930; L/P&S/12/4163-7900, Dr. Ram to Superintendent Punjab Hill States, 3-9 August 1931; L/P&S/12/4163-1165, Williamson report, 14 December 1932.
25 OIOC L/P&S/12/4163-1165, Williamson report, 14 December 1932.
26 OIOC R/1/4/992, Caroe to Gould, 4 April 1941.
27 Saker papers; copy of a report by Captain K.Saker, entitled 'The future of the British Trade Agency', c.1942; OIOC L/P&S/12/4191-2313, various correspondence.
28 Personal correspondence with H.Richardson, 19 October 1990.

CHAPTER TWELVE

1 OIOC L/P&S/12/4193-5552, Lhasa mission report, May-June 1937.
2 OIOC L/P&S/12/4201-4839; Lhasa mission report, week ending 17 May 1942; L/P&S/12/2859, Lhasa mission report, week ending 13 May 1945; L/P&S/12/4193, Lhasa mission report, week ending 29 September 1937.
3 Gould 1957, p. 238.
4 Lamb 1989, p. 310.
5 Mainprice papers, Mainprice diary entry, 15-19 October 1943; OIOC MSS Eur D998-17, Hopkinson's mission diary.

6   OIOC L/P&S/12/4175-1922, Weir report, 1 March 1933, attached medical report by M.R.Sinclair IMS.
7   Interview with H.H. the Dalai Lama, March 1994; OIOC L/P&S/12/4202-4485, Lhasa mission report, week ending 12 August 1945.
8   NAI FD, 1906 External B March 19-31, file note by Younghusband, 4 November 1904.
9   OIOC L/P&S/12/4206-4830, Gould to India, 15 September 1944.
10 Interview with Dr M.V.Kurian, January 1994.
11 Interview with A.Robins, April 1993.
12 OIOC MSS Eur D998-17, Hopkinson to Mrs Hopkinson, 21 April 1946.
13 OIOC MSS Eur D998-18, Hopkinson to Mrs Hopkinson, 19 May 1945.
14 OIOC MSS Eur D998-16, Hopkinson to Mrs Hopkinson, 3 September 1945; pesrsonal correspondence with Sir Stephen Olver, March 1993; Hopkinson 1950, p. 239.
15 Maraini 1952, p. 221.
16 Sangharakshita 1991, pp. 30-31.
17 Datta-Ray 1984, pp. 56, 70; also see Maraini 1952, numerous entries.
18 'Western Visitors to Lhasa: A Chronological List', Tibet Society UK, information sheet by James Cooper. Eight Japanese also visited Lhasa in 1901-50; see Berry 1995.
19 There are a wide variety of primary sources concerning British control of access to Tibet. See, for example, OIOC L/P&S/12/4201-6471, Lhasa mission report, 24 August 1942, regarding Richardson's obtaining permission for the visit of two American officers.
20 NAI FD, 1907 Secret E October 381-387, Consulate-General Chengdhu to India, 13 June 1907, and Thakur Jai Chand to India, 12 July 1907; also see FD, 1909 External B January 16-21, various correspondence re W.S.Paxton.
21 OIOC L/P&S/10/716-140, Teichman report, 29 February 1920.
22 OIOC L/P&S/12/4325, India to Government of Bengal, 23 October 1936.
23 OIOC L/P&S/12/4197-3864, Gould report, 30 April 1937.
24 OIOC L/P&S/12/4175-8833, article No.5 by Captain R.K.M.Battye.
25 OIOC MSS Eur D979, Ludlow diary entry, 30 September 1926; L/P&S/12/4332, Richardson to India, 5 June 1937; NAI EAD, 1940 Index File No 102 (5)-X; Interview with Mrs A.Saker, April 1993; Williamson 1987, pp. 225-26.

26 OIOC L/P&S/12/4202-2424, Lhasa mission report, 3 March 1946. The ban was ineffective. Such edicts often appear to have been moral guidelines, rather than laws in the European sense.
27 OIOC MSS Eur F80 5a 130, Rev. Tharchin to Bell, 11 December 1937; L/P&S/12/4193, Lhasa mission diary entries, 24 June 1937, & 4 September 1937; L/P&S/12/4202-6154, Lhasa mission report, 16 February 1947. Re Bernard, see Cooper (1986); Bernard's own account (1939) is unreliable.
28 Examples of religious seekers in this 'acceptable' category include the American, Edwin Schary, and the German-Bolivian, Lama Anagorika Govinda, who travelled in western Tibet during World War One, and in the 1940s, respectively. Neither ever commented on political matters.
29 OIOC L/P&S/12/4247, various correspondence; this file contains a detailed record of Tucci's applications.
30 OIOC L/P&S/12/4247, Gould to E.P.Donaldson (India Office), 6 April 1946.
31 For example, in 1930 the cadre arranged for a particular caravan leader to accompany the wealthy American traveller, Suydam Cutting; OIOC MSS Eur F157-236, Laden La to Bailey, 18 September 1930.
32 This account, where not otherwise indicated, is taken from various correspondence contained within OIOC L/P&S/12/4343.
33 Greve,R., 'Das Tibetbild im Nationalsozialismus,' paper given at the *Mythos Tibet* symposium, Bonn, May 1996.
34 Interview with H.Richardson, November 1990.
35 OIOC L/P&S/12/4165-7795, Lhasa mission report, October 1938-October 39, by H.Richardson, in Gould to India, 24 October 1939.
36 See, Sinclair 1965; OIOC L/P&S/12/4201, Lhasa mission reports, December 1943.
37 See Harrer 1954; also see OIOC MSS Eur F157-259, Richardson to Bailey, 30 March 1956.
38 Mainprice papers, Mainprice diary entry, 16 June 1944; also see NAI FD, 1909 Establishment B February 57-58, file note by M.Wood, 25 January 1909, which notes Secret Service expenditure records will be dispensed with; EAD, Index 1945 File No 118 (2) C.A. contains 'Reports on Tibet from a Secret Agent'.
39 *Asian Affairs*, (61) 1974, pp. 119-21, letters of Richardson & Caroe.
40 NAI FD, Index 1936, lists a classified file No 434-X Secret, containing 'Arrangements for intelligence on the NE Frontier' that may detail this reorganisation.
41 Griffiths 1971, pp. 342-52; Lha Tsering inherited Lambert's post in August 1947; NAI EAD, Index 1944 File No.188 C.A.; Interview with Namgyal Tsering, February 1944.

Notes 303

42 NAI EAD, Index 1944, File No.592 C.A. Secret, Lambert to Sir Denys Pilditch (Director, Intelligence Bureau), 18 September 1944.
43 OIOC MSS Eur D 998-39, 'Report on Tibet August 1945-August 1948', by A.J.Hopkinson.
44 Interview with H.Richardson, November 1990; 'Cess' has two dictionary meanings; 'tax' or 'rate' and, appropriately given the results noted next, 'bad to' or 'may evil befall'.
45 OIOC L/P&S/12/4202-6154, Lhasa mission report, week ending, 23 February 1947.
46 OIOC MSS Eur D998-39, 'Report on Tibet August 1945-August 1948', by A.J.Hopkinson.
47 Ibid.
48 OIOC MSS Eur F157-259, Richardson to Bailey, 18 July [1945?]; Re bribery of Regents, see L/P&S/12/4197-6072, Lhasa mission Annual Report, 1946, by H.Richardson; Lamb 1989, p. 310; Kimura 1990, p. 172; Goldstein 1989, pp. 364, 375, 448-49. An alternative interpretation is that that discourse represents a realistic picture of a society more commonly depicted in idealised terms and images.
49 Tada 1965, pp. 33-34. Whether this is true is not at issue, the point is the articulation of a religious ideal as the basis for the aspirations of the society, and the British acceptance that this was the basis of that society.
50 OIOC MSS Eur D998-39, 'Report on Tibet August 1945-August 1948', by A.J.Hopkinson; MSS D979, Ludlow diary entry, 1 February 1924.
51 Hopkinson ibid.; NAI FD, 1906 Secret E February 98-109, White to India, 31 October 1905.
52 OIOC MSS Eur F157-241, Ludlow to Bailey, 3 November 1926.
53 OIOC L/P&S/12/4223-6535, Hopkinson to India, 31 October 1945.
54 OIOC L/P&S/10/218-2134, Yatung Annual Report, 1921-22.
55 OIOC MSS Eur F157-259, Richardson to Bailey, 5 December 1949.
56 Ibid.

CHAPTER THIRTEEN

1 Interview with R.Ford, March 1993; Lamb 1989, p. V1; Addy 1985, p. 193.
2 As scholars such as Clive Dewey and David Fieldhouse have argued, 'vested ideas, rather than vested interests, are the great determinants of human behaviour'; Dewey 1993, p. V11; also see Feildhouse 1981, p. 230.
3 Personal correspondence with H.Richardson, June 1992; re lack of patronage, see OIOC MSS Eur F157-236, Laden La to Bailey,

18 September 1930, [concerning a Major Lock's hopes of a Tibet posting].
4 OIOC L/P&S/7/183-168, O'Connor to India, 19 November 1905; MSS Eur D998-39, 'Report on Tibet August 1945-August 1948', by A.J.Hopkinson.
5 NAI FD, 1913, Secret E January 120, file note by A.H.Grant, 10 September 1912.
6 These files are contained in the NAI Foreign Department Establishment B series, e.g. Gould – FD, 1913 Establishment B May 168-173, and FD, 1932 Establishment B 180. Williamson's preferences are shown in his personal file; OIOC R/1/4/1319, Williamson to India, 18 August 1923; re Hopkinson, NAI FD, 1928 Establishment B, 47 (14) E/28.
7 Bell 1992, p. 259; OIOC MSS Eur D998-39, 'Report on Tibet August 1945-August 1948' by A.J.Hopkinson.
8 NAI FD, 1913 Establishment B May 168-73, File Note, 20 February 1913, signature unclear. OIOC L/P&S/12-2345, India to Secretary of State, 19 May 1945; Mainprice papers, various correspondence, 1943-44.
9 OIOC MSS Eur F157-166, Bailey to his parents, 13 January 1908; NAI FD, 1911 Establishment B March 10-17, Bell to India, 23 December 1910.
10 OIOC MSS Eur F157-236, Laden La to Bailey, 18 September 1930; MSS Eur F157-269, Weir to Bailey, January 1929; Weir Papers, Weir to Mrs Weir, 9 December 1930. Although Gould ranked personally as a Second-class Resident, the Sikkim post was not made a Second-class Residency until Hopkinson took over.
11 OIOC MSS Eur D979, Ludlow diary entry, 10 November 1926.
12 Macdonald 1991, p. 121.
13 Interview with A.H.Robins, April 1993; Interview with R.Ford, March 1993; personal correspondence with R.Ford, October 1994; Walter's papers, 'Gyantse to Tibet 1940/1', (unpublished[?] article) p. 7.
14 Weir papers, Weir to Mrs Weir, 24 October 1929; OIOC R/1/4/986, file note by B.Gould, 14 August 1940, file note (unsigned), 27 May 1940 & related correspondence; R/1/4/992, Gould to India, 25 March 1941.
15 Mainprice papers, various diary entries, May to August 1944; Personal information courtesy of his sister, L.J.Mainprice.
16 Weir papers, Weir to Mrs Weir, 6 May 1930; OIOC MSS Eur F89 5a 92 & 5a 93 both contain reports on Fletcher sent from Tibet, dated 7 December 1930, [apparently by David Macdonald]; Interview with Mrs J-M.Jehu, March 1993.
17 MacLeod 1973, p. 1403; Potter 1986, pp. 34, 74-75; Robb 1992, p. 38.
18 Interview with Mrs E.Hopkinson, April 1993.

19 OIOC L/P&S/12/2345-3200, copy of Hansard entry of 21 May 1930.
20 Interview with R.Ford, March 1993.
21 Copland 1978, p. 287, also see pp. 277 & 289; In contrast see Dewey 1993, pp. 5, 7; Misra 1970, pp. 178-79, 246.
22 Landon 1988 (2) p. 152; OIOC MSS Eur F157-241, Ludlow to Bailey, 3 June 1930 & 20 June 1943; MSS Eur D979, Ludlow diary entry, 8 November 1926; Fletcher 1975, p. 233.
23 Williamson 1987, pp.186-87.
24 Mainprice papers, Mainprice diary entry, 15-19 October 1943; Interview with A.H.Robins, April 1993.
25 Interview with Dr T.W.Pemba, March 1994; also see OIOC L/P&S/12/4201-1863, Lhasa mission reports, 1942-45, comment by Sherriff, week ending, 19 March 1944; L/P&S/12/4193, Gould mission diary, 25 August 1936 &13 September 1936.
26 Interview with R.Ford, March 1993; Interview with A.H.Robins, April 1993; Interview with Mrs A.Saker, April 1993.
27 Interview with Mrs E.Hopkinson, April 1993.
28 Williamson 1987, pp. 39 & 207; Younghusband 1918, pp. 407-08.
29 Williamson 1987, pp. 39, 207; Weir papers, Weir to Mrs Weir, 7 September 1930.
30 Interview with R.Ford, March 1993; Interview with Mrs E.Hopkinson, April 1993.
31 Bishop 1989, p. 111.
32 Concerning the Punjab tradition, see Wurgaft 1983; van den Dungan 1972. George Orwell's description of the ethos of these magazines has not been bettered, see Orwell 1957.
33 Wurgaft 1983, p. 37. Re Curzon and Younghusband in the 'Great Game', see French 1994, and the popular account by Hopkirk 1990.
34 Younghusband 1985, pp. 434-38. Re Younghusband's spiritual character and beliefs, see French 1994.
35 Gould 1957, p. 19.
36 OIOC MSS Eur D979, Ludlow diary entry, 12 September 1924.
37 OIOC MSS F157-258, Hopkinson to Bailey, 5 December 1949.
38 OIOC MSS Eur F157-259, Richardson to Bailey, 25 February 1949.
39 OIOC MSS Eur F157-144, Younghusband to Bailey snr., 6 February 1906; also see MSS Eur F157-219, Younghusband to (F.M.) Bailey, 10 May 1906.
40 OIOC MSS Eur F80 5a 127, Gould to Bell, 22 March 1936.
41 OIOC L/P&S/12/4247-1517, cutting from *The Times*, 9 January 1934; also see Caroe 1974; Richardson 1974.

306 Tibet and the British Raj

42 Ewing 1980, pp. 181-84, 382, 389 & *passim;* Spangenberg 1976, pp. 53-54; Wurgaft 1983, pp. XVII, XIX, 83, 170.
43 OIOC MSS Eur F157-241, Ludlow to Bailey, 26 November 1934, & 4 December 1945, Gould 1957, p. 3; Re criticisms see, for example, Copland 1978, pp. 277-78, 289, 299; Wurgaft 1983, pp. XVII-XIX.
44 OIOC MSS Eur F157-166, Bailey to his parents, 2 May 1909.
45 Shils 1981, p. 14.
46 Interview with H.Richardson, November 1990.

CHAPTER FOURTEEN

1 See the various works by White, Bailey, Bell, Gould, Macdonald, O'Connor, Richardson and Younghusband listed in the bibliography.
2 OIOC L/P&S/12/4605, India to India Office, 27 July 1942.
3 Anderson 1992, esp. pp. 113-19; Dreyfuss 1995, p. 205; Robb 1994, pp. 2-5; Smith 1986, esp. pp. 134-36.
4 For example, see Cassinelli & Ekvall 1960; Ekvall 1969; Samuel 1994. Regarding the Sikkimese and Bhutanese enclaves, see Bray 1995, Dutta-Ray 1984, p. 42; Pranavananda 1983, pp. 81-82.
5 Regarding these social factors, see Snellgrove and Richardson 1968; Stein 1972.
6 Dreyfuss 1994, p. 210; Ekvall 1960. Dreyfuss's excellent essay examines the origin of this identity.
7 Bray 1993, p. 181; Tucci 1980, p. 111.
8 Bernard 1939, p. 120, quoting a telegram from the Kashag to himself; Goldstein 1989, p. 542, quoting the Kashag to Chang Kai-chek in 1946. Battye papers, (unpublished) 'Note on the present condition of Trade between Tibet and other countries', by Captain Battye, 28 April 1936.
9 Anderson 1992, p. 19. For further discussion of the Tibetan polity see, for example, Samuel 1993; Dreyfuss 1994.
10 Robb 1994, p. 2-4.
11 Ibid esp. p. 2. For a valuable discussion of the process by which South Asia's traditional frontiers were transformed into boundaries, see Embree 1977, pp. 255-80.
12 For example, the Chumbi was returned directly to the Tibetan Government in 1908, rather than to the Chinese authorities; OIOC L/P&S/7/210-602, Frontier Confidential Report, 14 February 1908.
13 Allen 1982, p. 201.
14 See, for example, Chandler 1905; Landon 1905; Ottley 1906.

15 Landon 1988, p. 107.
16 NAI FD, 1910 External B April 12-13, 'Military Report on Tibet', by Captain V.E.Gwyer. An attached file note states that this report was compiled with Bell's assistance. The report is also in OIOC L/Mil/17/14/92.
17 Bailey 1911; White 1984 (1909); Younghusband 1985 (1910).
18 O'Connor 1988, p. 352.
19 Bell 1987, pp. 65-66.
20 Anderson 1992, p. 179 fn.30, quoting a speech by Lord Curzon.
21 OIOC L/P&S/11/123-2400, Yatung Annual Report, 1916-17, cover note by Bell; Normanton 1988, p. 122 quoting Richardson [no source given]; McKay 1992b, p. 122, fn.13.
22 OIOC, L/P&S/7/249-1151, Gyantse Annual Report, 1910-11, cover note by Charles Bell.
23 Normanton 1988, p. 122 quoting Richardson (no source given).
24 NAI FD, 1905 Secret E March 341-368, Gyantse diary entry, 18 December 1904; OIOC L/P&S/12-4201-1863, Lhasa mission report, week ending, 19 March 1944.
25 NAI FD, 1930 Estimate 45E 1-9, personal file of H.Martin; re Luff, see Bell 1987, pp. 97-99; OIOC MSS Eur F157-240, Norbu Dhondup to Bailey, 17 September 1929 & 30 September 1929; MSS Eur F157-241, Ludlow to Bailey, 3 September 1931; The most detailed account of Fox's career, perhaps significantly, is by an American, see Thomas 1950, pp. 284-288.
26 OIOC MSS Eur F157-214, O'Connor to Bailey, 22 June 1907.
27 Suyin 1977; OIOC MSS Eur F226/34, M.Worth, IPS Collection. Due to illness and age, Mr Worth was unfortunately unable to respond to my request to discuss his recollections in more detail; personal correspondence with Mrs Olga Worth, 22 August 1993.
28 Mainprice papers, Mainprice diary entry, 22 July 1944.
29 Mainprice stayed on in Pakistan after 1947, but died of polio in Swat three years later; personal correspondence with L.J.Mainprice, 28 April 1993; Mainprice papers, *passim*.
30 David-Neel 1927; Younghusband 1925.
31 OIOC MSS Eur F157-319, anonymous comments on (unpublished) manuscript by F.M.Bailey, [original emphasis].
32 I have favoured the term 'mystic Tibet' here rather than the terms 'mythic Tibet' or 'mythos Tibet' to emphasise the fundamental attraction of mystical spiritual experiences associated with these exotic constructions of Tibet in the 20th century, although those alternative terms better embrace many older constructions including 'gold-digging ants',

'forbidden cities' and so on.
33 The seminal account of this process is by Bishop 1989.
34 Younghusband 1985, p. 2; Chapman 1992, p. 214.
35 Macdonald 1991, p. 201; OIOC MSS Eur F80 5h 2, unpublished manuscript by Bell entitled 'A Year in Lhasa', [apparently a draft autobiography, and unrelated to his (1924) article of that title], chapter three.
36 OIOC MSS Eur D979, Ludlow diary, various entries, 13 June 1926 to 1 August 1926, describes one such eccentric. Sven Hedin was one famous traveller who, after World War One, was considered undesirable on political grounds; see MSS Eur F157-221, Arthur Hirtzel to Bailey, 15 November 1922.
37 Sikkim State Archives, General 1916 (7)10/3(XXII)/1916; David-Neel to Bell, 31 August 1916; here David-Neel describes herself as 'a loyal friend of England'.
38 OIOC L/P&S/12/4247, Gould to E.P.Donaldson (India Office), undated, c.February 1946.
39 Bell 1992, pp. 5, 126, 139, 140, 213-14, 269.
40 'Tibet: A Reading List', information sheet available from The Tibet Society of the U.K.
41 Hopkinson 1950, p. 230; Chapman 1992, pp. 178-79.
42 Chapman 1992, p. 194.
43 Macdonald 1991, p. 57.
44 Richardson 1984, p. 10.
45 Interview with H.H. the Dalai Lama, March 1994.
46 Ibid; also see Shakya, 1992.
47 Bell 1987, p. 56.
48 Richardson 1994.

CHAPTER FIFTEEN

1 Younghusband 1910, p. 4.
2 NAI FD, 1912 External B August 71, Bell to India, 6 June 1912; FD, 1912 External B May 207, Bell to India, 26 March 1912; FD, Index 1934 File No 458-X Secret; Bell 1992, pp. 198, 268.
3 OIOC L/P&S/12/4197-3864, Gould report, 30 April 1937.
4 OIOC L/P&S/12/4193, Gould mission diary, various entries, Viceroy to Secretary of State, 18 July 1936, Press release entitled 'On the Road to Lhasa', issued on 17 September 1936.
5 NAI EAD, Index 1944 File No 10 (60) F.P; EAD, Index 1946, Files No

10 (2), & (3) N.E.F; OIOC L/P&S/12/4165-3578, Richardson to Gould, 9 July 1944; L/P&S/12/4201, Lhasa mission reports, 1942-45, various entries, esp. (4418) cover note by J.P.Ferriss, 3 September 1944; Interview with S.S.Tharchin, February 1994; Lamb 1989, p. 332. Re Steele, see Baker & Steele 1993; Re the Reverend Tharchin, see Norbu 1975.

6   OIOC MSS Eur F157-290, Bailey to Mr Parsons, undated [c1924/25]; L/P&S/12/1176, various correspondence, (original emphasis); RGS Everest Collection, EE 24/2/1, Bailey to Hinks, 18 November 1924; also see Hansen, 1996.

7   OIOC L/P&S/12/4201-7096, Lhasa mission report, week ending, 20 September 1942; MSS Eur F80 5a 88, Bell to the Dalai Lama, 31 January 1928; NAI EAD, Index 1945 File No.148 C.A.

8   OIOC L/P&S/12/4605-5261, C.Rolfe (India Office) to Film Section, British Council, 3 May 1943, (3894) British Embassy, Chungking, to Far Eastern Section, Ministry of Information, 27 May 1942; NAI EAD, Index 1945 File No. 148 C.A.

9   Baker & Steele, 1993, p. 68; Correspondence between the Panchen Lama and Mr B.Crump, *Journal of the Royal Central Asian Society,* 23, 1936, p. 720.

10 FO 371/84449 (170649), 'Notes on a conversation with Mr J.E.Reid', 19 January 1950.

11 OIOC L/P&S/12/3977-206, undated memo to Mr Walton. The 'Government Servants Conduct Rules of 1904' and the 'Army Regulations India, Volume 2, paragraph 423 of the King's Regulations' both governed publications by government officials; NAI FD, 1906 External B July 15.

12 NAI FD, 1910 General B April 156, file notes by E.H.S.Clarke, 2 March 1910, & Viceroy Minto, 25 March 1910; White 1984, pp. 110, 283, also see 166, 200, 284.

13 OIOC L/P&S/12/3982, various correspondence. Bell's papers include a copy of the Official Secrets Act. NAI FD, 1928 Establishment B 253-E, Secretary of State to India, 28 June 1928.

14 NAI FD, External B July 16-60, various correspondence.

15 NAI FD, 1906 External B July 15, anonymous file note, May 1906.

16 OIOC L/P&S/12/3982, various correspondence; L/P&S/12/3977, various correspondence; Bell 1992, p. 162.

17 OIOC L/P&S/10/1011-3605, India to India Office, 5 September 1923.

18 For example, the India Office supplied the RGS with a copy of Williamson's confidential report on his journey to western Tibet; OIOC L/P&S/12/4163-1165, E.P.Donaldson (India Office) to Arthur Hinks, 21 March 1933; also see Bishop 1989, pp. 13-14; Kaminsky 1986, pp. 176-77.

19 OIOC L/P&S/12/4193-3143, Hinks to J.C.Walton, 3 May 1938, 12 May 1938.

EPILOGUE

1. OIOC L/P&S/12/4197-7218, UK High Commission to India Office, 2 July 1947 and related correspondence.
2. Hopkinson 1950, p. 234.
3. Richardson 1984 p. 173; Diary entry of Mrs E. Hopkinson, 1 September 1948, courtesy of Mrs Hopkinson.
4. OIOC MSS Eur F157-258, Hopkinson to Bailey, 5 December 1949; Interview with J.Lall, October 1993.
5. See Ford, 1990.
6. The text of this agreement is given in Richardson 1984, pp. 293-300.
7. Interview with Dr T.W.Pemba, March 1994.
8. Goldstein 1989, pp. 703-04; Richardson 1984, pp. 179, 197-99, 231-32.
9. Addy 1994, p. 28.
10. OIOC MSS Eur D998-39, 'Report on Tibet August 1945-August 1948', by A.J.Hopkinson; Saker papers, copy of an undated (c1948-50) 'Top Secret' report for the Pakistan Government, entitled 'Tibet'.
11. OIOC L/Mil/7/19395, unsigned/undated report, c1927; Goldstein 1989, pp. 611-12, 623.
12. Interview with J.Lall, October 1993.
13. Bell 1992, p. 247.
14. Ford 1990, p. 195.
15. Interview with Dr T.W.Pemba, March 1994.
16. Interview with Mrs J-M.Jehu, March 1993.
17. Interview with H.H. the Dalai Lama of Tibet, March 1994.
18. Personal information courtesy of George Tsarong, March 1994.

Bibliography

This study is principally based on the English-language primary source material of the Oriental and India Office Collection and Records (London) and the National Archives of India (New Delhi), supplemented by material from other public and private archives. These records consist largely of official and private correspondence to and from the Tibet cadre. This written material was supplemented by a series of interviews with British, Tibetan and Indian officials who served in Tibet, or with the families of those who did so.

SECTION ONE: PRIMARY SOURCES

Section 1.1: The Oriental and India Office Collection and Records.

L/P&S/7	Political and Secret Despatches to, and Letters Received from, India.
L/P&S/10	Political and Secret Subject Files.
L/P&S/11	Political and Secret Annual Files.
L/P&S/12	Political and Secret (External) Files and Collections.
L/P&S/18	Selected Political and Secret Memoranda.
L/P&S/20	Selected Political and Secret Library.
MSS Eur D 979	The Ludlow Collection.
MSS Eur D 998	The Hopkinson Collection.
MSS Eur F 80	The Bell Collection.
MSS Eur F157	The Bailey Collection.
MSS Eur F 112/82	The Curzon Collection, Younghusband correspondence.
MSS Eur F 203	The Caroe Collection
R/1/4	Selected Indian Foreign Department Personnel Files.
V/12/53	Selected Indian Public Works Department services 1905-06.
V/13/77	Civil Lists, Indian Foreign Department.

V/12/12   History of Services.
L/Mil/17/14/92   'Military report on Tibet', Calcutta 1910.
Biographical Indexes of the Oriental and India Office Collection and Records.
Indian Army Lists 1905-1947.

Section 1.2: The National Archives of India

Foreign and Political Department Proceedings, Secret-External, A and B, 1905-13.
Foreign and Political Department Indexes, 1914-36.
External Affairs Department Indexes 1937-46.
Selected Foreign and Political Department Establishment, 1905-30.
Selected Foreign and Political Department General, 1905-30.

Section 1.3: Other Collections

The British Museum.
   Bell papers.
The Cambridge South Asia Library.
   Mainprice Papers.
The Public Records Office.
   Selected papers.
The Royal Society for Asian Affairs Library.
   Bell collection.
The Royal Geographical Society Library.
   Everest papers.
   Bailey papers.
The Sikkim State Archives.
   Judicial 1934–42 [Incomplete].
   General 1916–48 [Incomplete].

Section 1.4: Private Papers

Private papers:- I am indebted to the following families for access to private papers;

The Battye family (Battye papers), U.K.
The Jehu family (Weir papers), U.K.
Mr & Mrs R.Mouland (Walters papers), U.K.
Mrs E.Hopkinson (personal Gangtok diary), U.K.

Mrs A.Saker (Saker papers, and personal Tibet diary of Mrs Angela Saker), U.K.
The Macdonald family and Dr K.Sprigg (Macdonald papers), India.

Selected correspondence as per cited references.
Gyatso papers: copies in the possession of the author.

SECTION TWO: INTERVIEWS

Formal interviews were conducted with the following persons, whose status is shown briefly after their name.

Mr H.E.Richardson   Head of British Mission Lhasa, Trade Agent Gyantse, Acting Political Officer Sikkim.
Interviewed in London, 29 November 1990.

Dr K.Sprigg   To Gyantse in 1950, married into the family of David Macdonald.
Interviewed in Kalimpong, various dates in January 1992.

Mrs R.Collett   Daughter of Sir Charles Bell.
Interviewed in South Warnborough, 1 March 1993.

Mr R.Ford   Radio Officer, Lhasa and Chamdo.
Interviewed in London, 11 March 1993.

Mrs J-M.Jehu   To Lhasa in 1932, daughter of Lieutenant-Colonel J.L.R.Weir.
Interviewed in Bordon (Hants.), 26 March 1993.

Mrs E.Hopkinson   To Gyantse 1946 & 47, wife of Mr A.J.Hopkinson.
Interviewed at Welwyn Garden City, 20 April 1993.

Mr A.H.Robins   ECO Gyantse, BTA Gyantse. To Lhasa September 1945.
Interviewed at Carshalton, 23 April 1993.

Mrs A.Saker   Spent 6 months in Gyantse, wife of Major K.Saker.
Interviewed at Chichester, 27 April 1993.

Mr J.Lall   IAS. Maharaja of Sikkim's Prime Minister 1949-54.
Interviewed at Delhi, 12 October 1993.

Dr M.V. Kurian   Gyantse Medical Officer, two visits to Lhasa.
Interviewed at Coimbatore [India], 12 January 1994.

Mr S.S.Tharchin   Son of Reverend Tharchin.
Interviewed at Kalimpong, 22 February 1994.

Mr Namgyal Tsering Son of Lha Tsering, grandson of A-chuk Tsering.
Interviewed at Kalimpong, 23 February 1994.

Dr T.W.Pemba   Son of Rai Bahadur Pemba Tsering. Author of *Young Days in Tibet* etc.
Interviewed at Kalimpong, 6 March 1994.

His Holiness the 14th Dalai Lama of Tibet.
Interviewed at McLeod Ganj [Dharamsala], 31 March 1994.

SECTION THREE: SECONDARY SOURCES

Where additional dates and/or place of publication are given in brackets, this indicates the original publication.

Addy, P. 1984. *Tibet on the Imperial Chessboard: the making of British policy towards Lhasa, 1899-1925,* Calcutta.

—1994. 'British and Indian Strategic Perceptions of Tibet', in Barnett, R. & Akiner, S.(eds.) *Resistance and Reform in Tibet,* London.

Ahmad, A. 1991. 'Between Orientalism and Historicism: Anthropological Knowledge of India', in *Studies in History* (7.1), New Delhi.

Alder, G.J 1963. *British India's Northern Frontier 1865-1895,* London.

Allen, C. 1982. *A Mountain in Tibet; the Search for Mount Kailas and the Sources of the Great Rivers of India,* London.

Allworth, E.(ed.) 1967. *Central Asia. A Century of Russian Rule,* Columbia.

Anderson, B. 1992. *Imagined Communities,* London (1981).

Andreyev, A. 1994. 'The Buddhist temple in Petersburg and the Russo-Tibetan rapprochement', in Kvaerne, P. (ed.), (1994).

Anon. 1924. 'Dr McGovern's Visit to Lhasa', in *The Geographical Journal* (63. 2).

Aris, M., & Aung San Suu Kyi(eds.) 1979. *Tibetan Studies in Honour of Hugh Richardson,* Warminster.

Ashton, S.R. 1982. *British Policy towards the Indian States,* London.

Avedon, J.F.1984. *In Exile from the Land of Snows,* London.

Bailey, F.M. 1911. 'From the Outposts. A quiet day in Tibet', in *Blackwoods* (189.2)

—1945. *China - Tibet - Assam. A Journey, 1911,* London.

—1946. *Mission to Tashkent,* London.

—1957. *No Passport to Tibet,* London.

Bibliography 315

Baker, B., & Steele, A. 1993. *In The Kingdom of The Dalai Lama*, Sedona, (Arizona).
Ballhatchet, K. 1980. *Race, Sex and Class under the Raj,* London
Battye, E.D. 1984. *The Fighting Ten*, London.
Bayley, C.(ed.) 1989. *Atlas of the British Empire*, London.
Beaglehole, T.H. 1977. 'From Rulers to Servants: The I.C.S. and the British Demission of Power in India', in *Modern Asian Studies* (11.2).
Becker, S. 1968. *Russia's Protectorates in Central Asia: Bukhara and Khiva*, Harvard.
Beger, B. 1994. 'The Status of Independence of Tibet in 1938/39 according to the travel reports (memoirs)' [sic], printed by the Tibet Society (U.K), London.
Bell, Sir C. 1924a. 'The Dalai Lama; 1921', in *Journal of the Central Asian Society* (11.1).
—1924b. 'A year in Lhasa', in *The Geographical Journal* (63.2).
—1928. *The People of Tibet,* Oxford.
—1930. 'The North-Eastern Frontier of India', in *Journal of the Central Asian Society* (27.2).
—1931. *The Religion of Tibet,* Oxford.
—1949. 'China and Tibet', in *Journal of the Royal Central Asian Society* (36.1).
—1987. *Portrait of a Dalai Lama*, London (1946).
—1992. *Tibet Past and Present*, Delhi (Oxford 1924).
—1996. *Grammar of Colloquial Tibetan* London. (1905)
Bernard, T. 1939. *Penthouse of the Gods: a pilgrimage into the heart of Tibet and the sacred city of Lhasa*, N.Y.
Berry,S. 1991. *A Stranger in Tibet; The Adventures of a Zen Monk*, London (1990).
—1995. *Monks, Spies and a Soldier of Fortune: The Japanese in Tibet*, London.
Bharati, A. 1974. 'Fictitious Tibet: The Origin and Persistence of Rampaism', in *The Tibet Society Bulletin* (7).
Billington, R.A.(ed.) 1986. *The Frontier Thesis: Valid Interpretation of American History?,* N.Y.
—1972. 'Frontier Democracy: Social Aspects', in Taylor, G.R.(ed.) *The Turner Thesis: Concerning the Role of the Frontier in American History,* Lexington, (1949).
Bishop, P. 1989. *The Myth of Shangri-La: Tibet, Travel Writing and the Western Creation of Sacred Landscape,* London.
Black, C.E. 1908. 'The Trade and Resources of Tibet', *Asian Review* (26)
Blunt, E. 1937. *The I.C.S.,* London.

Bormanshinov, A. 1992. 'A Secret Kalmyk Mission to Tibet in 1904', in *Central Asiatic Journal* (36.3-4).
Bose, M. 1979. *British Policy in the North-East Frontier Agency*, Delhi.
Bower, H. 1976. *Diary of a Journey Across Tibet*, Kathmandu (London 1894).
Bray. J. 1990. 'The Lapchak Mission from Ladakh to Lhasa in British Foreign Policy', in *The Tibet Journal* (15.4).
—1992. 'Christian Missionaries on the Tibetan Border: the Moravian Church in Poo (Kinnaur), 1865-1924', in *Tibetan Studies, Proceedings of the 5th Seminar of the International Association of Tibetan Studies, Narita 1989*, Narita (Japan).
—1993. 'Christian Missionaries and the Politics of Tibet 1850-1950', in Wagner, W.(ed) *Kolonien und Missionen*, Bremen.
—1994. 'Towards a Tibetan Christianity? The lives of Joseph Gregan and Eliyah Tsetan Phuntsog', in Kvaerne, P.(ed)(1994).
—1995. 'Ladakhi and Bhutanese Enclaves in Tibet', paper presented at the 7th Conference of the International Association of Ladakhi Studies, Bonn, June 1995.
Breckenridge, C.A., & van der Veer, P.(eds.) 1994. *Orientalism and the Postcolonial Predicament*, New Delhi, (Uni. of Pennsylvania 1993).
Burman, B.R. 1977. 'The Regents of Tibet', in *Tibetan Review* (10.5).
Busch, B.C. 1980. *Hardinge of Penshurst*, Hamden (Connecticut).
Byron, R. 1933. *First Russia, Then Tibet*, London.
Cain, P.J. 1980. *Economic Foundations of British Overseas Expansion 1815-1914*, London.
Camman, S. 1951. *Trade Through the Himalayas. The Early British Attempts to Open Tibet*, Princeton.
Campbell, J. 1988. *The Power of Myth*, N.Y.
Caplan, L. 1991. "Bravest of the Brave": Representations of "The Gurkha" in British Military Writings', in *Modern Asian Studies* (25.3).
Carey, W. 1902. *Travel and Adventure in Tibet*, London.
Caroe, O. 1960. *Englishmen in Tibet from Bogle to Gould*, (printed by the Tibet Society U.K.), London.
—1974. Correspondence; *Asian Affairs* (61.1).
Cassinelli, C.W., & Ekvall, R.B. 1969. *The Political System of Sa sKya*, N.Y.
Chandler, E. 1905. *The Unveiling of Lhasa*, London.
Chandola, K. 1987, *Across the Himalayas Through the Ages*, Delhi.
Chapman, F.S. 1992. *Lhasa: The Holy City*, Delhi, (London 1940).
Charlesworth, N. 1982. *British Rule and the Indian Economy 1800-1914*, London.
Christie, C. 1976, 'Great Britain, China and the Status of Tibet, 1914-21', in *Modern Asian Studies* (10.4).

—1977. 'Sir Charles Bell; A Memoir', in *Asian Affairs* (64.1).
Coates, P. 1990. 'The China Consuls', in *Asian Affairs* (21.1).
Cocker, M. 1994. *Loneliness and Time: British Travel Writing in the Twentieth Century*, London (1992).
Coen, Sir T. 1971. *The Indian Political Service*, London.
Cohn, B.S. 1983. 'Representing Authority in Victorian India', in Hobsbawn, E., & Ranger, T., (eds.) (1983).
—1985. 'The Command of Language and the Language of Command', in Guha, R. (ed.) *Subaltern Studies IV*, Delhi.
Collister, P. 1987. *Bhutan and the British*, London.
Connell, J. 1959. *Auchinleck*, London.
Cooper, J. 1986a. 'Theos Bernard, Fact and Fiction', in *Tibetan Review* (21.4).
—1986b. 'The West and the Modernisation of Tibet; 1900-1950' in *Tibetan Review* (21.11).
Cooper, T.T. 1869. *Journal of an Overland Journey from China towards India*, Calcutta.
Copland, I. 1978. 'The Other Guardians: Ideology and Performance in the Indian Political Service', in Jeffrey, R.(ed.) *People, Princes and Paramount Power*, Delhi.
—1982. *The British Raj and the Indian Princes, Paramountcy in Western India, 1857-1930*, Delhi.
Crawford, D.G. 1930. *The Roll of the Indian Medical Service 1615-1930*, London.
Curzon, Lord G.N. 1889. *Russia in Central Asia*, London.
—1907. *Frontiers*, (Romanes Lecture), Oxford.
Cutting, S. 1947. *The Fire Ox and Other Years*, N.Y.
Das, S.C. 1902. *Journey to Lhasa and Central Tibet*, Delhi.
Datta-Ray, S.K. 1984. *Smash and Grab. Annexation of Sikkim*, New Delhi.
David-Neel, A. 1927. *My Journey to Lhasa*, London.
—1931. *With Mystics and Magicians in Tibet*, London.
Dewey, C. 1973. 'The education of a ruling caste: the Indian civil service in the era of competitive examination', in *English Historical Review* (88.2).
—1978. 'Patwari and Chaukidar: Subordinate Officials and the Reliability of India's Agricultural Statistics', in Dewey, C., & Hopkins, A.G.(eds.) *The Imperial Impact: Studies in the Economic History of Africa and India*, London.
—1993. *Anglo-Indian Attitudes: The Mind of the Indian Civil Service*, London.
—1995. "Socratic Teachers": Part 1 – The Opposition to the Cult of Athletics at Eton, 1870-1914', in *The International Journal of the History of Sport* (12.1).

Dhondup, K. 1986. *The Water-Bird and Other Years*, Delhi.
Dilks, D. 1969. *Curzon in India*, (2 vols.) London.
Dirks, N.B. 1994. 'Colonial Histories and Native Informants: Biography of an Archive', in Breckenridge, C.A., & van der Veer, P. (1994).
Dreyfus, G. 1994. 'Proto-Nationalism in Tibet' in Kvaerne, P.(ed.), (1994).
Duby, G. 1985. 'Ideologies in social history', in le Goff, J., & Nora, P.(eds.) (1985).
Edwardes, H.B. 1851. *A Year on the Punjab Frontier*, London.
Edwardes, M. 1967. *The West in Asia, 1850-1914*, London.
—1975. *Playing the Great Game*, London.
Ekvall, R.B. 1960. 'The Tibetan Self-Image', in *Pacific Affairs* (33.4).
Eliade, M. 1955. *The Myth of the Eternal Return*, N.Y.
Elridge, C.C.(ed.) 1984. *British Imperialism in the Nineteenth Century*, London.
Embree, A.T.1977. 'Frontiers into Boundaries: From the Traditional to the Modern State', in Fox, R.G.(ed.) *Realm and Region in Traditional India*, New Delhi.
Etherington, N. 1984. *Theories of Imperialism*, N.J.
Everest-Phillips, M. 1991. 'British Consuls in Kashgar', in *Asian Affairs* (22.1)
Ewing, A. 1980. 'The Indian Civil Service, 1919-42', unpublished PhD. dissertation, Cambridge University.
—1984. 'The Indian Civil Service 1919-1924: Service Discontent and the Response in London and Delhi', in *Modern Asian Studies* (18.1).
Field, H.J. 1982. *Towards a Programme of Imperial Life*, Westport (Connecticut).
Fieldhouse, D.K. 1981. *Colonialism 1870-1945: An Introduction*, London.
Fisher, M.H. 1987. *A Clash of Cultures: Awadh, The British, and the Mughals*, Delhi.
—1991, *Indirect Rule in India*, Delhi.
Fleming, P. 1986. *Bayonets to Lhasa*, London (1961).
Fletcher, H.R.1975. *A Quest for Flowers, the plant explorations of Frank Ludlow and George Sherriff*, Edinburgh.
Ford, R. 1990. *Captured in Tibet*, Oxford, London (1957).
Fraser, D. 1907. *The Marches of Hindustan*, London.
French, P. 1994. *Younghusband: The Last Great Imperial Adventurer*, London.
Frykenberg, R.G. 1965. *Guntur District 1788-1848: A History of Local Influence and Central Authority in South India*, Oxford.
Gallagher,J., & Robinson, R., 1976. 'The Imperialism of Free Trade', in Louis, W.R.(ed.) (1976).
Gellner, E. 1983. *Nations and Nationalism*, Oxford.

Girouard, M. 1981. *The Return to Camelot*, London.
Goldstein M. 1989. *A History of Modern Tibet, 1913-1951: The Demise of the Lamaist State*, London.
Gould, Sir B.J. 1941. *Report on the Discovery, Recognition and Installation of the Fourteenth Dalai Lama*, New Delhi.
—1957. *The Jewel in the Lotus*, London.
Griffiths, Sir P. 1971. *To Guard My People: The History of the Indian Police*, London.
Grove, L.T. 1931. 'Two Sapper Subalterns in Tibet,' in *Royal Engineers Journal* (45).
Guha, R. 1988. *An Indian Historiography of India: A Nineteenth Century Agenda and its Implications*, Calcutta.
—1989. 'Dominance Without Hegemony And Its Historiography', in Guha, R.(ed.) *Subaltern Studies VI*, Delhi.
Gupta, K. 1974, *The Hidden History of the Sino-Indian Frontier*, Calcutta.
Hansen, P.H. 1996 'The Dancing Lamas of Everest: Cinema, Orientalism, and Anglo-Tibetan Relations in the 1920s', in *The American Historical Review*, (101.3).
Harrer, H. 1954. *Seven Years in Tibet*, London.
Hayden, H.H., & Cosson, C. 1927. *Sport and Travel in the Highlands of Tibet*, London.
Heathcote, T.A. 1974. *The Indian Army*, London.
Hedin, S. 1909. *Transhimalaya*, London.
Heussler, R. 1963. *Yesterday's Rulers: The Making of the British Colonial Service*, London.
Hilton, J. 1933. *Lost Horizon*, London.
Hilton, R. 1955. *Nine Lives: the autobiography of an old soldier*, London.
Hobsbawn, E. & Ranger, T.(eds) 1983. *The Invention of Tradition*, London.
Hogben, W.M. 1981. 'An Imperial Dilemma: The Reluctant Indianization of the Indian Political Service', in *Modern Asian Studies* (15.4).
Holditch, Sir T. 1916. *Political Frontiers and Boundary Making*, London.
Hopkirk, P. 1984. *Setting the East Ablaze*, Oxford.
—1990. *The Great Game; On Secret Service in High Asia*, London.
Hopkinson, A.J. 1950. 'The Position of Tibet', in *Journal of the Royal Central Asian Society* (37.3-4).
Hunt, R., & Harrison, J. 1980. *The District Officer in India: 1930-1947*, London.
Hutchinson, J., & Vogel, J.P. 1933. *History of the Punjab Hill States*, (2 vols.), Lahore.
Hyam, R. 1979. 'The Colonial Office Mind 1900-1914', in *Journal of Commonwealth and Imperial History* (8.1).

—1990. *Empire and Sexuality,* Manchester.
Inden, R. 1986. 'Orientalist Constructions of India', in *Modern Asian Studies* (20.3).
Johnson, K.P. 1994. *The Masters Revealed: Madame Blavatsky and the Myth of the Great White Lodge,* N.Y.
Jones, R.L. 1985. *A Fatal Friendship,* Delhi.
Kaminsky, A.P. 1986. *The India Office,* London.
Kawaguchi, E. 1979. *Three Years in Tibet,* Kathmandu, (Benares, 1909).
Kimura, H., & Berry, S. 1990. *Japanese Agent in Tibet,* London.
King. L.M. 1927. *China in Turmoil. Studies in Personality,* London.
King, W.H. 1924. 'The Telegraph to Lhasa', in *The Geographical Magazine* (63.6).
Klein, I. 1971a. 'British Imperialism in Decline: Tibet, 1914-1921', in *Historian* (34.1).
—1971b. 'The Anglo-Russian Convention and the Problem of Central Asia, 1907-1914', in *Journal of British Studies* (11.1).
Kolmas, J. 1979. 'The Further Development of the Disputed Frontier', in Aris, M., & Aung San Sui Kyi, (eds.) (1979).
—1992. 'A Chronology of the Ambans of Tibet. Part I: The Ambans and Assistant Ambans in the Yongzheng and Quianlong Period (1727-1795)' in *Tibetan Studies. Proceedings of the 5th Seminar of the International Association for Tibetan Studies, Narita,* (Japan).
—1994. 'The Ambans and Assistant Ambans of Tibet (1727-1912): Some Statistical Observations', in Kvaerne, P.(ed) (1994).
Kuleshov, N. 1992. 'Agvan Dorjiev, the Dalai Lama's Ambassador', in *Asian Affairs* (23.1).
Kvaerne, P.(ed) 1994. *Tibetan Studies: Proceedings of the 6th Seminar of the International Association for Tibetan Studies Fagernes, 1992, (2 vols.)* Oslo.
Kwanton, L. 1969. 'Indian Trade Marts in Tibet', in *Courrier de l'Extreme Orient* (29.3).
Lamb A. 1959. 'Some Notes on Russian Intrigue in Tibet', in *Journal of the Royal Central Asian Society* (46.1).
—1960. *Britain and Chinese Central Asia: the Road to Lhasa 1767-1905,* London.
—1966. *The McMahon Line,* (2 Vols.), London.
—1971. 'War in the Himalayas. "India's China War" by Neville Maxwell', in *Modern Asian Studies* (5.3).
—1986. *British India and Tibet. 1766-1910,* London. (A revised edition of his 1960 work.).
—1989. *Tibet, China and India 1914-1950,* Hertingfordbury (U.K).

Landon, P. 1988. *Lhasa*, (2 Vols.), Delhi, (London 1905).
le Goff, J. 1985. 'Mentalities: a history of ambiguities', in le Goff, J., & Nora, P.(eds.) *Constructing the Past: Essays in Historical Methodology*, Cambridge, (First published as *Faire de l'Historie*, Paris 1974).
Louis, J. 1894. *The Gates of Thibet*, Calcutta.
Louis, W.R.(ed.) 1976. *The Robinson and Gallagher Controversy*, N.Y.
Ludden, D. 1993. 'Orientalist Empiricism: Transformations of Colonial Knowledge', in Breckenridge & van der Veer, (1993).
Lyall, A. 1973. *The Rise and Expansion of British Dominion in India*, London, (1891).
Macdonald, D. 1991. *Twenty Years in Tibet*, London, (1932).
MacLeod, R.M. 1973. '*Statesmen Undisguised*', in *American Historical Review* (78.5).
McGovern, W. 1924. *To Lhasa in Disguise*, London.
McKay A.C. 1992a. 'The Establishment of the British Trade Agencies in Tibet: A Survey', in *Journal of the Royal Asiatic Society* (3.2.3).
—1992b. 'The Cinderella of the Foreign Service', in *South Asia Research* (12.2).
—1992c. 'David Macdonald: The Early Years', in *The Tibet Society of the United Kingdom Newsletter* (4).
—1994a. 'The Other "Great Game": Politics and Sport in Tibet, 1904-47', in *The International Journal of the History of Sport* (11.3).
—1994b. 'Major Cairncross: A Rogue on the Tibetan Frontier', in The *Tibet Society of the United Kingdom Newsletter* (4).
—1995. 'Tibet and the British Raj, 1904-47: The Influence of the Indian Political Department Officers', PhD. thesis, S.O.A.S., London University.
—1997. 'Tibet 1924: A Very British Coup Attempt?', in the *Journal of the Royal Asiatic Society* (forthcoming).
Madden, F., & Fieldhouse, D.K.(eds.) 1982. *Oxford and the Idea of Commonwealth*, London.
Mangan, J.A. 1986, *The Games Ethic and Imperialism*, London.
Maraini, F. 1952. *Secret Tibet*, London.
Marshall, J. 1977. *Britain and Tibet 1765-1947. The background to the India China Border Dispute. A select annotated bibliography of printed material in European languages*, University of La Trobe, (Melbourne).
Marshall, P.J., & Williams, G. 1982. *The Great Map of Mankind*, London.
Mason, P. 1954. [as Woodruff, P.] *The Men Who Ruled India*, (2 vols.), London.
—1974. *A Matter of Honour: An account of the Indian Army, its officers and men*, London.

Maxwell, N. 1970. *India's China War,* London.
Mehra, P. 1958. 'Tibet and Russian Intrigue', in *Journal of the Royal Central Asian Society* (45.1).
—1967. 'Beginnings of the Lhasa Expedition: Younghusband's own words', in *Bulletin of Tibetology* (4.3), Gangtok.
—1969. 'The Mongol-Tibetan Treaty of January 11, 1913', in *Journal of Asian History* (3.1).
—1974. *The McMahon Line and After,* Delhi.
Mersey, Viscount. 1949. *The Viceroys and Governors-General of India:* 1757-1947, London.
Misra, B. 1970. *The Administrative History of India, 1834-1947,* Bombay.
Moir, M.I. 1966. *Political and Secret Department: Index to Records, India Office Library,* London.
Mommsen, W.J. 1980. *Theories of Imperialism,* London, (Gottingen, 1977).
Moore, R.J. 1993. 'Curzon and Indian Reform', in *Modern Asian Studies* (27.4).
Morgan, G. 1971. *Ney Elias,* London.
—1973. 'Myth and Reality in the Great Game', in *Asian Affairs* (60.1).
—1981. *Anglo-Russian Rivalry in Central Asia 1810-1895,* London.
Morris, P.(ed.) 1984. *Africa, America and Central Asia: Formal and Informal Empire in the Nineteenth Century,* Exeter.
'Mugger' [Huelin H.W?] 1936. 'With the Tibet Detachment', in *Journal of the United Service Institute of India* (66.3)
Murty, T.S. 1978. *Frontiers: A Changing Concept,* New Delhi.
Neame, P. 1939. 'Tibet and the 1936 Lhasa Mission', in *Journal of the Royal Central Asian Society* (26.2).
—1947. *Playing with Strife: the autobiography of a soldier,* London.
Nilsson, S. 1968. *European Architecture in India, 1750-1850,* London.
Noel, J.B. 1989. *Throgh Tibet to Everest,* London (1927).
Norbu, Dawa. 1974. *Red Star Over Tibet,* London.
—1975. 'G.Tharchin: Pioneer and Patriot', in *Tibetan Review* (8.12).
Normanton, S.1988. *Tibet: The Lost Civilisation,* London.
Nyman, L-E. 1973. 'The Great Game; A Comment', in *Journal of the Royal Central Asian Society* (60.3).
O'Connor Sir F. 1931. *On the Frontier and Beyond: A Record of Thirty Years Service,* London.
—1940. *Thing Mortal,* London.
—1988. 'The Present Condition and Government of Tibet', appendix 'D' in Landon P., (1988).
O'Malley, C.S.S. 1965. *The Indian Civil Service 1601-1930,* London (1931).

Orwell, G. 1957. *Selected Essays*, London.
Ottley, W.J. 1906. *With Mounted Infantry in Tibet*, London.
Pemba, Tsewang.W. 1957. *Young Days in Tibet*, London.
Pereira, G. 1924. 'Peking to Lhasa (from the diaries of the late Brigadier-General George Pereira)', in *The Geographical Journal* (64.2).
Potter, D. 1973. 'Manpower Shortage and the End of Colonialism: The Case of the Indian Civil Service', in *Modern Asian Studies* (7.1).
—1977. 'The Shaping of Young Recruits in the Indian Civil Service', in *Indian Journal of Public Administration* (23.4).
—1986. *India's Political Administrators 1919-1983*, Oxford.
Praag, M.C.v.W.van. 1987. *The Status of Tibet: History, Rights, and Prospects in International Law*, Boulder, Colorado.
Pranavananda, Swami. 1983. *Kailas-Manasarovar*, Delhi (Calcutta 1949).
Prasad, B. 1979. *Foundations of India's Foreign Policy*, Calcutta.
Prescott, J.R.V.1965. *The Geography of Frontiers and Boundaries*, Chicago.
—1972. *Political Geography*, London.
Ranger, T. 1983. 'The Invention of Tradition in Colonial Africa', in Hobsbawn, E., & Ranger,T. (eds.) (1983).
Rawling, C.G. 1905. *The Great Plateau*, London.
Rayfield, D. 1976. *Dream of Lhasa: The Life of Nikolay Przhevalsky*, London.
Razzell, P.E. 1963. 'Social Origins of Officers in the Indian and British Home army: 1758-1962', in *British Journal of Sociology* (14.2).
Reincourt, A. de 1950. *Roof of the World. Tibet, Key to Asia*, N.Y.
Richards, T. 1993. *The Imperial Archive: Knowledge and the Fantasy of Empire*, London.
Richardson H.E. 1945. *Tibetan Precis*, Calcutta.
—1951. 'The State of Tibet', in *Journal of the Royal Central Asian Society* (38.2).
—1974. Correspondence, *Asian Affairs* (61.1).
—1979. 'The Rva-screng Conspiracy of 1947', in Aris,M., & Aung San Suu Kyi, (eds) (1979).
—1984. *Tibet and its History*, (revised edition) Boston/London (London, 1962).
—1985. 'British Policy Towards Old Tibet', (review of Addy, P., 1984) in *Tibetan Review* (20.1).
—1988. 'Tibetan Lamas in Western Eyes', in *Bulletin of Tibetology* (1) Gangtok.
—1992. 'Reminiscences of Life in Old Tibet', in *Bulletin of the Department of Sanskrit and Indian Studies, Harvard University*, (2.3).
—1993. *Ceremonies of the Lhasa Year.* M.Aris (ed.) London.
—1994. 'My Direct Experience of Independent Tibet', Tibet Society of the U.K. Information Sheet, London.

Richardson, H.E., & Skorupski, T. 1986. *Adventures of a Tibetan Fighting Monk*, Bangkok.
Richardus, P. 1989. *The Dutch Orientalist Johan van Manen: His Life and Work*, Leiden (Kern Institute).
Robb, P. 1987. 'New Directions in South Asian History', in *South Asia Research* (7.2).
—1992. *The Evolution of British Policy Towards Indian Politics 1880-1920*, Delhi.
—1994. 'The colonial state and constructions of Indian identity: an example on the north-east frontier in the 1880s', paper given to the Calcutta-S.O.A.S. Conference, Calcutta, March 1994.
Robinson, R. 1982. 'Oxford in Imperial Historiography', in Madden, F., & Fieldhouse, D.(eds.) (1982).
—1976. 'Non-European Foundations of European Imperialism: Sketch for a Theory of Collaboration', in Louis, W.R., (ed.) (1976).
Rockhill, W.W. 1891. *Land of the Lamas. Notes of a Journey through China, Mongolia and Tibet*, London.
—1910. *The Dalai Lamas of Lhasa*, Leiden.
Rudolph, S.H & L.I. 1984. *Essays on Rajputana: Reflections on History, Culture, and Administration*, Delhi.
Rupen, R.A. 1979. 'Mongolia, Tibet, and Buddhism or, A Tale of Two Roerichs', in *The Canada-Mongolia Review* (5.1) Saskatchewan.
Ruttledge, H. 1928. 'Notes on a visit to Western Tibet in 1926', in *The Geographical Journal* (71.5).
Rywkin, M.(ed.) 1988. *Russian Colonial Expansion to 1917*, London.
Samuel, G. 1993. *Civilized Shamans*, Washington.
Sandberg, G. 1987. *The Exploration of Tibet*, Delhi, (Calcutta, 1904).
Sangharakshita, (Lingwood, D.P.) 1991. *Facing Mount Kanchenjunga*, Glasgow.
Schary, E. 1937. *In Search of the Mahatmas*, London.
Scwartz, R.D. 1994. *Circle of Protest; Political Ritual in the Tibetan Uprising*, London.
Seaver, G. 1952. *Francis Younghusband: Explorer and Mystic*, London.
Seldon, A., & Pappworth, J. 1983. *By Word of Mouth - Elite Oral History*, London.
Shakabpa, W.D. 1984. *Tibet: A Political History*, N.Y.
Shakya, T. 1985. 'Tibet and the League of Nations with reference to letters found in the India Office Library, under Sir Charles Bell's Collections', in *The Tibet Journal* (10.3).
—1986. 'Making of the Great Game Players. Tibetan Students in Britain Between 1913 and 1917', in *Tibetan Review* (21.1).

—1992. 'Tibet and the Occident: The Myth of Shangri-la', in *Tibetan Review* (27.1).
Shepperd, A. 1980. *Sandhurst; The Royal Military Academy,* London.
Sherring, C. 1906. *Western Tibet and the British Borderland,* London.
Shils, E. 1981. *Tradition,* London.
Simon, H.A. 1961. *Administrative Behaviour,* N.Y.
Sinclair, W.B. 1965. *Jump to the Land of God,* Caldwell (Idaho).
Singh, A.K.J. 1988a. *Himalayan Triangle,* London.
—1988b. *A Guide to the Source Materials in the India Office Library and records for the History of Tibet, Sikkim and Bhutan, 1765-1950,* London.
Sinha, A.C. 1975, *The Politics of Sikkim,* Faridabad.
Smith, A.D. 1986. *The Ethnic Origin of Nations,* Oxford.
Snellgrove, D. 1979. 'An Appreciation of Hugh Richardson', in Aris, M., & Augn San Suu Kyi, (1979).
Snellgrove, D., & Richardson, H. 1968. *A Cutural History of Tibet,* London.
Snelling, J. 1990. 'Agvan Dorjiev: Eminence Grise of Central Asian Politics', in *Asian Affairs* (21.1).
—1993. *Buddhism in Russia; The story of Agvan Dorzhiev, Lhasa's Emissary to the Tsar,* Shaftsbury, (U.K.).
Spangenberg, B. 1971. 'The Problem of Recruitment for the Indian Civil Service in the Late Nineteenth Century', in *Journal of Asian Studies* (30.2).
—1976. *British Bureaucracy in India; Status, Policy and the ICS in the late 19th century,* Delhi.
Spear, T.G.P. 1978, 'Stern Daughter of the Voice of God: Ideas of Duty among the British in India', in O'Flaherty, W.D., & Derrett, J.D.M.,(eds.) *The Concept of Duty in South Asia,* London.
Spence, H. 1991. 'Tsarong 11, the Hero of Chaksam, and the Modernisation Struggle in Tibet, 1912-1931', in *The Tibet Journal* (26.1).
Spengen, W.van, 1992. 'Tibetan Border Worlds: A geo-historical analysis of trade and traders', PhD. thesis, University of Amsterdam.
Spitzer, A. 1973. 'The Historical Problem of Generations', in *American Historical Review* (78.5).
Stein, R.A. 1972. *Tibetan Civilization,* London.
Stewart, J. 1989. *Envoy of the Raj,* Maidenhead.
Suyin, H. 1977. *Lhasa the Open City,* N.Y.
Swinson, A. 1971. *Beyond the Frontiers: the biography of Colonel F.M.Bailey, explorer and secret agent,* London.
Sykes, P. 1945. 'Obituary' [of Sir Charles Bell], in *Journal of the Royal Central Asian Society* (32.2).
Symonds, R. 1991. *Oxford and Empire,* Oxford (1986).
Tada, T. 1965. *The Thirteenth Dalai Lama,* Tokyo.

Taring, R.D. 1983. *Daughter of Tibet*, London (1970).
Teichman, E. 1992. *Travels of a Consular Officer in Eastern Tibet*, Cambridge.
Templeman, D. 1994. 'The Lotus and the Snow Lion: Notes from Six Lectures on the Culture and History of Tibet,' given at the Australian Museum, April to June 1994, printed by the Australian Tibet Society, Sydney 1994.
Tenzin Gyatso, (H.H. the 14th Dalai Lama), 1962. *My Land and My People*, London.
Thomas, L. jnr. 1950. *Out of This World: Across the Himalayas to Forbidden Tibet*, N.Y.
Thornton, T.H. 1895. *Sir Robert Sandeman*, London.
Trench, C.C. 1987. *Viceroy's Agent*, London.
Tucci, G. 1956. *To Lhasa and Beyond*, Rome.
—1980. *The Religions of Tibet*, London, (first published as 'Die Religionen Tibets', in Tucci, G. & Heissig, W. *Die Religionen Tibets und der Mongolei*, Stuttgart, (1970).
Turner, F.J. 1963. 'The Significance of the Frontier in American History' (1893), in Simonson, H.P.(ed.) *The Fronteir in American History*, N.Y.
Ullman, J.R. & Tenzing Sherpa, 1955. *Man of Everest: The Autobiography of Tenzing*, London.
Unsworth, W. 1981. *Everest*, N.Y.
van den Dungen, P.H. 1972. *The Punjab Tradition*, London.
Verrier, A. 1992. 'Francis Younghusband and the Great Game', in *Asian Affairs* (23.1).
Virk, D.S. 1989. *Postal History of Indian Campaigns: Sikkim – Tibet, 1903-1908*, New Delhi.
Waddell, L.A. 1899. *Among the Himalayas*, London.
—1905. *Lhasa and its Mysteries*, London.
Wakefield, E. 1961. 'A Journey to Western Tibet, 1929', in *Alpine Journal* (66).
—1966. *Past Imperative. My Life in India 1927-1947*, London.
Waller, P. 1990. *The Pandits: British Exploration of Tibet and Central Asia*, Lexington, (Kentucky).
Walsh. E.C.H. 1945. 'Obituary' [of Sir Charles Bell], in *Journal of the Royal Asiatic Society* (16.1).
Waterfall A.C. 1965. *The Postal History of Tibet*, London.
Webb, M. 1985. *The Last Frontier*, Albuquerque.
Weir, T. 1932. 'The Impressions of an Englishwomen in Lhasa', in *Journal of the Royal Asiatic Society* (3.1).
White, J.C. 1984. *Sikkim and Bhutan*, Delhi (London 1909, as *Sikhim and Bhutau*).

Williamson, M.D., with John Snelling, 1987. *Memoirs of a Political Officer's Wife in Tibet, Sikkim and Bhutan*, London.
Wolpert, S. 1967. *Morley and India: 1906-1910*, Berkeley.
Woodcock, G. 1971. *Into Tibet: The Early British Explorers*, London.
Woodman, D. 1969. *Himalayan Frontiers; A Political Review of British, Chinese, Indian and Russian Rivalries*, London.
Wright S.F. 1950. *Hart and the Chinese Customs*, Belfast.
Wurgaft, L.D. 1983.*The Imperial Imagination*, Middletown (Connecticut).
Yapp, M.E. 1980. *Strategies of British India; Britain, Iran and Afghanistan, 1798-1850*, Oxford.
—1990. Review of Kaminsky, A.P. (1986), in *Bulletin of the School of Oriental and African Studies* (53. 3).
Younghusband, F.E. 1910. 'Our Position in Tibet', in *Proceedings of the Central Asian Society* (11).
—1918. (as 'F.E.Y.') 'Obituary: John Claude White', in *The Geographical Journal* (51.6).
—1925. (ed.) *Peking to Lhasa: the narrative of the journeys in the Chinese Empire made by the late Brigadier-General George Pereira*, London.
—1949. *Everest; the Challenge*, London (1936).
—1985. *India and Tibet*, Oxford (London 1910).
Zinkin, M. 1994. 'ICS Revisited', in *Asian Affairs* (25.3).

Index

A

A-chuk Tsering, 77, 198
Addy, P., 205
Afghanistan, 5
Albanian deserter, Bailey disguised as,, 117
Almora, 172,179-180
Amban(s), xx, 9, 20, 24, 27, 38, 52-53, 79
American travellers to Tibet, vi, 104, 106-107, 119, 191, 193
Amitabha, 59
Amo River, 98-99
Ampthill, Lord, 19, 177
Anderson, B., 2
Andrews, Lt. J.A., 111
Anglo-Chinese Agreement of 1908, 47, 53
Anglo-Chinese Convention of 1890, 10
Anglo-Chinese Convention of 1906, 47
Anglo-Chinese trade, 23
Anglo-Chinese Trade Regulations of 1893, 10, 23, 47, 64, 103, 263
Anglo-Indians, 36, 51, 53, 77, 141, 145
Anglo-Russian Convention of 1907, 47, 51, 60, 64, 67, 71-72
Anglo-Tibetan Convention of 1904, xxiii, 20

Anzacs, 172
Arms supplies to Tibet, 27, 40, 68-69, 74, 174, 243-244, 276 n.16.
Assam, 117, 122, 127, 198, 207, 230
Astor, Lord, 194
Auchinleck, Field-Marshal Claude, 108
Aufschnaiter, P., 197
A Year on the Punjab Frontier, 94
Ayi-la, xxix

B

Babu, 50
Baghelkhand, 151
Bailey, Lt-Col.F.M., vii, xxviii-xxix, 12, 29-30, 33-35, 37-39, 47, 50, 81, 87-88, 90, 93, 101-103, 105, 108-109, 112-113, 115-130, 132-135, 137, 144, 150-151, 165, 187, 202, 206-207, 212-213, 215-217, 224, 229-231, 240, 244, 248, 251, 253-254
Bailey, Mrs I., 213
Bailey mission to Lhasa, 120-124
Bailey, Lt-Col.,snr., 33, 88, 216
Baluchistan, 94, 206
Baroda, 136, 151, 172
Battye, Major R.K.M., xiv, 158-160, 166, 206, 253
Battye, T., 253

Bell, Sir C.A., x, 49-50, 54, 56-60, 63-64, 66-85, 88-92, 95-96, 106, 109, 115-120, 122, 124-125, 127, 129, 133-135, 137-141, 146, 151-153, 155-158, 161-162, 164, 166-167, 171-174, 186, 190, 198, 206-208, 210-212, 215-217, 223-227, 231-232, 234-236, 239, 241-245, 251-252, 254
Bell, Mrs C., 77, 157
Bell mission to Lhasa, 71-78, 80, 106, 115-116, 118, 122, 124, 134, 141
Bengal, 49
Bengal Civil Service, 7
Bengal Eastern Frontier Regulations, 190
Bengal, Lieutenant-Governor of, 143
Berlin, British Ambassador in,, 195
Bernard, T., 193
Bhotia Boarding School, 8, 50
Bhotias, 180
Bhutan, xiii, xxiv, 1, 10, 13, 35, 42, 49, 64, 84, 140, 152, 187, 206, 221, 242, 250
Bhutanese officials, 27
Bihar, 49
Bishop, P., 82, 214
Blackwoods magazine, 101, 224
Boer War, 15
Bogle, G., 7, 22, 41, 88
Bolsheviks/ism, 117-118
Bombay, 104, 113, 161, 199
Bön, 221
Bo Tsering, 144, 197
Bower, General H., xxvii
Boys Own Paper, 214
Brahmaputra, *See* Tsangpo
Bray, Sir D., 132
Britain, xxiii, xxv, 3, 12, 15, 28, 31, 47, 62, 64-65, 67, 70, 102, 106, 117, 120, 127, 138, 155-156, 164, 173, 179, 185, 194, 197, 223, 251-252
British Army, 104
British Buddhist Mission, 119
British Envoy to the Court of Nepal, 115
British Government, xxiv, 5-6, 12, 15-16, 21, 33, 38, 52, 70, 75, 160, 165, 227, 237, 250, 253 (also see, Whitehall)
British Intelligence, 105
British Legation Peking, 71, 74, 121
British Legation Berne, 105
British Mission Lhasa, xiii, xxiii, 1, 22, 65, 78-79, 166-173, 175, 185-186, 190, 197, 211, 228, 240-241, 247-249
Broderick, St. John,, 15
Buddhism, ix, xxi, 6, 11, 20, 63, 84, 157, 192-193, 222, 224
Buddhism in Russia, 63
Buffer states, 14
Buriats, 11, 52, 118, 138
Burma, 112, 250
Bushir (Persian Gulf), 59
Byron, R., 109-111

C

Cairncross Major W.H., 104-106
Calcutta, 10, 29-30, 104, 106, 109, 128
Calcutta university, 128
Calvert, H., 180, 216
Cambridge university, xvi, 89, 149
Campbell, Major W.L., xvi, 71-72, 104, 109-110, 146, 164
Canada, 109, 157
Caplan, L., 141
Caroe, Sir O., 157, 166, 171, 251
Carpenter, H.A., 106

Cars (gift to Panchen Lama), 39
Cassels, W.S., 180
Cavignari, Capt., 214
Central Intelligence Bureau, 198
Central Intelligence Officer, Assam., 198
Cemeteries, (British in Tibet), 99, 109, 160, 248
Chaksam Ferry, 53, 61
Chamberlain, Sir N., 195
Chamdo, 248
Chandra, Pedma, 8, 60, 128, 138-139, 220
Chand, Thakur Jai, 179-181
Chang lo, 19, 44, 99
Chang Yin-tang, 38
Chao Er-feng, General, 45, 53
Chaplin, C., 241
Chapman, F.Spencer, 132, 167, 169, 235, 244
Charterhouse school, xxvi
Chatterjee, Lt G.N., 110-111, 141
Chengdu, 248
Chengdu, British Consul, 53
Chenrezi, 6, 55
Chensal Namgang *See* Tsarong Shapé
Chiang Kai-shek, 154
China, viii, xii, 2-4, 6, 9-10, 13-14, 16, 20-21, 23-24, 26, 28, 31, 33, 36-40, 44-45, 47-48, 51-52, 54-55, 58, 62-63, 65-67, 71-72, 74, 79-80, 103, 106, 117, 122, 134-136, 149-150, 154, 156, 159, 170, 173, 176, 178, 185-186, 188-189, 194, 197, 200, 202-203, 222, 229, 232, 234-235, 240-241, 248-250
China Consular Service, 71
China Maritime Customs Services, 23
China, People's Republic of, 250
China Treaty Ports, 23

Chinese mission in Lhasa, 72, 154, 158-159, 196, 284 n.42.
Ch'ing dynasty, 6, 21, 59
Chitral, Relief of, xxv
Chomolahari, Mount, 99
Christianity, 89, 103
Chumbi Valley, xxiii-xxiv, xxix, 35, 37, 45-46, 49, 64-65, 73, 98-99, 104, 112, 164, 223, 232
Clifton college, xxv
Cobbett, Capt. J.E., 108
Collett, C.M., 181
Congress party, 248
'Coo-Coo la', 189
Cossacks, 21
Cozens-Hardy family, 117
Crozier, Lt. R.E., 197
Curtis, Alice, *See* Macdonald, D., family of
Curzon, Lord G.N., v, xvi, xxiv-xxvii, 9, 11-13, 15, 19, 22, 30-31, 34, 40-41, 47-48, 50, 52, 60, 73-74, 76, 79, 87-90, 95, 117-118, 162-163, 177, 198, 200, 214, 223, 226, 250
Curzonism, 31

D

Dagg, Sgt., 167, 185
Daily Mail, 112
Dak bungalows, 54, 98, 100, 108, 192
Dalai Lama[s], vii-viii, xi, xv, 4, 6, 9, 11, 12, 20-23, 28, 31, 34, 40-41, 51-67, 71, 75-76, 79, 81, 83-84, 104-105, 112, 116, 118-131, 133-136, 142, 145, 150-158, 161, 167-168, 170-171, 176, 185, 187, 197, 200, 225-226, 228, 234-236, 239-241, 248, 252-253
Dane, L. Sir, xxvii, 13, 23, 29-31, 40, 43-45, 94, 177-178, 225

332 *Tibet and the British Raj*

Darjeeling, xxvi-xxvii, xxix, 8, 19, 36, 49-50, 121, 125, 138-139, 142, 144, 228, 253
Darjeeling High School, 139, 142, 144
Das, Lala Devi, 181
Das, Sarat Chandra, 8-9, 60, 138-139, 220
David-Neel. A., 162, 230, 233
Dayal, H., 247
Dekyi Lingka, 152, 185
Delhi, ii, ix, xv, xxvii, 5, 25, 59, 74, 77, 111, 120, 167, 193, 201, 226, 247
Dharamsala, 253
Dhondup, K., 3
Dhondup, R.S.Norbu *See* Norbu Dhondup
Domville, Admiral Sir B., 195
Dongtse, 9
Dorzhiev, A., 11, 21, 52, 62, 70, 84, 118, 139, 157
Drepung monastery, 11, 21, 65, 77, 118, 175
Durbar, 59
Dyer, Dr., 77, 141

E

Eastern Tibet, 4, 25, 45, 53, 68-69, 71, 74, 117, 191, 194, 221, 230, 235
Edgar, J.H., 25
Edinburgh Academy, xxviii
Edwardes H.B., 94
Eliade, M., 85
Ellis, R., 253
Emperor (of China), 51-52
Empress Dowager, 52
Enga, Teremoto, 27
Escort Commanding Officer (Gyantse), 107-108, 110-111, 121, 141, 152, 164, 172, 188, 207-208, 212, 253, 265
Escort, Gyantse Trade Agent's, 43, 46, 64, 164
Eton school, 88
Everest, Mount, 78, 119, 124, 136, 182, 240

F

Fairley, J., 74-75
Fenton, Capt. L.S., 107
Fletcher, Lt-Col.E.W., 90, 93, 209
Football, 70, 90, 101, 130-132, 143, 168-169
Ford, R., 173, 203, 205, 212, 248, 253
Foreign and Political Department, *See* Political Department
Foreign Office, British, 4, 16, 24, 60, 74, 196, 247
Foreign Secretary, British, 74, 117
Foreign Secretary, Indian, xxvii, 6, 13, 23, 63, 94, 132, 135, 155, 157, 166, 171, 183, 193, 251
Foreign Minister, China, 157
Foreign Minister, India, 188
Forward policy/school, 14, 16, 33-34, 40, 48-49, 63, 66, 95, 118, 127, 177, 215, 254
Foucault, M., 224
Fox, R., 185, 228
France, 194

G

Gabet, Abbé, 7
Gallacher, W., 160
Gallipoli, 117, 172
Ganden monastery, 21
Gandhi, M.K., 202
Gangtok, xv, xxvi, 10, 27, 42-43, 54, 67, 71, 74, 88, 96-98, 102, 115,

Index 333

133-134, 136, 145, 150-153, 156, 158, 161, 164, 174, 184, 188-189, 206-210, 213, 228, 232
Gangtok Residency, 27, 213, 228, 232
Gartok, iii, xxiii, xxviii-xxix, 19, 22, 58, 81, 137, 172, 177-184, 188, 216, 243
Gartok Trade Agency, xxviii, 81, 172, 177, 243
Gartok Trade Agent, 19, 58
Garwhal, D.C. of, 181
Gelugpa, 6, 21, 221
Gem, 214
George V, King, 56
Germany, 14, 65, 194-197
Gnatong, 54
Gordon, General, xxv, 214
Gould, Sir B., vi, x, 88-89, 94, 139, 142, 157, 161-162, 165-171, 173-175, 184-186, 188-189, 192-193, 195-196, 198, 205-206, 208, 215-217, 232, 235, 239-241, 251-252
Government of Bengal, 10
Government of India, iv, xxiii, xxvi, xxix, 4-5, 7, 10, 12-14, 16, 23-25, 29, 34, 36, 46, 51, 55, 59-60, 64-65, 67, 77-78, 84, 88, 104-106, 112-113, 117, 121, 125-126, 133, 139, 150, 154, 156, 160, 165, 167, 174, 177, 179-180, 182-183, 191, 193-195, 197-198, 220, 227, 242-244, 247
Government of Pakistan, 249
Government of the Punjab, 177, 179, 181
Government of the United Provinces, 179
Gow, Mr., 38-39, 41, 44
Grammar of Colloquial Tibetan, 70
'Great Game', ix, xxv 52, 150, 214, 249

Grey, P., 16
Grist, Lt.R., 208
Guthrie, Dr.J., 142, 158-159, 187, 212, 247
Guthrie, Mrs., 142
Gyantse, vi, xxi, xxiii-xxiv, xxvi, xxviii-xxix, 1, 19, 22-23, 25-28, 30, 33, 35-39, 43-44, 46-47, 50, 53-54, 57-58, 60, 63, 67, 70-72, 74-75, 77-78, 94, 96-102, 104, 106-113, 116-119, 121-125, 128-137, 140-143, 146, 149-153, 155, 158, 160-162, 164-167, 170, 172, 184-190, 195, 198, 201, 205-212, 227-229, 248-249, 252-253
Gyantse *dzong* (fort), 100
Gyantse (English) school, vi, 105, 125, 129-132, 153, 186, 201-202
Gyantse Trade Agency, 19, 99, 104, 146, 155, 188, 227, 248
Gyantse Trade Agent, xxiv, xxvi, 63, 71, 109, 122, 133, 158, 166, 184, 188, 198, 249
Gyantse monks to Europe, 119, 124
Gyatso, Sherab, *See* Shabdrung Lama
Gyatso, Urgyen, 8-9, 138, 143

H

Hailey, Major P.C., 94, 208
Hailey's comet, 53
Hailey, Sir W., 94
Haldenov, Z., 118
Hamilton, Lord G., 162
Hann, Sgt., 100
Hardinge, Lord C., 60-61
Harnett, Lt-Col., 155-156
Harrer, H., 197
Hart, Sir R., 24
Hastings, W., 7
Head Clerk, Gyantse, 108
Head Clerk, Yatung, 144

Head of British Mission Lhasa, 1, 169
Hedin, S., 61, 95, 217, 223
Henderson, V., 23-25, 37
Himalayan Hotel, 112, 252
Himalayas, 7, 29, 40, 55, 133, 150-151, 184, 232
Himmler, H., 195-196
Hindus, 141
Hinks, A., 120, 244-245
Hislop, Major J.H., 122, 187
Holditch, Sir T., 13
Home Affairs Dept., 198
Hopkinson, A.J., 88, 90-91, 94, 102, 188-189, 199-201, 206-207, 215-216, 233, 235, 247-249, 252
Hopkinson, Mrs E., 247
House of Commons [British], 160
Howell, Sir E.B., 193
Huang, General Mu-sung., 154, 166, 174
Huc, Abbé, 7
Humphreys, Dr G.F., 141
Humphreys, Sgt., 54
Hunza, xxv

I

Imperial history, 2
India, iv-v, viii, xi, xv-xvii, xxiii-xxix, 2, 4-5, 7, 9-11, 13-15, 22-31, 34, 36, 39-41, 43, 45-47, 49-52, 54-55, 58-61, 64-65, 67-69, 71, 73-74, 76-80, 83-84, 87-88, 91, 94-95, 102, 104-107, 111-113, 115, 117-121, 123-127, 132-133, 136, 138-141, 144-147, 149-150, 152-154, 156-157, 159-165, 167, 172, 174, 176-177, 179-183, 185, 191, 193-202, 206-207, 209, 213-215, 217, 220-223, 225-229, 233-234, 236, 239-240, 242-245, 247-250, 252-253
India and Tibet, 7, 58, 145, 191, 215, 223
Indian Army, xxvii, xxviii, 5, 19, 30, 33, 74, 90-91, 93, 95, 107, 211, 250
Indian Civil Service [ICS.], 5
Indian Education Department, 130
Indian Government [post-1947], 166, 247-248
Indian Medical Service [IMS], 19
Indian 'Mutiny', 166
Indian National Archives [National Archives of India], 125
Indian Police, 5, 110, 144
Indian Political Department;
 See Political Department
Indian Trade Agencies, 248
India Office, xvi, 4, 6, 52, 56, 240, 242-245
Indo-China war, 1962, 65
Indo-Chinese Agreement of 1954, 248
Indus river, 172
Intelligence, xxvii, 25-27, 35, 77, 105, 117, 122, 126, 145, 150, 178, 190, 198, 220
Irwin, Miss., 105
Italy, 194

J

Jacob, General Sir J., 14
Jameson Raid, xxv
Japan, 14, 28, 74, 170, 194
Japanese in Lhasa, 26
Jebtsundamba Khutukhtu, 20
Jehu, Mrs J-M., xiv, 252
Jelep la, 35, 54, 98
Johnson, J., 109
Jongpon [Gartok], 178-180, 182
Jongpon [Gyantse], 27, 110
Journal of the Royal Central Asian Society, 241

Journal of the Royal Geographical Society, 245

K

Kabul, 206, 214
Kailas, Mount, 172, 231
'Kaiser', 196
Kalimpong, 98, 112, 142, 151, 154-156, 174, 198, 202, 240, 252
Kalmuck, *See* Buriat
Kamba valley, 98
Kansu Mission, 72, 80
Karnali river, 172
Kashag, *See* Tibetan Government
Kashgar, xxv, 78, 80, 150, 181, 186, 207
Kashmir, xxv, 33, 35, 61, 151, 177, 206, 230
Kathmandu, 25, 117, 127, 133
Kennedy, Lt-Col.R., 47, 77, 107, 212
Kew gardens, 252
Khenchung (Gyantse), 107, 124-125, 131
Khotan, 181
Kim, 21, 88, 213
King Arthur..., 131
Kipling R., 21, 88, 94, 213
Kitchener, Field-Marshal Lord, xxvii, 30
Kulu, D.C.'s of, 180
Kumaon, 182
Kundeling monastery, 152
Kunlun mountains, 177
Kurian, Capt. M.V., 141, 188, 253

L

Ladakh, 84, 140
Ladakhis (in Lhasa), 26, 76
Lahoul, 179
Laden La, Rai Bahadur, vii-viii, 60-61, 77, 122-126, 128, 131, 134, 137, 139, 143-147, 155, 239, 253
Lama Sengchen Tulku, *See* Sengchen Tulku
Lamb, A., 3, 76, 205
Lambert, E., 198-199
Lauder, H., 37
Laughton, Major., 209
Lazarists, 7
Lepcha, 50
Lhasa, iii, v-vii, xi, xiii, xx, xxiii-xxvi, xxix, 1, 3, 7, 9-11, 13, 15-16, 20-28, 30, 33-34, 36, 38, 40, 44-45, 47, 52-53, 56, 58, 60-61, 63, 65, 67, 69-80, 83-84, 93, 96, 101, 103-104, 106, 112, 115-116, 118-128, 131-145, 150-160, 165-176, 178, 185-191, 193-199, 202, 207, 211-212, 215, 221, 223, 228-230, 232-235, 239-241, 244, 247-249, 252-253
Lhasa [English] school, 175
Lhasa Government, *See* Tibetan Government
Lhasa Mission; *See* British Mission Lhasa
Lhasa Police, 112
Lhasa: The Open City, 229
Lhasé Kusho, 72
Lha Tsering, Lt., 198
Liberal government, 1905, 15
Linlithgow, Lord, 93
Little, Sgt., 110
Lohit, 207
Lönchen Shatra, 64, 72
London, 6, 31, 56, 61, 78, 112, 119, 136, 157, 194, 216, 224, 239, 244
Longstaff, T., 180
Loseling college (Drepung), 65
Ludlow, F., 125, 129-132, 149-150, 152-153, 172, 186, 192, 201-202, 208, 211-212, 216-217, 252

336 Tibet and the British Raj

Luff, Sgt., 54, 110-111, 228
Lyall, Sir A., 94-95

M

Macdonald, D., 50, 54, 58, 60-62, 65, 72, 77, 81, 85, 92-93, 105, 110-113, 115-117, 121, 125, 134, 137-138, 144-145, 149, 151-153, 155, 158, 163, 167, 173-174, 183, 208, 215, 217, 224, 226, 232, 242, 244-245, 252
Macdonald, D., family of, 50, 110-112, 252
MacDonald, General J., 42
Macgregor, Field-Marshal Sir C., 95
Macready, Lt. W., 107
Magnet, 214
Maharaja of Sikkim, 26, 72, 189
Mainprice, F., 146, 198, 207, 209, 229-230
Manasarovar, Lake, 80, 231
Manchuria, 44, 149, 157
Manning, T., 7
Marlborough school, 88, 91
Marshall, Capt.W., 108, 152-153
Marshall, M., *See* Williamson, Mrs M
Martin, H., 110-111, 228
McGovern, W.M., 119-120, 125, 146, 194, 244-245
McLeod Gang, 253
McMahon, Sir H., 63
Medical Officers, 26, 39, 47, 77, 104, 107, 110, 122, 135, 152, 155, 158, 167, 172, 182, 187-188, 207
Medical Officers (Gyantse), 26, 39, 47, 77, 104, 107, 110, 135, 141, 152, 158, 188
Menon K.P.S., 188
Mesopotamia, 104, 149
Michael, E.A., 104
Minto, Earl of, 31, 40, 56, 76, 242
Mishmis, 230

Missionaries (Christian), 25-26, 78, 97, 103, 117, 202
Mondo [Möndrong], 182
Mongolia, 12, 20, 62, 84, 157
Mönlam; *See* Tibetan New Year
Morgan, Capt.W., 167
Morley, Lord John, 31, 40-41, 47-49, 56, 73, 76
Mughals, 162
Muir, Rev.J.R., 25-26
Mukden (Manchuria), 44
Murree, xxv
Muslims, 140-141, 168, 221, 230
Mussolini, 194
Mysore, 206

N

Nathu la, 35, 98
Neame, General P., 68, 142, 167
Nehru, Jawaharlal, 249
Nepal, 5, 7, 25, 71, 78, 115, 124, 151, 195-196
Nepalese Prime Minister, 25
Nepalese representative in Tibet, 25, 75-76, 168, 249
Nepean, Sgt.E., 167
Nevill, Capt. G.A., 117, 122, 127
New Zealand, 133, 253
Nichols, F., 104
Nobel Peace Prize, 253
Norbu Dhondup, R.B., 61, 77, 82, 85, 90, 92, 125, 134, 137, 142, 145, 147, 152, 154, 158, 166, 185-186, 241
North-West Frontier (Province), xxvii, 214
Nyang chu, 99
Nyingma, 221

O

O'Connor, Lt-Col Sir F., viii, xxvi-xxix, 3, 12, 19, 22-25, 27-31, 33,

36-37, 39-45, 47, 49-51, 58-59, 65, 73, 88, 90, 94-95, 99, 101, 104, 107, 109, 115-117, 124, 127, 138-139, 142, 151, 189, 198, 206, 211-212, 214-217, 223, 225, 227, 229, 252
Official Secrets Act, 242
Old Bailey, 253
Old Yatung, 98
Olver, Sir S., 189
Oracle, Tibetan State, 173
Orissa, 49
Oxford university, 49, 89, 97, 119, 166

P

Pakistan, xxv, 249, 253
Palhe family, 138
Palhesé, Kusho, 138-139, 146
Pallis, M., 193-194
Panchen Lama, xxviii, 4, 7, 9, 22-23, 27-31, 33, 37-41, 43, 52, 58, 69, 99, 115-116, 119, 122-123, 127-128, 130, 135-136, 149, 153, 158-159, 166-167, 170, 223, 241
Panchen Lama's Prime Minister, 9
Panchen Lama's visit to India, 28-30, 37, 41
Pandits, 8, 220
Pan-Mongolian state, 63, 157
Parker, Capt. E., 111-112
Parr, Capt.W.R.M., 23, 103
Patterson, Sgt., 100
Pekhor Chödé monastery, 99
Peking, xxv, 3, 10, 26, 41, 44, 51, 71, 74, 106, 118, 121, 150, 157, 252
Pemba Tsering, R.S., 92, 137, 140, 144, 184, 186-187, 248, 251
Pereira, General G., 121, 126, 230
Perry, Capt. F., 110-112
Persia, 58-59, 90, 117

Phari, 10, 22, 53-54, 98-99
Pierpoint, Mr., 108-109
Pipitang, 98
Political Department, 4-5, 9-10, 13, 34, 78, 87, 89-90, 92-94, 112, 116, 133, 137, 151, 179-180, 183, 186, 189, 198, 205, 208, 210-211, 213-214, 217, 230
Political Department *Manual of Instructions*, 79
Political Officer Assam, 117, 122, 127
Political Officer Sikkim, xxvi, xxix, 1, 4, 10, 27, 33, 38, 49, 55, 67, 72, 77, 105, 112-113, 115, 133, 150, 157, 159, 161, 164, 166, 169, 178, 184, 188, 196, 198, 205, 207, 233, 243, 247
Potala (Palace), 12, 118, 201, 212
Prince and Princess of Wales, 28, 30
Public Works Department (Indian), 10, 41
Punjab, 44, 94, 177, 179, 181, 214-215
Purang, 178, 184
Pursing Karthak, 109

Q

Quetta Military College, 121

R

Rabgyeling monastery, 216
Raj, i, viii, xiii, xv, xxix, 1-2, 4, 7-8, 12-15, 21, 24-25, 29-31, 33-34, 37, 51, 55, 64, 66-67, 70, 72, 76, 78-79, 81, 83, 87, 92, 94, 109, 120, 128-129, 137-139, 146-147, 153, 155-156, 160, 162-165, 171, 183-184, 210, 217, 247, 249, 251-252, 254
Ram, Dr. K., 182-184

338 Tibet and the British Raj

Ram, Pala., 181-182
Rangoon, 133
Rawalpindi, 30
Rawling, Capt.C.G., xxviii-xxix, 184, 243
Regent, 6, 21, 52, 154, 156-159, 169, 186 See also Reting Regent
Reid, J.E., 241
Residency, Gangtok, 27, 213, 228, 232
Reting monastery, 154
Reting Regent, 154, 156-159, 169, 200
Reuters (News Agency), 244
Richardson, H.E., x-xi, xiii, 65, 85, 88-90, 94, 129, 141, 166-167, 169-170, 173, 175, 185-186, 189, 192, 194-200, 203, 205, 207-208, 211-212, 216, 231, 234, 236, 240-241, 247, 251-252
Rivett-Carnac, Major H.G., 113, 146, 172, 206, 211
Robins, Capt.A., 188, 208, 212, 253
Rome university, 194
Rosemeyer, W.P., 53, 75, 145
Rothschilds, 177
Royal Air Force, 159
Royal Geographical Society (RGS), 13, 83, 120, 190, 244-245
Royal Military Academy Woolwich, xxvi
Rugby school, 129, 161
Russell, Major A.A., 90, 93, 206, 208-209
Russia, xxiii, 4, 8, 11, 13-14, 21, 28, 31, 33, 45, 56, 60, 62-63, 67, 72, 104, 118, 120, 126, 178, 194, 214, 249
Russian Tsarist Government, 11
Russian Communist Government, 72, 126, 160
Russian secret police, 117
Russo-Japanese war, 21
Ruttledge, H., 182
Ryder, Capt.C.H., xxviii

S

Sadiya, 118
Said, E., 224
Saker, Major R.K.M., 143, 172, 184-185, 212, 249, 253
Saker, Mrs A. 172, 212
Salween river, 104
Samye monastery, 197
Sandeman, Sir R., 94-95, 213-214
Sandhurst (military academy), xvi, xxv, xxviii, 89
Schäfer mission, 197
School of Oriental Studies, 119
Secret Agents/Service; See Intelligence
Secretariat (Political Department), 5, 43, 68, 73, 85, 87, 93, 108, 133, 160, 172, 205, 225, 242
Secretary of State, 4-5, 15, 31, 40, 46, 61, 73, 75, 92, 162
Sengchen Tulku, 9, 138
Sera monastery, 21, 159, 175
Seven Years in Tibet, 197
Shabdrung Lama (Sherab Gyatso), 138-139
Shakabpa W.D., 83
Sherriff, Major G., 93, 142, 150, 152, 186, 197, 212, 252
Sherriff, Mrs B., 142, 197
Sherring, C., 179-180, 243
Shigatse, xxviii, 6-7, 9, 22, 28, 36-38, 40-41, 52, 58, 107, 119, 122-123, 128, 135-136, 153, 155-156, 158, 191, 221
Shigatse representative in Lhasa, 28
Shillong, 198
Shils, E., 217

Sikhim and Bhutan, 42, 242
Sikh Pioneers, 32nd, xxix
Sikkim, vi, xv, xix, xxiii-xxiv, xxvi-xxvii, xxix, 1-2, 4-5, 10, 26-28, 33, 35, 38, 41-42, 45, 49, 53, 55, 67, 72, 77, 84, 97, 105-106, 109, 112-113, 115-117, 124, 126, 128, 133, 140, 146, 150-151, 155, 157, 159, 161-162, 164, 166-167, 169, 178, 184, 188-190, 195-199, 205-207, 221, 233, 243, 247
Simla, xxvii, 5, 16, 44-45, 63-68, 71, 82, 109, 124, 161, 179-181, 222-223, 249
Simla Convention, 1914, 63-68, 71, 82, 109, 124, 161, 222-223, 249
Sinclair, Lt. M.R., 135
Sinclair, Major M.C., 206, 209
Sind, 14
Singh, Thakur Hyatt, 182
Slate letters, 27
Smith, Capt. D.R., 209
Snelling, J., 63
Somners, Thyra, *See* Weir, Mrs T.
Sprigg, Dr & Mrs K., 252
Stalin, 157
Steele, A. 240-241
Stiffe, N.C., 180, 182
St. Paul's Cathedral, 241
St. Petersburg, 12
Sun Yat-Sen, 59
Supply and Transport Department, 107, 110
Sutlej river, 172
Suyin, H., 229
Suzerainty, 47, 56, 234, 276 n21.
Swiss Tourist Board, 105
Switzerland, 105, 253

T

Tachienlu, 71
Tada Tokan, 124
Tashkent, 117
Tawang, 64-65, 77, 223, 249
Taylor, Miss A., 36, 103-104
Teichman, Sir E., 71, 191, 252
Telegraph, 19, 26, 53, 61, 74-75, 99, 102, 110, 113, 118, 145, 154, 167, 248
Telegraph sergeants (Gyantse), 19, 167
Tennant, Capt.D., 152
Terry, Dr.G., 172
Tharchin, Rev., 240
The Defence of India, 95
Theosophists, 191
The Rise and Expansion of Brtish Dominion in India, 94
The Times, viii, 58, 90, 102-103, 145, 221, 236
Thornburgh, Capt D.G., 185
Thornton, T., 94-95, 213
Tibet *passim*
Tibetan Army, 12, 67-68, 77, 121, 240
Tibetan Autonomous Region, 4
Tibetan Chief Minister, 164
Tibet and its History, 65
Tibetan Frontier Commission, *See* Younghusband mission
Tibetan Government, xxiii, xxvi, 7, 9-10, 28, 65, 68-69, 74, 116, 120-121, 123, 128, 130-132, 135, 138, 145, 147, 155-156, 158-159, 167, 169-171, 175, 190-192, 194-195, 197, 199, 202-203, 222, 224, 227, 234, 236, 242-243, 245, 248
Tibetan Government-in-Exile, 147, 203, 234, 236, 245
Tibetan New Year, 39, 76, 169
Tibet: A Political History, 83
Tibet cadre, 1-4, 14, 16, 21, 23, 38,

42, 46, 55, 58, 60, 62, 65, 71, 87, 91-95, 112, 137, 141, 205, 210-211, 215, 228, 233, 244, 249, 252
Tibet-Mongolia Treaty, 1913, 63
Tibet Past and Present, 78
Tibet Society of the U.K., 251
Tobden, Sonam, 137
Tournament of Shadows, *See* Great Game
Trade Agents, *See* Tibet cadre
Trans-Tibet Transport Scheme, 186, 200
Trapchi regiment, 168
Treasure, thefts of, 43
Treaty of Tumlong, 10
Tromowas, 36
Tsangpo (Brahmaputra) river, 53
Tsarong, G., 253
Tsarong Shapé, 53-54, 59, 76, 115, 121-124, 126-127, 131, 134-135, 153, 253
Tseuden Pemba, *See* 'Coo-Coo la'
Tucci, G., 193-194, 216, 241
Turner, Capt.S., 7, 22, 41

U

U.K. High Commission, Delhi, 247
Union Jack, 164, 185, 247
United States of America, 14, 106, 185, 194, 240
University College Swansea, 106
Urga (Ulan Bator), 20-21, 122
U.S. Air Force, 197

V

Vatican, 201
Viceroy (of India), xxiv, xxvii, 5, 11-12, 15, 19, 29-31, 40, 42, 46, 56, 60, 74-75, 92, 104, 109, 124, 177, 192, 195, 242

W

Wakefield, Sir E.W., 182-183
Walters, Lt-Col. D.A., 100, 208
Warren, Lt., 208
Weir, Lt-Col. J.L.R, iii, 94, 133-137, 143, 149-153, 172, 187, 207, 210, 215, 228, 252
Weir, Miss J-M, *See* Jehu, J-M.
Weir, Mrs. T., 133, 135
Weir mission to Lhasa, 133-136, 153
Weir snr., Colonel, 94, 133
Wellington school, xxviii
Western Tibet, xxiii, xxviii, 22, 36, 68, 149, 177-178, 182-184, 197, 216, 243, 249
Whitaker's Almanack, 240
Whitehall, ix, xxiv, 2, 4, 7, 14-15, 21-24, 31, 33-34, 38, 40, 44-47, 53, 55, 57, 60, 63, 65, 67, 71-72, 74-76, 80, 121-123, 128, 133-134, 136, 145, 150, 152, 154-155, 166-167, 169-171, 178, 194, 199, 202, 223, 226, 236, 247, 249-251
See also British Government
White, J.C., xxvi, xxix, 10, 28-29, 33, 97, 146, 211, 213
White Memorial Hall, 152
Wiggins, Miss, 98
Williamson, F., 80, 90, 95, 149-157, 159-160, 166, 172, 183-184, 202, 206, 211, 213, 215, 248
Williamson, Mrs M.D., 95, 153, 158-160, 213
Williamson missions to Lhasa, 150-160, 166, 211
Winchester school, 49, 88-89
Winter, travel and conditions, xxviii, 54, 75, 150, 156, 181, 184
Wood, Lt., xxviii

World War One, xxviii, 14, 90, 104, 117, 149
World War Two, 92, 108, 112, 171, 173, 185, 197
Worth, M., xiv, 208, 229-230

Y

Yatung, xxiii, 10, 22-23, 25, 36, 39, 46-47, 50-51, 54-55, 61-62, 72, 75, 77-78, 97-99, 103, 105-106, 110-112, 116, 123, 125, 137, 140, 143-145, 164, 166, 184, 186-187, 207-208, 226
Yatung Customs House, 103
Yatung mint, 123
Yatung Trade Agency, 39, 46, 98, 166
Yatung Trade Agent, 50, 125, 140, 143
Younghusband, Col. Sir F., iii, v-vi, xi, xxiii-xxix, 2, 6, 9, 12-13, 15, 17, 19-21, 23, 30, 33-34, 36-37, 40-43, 45, 47-49, 56, 58, 60-61, 64, 66, 73, 78, 80, 90, 93, 95, 98, 100-103, 116, 138-139, 142, 160, 162-163, 165, 167, 174, 179, 187, 190, 198, 200, 213-216, 219-220, 223-224, 228, 232-233, 239, 250, 252
Younghusband mission, v-vi, xi, xxvii-xxviii, 6, 19, 21, 30, 36-37, 40-41, 49, 58, 60, 66, 80, 98, 100, 102-103, 116, 138-139, 142, 160, 163, 167, 190, 220, 223, 228
Young, M., 181
Yutok Dapön, 168

Z

Zyrianin, 122